SECOND EDITION

# READING-WRITING CONNECTIONS

## From Theory to Practice

### MARY F. HELLER

Kansas State University

MARY F. HELLER

Kansas State University

 **LAWRENCE ERLBAUM ASSOCIATES, PUBLISHERS**
Mahwah, New Jersey

Lawrence Erlbaum Associates, Inc., Publishers
10 Industrial Avenue
Mahwah, New Jersey 07430

**ISBN 0-8058-3451-6**

Books published by Lawrence Erlbaum Associates are printed
on acid-free paper, and their bindings are chosen
for strength and durability.

Printed in the United States of America

10 9 8 7 6 5 4 3 2 1

*For Daniel, Michael, David, and Steve*

# CONTENTS

# FOREWORD

In the foreword to the first edition of *Reading-Writing Connections: From Theory to Practice,* I took note of Seymour B. Sarason's foreword to another book, *The Politics of Reading,* by Jo Michelle Beld Fraatz. One pervasive theme that runs through Fraatz's book is the "pursuit of routines" by teachers, school administrators, and special personnel. Routines are seen as a source of comfort and control, as means of coping with too many students and with multitudinous responsibilities. "In the culture of the school, as in any complicated social organization," Sarason says, "the need for routine too easily becomes an end in itself and individual needs and differences go by the boards. . . . There is a culture of the school that, when not understood, works against outcomes consistent with stated goals."

I'd found Fraatz's observations and Sarason's elaboration disturbing because they reminded me that the high price for "comfortable" routines is paid not out of apathy or ignorance but out of frustration. I thought, and I continue to think, that the frustration stems largely from an abiding belief that school curricula, particularly in reading and writing, are materials-driven. With all that material to cover—never mind where it came from or why—the promise of comfort and control offered by routines is irresistible. The frustration is compounded because even when there is a will, there are no perceived *ways* to proceed otherwise.

Not that there's ever been a dearth of advice. The "experts" continue, some with strident and some with seductive voices, to offer advice. And teachers continue to be neither impressed nor empowered by advice that has little basis in classroom realities or scant theoretical and empirical support.

Then there was *Reading-Writing Connections,* sound advice rooted in theory and enriched by the commonsense perspectives that derive from active, introspective experiences in real classrooms. Mary Heller described methods and practices that were both grounded in theory and enlivened by examples of classroom applications by actual teachers—palatable alternatives to the pursuit of routines.

And now there's *Reading-Writing Connections,* Second Edition. What I like best about this revised and expanded edition is Professor Heller's straightforward treatment of implications associated with the "whole language" philosophy in education. Rather than get embroiled in the either-or arguments that seem increasingly to surround the whole language "movement" these days, Professor Heller reminds us that "change in educational practice is a process, not an event." So she offers, throughout the book, integrated instructional practices that are wise meldings of child-centered and direct instruction.

There's more, lots more, but don't take *my* word for it. Have a look at the book. This is not just another kiss-and-a-promise revision.

WAYNE OTTO
UNIVERSITY OF WISCONSIN–MADISON

# PREFACE

*Reading–Writing Connections: From Theory to Practice,* Second Edition, is a primary language arts methods text written for preservice and in-service teachers who are studying ways to develop integrated curricula. Like the first edition, this text reflects the *whole language* approach in its most practical sense, connecting listening, speaking, reading, and writing in the context of developmentally appropriate methods and materials. Children's literature is central to my practical applications, as are reading and writing processes. Overall, what makes my book unique among language arts methods texts is its theory-to-practice perspective embedded within a developmental viewpoint.

The content and organization of this text once again reflect my belief that teachers will not own a method or procedure, will not permanently incorporate a practical activity into their repertoire of teaching methods, unless they understand the theory behind the technique. At the same time, both undergraduate and graduate students of the art of teaching need examples of real classroom practice that make sense to them. This text allows both preservice and in-service professionals to put theory and research into proper classroom perspective by encouraging them to become reflective practitioners.

## NEW IN THIS EDITION

To accomplish my goals, I take an integrated, developmental approach, moving from theory to classroom practice through description, example, and reflection. This edition continues to provide teachers with a strong foundation in how writing and reading processes can be used as the basis for effective language arts instruction from kindergarten through the middle school years.

The following features distinguish the second edition:

- *Whole Language Defined*—In Chapter 1 I provide a historical perspective on the whole language movement and its growing influence on teaching the language arts, in general, and reading and writing across the curriculum, in particular. In subsequent chapters, I describe integrated instructional practices through a variety of model lessons and genuine classroom scenarios, based on my elementary and middle school field-based research.

- *Cultural Diversity Examined*—Throughout the text, I describe the influence of cultural diversity on classroom instruction, organization, and management. New literature-based model lessons and classroom scenarios feature multicultural and multiethnic children's literature. To help teachers in their effort to inform children about other cultures, I include a Bibliography of Multicultural Children's Literature at the end of Chapters 2 through 5.

- *Alternative Assessment Explained*—In Chapter 7 I describe alternative evaluation strategies and explain how teachers go about organizing a language arts portfolio system, which utilizes assessment by observation, reaction, analysis, and grading.

- *Emerging Technologies Explored*—The technology section of Chapter 8 includes information about HyperCard, hypertext, and virtual reality—the newest technologies with the potential to revolutionize language arts instruction.

- *The Multiage Classroom Introduced*—In the final chapter, I describe the multilevel, multiage classroom management system. Special emphasis is placed upon small-group cooperative learning and individualized instruction.

- *New Pedagogical Illustrations Included*—This edition further highlights literature-based language arts instruction and reading and writing processes in the following ways:

  *Reader Response to Literature* is described and illustrated using classroom scenarios and child/teacher dialogue.

  *Thematic Teaching* is defined and examples are included of how to develop functional thematic units that integrate a variety of subject areas.

- *New Teacher Resources Provided*—This edition includes new sections with detailed information important to language arts lesson planning:

  *Your Handwriting Notebook:* Practical suggestions for teaching emergent, manuscript, and cursive handwriting in grades K–3

  *Multicultural Children's Literature Booklists:* Included at the end of Chapters 2, 3, 4, and 5

  *Bibliographies of Selected Dictionaries, Thesauri, and Periodicals for Children and Adolescents:* Included at the end of Chapter 6

  *Appendix A:* Making Puppets

  *Appendix B:* Making Books

  *Appendix C:* Handwriting Models

  *Appendix D:* Thematic Units

- *Newly revised features*—the first and second editions both include the following:

*Children's Literature Bibliographies:* Age-appropriate fiction, nonfiction, and poetry listed at the ends of Chapters 2–5.

*Inside the Classroom:* Authentic classroom scenarios that serve to demonstrate integrated instructional practice; new glimpses into literature-based, reader response lessons.

*Instructional Guidelines:* Step-by-step procedures for organizing and implementing integrated approaches, including "Creating a Thematic Unit" and "Conducting an Individual Writing Conference."

*For You to Try:* Activities that encourage the methods student to experience the comprehending and composing process. Students put theory into practice as they try new methods and procedures, such as "Writing from the Heart," a poetry-writing exercise.

*For Your Journal:* Practical journal-writing exercises that encourage preservice and in-service teachers to be reflective practitioners.

## ACKNOWLEDGMENTS

I am deeply indebted to the children, classroom teachers, and administrators who have allowed me into their schools to observe, interact, teach, and record, in order to provide visions from the real world of the classroom. My heartfelt thanks go to the following educators: Dr. Teresa Miller, Principal, Eugene Field School, and staff members Laura Renfro, multiage classroom, K–3, Kay Hendricks, grade K, Nancy Havenstein, grade 2, Betty Rae Wallace, grade 1, Nancy Evans, grade 3, Mitzi Eyestone, grade 4; Pat Tippin, grade 5; Oceana Wright, Principal, Woodrow Wilson School, and staff members Lori Thompson and Melisa Hancock, grade 5; Marvin Marsh, Principal, Manhattan Middle School, and staff member Dr. Donna Sears, Reading Teacher, grades 7–8; Raymond Thomas, Principal, Roosevelt School, and staff members Dr. Mary Ellen Titus, grades K–3, multiage classroom teacher and Diane DeNoon, grades 4–5.

To all of the children whose oral and written language appears in the book, I want to express my sincerest gratitude for allowing me to publish your thoughts and writing. Many thanks also to Eugene Field and Manhattan Middle School parents who gave permission to photograph their children.

Special words of appreciation go to photographer Don Feuerborn for the care that he took in taking the new pictures that appear in this edition.

I extend my sincerest gratitude to Mary Hammel, graphic artist at Kansas State University, for her professional and meticulous preparation of the new figures, appendices, and logos that appear in this edition. I also wish to thank Denise Rowley, undergraduate education major at Kansas State, for the care that she took in the initial preparation of new figures.

I would like to thank the reviewers who helped me shape the manuscript in progress. Their kind words of encouragement and thoughtful suggestions enabled me to write a better second edition. The reviewers are as follows:

Kathy Danielson, University of Nebraska at Omaha

Dolores Dickerson, Howard University

Karen Dunnagan, Western Illinois University

Patricia Grasty Gaines, West Chester University of Pennsylvania

Jane Meeks Hager, Old Dominion University

Warren Heydenberk, Lehigh University

Reta Hicks, Western Kentucky University

Rosalind Horowitz, University of Texas, San Antonio

Gayle Luck, Cornell College

Linda Jones McCoy, Pittsburgh State University

Mary Mosley, University of Central Arkansas

Deborah Norland, Luther College

Barbara Samuels, University of Houston, Clear Lake

Milagros Seda, University of Texas, El Paso

Barbara Steele, University of Massachusetts, Dartmouth

Many thanks also to Laura McKenna, Senior Editor, and Rebecca Mabry, Editorial Assistant. Your support and patience throughout the preparation of this second edition were very important to the successful completion of my book.

Finally, I wish to express love and appreciation to my family, who supported me throughout the summer of no-summer at the computer. Thanks guys. I couldn't have done it without you.

# BECOMING LITERATE

*Reading is when someone can't hear you, so you write them a letter.*

*Jamie, age 5*

## CHAPTER CONCEPTS

Reading, writing, listening, and speaking are the language arts.

How we view reading and writing influences how we teach.

Reading and writing may be defined as skills, products, and processes.

The social aspects of language are important to learning.

Reading and writing provide access to literacy. We learn the value of communication through the written word very early as children struggling to master print in our environment. From the posters on the nursery room wall, to the bedtime storybooks, to the signs around town, letters and words quickly become a part of our consciousness. The need to know what the words mean is at first a curiosity soon replaced by the desire to communicate. We learn to communicate our desires first through listening and oral language, the very foundations of literacy. Ultimately, the acquisition of reading and writing enables us to develop into the unique individuals we are all capable of becoming. To be lifelong readers and writers is our goal as well as the goal of parents and teachers for us. Home and the schools, then, are the main forums for literacy development. The connections that can be made between reading and writing, listening and speaking bond in those arenas.

The primary focus of this book is on the translation of theory and research into effective classroom practice. In this text you will learn how language, cognitive, and social development theory and research can be used to integrate reading, writing, listening, and speaking in the language arts classroom. Chapter 1 provides the foundation for all subsequent chapters, as I first describe the nature of reading and writing. In this context, I also attend to the primacy of oral language and listening during the processes of teaching and learning. Included in this chapter are perspectives on how educators have historically defined reading and writing and ultimately conceptualized the interrelationships among all of the language arts.

As students read and write to learn, the processes of comprehending and composing reinforce one another.

In order to fully inform the reader, I provide contrasting definitions and philosophical points of view that influence today's elementary and middle school language arts instruction. These pedagogical positions range from traditional skills-based, text-driven models to more holistic, process-oriented approaches associated with integrating the language arts. New to this chapter is a description of the whole-language movement and its impact on classroom instruction across all content areas. The discussion provides a forum for the introduction of important theory into practice issues relative to integrating reading, writing, listening, and speaking. These issues include the importance of prior knowledge (schema theory); the construction of meaning (response theory); the structure of text (genre studies); the concept of learning to learn (metacognitive theory); and the social nature of language acquisition and development (sociocultural theory).

As teachers of language, we have the power to create an environment where all children can become literate, regardless of race, gender, or socioeconomic background. The power is manifest in pedagogically sound methods and procedures that have as their base the best of all possible theory and research. To empower teachers and learners is the ultimate goal of this book.

## THE NATURE OF READING AND WRITING

### Alternative Viewpoints

Both reading and writing are skills, products, or processes, depending on the theoretical point of view. Differing viewpoints lead to alternative definitions of reading and writing. For example, reading and writing are complex unitary *skills* made up of numerous subskills acquired through instruction. Reading and writing are the *products* of skills acquisition, with comprehension and composition being the observable elements. Reading and writing are *processes* an individual undertakes to construct meaning from print or to construct meaning using print, respectively. How we view reading and writing influences how we teach these essentials of literacy.

Regardless of our description, the interrelationships among the language arts are complex, are not readily apparent or clearly understood, and yet today are often taken for granted (Langer, 1986). To understand how reading and writing are connected, it is important first to discuss them separately and to look at the differences as well as the similarities. Ironic as this may seem, the traditional viewpoint is that reading and writing are "basic skills," treated as separate subjects in the schools. Reading is a receptive skill, whereas writing is expressive in nature. This very viewpoint is what has influenced textbook contents as well as classroom methods for generations. To create *skillful* readers and writers is the ultimate goal of schooling. The language of skills remains integral to pedagogy. Yet much is to be learned from each perspective as we begin to apply theory to practice.

***The Skills of Reading and Writing.***     Traditional language arts programs support the notion of sequentially ordered reading and writing skills. The global skills of reading include word recognition and comprehension. The skills of writing are more extensive and incorporate grammar, usage, and spelling, as well as matters of style and forms of discourse. Whether it is intended or not, scope and sequence charts imply that language development through reading and writing is hierarchical in nature. First we learn to recognize the alphabet letters; then we learn to decode words. First we learn to write a sentence; then we learn to write a paragraph. However, there is little evidence to support the idea that a true hierarchy of skills exists in reading (Downing, 1982; Samuels, 1976).

Skills approaches necessitate breaking down reading or writing into more *manageable* and, theoretically, more *teachable* units. William Gray's (1960) skills model of reading suggests that individuals learn to read by first matching sounds to letters before progressing to whole-word identification. Though Gray discusses the component parts of reading separately, he nevertheless believes that reading is a complex unitary skill made up of numerous subskills that not only are closely interrelated but also function simultaneously. The concept of automaticity is fundamental to reading skills models. Fluency in reading is achieved through instantaneous recognition of words without conscious effort. Automatic word recognition allows the reader to give full attention to the ultimate goal of reading: comprehension of the text (LaBerge & Samuels, 1976).

Traditional models of writing also focus on the parts in relation to the whole. Richard Young (1978) describes the characteristics of the current traditional paradigm that has dominated the content and organization of hundreds of anthologies and composition texts for decades. The distinguishing features of the traditional rhetorical paradigm include ". . . the analysis of discourse into words, sentences, and paragraphs; the classification of discourse into description, narration, exposition, and argument; the strong concern with usage (syntax, spelling, punctuation) and with style (economy, clarity, emphasis) . . ." (p. 31).

Arthur Applebee (1986) notes that textbooks perpetuate traditional models. Composition textbooks are the primary influence in classroom writing instruction. We need take only a cursory look at elementary or secondary language arts texts to see the truth in his observation. The lists of writing skills go on for pages. The complexity of writing is highlighted by lessons that first break down written expression into component parts and then proceed to the application of newly acquired skills. The automatic application of skills during the composing process equals success in writing. Theoretically, if students know the rules of grammar, they will use them correctly when writing a sentence. However, decades of research into the teaching of writing reveals that knowledge of grammatical rules alone does not improve one's writing (Hillocks, 1987). The sum of the parts do not necessarily equal the whole product or process in writing or reading.

On the surface, a skills viewpoint appears to eliminate the need to make connections among the language arts. What do word recognition and comprehension skills have in common with sentence construction, paragraph development, spelling, grammar, punctuation, or text structure? Studies in the 1960s and 1970s attempted to show a correlation between the skills of reading and writing as measured by standardized achievement tests. Sandra Stotsky (1983) reported a number of research projects in which better reading comprehension and vocabulary scores were positively related to good-quality writing as determined by a variety of measures, including normed tests of writing, holistic assessments, composition writing scales, sentence length and complexity, and grammar and usage achievement test scores. The more skillful readers appeared to be the more skillful writers.

The better reader/better writer phenomenon was most extensively researched and documented by Walter Loban (1963, 1976), who undertook longitudinal studies of children's language development as they progressed from kindergarten through grade 12. Loban was concerned not only with reading and writing abilities but also with the children's oral language and listening. At the end of his thirteen-year study, Loban described language-proficient children:

> They had an overview, a plan for their talk and writing that showed coherence and unity. They spoke not only freely, fluently and easily, but also effectively, using a rich variety of vocabulary. . . . They were, themselves, attentive and creative listeners. . . . Both in reading and in written composition, the proficient subjects excelled, and they were superior in using connectors—like *meanwhile, unless* . . . those superior in oral language in kindergarten and grade one *before they learned to read and write* are the very ones who excel in reading and writing by the time they are in grade six. (pp. 70-71)

Studies examining the influence of reading on writing and of writing on reading generally support the idea that growth in one area will probably carry over into the other. In an essay on the value of connecting reading and writing, Tierney and Leys (1986) conclude that research to date shows that ". . . the general correlation between reading and writing is moderate and fluctuates with age, schooling, and other factors" (p. 25). They nevertheless agree that certain reading and writing experiences have an influence on reading and writing performance. Some influential activities have as their basis a skills viewpoint. For example, highlighting the structural characteristics of a text before reading appears to influence the writing of similarly structured texts (McGee & Richgels, 1985). Teaching expository text structure as well as story grammars also influences both written composition and reading comprehension (Gordon & Braun, 1984; Taylor & Beach, 1984). Chapters 3 through 6 contain practical applications of text structure theory and research.

***The Products of Reading and Writing.***    The product view of reading and writing is the direct result of a skills orientation. The ultimate reading product is comprehension, which occurs automatically as a result of word recognition, or decoding (Fries, 1962). This view of reading comprehension dominated reading research in the 1960s and 1970s and still influences classroom instruction today (J. D. Cooper, 1986). *Read the story and answer the comprehension questions* is a familiar sequence of events, which is very much a part of a product-centered language arts curriculum. We test reading comprehension through questioning. The product is then quantifiable, and reading comprehension scores represent what the student understands about the text.

The products of writing are visible: the sentence, the paragraph, the essay, the short story. Traditional approaches to writing instruction focus on written products and take a prescriptive stance (Applebee, 1986). Teachers evaluate the written product, judge its form and content, according to a set criteria, and prescribe remedial action if necessary. Society holds the perfected final written product in high esteem because it is the very essence of literacy—communication through the written word.

Comparing the products of reading and writing renders a limited understanding of the nature of reading and writing connections. Better readers are often better writers and vice versa, as measured by quantifiable factors (Stotsky, 1983). Skills and product-oriented definitions also limit research implications for classroom instruction. We rely on the idea that facility in one area carries over into another. But mere practice in reading does not guarantee quality writing. Why are better readers better writers? What happens during reading that is similar to what happens during writing? These are the kinds of questions researchers began to ask in the mid- to late 1970s as a shift in the theoretical views of reading and writing emerged.

## Changing Perspectives

***Schema Theory.***    Current theories of reading and writing go beyond the skills and products perspectives to take into consideration the interactive nature of language acquisition and development. Schema theoretic models of reading, for example, describe how prior knowledge of the world enables readers to construct meaning from print (Anderson, 1984). *Schema* (or *schemata*) refers to the structures that we use to organize information in our memory (Rumelhart, 1981). According to schema theory, reading comprehension is an interactive process whereby the reader relates already existing knowledge to the meanings in the text. During the process, readers reconstruct the author's message and add to schemata present in memory. So defined, comprehension is much more than a product or an outcome. It is a process that enables the reader to learn from a written text.

Composition is also an interactive process, as the writer seeks to construct meaning for an intended audience. While composing, the ongoing activity is that of creating meaning. The writer joins together, coordinates, and structures information for the purpose of communicating ideas. The author-reader relationship is critical to reading comprehension because it is the author who is initially responsible for the comprehensible nature of a text (Adams & Bruce, 1982).

Prior world knowledge in general and knowledge of text structures in particular are important to a schema-theoretical viewpoint in both research and practice. One important source of prior knowledge in our lives is *script knowledge.* Script refers to the ordinary, everyday experiences (such as kite flying) that are stored in our memory. Script implies a story or narration, what happens when. . . . Examples are such experiences as going shopping, attending a surprise party, participating in a wedding, or flying a kite. We call on the appropriate script at the appropriate moment while reading in order to make sense of the text.

The following conversation illustrates the emergence of a script for going to the movies. David, age three, discusses with his mother the events that took place the night before when he went with his father to see the movie *Pinocchio.*

**MOTHER:** Did you see *Pinocchio* last night with Daddy?

**DAVID:** Oh, yeah. It's coming on!

**MOTHER:** Did you have a good time?

**DAVID:** Oh, yeah. We got some gas.

**MOTHER:** What did you do at the movies?

**DAVID:** I sat down in my seat.

**MOTHER:** What else did you do?

**DAVID:** I spilled the popcorn.

**MOTHER:** What else happened?

**DAVID:** I spilled the popcorn.

**MOTHER:** What happened to Pinocchio in the movie?

**DAVID:** He gots to go to school.

**MOTHER:** Was Pinocchio put in a cage?

**DAVID:** Oh, yeah. He was sad. I want him out.

David's first experience at the movies provides him with information about moviegoing that will remain in his memory, ready to be recalled whenever needed to communicate through speaking, reading, or writing. Facts like "It's [the movie] coming on," "I sat down in my seat," and "I spilled the popcorn" are all important to the experience. Because it was his first experience as a moviegoer, David did not realize that spilling popcorn is quite common and therefore acceptable behavior at the movies. The fact that he repeated twice "I spilled the popcorn" implies that this was a significant event, one that he very likely had to accommodate to his already-existing knowledge about spilling popcorn in other, less appropriate settings such as the living room. Other accommodations will be made as he becomes more experienced. He will learn, for example, that we do not necessarily go to the gas station before going to the movies.

For script knowledge to be useful to readers and writers, it must be easily retrieved from memory. As illustrated by the example conversation between David and his mother, oral language and listening facilitate retrieval of information imbedded within memory. Prereading or prewriting discussions are highly recommended activities that help activate elementary and middle school students' prior knowledge of concepts crucial to comprehension and composition (Anderson, 1984). Focused conversation and discussion *before* reading and writing enable children to use their prior knowledge of the world to greater advantage *during* comprehending and composing. Chapters 2 through 5 include practical ways to encourage children to talk about what they already know before engaging in the reading or writing process.

***Text Structure.***    Knowledge and understanding of text structure are also important to comprehension and composition. Text structure refers to those aspects of language that signal how content is organized and related. In the language arts curriculum, we are concerned with text structure at three levels: sentence, paragraph, and whole text. Attention to the structure of a sentence occurs throughout the composing process, as the writer decides how best to word a sentence in order to communicate clearly. If ambiguities exist then the reader may not comprehend the author's intention.

At the sentence level, anaphoric relationships are the most frequently occurring structures that assist communication. Anaphora is "the use of a word as a substitute for a preceding word or group of words" (Harris & Hodges, 1981, p. 15). Pronouns and nouns used as pronouns are the most commonly used words to signal references made earlier in a sentence or paragraph, as in the following story dictated by a kindergartner:

## PARENT STORY

by Daniel

*Once upon a time and a long time ago,* I *saw Mommy taking care of the baby in the hospital. And* she *was so pretty. And then* I *had an adventure with Dad on a sailboat called the Argo. We* catched fish. It *was fun.*

Daniel's story contains five instances of anaphora. To comprehend the story, readers must recognize to whom or what the pronouns *I, she, we,* and *it* refer. Although the narrative is simple enough to understand, ambiguities nevertheless exist, as we are not sure if *she* refers to the mother or the baby. During the composing process, writers are necessarily concerned with constructing an unambiguous message.

Clear pronoun-noun referential relationships bring cohesion to texts and make it easier for the reader to reconstruct the author's intended meaning. King and Rentel (1981) found in a longitudinal study of coherence in children's writing that by the time they enter first grade, most have acquired a basic understanding of the cohesive devices that hold a text together. How children use cohesive devices varies according to genre. Text genre, or form, influences comprehension and composition at paragraph and whole-text levels. The basic forms of oral and written discourse are narration, exposition, and poetry. Each form denotes a specific purpose for communicating ideas. Narrative writing tells a story. Stories may be fictional short stories and novels, historical fictions based on facts, or personal narratives telling a true story, as in autobiography and biography. Expository prose explains or clarifies a subject. Exposition can be developed through definition, description, process, comparison, classification, analysis, and persuasion. Poetry is personal expressive writing. Poetic structures are characterized by rhythm, meter, and sometimes rhyme. The importance of providing excellent models in each genre is discussed throughout the book.

Traditional language arts curricula include a good deal of narrative reading and writing, especially in the primary grades, K–3. There are several research-based reasons for focusing on stories in the early grades. In general, narrative writing is less syntactically complex and therefore more comprehensible to the beginning reader than exposition. Studies of syntactic complexity show persuasive writing to be the most complex in terms of sentence structure (Hunt, 1977). On entering school, most children have extensive prior knowledge of narrative form, mainly from bedtime storybooks. Thus by the time children enter formal schooling, they have internalized the underlying structure of stories (Applebee, 1978; Stein & Glenn, 1979). Reading to children both at home and at school helps them to internalize narrative and other forms of discourse. A child's concept of story influences comprehension and composition.

Narrative writing is also emphasized in the early grades as we encourage children to compose fictional and personal narratives. Narratives are easier for children to write because of their prior knowledge of the form. Teachers assign or children choose story writing more frequently than any other writing form in the elementary grades (M. F. Heller, 1987). D. H. Graves's (1983) text on teaching the writing process highlights the importance of children developing topics of their own choice. Topics that children choose almost always evolve into fictional or personal narratives, unless the teacher intervenes with an alternative assignment.

Children often keep their personal narratives and stories in journals. Daily journal writing is an important management tool that supports writing and reading fluency. Dialogue journals (Staton, 1988) support narrative writing by encouraging a written conversation between teacher and child. (See Chapter 8 for more on journal writing.)

As children move into the intermediate grades (4–6), there is an increased need to comprehend and to compose more complex forms of discourse in a variety of

Early experiences with print help children develop
the concept of word.

content areas. Content area reading and writing often makes learning difficult because children do not know how to recognize and use a variety of text structures to comprehend and compose effectively. Unlike narratives, prior knowledge of expository forms is less extensive. Text structures can be directly taught through teacher modeling and graphic organizers (Flood et al., 1986; McGee & Richgels, 1985). Knowledge of the organizational patterns of text helps students to remember better what they read. Wide-ranging experience in reading and writing in the content areas enhances both comprehending and composing the next time the form is encountered (Pearce, 1984). Chapters 4 and 5 elaborate on methods that are effective when teaching traditional text structure through reading and writing experiences. The concept of nonlinear text, or hypertext, is discussed in Chapter 8. Hypertext may be the ultimate example of schema theory applied to language arts instruction via educational technology.

***The Processes of Reading and Writing.***     Perhaps more than any other theoretical paradigm, interactive models of reading and writing help us to conceptualize how the language arts are interrelated. Both readers and writers are involved in similar if not identical thought processes during the acts of comprehending and composing (Squire, 1983). This phenomenon is not surprising since thought and language are virtually inseparable (Vygotsky, 1962, 1979). What readers and writers think about during comprehending and composing is the subject of both theoretical and applied research into reading-writing connections.

James Squire's (1983) model of how reading and writing are related is based on the premise that reading and writing place similar demands on our thinking skills. These demands can best be illustrated by comparing the concerns of the reader and the writer *during* the process of comprehending or composing. For example, before reading a text, the reader prepares to comprehend by establishing a purpose for reading and recalling or activating prior knowledge of the reading topic. Similarly, before writing a text, the writer prepares to compose by establishing a purpose for writing and calling to mind all prior knowledge of the topic. Prereading and prewriting time are critical to the overall processes of comprehending and composing. Conversation and discussion are essential during this stage. Quality time spent during these initial stages prepares readers and writers to construct meaning more effectively.

We can also compare readers and writers during the acts of comprehending or composing. For example, while reading, the reader is actively involved both intellectually and emotionally in reconstructing the author's meaning. The reader consciously monitors his or her comprehension, that is, actively planning, regulating, checking, and rechecking one's thinking while reading (Palinscar & Brown, 1984). Metacognitive theory (Flavelle, 1976) is the basis for much research into the conscious orchestration or manipulation of thinking while reading. Metacognition also refers to our knowledge about thinking, or awareness of our own cognitive abilities. Metacognitive skills can be modeled and directly taught (M. F. Heller, 1986b). Teaching children to articulate what they were thinking while they were reading is helpful in assessing comprehension difficulties that may otherwise remain overlooked.

Writers are also actively involved intellectually and emotionally in constructing meaning. The writer consciously monitors his or her word choice, sentence structure, or paragraph organization in order to achieve a purpose for writing. Unique to the process is the fact that writers are constantly reading and rereading what they have written during the act of composing. Tierney and Leys (1986) note, "Writers use reading in a more integrated fashion [than readers use writing] for . . . they are constantly involved in reading their own writing, reading other materials, and using understandings they have acquired from past readings" (p. 23). Reading during the composing process directly affects the quality of the written product (Birnbaum, 1982; Perl, 1979). Oral language also advances the composing process, as writers talk about their work in progress with teachers and peers. The interrelationships among reading, writing, listening, and speaking during the composing process have important pedagogical implications that are explored in Chapters 2 through 5.

We can also compare what readers and writers think about *after* they are finished with their respective texts. For example, a reader who has reconstructed the author's meaning will be able to reflect on any number of ideas that demonstrate comprehension. After reading an article, readers can talk about the facts or main ideas, analyze the parts in relation to the whole, or make value judgments such as "I like what I read because. . . ."

Similarly, on finishing the piece, writers check to make sure they have constructed something meaningful. The questions that a writer might ask about his or her own work are similar to the reader's reflections. A writer might wonder, "Have I included enough facts to support my main ideas?" Writers also pass judgments on their own work, often reflecting, "I like my article because. . . ." Peer reviews also help writers to become more reflective. During Writers' Workshop (described in Chapter 8), students read each other's initial and final drafts and talk about form and content. Oral and written responses to work in progress are a valuable aid to writers of all ages striving to communicate clearly.

The concept of reflective thought is important to both the reading and writing processes. June Birnbaum (1986) describes a number of studies concerned with the reflective thinking of good and poor readers. These studies demonstrated that "reflective thinking is central to proficiency in written language" (p. 31), whether the individual is engaged in reading or writing. Better readers, who also happen to be the better writers, are fundamentally better thinkers throughout the reading and writing processes. Reflective thinkers are more capable of articulating what it is they do to construct meaning before, during, and after reading and writing. Birnbaum analyzed her subjects' oral or written protocols taken at each stage of the reading and writing process in order to demonstrate this point. What readers and writers think about is directly related to their prior knowledge of and experiences in reading and writing about a specific topic or within a certain genre. One example cited is that of Kathy, a seventh-grader, who upon completing the third draft of a poem reflected, "I've been reading a lot of Nikki Giovanni's poems lately, and I'm trying to use (in my own poetry writing) images in the same way" (p. 36).

Though the ability to pause and reflect on what one is reading and writing varies with age and cognitive level, Birnbaum (1986) found *reflectiveness* to be a significant factor in the better reader/better writer studies of elementary- through college-level students. Further a *reciprocal influence* of the processes of reading and writing appears to exist, which explains in part the reason why better readers are usually better writers and vice versa. Examples of reflective thinking by teachers and students are presented throughout the text.

***Literature-Based Instruction.***     Children's literature is currently experiencing a renaissance in the language arts classroom. Literature-based language arts instruction underscores the importance for educators to understand how readers and writers interact with and respond to prose and poetry. Reader response theory is grounded in literary criticism and describes how readers read and interpret literature (Tomkins, 1980). Like schema-theoretical views of reading and writing, Louise Rosenblatt's (1978) transactional theory of literature defines reading as an active transaction between the reader and the text. During the comprehending process, the reader creates personal meaning inspired by literature. Meaning, therefore, resides within the exchange and not in the text alone. Within the context of responding to literature, prior knowledge is extremely important to the reader who draws upon past experiences, images, and feelings in order to comprehend.

Rosenblatt (1991) makes a distinction between responding from an aesthetic and an efferent stance or point of view. Readers maintain an efferent stance when reading for the purpose of gaining information from the text. For example, a teacher might ask her students to listen for the kinds of animals that live in a rain forest, as she reads aloud *The Great Kapok Tree* by Lynne Cherry (1990). Conversely, when reading for purely aesthetic reasons, readers focus more on feelings, images, and personal thoughts and associations aroused by the text. "Tell me what you thought about Lynne Cherry's book about the destruction of the Amazon rain forest," is an open-ended question designed to elicit a personal response, rather than specific information learned from the text.

Although readers may approach a text with a specific purpose in mind, they often move along a continuum from efferent to aesthetic and back again, as illustrated by Purves (1990):

> As readers enter into the transaction, they may decide to treat the text as if it were providing them with information or teaching them a lesson, or seeking to persuade them, or providing them with an aesthetic experience. . . . People often pick up a text with a purpose and find that, as they proceed through it, their purpose shifts. . . . A reader may have opened a book with the intention of finding a specific item of information thought to be in it. Four hours later he could be writing an essay about the book and have completely forgotten what it was he was searching for. (pp. 82–83)

In a descriptive study of reader response to environmental children's literature, students in a multiage K–3 classroom listened to *The Great Kapok Tree* and engaged in a discussion stimulated by open-ended questions (Heller, 1992). Third-grader Molly's oral response demonstrates naturally occurring shifts in reader perspective:

MRS. R.: *Tell me what you thought about* The Great Kapok Tree.

MOLLY: *Well, I thought it was beautiful. I think the author should win a prize for this story. It made me want to go to a rain forest and just lie down and look at the canopy. The animals were really smart to talk to the wood chopper man. I didn't know that porcupines lived in trees in the rain forest. Can you read it again?*

A cursory analysis of Molly's comments reveals that she responded aesthetically to the book (i.e., "I thought it was beautiful.") and at the same time articulated new information ("I didn't know that porcupines lived in trees in the rain forest."). Inspired by the book, she later wrote a fictional narrative about a unicorn who lives in a rain forest. Michael, a third-grade peer in the same class, wrote a free verse poem (Figure 1.1), "Climbing Trees Is Freedom."

## Climbing Trees Is Freedom

### By Michael

Climbing trees is freedom.
You can do whatever you
  want in a tree.
You can build a tree house in a tree.
You can swing on a vine in a tree.
You can hang from branches in a tree.
You can climb as high as you can in a tree.
You can eat fruit in a tree.
So ends my poem and now begins yours.

**FIGURE 1.1** "Climbing Trees Is Freedom," by Michael, grade 3

It is important for language arts teachers to remember that setting purposes for children's reading or writing may not necessarily bring about an established curricular objective. Children read and write for a variety of purposes and audiences. Like adults, their intentions will change while they are engaged in the meaning-making process. Throughout this book are many examples of children's oral and written responses to literature, as well as developmentally appropriate lessons that nurture aesthetic and efferent points of view. Also included at the ends of Chapters 2 through 5 are bibliographies of quality children's literature written for elementary and middle school students.

## THE SOCIAL ASPECTS OF LANGUAGE

How we view reading and writing—as a skill, as a product, or as a process—does not alter the fact that language is social in nature. The social processes of reading, writing, listening, and speaking occur in a variety of settings, where children and parents, students and teachers, students and peers, teachers and parents, as well as authors and readers meet to communicate ideas.

Sociocultural theories of language acquisition and development emphasize the importance of the environment as a child learns to speak, read, and write. A sociocultural view of reading and writing recognizes "that all learning is socially based, that language learning is ultimately an interactive process, that cognitive factors are influenced by context, and that they, in turn, affect the meanings that are produced" (Langer, 1986, p. 7). Vygotsky (1978), an early twentieth-century Russian psychologist, examined the social structure that surrounds learning. In part, he was interested in describing how a child's interaction with adults or more able peers contributes to cognitive and language development. Vygotskian theory suggests that human activity supports language development within the sociocultural contexts of play, formal education, and work (Wertsch et al., 1984). In hypothesizing the best environment for learning, Vygotsky conceptualized the "zone of proximal development," which he defined as "the distance between the actual developmental level as determined by independent problem solving and the level of potential development as determined through problem solving under adult guidance or in collaboration with more capable peers" (p. 86). This theoretical space represents the most opportune time to stimulate language growth both at home and in the schools. The concept of mediation lies central to Vygotskian theory, which claims that cognitive processes can be understood only if we understand the "tools and signs that mediate them" (Wertsch, 1985, p. 15). Adults and other children mediate language learning at home and in the schools.

In the classroom it is frequently the teacher who provides supportive tools for each learner, "which extend his or her skills and thus allow the learner to accomplish successfully a task not otherwise possible" (Greenfield, 1984, p. 118). Teacher support during the learning process takes many forms as illustrated by direct instruction, teacher modeling, and positive responses to work in progress. Children may also develop their language in collaboration with peers as they interact in settings structured by cooperative learning groups or peer tutoring. At home parents, siblings, and child-care providers also support everyday experiences that encourage the development of literacy. For example, conversation that occurs between parent and child on a simple trip to the grocery store can reinforce the child's concept of word, as the adult draws attention to environmental print as in labels and advertisements. Rogoff (1990) suggests that children are "apprentices in thinking, active in their efforts to learn from observing and participating with peers and more skilled members of their society, developing skills to handle culturally defined problems with available tools, and building from these givens to construct new solutions within the context of sociocultural activity" (p. 7).

In his description of reading as a social process, David Bloome (1985) discusses the social aspects of reading according to three dimensions: (1) reading as a social context, (2) reading as a cultural activity, and (3) reading as a sociocognitive process. For some children the very first social context in which reading occurs is at home, where parents and child-care providers read bedtime stories aloud. Here we envision the emergence of literacy, as children listen and begin to internalize the concept of word, perhaps memorizing word for word their favorite stories. Just as important as learning about words and print is learning socially acceptable behavior when being read to. Parental expectations when reading to their children help to mold the child's behaviors toward reading. For example, successful read-aloud strategies require the child's attention to the print and pictures for the communication process to work (Trelease, 1989).

The social context for writing also begins at home, where language learning in general has been studied and described as "natural, pleasurable, and highly practical" (Piazza & Tomlinson, 1985). In the home, parents, child-care providers, and siblings can influence children's early writing experiences by encouraging children to write and by modeling the forms and functions of written discourse. Studies of home writing show that children use written language play for a variety of practical reasons as well as for self-expression of ideas and feelings (Clay, 1975). Chapter 2 elaborates on the social impact of the home environment on reading and writing and discusses ways to take advantage of parent-child interactions as communication skills begin to emerge.

When children enter school, they encounter different, more formal social contexts for reading and writing, which are not necessarily viewed as naturally occurring events but are instead planned parts of a highly structured, well-defined curriculum. Under the guidance of the teacher, students read and write for numerous purposes, including reading directions, self-selected books, signs, and labels and writing in journals or writing letters, narratives, and reports. The language arts curriculum is frequently implemented in a rule-governed classroom, where there are definite expectations about appropriate reading and writing behaviors among class members. Child-centered methods for organizing the language arts classroom include cooperative learning, Writers' and Readers' Workshops, and peer tutoring (discussed in Chapter 8). These are all positive classroom management systems that capitalize on the social nature of learning and make the transition from home to school and back again more pleasurable.

Bridging the gap between the home and school cultural contexts is an important step in helping students develop their language abilities within an environment that makes sense both socially and culturally. The value that we place on reading and writing arises out of our shared need to be a literate people. This need is a function of our society and of our culture. Reading and writing are cultural activities with roots in family and historical traditions that are imparted by parents long before children get to kindergarten. Our classrooms are a reflection of the diverse world in which we live and work. The values that families place upon reading and writing vary greatly within and across social, cultural, and economic boundaries (Crawford, 1993). Some children may come to us from families for which reading and writing are valued and integral parts of daily routines. Others may have never considered reading and writing for pleasurable or even practical reasons. Respect for such differences in family literacy values helps us to deal with the complex nature of our classroom as a social arena.

Our goal as teachers is to nurture the development of thought and language by providing a classroom environment that stimulates learning in challenging yet developmentally appropriate ways. Applying Vygotskian theory to practice involves the consideration of factors that influence lesson planning and classroom organization and management. A classroom environment that is child-centered, activity-based, and inquiry-driven supports Vygotskian principles. Chapters 2–5 contain model lessons that demonstrate the social interactions that support language development in the real world of the classroom. Chapter 8 discusses classroom management systems that have as their basis sociocultural theories of learning.

## FROM THEORY TO PRACTICE

The primary goal of educators worldwide is to provide a classroom environment where all children, regardless of race, gender, or social background, have the best chance of becoming lifelong readers and writers. Historically, reading and writing instruction in American schools has been influenced by a wide range of educational reforms, including learning by doing, mastery learning, outcomes-based education, individualized instruction, the open classroom, and effective teaching. A recent effort to influence change in instructional practice is reflected in the whole-language philosophy of education.

Whole language is an educational reform movement grounded in child-centered theory and practice. Although a phenomenon of the 1980s and 1990s, the origins of whole-language perspectives can be traced to major theorists of the twentieth century, including John Dewey, Lev´Vygotsky, Jean Piaget, M. A. K. Halliday, and Louise Rosenblatt. Viewed as more than mere practice, Edelsky (1991) suggests that whole language "is a set of beliefs, a perspective, a theory in practice." Sometimes characterized as a "grassroots" movement (Y. Goodman, 1989), the whole-language philosophy is often embodied in a variety of time-honored educational practices. For example, whole-language advocates believe that language cannot and therefore should not be fragmented, analyzed, and then put back together. In practice, emphasis is on the importance of whole or authentic texts, identified as the children's own oral and written language, as well as quality children's literature. There are no skill-drill work-sheets but rather more time is spent reading, writing, and responding to whole pieces of prose and poetry. We see the integration of listening, speaking, reading, and writing across all subject areas and the use of thematic units to integrate concepts across disciplines. Definitions of reading and writing are interactive in nature, as learners interact with one another in order to construct meaning through print (Edelsky, 1992). In whole-language classrooms, there is an emphasis on process instruction, where children have a voice in their own literacy learning. Assessment of reading and writing occurs through observation of language growth over time, documenting what the individual child communicates and creates. Readers' and Writers' Workshops play a prominent role in whole-language lesson planning. It is within these holistic and highly social contexts that the connections among all of the language arts, in general, and reading and writing, in particular, are clearly relevant to the development of literacy.

Overall, the whole-language philosophy seeks to empower both teachers and learners in the social context of a democratic classroom environment. Here, all children have total access to comprehending and composing processes and the freedom to take charge of their own language learning (Hoffman, 1992). Teachers are free to make decision at all levels of the curriculum and to eliminate educational activities that tend to test, track, and stratify children in the classroom (Edelsky, 1991). This latter point is what has made the idea of whole language politically volatile. Progressive critics express concerns that the whole-language movement could create a "separatism that will ultimately work against their goals. They run the risk of over-whelming us with too much too fast" (Pearson, 1989, p. 240). The separatism of which Pearson speaks can be seen in situations where teachers may take an either/or stance, choosing sides (text-driven, skills paradigms versus whole language) and voicing criticisms over which instructional approach is most effective. While lively discussions about effective teaching are essential to professional development, we must remember that change in educational practice is a process, not an event. Even classroom environments that reflect the whole-language philosophy "would not be effective without the wise combination of child-centered and direct instruction" (Heller, 1991). We must in the end strive to create schools that meet the needs of every child.

## FOR YOUR JOURNAL

1. Describe your very first memories of listening, talking, reading, and writing at home. Who was most influential in your early literacy development?

2. What are your memories of language arts instruction in elementary and middle school? How did oral language and listening influence in your classroom experiences? What and when did you read and write during the school day?

3. Think about how you define reading and writing. How do (will) your definitions influence your classroom teaching?

# 2 THE EMERGENCE OF READING AND WRITING

*I live in gratitude to my parents for initiating me—and as early as I begged for it, without keeping me waiting—into knowledge of the word, into reading. . . .*

*Eudora Welty*, One Writer's Beginnings *(1984, p. 9)*

*Once upon a time there was a real hungry butterfly and he ate up everything for dinner on Saturday. Then he ate a leaf. And he was very, very happy. The End.*

*Michael, age 3 (retelling of Carle, 1969, 1987)*

## CHAPTER CONCEPTS

Preschool and kindergarten children emerge into literacy.

The home environment influences experiences with print.

Kindergartners' knowledge of print is predictable and developmental.

Daily reading and writing is part of a risk-free kindergarten classroom.

Parents can help to bridge the gap between home and formal schooling.

Daniel is a two-and-a-half-year-old child who often entertains his parents' guests by "reading" verbatim Maurice Sendak's (1963) classic tale, *Where the Wild Things Are.* During these highly social literacy events, Daniel carefully holds the book, turning the pages only after perusing each picture and pointing out important details relative to the story. "This is the most scariest wild thing of all," he says as he gestures toward the illustrations. Daniel's oral interpretation is filled with adultlike intonation and expression as he reenacts his favorite bedtime story, "reading" loudly and clearly: "Now stop! Max said and sent the wild things off to bed without their supper." If asked how he learned to read at such a young age, he responds astutely, "I just know it [the story] because Mommy and Daddy read me the book." Indeed, Daniel's parents had read him *Where the Wild Things Are* every night for several months. The read/reread strategy they employed was as natural as tucking him into bed. The effects of their technique are startling, for not only has Daniel memorized the story word for word but also he has articulated how he came to know what he knows.

Michele is three years old and independently writes messages that she proudly shares with her parents. Michele's first written message (Figure 2.1) is indicative of a beginning writer who is learning the standard conventions of print. Filled with lines, circles, scribbles, and drawings, yet devoid of discernable letters, Michele's communication is nonetheless real to her, as she easily "reads" her own work to any willing audience. The note is posted on the refrigerator door for all to admire. Michele understands the importance of print. When asked to read her message, she reflects on the value of the written word in this way: "This is my note. It says I'll be in my room playing if you need me. This is a *M* and this is a *Q* and this is a *R*. Keep it [the message] on the 'frigerator so you don't forget. Bye-bye." Michele pretend-

**FIGURE 2.1**    First written message, by Michele, age 3

writes whenever her mother makes a list or writes a note or a letter. She imitates writing behaviors and often translates the behavior into a situation that is meaningful to her.

Daniel and Michele are emergent readers and writers. They are learning to read and write at home, seemingly effortlessly, without the trappings of formal instruction associated with the schools. Daniel's *metacognitive* awareness (Flavelle, 1976), or his ability to talk about what he knows about his own emergent reading and writing behaviors, is typical of some children, who enter school already knowing a great deal about books and reading. Michele's *metalinguistic* awareness, or her ability to articulate what she knows about language, reflects the thoughtful mind of an emergent writer who knows far more about written language than educators, until recently, could ever imagine.

## EMERGENT LITERACY

*Emergent literacy,* a term first introduced by Marie Clay (1966), is a concept that has come to replace our former notions of "readiness" to read and write. Research during the 1980s into young children's reading and writing behaviors challenges the traditional idea that children entering school for the first time must pass through an organized sequence of skills before they will benefit from formal reading and writing instruction. Instead, we have learned that oral language, reading, and writing begin to develop concurrently and interrelatedly long before children enter school (Martinez & Teale, 1987). Our growing knowledge of how reading and writing emerge helps us to develop an instructional program in which the natural relationships among oral language, listening, reading, and writing play a prominent role early in a child's schooling.

Reading and writing, like listening and speaking, begin at home. Recent home and preschool developmental research enables us to develop a profile of a kindergartner's reading and writing knowledge. The following characteristics of emergent readers and writers reveal important information to guide the development of an effective kindergarten environment.

### What Emergent Readers and Writers Know

1. Young children know that reading and writing are purposeful means of communicating ideas and feelings (Klein & Schickendanz, 1980; Teale, 1982).

2. These children have internalized many of the forms and functions of environmental print (Hiebert, 1981).

3. Their knowledge of the conventions of print enables them to understand the concept of word. That is, they know that reading and writing progress from left to right on the printed page, that spaces are necessary between words, that letters and words have uniform shapes and sizes, and that definite patterns and repetitions occur in print for a meaningful message to evolve (Clay, 1982; DeFord, 1980).

4. Their knowledge of sound-symbol correspondences enables them to reconceptualize their ideas about language in order to make the crucial transition from

Reading and writing begin at home.

oral to written language. Conversation and discussion facilitate comprehension after listening activities. Oral language also fosters planning during the composing process. (Dyson, 1981; Geller, 1983; Mason, 1980; Smith, 1981; Sulzby, 1985).

5. They have the ability to talk about language, using their intuitive understanding of environmental print. Emergent readers and writers use such metalinguistic terms as *alphabet, letters, words,* and *sentence* or terms that communicate thought processes, such as *think, mean,* and *remember* (Templeton, 1986).

6. Emergent readers and writers expect reading and writing to be interactive, social events (Templeton, 1986). Parents, siblings, teachers, and child-care providers all contribute to the interactive nature of reading and writing development by helping to shape dozens of literacy events each day during a young child's lifetime (Rasinski & Fredericks, 1988; Teale, 1982).

7. Young children enter school enthusiastic about reading and writing, often already thinking of themselves as writers, but not necessarily as readers just yet. They enjoy books and stories of all kinds and are curious about print (Graves, 1983; Holdoway, 1979).

## Reading and Writing Begin at Home

According to constructivist theories of "natural" literacy development, children acquire the ability to read and write by interacting with the environment. The developmental process of becoming literate is initiated by the child and is "mediated by literate adults, older siblings, or events in the child's everyday life" (Teale, 1982, p. 559). Another person in the child's life, usually an adult, helps to shape the environment by verbally interacting in situations in which the child begins to internalize appropriate reading and writing behaviors. This shaping of the environment reflects the society and culture in which the child and parent reside. Teale and others (Mehan, 1981) believe that becoming literate is an interactive process involving both learning and teaching, thus challenging the Piagetian (Piaget, 1955, 1973) idea that natural literacy development is a somewhat isolated and individualistic learning process. Instead, the total home environment is crucial to early literacy.

Every day children are actively involved in a variety of *literacy events* that may require listening, speaking, reading, and writing. A literacy event "is a set of reading and writing routines embedded within common events in a modern industrial culture, such as banking, mailing, phoning, shopping" (Roskos, 1988, p. 564). Literacy events often involve more than one person, and the use of print through composing or comprehending activities is significant to the event. Interactive literacy events are essential to children's growth in reading and writing (Teale, 1982).

Typical home situations that occur dozens of times a day and lend themselves to reading and writing behaviors include the following: reading bedtime storybooks; reading grocery labels and advertising; reading words in newspapers, magazines, and advertisements; reading captions that appear on television programs; reading and writing letters, birthday, and holiday greetings; writing notes to immediate family members; making lists of all kinds; writing checks; writing phone messages; and writing "welcome home" greetings. Studies of parent-child interactions during home literacy events give us insight into "natural" reading and writing regimes that can be translated into classroom settings.

The most often recorded and most influential home literacy event is a parent reading aloud to a child (Anderson, Hiebert, Scott, & Wilkinson, 1984). The books that parents read are of interest to their children and almost always include content relative to the child's experiential background. Studies of parent and child read-aloud sessions articulate the highly social, interactive nature of bedtime storybook reading. For parents, reading aloud to their child provides a sense of satisfaction and enjoyment; for the child, it is a happy, secure event that contrasts with the more mundane, daily household routines (Holdoway, 1979). From a parental point of view, the main purpose for reading to their children is to provide a pleasurable experience: Storybook reading "is simple giving and taking of pleasure in which the parent makes no demands on the child, but is deeply gratified by the lively responses that normally arise" (p. 39).

The verbal interaction that ordinarily takes place between parent and child during storybook reading often illustrates the concept of *mediation*. A mediated bedtime story routine is one in which the parent shapes the experience by pausing to reflect on what has just been read, pointing to pictures as well as to individual words, asking questions at a variety of cognitive levels, and responding to the child's reactions in such a way as to encourage active involvement in the unfolding story. This social interaction is the teaching aspect of natural literacy development. The parent as teacher nurtures learning to read and write through spontaneous yet normal routines.

During home literacy events, children begin the process of internalizing the concept of word as the parent or child-care provider draws attention to the print. Ultimately, many young children are able to read a few words themselves, although most are quite happy to allow the parent to do most of the reading. A stable concept of word is prerequisite to building a sight-word vocabulary for reading (Gillet & Temple, 1986) and a working written vocabulary for composing. Read-aloud sessions enhance the child's ability to match speech to print, especially when words are pointed to and discussed. By listening to stories again and again, children also come to know how stories are structured. The conceptual knowledge of text structure is fundamental to comprehending and composing.

## MOVING INTO KINDERGARTEN

### VIGNETTE

*"How was your first day of kindergarten?" asked Michael's mother, after picking him up from school. In an exasperated voice he replied, "What's the use, Mom? I can't read, I can't write, and they won't let me talk."*

*"What do you mean they won't let you talk?" she asked with some trepidation.*

*"Well, we just sit around and be quiet and listen to the story. I wanna talk about stuff. But no. We have to just sit and be quiet. Even when we have art we have to be quiet. Kindergarten's no fun."*

## Cultural Diversity

The account of Michael's reaction to the first day of kindergarten illustrates fundamental differences between the culture of the home and the school. Even though this five-year-old comes from an English-speaking, middle-class home where verbal communication is valued, kindergarten for Michael was nevertheless a rule-governed environment where he perceived talking to be a delegated privilege rather than a natural tool to communicate. Hence his frustration.

Theories of cultural discontinuity, or the mismatch between home and school cultures, are sometimes blamed for student failure to learn, especially when a child's home language and culture are either suppressed or ignored (Erickson, 1987). The children in our classrooms come from diverse backgrounds, when values and beliefs of the family and community influence their thoughts, feelings, and behaviors toward schooling. It is important for teachers to remember that all children bring with them a richness of experience from which to draw upon during the process of becoming literate.

Learning to read and write standard English is a fundamental objective in the language arts curriculum, beginning in kindergarten. Kathryn Au (1993) suggests that teachers need to allow students of diverse backgrounds "to use strengths in their home languages as the basis for becoming proficient in reading and writing in English" (p. 21). "Share and tell" is an important time during the kindergarten day in which children should be allowed to talk freely, using their home language. The teacher models standard English while talking with the children about their experiences. Another opportunity occurs after children have listened to, read, or written a story, poem, or nonfiction. Here they could engage in discussions using their home language, such as Spanish, Vietnamese, or any of the nonstandard English forms, including pidgin English, Creole English, and Black dialect. Au suggests that during such discussions the teacher model standard English to express similar ideas and to encourage the children's use of conventional vocabulary and sentence structure.

Talk is fundamental to the process of learning to read and write. The following sections describe language arts methods that encourage young children to engage in oral language play throughout the kindergarten reading and writing curriculum.

## Oral Language and Reading

Recent studies comparing home and kindergarten storybook reading describe the developmental nature of emergent reading behaviors. Sulzby (1985) discovered that kindergarten children's early reading attempts of favorite storybooks followed an organized pattern, which differs predictably from the emergent reading behaviors of preschool-age children. She categorized kindergartners' early reading attempts in the following way: Picture-governed attempts, which inspired labeling, commenting, and disjointed storytelling, followed by more coherent telling of the entire story, and print-governed attempts in which the child first ignores the print yet attempts the story by using pretend reading. Sulzby found that as children began to pay more and more attention to print, they progress through the following stages: (1) "high-level" refusals, based on a need to know more about print; (2) "aspectual reading," in which the child attempts only known words on each page; (3) and finally, holistic attempts in which the child successfully reads from print and ultimately becomes an independent reader.

***Kindergarten Storybook and Poetry Reading.***    Classroom read-aloud strategies should take into consideration emergent reading behavior as reflected in the developmental research on early literacy. Teachers reading stories aloud is a time-honored tradition in the kindergarten curriculum. Reading prose and poetry to kindergartners helps children to develop important concepts about written language, including the concept of word and the structure of texts.

Young children love oral language play involving rhyme, rhythm, and meter. Many children come to school already having memorized numerous nursery rhymes, lullabies, and preschool songs. They easily recite their favorite verse and feel a great sense of accomplishment at having "read" a rhyme in their favorite Mother Goose storybook. Pretend reading or reciting memorized verse while attending to print helps children to develop a sense of what words are. Studies of language acquisition and development reveal that children naturally segment and categorize speech sounds as they organize and make sense of the environment (Geller, 1983). Hearing differences and similarities of sounds in the environment is fundamental to literacy development and aids in comprehending and composing.

These kindergartners enjoy a private space to read picture books independently.

By reading aloud a variety of rhymed poetry to children, we take advantage of the child's natural interest and curiosity about the sounds in our world. Books that are especially fun to read aloud include classic nursery rhymes, such as *The Real Mother Goose* (1916, 1982), the not so classic *Father Gander Nursery Rhymes* (1985), books of nonsense verse like *A Great Big Ugly Man Came Up and Tied His Horse to Me* (1973), and more modern books of poetry such as Eve Merriam's *Blackberry Ink* (1985) and Jack Prelutsky's *Tyrannosaurus Was a Beast* (1988).

To whatever extent possible, it is desirable to replicate homelike settings within school read-aloud routines. In this way, a gradual transition between "natural" literacy development at home and more formal schooling can be achieved. The use of big books, lap techniques, read/reread, and storytelling methods are important strategies that make the transition easier.

***Big Books.***    Big books are giant-size books published along with a "little book" replica. These colorfully illustrated, highly predictable books can be used in small groups to recreate homelike reading routines. Big books are large enough for all the children in the group to see both print and pictures and to make the connection between oral and written language as the teacher reads aloud. Read-aloud strategies with big books are very similar to one-on-one storybook reading. The reader, who may be a teacher, paraprofessional, or parent volunteer, points to the print and pictures, models excellent oral reading behavior by using an expressive and enthusiastic voice, and pauses throughout to encourage predictions and active involvement in the process. Big books are inviting and allow teachers to engage children more readily in a conversation about the pictures and unfolding narrative, poem, or nonfiction. The children are then free to peruse or reread the small-book version that is available in the classroom library. A list of companies that publish big books is included at the end of this chapter.

## INSTRUCTIONAL GUIDELINES
## Reading to Kindergartners
**Encouraging Reader Response to Literature**

**BEFORE READING**

Begin your read-aloud session by asking the children to tell you everything they know about a major concept that underlies the meaning of the prose or poetry you are about to read. For example, "Tell me everything you know about birthday parties," and "Do you know what it means to be responsible?" are appropriate questions to ask before reading Robert Munsch's (1987) picture book, *Moira's Birthday*. By activating the children's prior knowledge of birthday parties and what it means to be responsible for one's behavior, you will prepare them to understand better the story they are about to hear. At this time you and the children can establish a purpose for listening, based upon the title of the book and the major concept(s) that have been discussed thus far.

**WHILE READING**

Next, read the prose or poetry straight through, pausing only to respond to the children's spontaneous comments about the emerging text and accompanying pictures. Stopping too often to ask for predictions while reading aloud can interfere with interest in and comprehension of the text (Zarillo, 1991).

**AFTER READING**

After reading the piece aloud, ask the following open-ended response questions (M.F. Heller, 1992) to frame the class discussion:

1. Tell me what you thought about (title of story, poem, or nonfiction).
2. How did it make you feel?
3. What was your favorite part?
4. Did the (story, poem, or nonfiction) leave you with a special message?
5. Did the (story, poem, or nonfiction) give you any ideas for writing your own (story or poem)?

The final question in the series is designed to encourage children to begin coming up with writing topics on their own. You may want to provide your own model story or poem inspired by the literature. In this way the children may begin to see the connections between children's literature and composing, between reading and writing.

By establishing an aesthetic purpose for listening (or reading), children are more likely to become personally involved in literature and, as a result, reach higher levels of personal understanding (Many, 1991). While not all literature read-aloud events need to culminate in a writing activity, it is important to ask open-ended questions, in order to promote critical and creative thinking. Figure 2.2 is a kindergartner's written response to *Moira's Birthday*, written after her teacher engaged the children in an open-ended discussion of the book using the five response questions.

**FIGURE 2.2**　Robyn's response (M.F. Heller, 1992) to *Moira's Birthday* (Munsch, 1987)

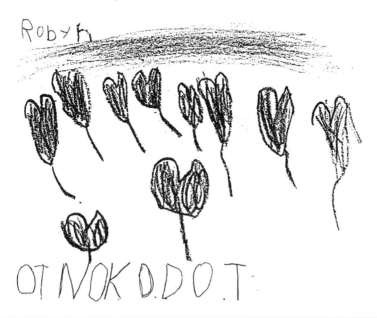

***Reading and Rereading.***   Repeated readings of favorite stories and poems is a valuable method because of its strong theoretical base. By virtue of hearing the same story again and again, children begin to internalize its form and content. The gradual process of becoming *linguistically aware* is a crucial factor in overall reading and writing development. As home observational studies have demonstrated, children often beg to hear the same story again and again. Repeated reading of favorite books encourages children to be more elaborate in their retellings, discussions, and interpretations of familiar stories (Morrow, 1989). Teachers and volunteers can capitalize on young children's enthusiasm by accommodating their wishes during read-aloud sessions. "Friday Favorites" is a time set aside once a week for books chosen by the children to be read again and sometimes again. Favorite books are always made available in both classroom and school libraries.

A note home about a child's favorite read-aloud books is also a good idea, so that parents can reinforce enthusiastic responses to stories. One resourceful kindergarten teacher read and reread Bill Martin's (Martin & Brogan, 1972) classic story "Brown Bear, Brown Bear" again and again the first week of the school year so that by Friday every child had memorized the story. She then sent home a letter describing what they had been doing all week and suggesting what parents could do to reinforce reading behaviors at home. One of her suggestions was that the "Brown Bear, Brown Bear" pattern be extended to include household members or items familiar to the child. For example, "Brown Bear, Brown Bear, What do you see? I see Mommy looking at me!" The result would be an enjoyable and meaningful oral language/listening game between parent and child.

Kindergartners also enjoy creating their own class versions of pattern books such as "Brown Bear, Brown Bear." When creating a class book, each child dictates and then illustrates an original page of the book, as in "Green snake, green snake, What do you see? I see a yellow chicky looking at me," by Michael. The teacher or aide then types, laminates, and assembles the class effort. Throughout the year the book may be sent home with each child to be read to parents and siblings. The result is a marvelous opportunity for children to share their published work with a captive audience.

***Telling and Retelling.***   Oral language and listening are the foundations of reading and writing. The development of listening and oral language communication skills in kindergarten cannot be overemphasized. Kindergarten storytelling is an informal listening activity during which the teacher or child tells a fictional or nonfictional story or retells a familiar tale. Compared to traditional read-the-story-answer-the-comprehension-question techniques, story retelling is a much more holistic and developmentally appropriate way to help children develop their knowledge and understanding of fiction and nonfiction (Morrow, 1989). Listening to, telling, talking about, and retelling a wide variety of literary forms—including poetry, predictable texts, narratives with strong story lines, simple nonfictions, and friendly letters— gives emergent readers and writers a wealth of information about the structure and purpose of written language. This knowledge is gradually internalized as children achieve linguistic awareness, a factor crucial to the process of becoming literate.

Eva has made a puppet that she will use to tell a story.

Stories and folktales with linear or circular plots as well as strong characterization make the best material (Bromley, 1988). For example, "Hansel and Gretel" contains a circular plot that begins and ends in the same setting. "The Gingerbread Man" has a linear plot that begins and ends in different settings. The teacher may choose to tell a classic tale; to make up a "tall tale"; or tell a true story, perhaps about a favorite childhood memory. After modeling storytelling, the teacher then encourages the children to tell a story that is familiar to them or a real tale about themselves. Storytelling and retelling often take place during "share and tell" time (see Appendix A).

Storytelling is even more enjoyable when props are used. Puppets, flannel boards, and "draw and tell" methods (Pflomm, 1986) add interest and curiosity to the unfolding narrative. Using draw and tell, the teacher or a child draws on chart paper or chalkboard parts of a character in the story as it is being told. By the end of the storytelling session, the character is fully drawn. Children have fun predicting what the character is as the picture is pieced together.

Although original storytelling is the preferred setting to instill a sense of narrative structure, single pictures and wordless picture books are often used as a stimulus for story-making activities. Wordless picture books can be a wonderful resource for storytelling, provided the teacher helps children to make the connections between events on each page (Hough, Nurss, & Wood, 1987). Inspired by the pictures, which tell a tale, children can (theoretically) create their own story. In the following oral rendition of Helen Oxenbury's *Beach Day* (1982), Stephen's telling of "The Boy Goes to the Beach" basically retells the literal events on each page, adding just a bit of dialogue.

### THE BOY GOES TO THE BEACH

by Stephen

*One day the little boy went to the beach. He played in the sand. He made a sand castle. A dog digged into it. The boy was mad. He poured water on his mom and dad. They were angry. Then a little girl came along with some ice cream. She gave the little boy some of hers. Then he buried his dad with sand. Then he buried himself with sand. Sometimes he plays beach ball. But one time he threw the beach ball into the man's lap by accident. It was "OK," he said. Suddenly he splashed in the water. He was wet and too wet. His mommy dried him off. Suddenly it was windy. They had to get away from the wind. They had their dinner. They had apples, cake, tea, chocolate milk, grapes, potato salad, napkins, plates, and knives.*

*The End*

Kindergartners will probably not fictionalize a wordless picture book or create a fiction from a single picture. Ironically, the picture as stimulus in each setting can inhibit the child's own creativity, which appears to be nurtured during original storytelling activities (Hough, Nurss, & Wood, 1987). According to the research literature, original storytelling activities ought to take precedence over single picture or wordless picture-book tellings, though the latter should not be eliminated from the kindergarten language arts program. There are many interesting pictures and beautifully illustrated wordless picture books that give children hours of pleasure, from Alexandra Day's (1985) *Good Dog Carl* to David Wiesner's (1991) *Tuesday.* Wordless picture books and picture files are an important part of kindergarten classroom libraries and learning centers.

Another level of story retelling involves either oral or written summaries of a story. These summaries closely parallel the actual story and reveal the children's listening and reading comprehension. Valuable insights can be obtained by listening closely to a kindergartner's rendition of a story just heard. We learn how well the child can reconstruct a fully formed story containing traditional parts—setting, beginning, reaction, attempt, outcome, ending (Mandler & Johnson, 1977). Storytelling and retelling helps children to internalize the concept of story and ultimately to comprehend and compose narratives of all kinds (Applebee, 1978).

You may want to tape-record the children's oral stories for later transcription and placement in a class book of stories. Word processors and typewriters make record keeping even more efficient, as you can type and print an immediate record as the children are telling their stories.

***Creative Dramatics.***    The American Alliance for Theater and Education (AATE) defines creative drama as "an improvisational, nonexhibitional, process-centered form of drama in which participants are guided by a leader to imagine, enact, and reflect upon human experiences" (Davis & Behm, 1978, p. 19). In kindergarten, creative dramatics typically includes movement activities, pantomime, improvisation, and dramatization of narratives and nonfiction. Young children often engage in spontaneous and imaginative play. Children's spontaneity can be channeled into dramatic play that supports language development, especially oral language and listening.

Creative drama also has the "potential to develop language and communication abilities, problem-solving skills, and creativity; to promote a positive self-concept, social awareness, empathy, a clarification of values and attitudes, and an understanding of the art of theater" (Davis & Behm, 1978, p. 10). While dramatizations of fictional stories are frequently used in kindergarten, nonfiction is also an important source for creative play. Putnam (1991) describes an inner-city kindergarten classroom in which the teacher, Mrs. Winslow, engaged the children in the dramatization of the concept "Civil Rights." Mrs. Winslow told the kindergartners (all of whom were African American) the story of Rosa Parks, a seamstress who was arrested for refusing to move to the back of a bus. She then described how Martin Luther King organized a peaceful boycott of the buses in Montgomery and how the police commissioner sent dogs to attack the demonstrators. The next day, Mrs. Winslow reviewed key points in the historical event and then organized a class dramatization. The following is a brief excerpt from Putnam's observations in Mrs. Winslow's classroom that day:

> "Now let's make a bus," she said. "How will we make a bus?"
> "Chairs!" chorused the children.
> After two rows of chairs were placed to simulate a bus, it was time to organize the cast of characters. As always, students were given choices . . .
> "All right, bus driver, drive your bus up to the corner. Come on, rmmm, steer your wheel. Brrmmmm. Brrrmm. Stop your bus at the corner. Now, white people, come get on the bus and sit in the front. Black people, to the back. Now, Mrs. Parks, on the bus, please. Mrs. Parks is getting on the bus. Look, look, her feet hurt. All right, start your bus." The bus driver made an "mmmmm" sound as he started the bus." (p. 467)

The dramatization of nonfiction helps children "to build their reservoir of scripts and scenarios for how the world works" (p. 468). Role-playing a concept such as civil rights is a powerful way to develop prior knowledge of ideas that are ultimately needed for comprehension and composition.

The kindergarten environment is a natural setting for dramatic play areas or centers. In a dramatic play center, students engage in role-playing activities such as housekeeping, grocery store, doctor's office, hospital, restaurant, fire station, post office, school room, parenting, and many more real-life scenarios. Here the teacher provides a well-defined area in the room and equips it with props that stimulate the children's imagination and language. Such props could include simple costumes (an apron for the kitchen area), imaginary people (puppets and dolls—see Appendix A, "Making Puppets"), writing stimuli (pads for taking food orders, charts for hospital rounds), or reading materials (books to read to baby). The overall goal of a dramatic play area is to encourage communication through oral language and listening.

Dramatic theme plays that include role-playing opportunities familiar to the children are important experiences that foster speaking, listening, and social interaction (Gentile & Hoot, 1983). The theme of a play center ordinarily changes weekly and ties in with daily reading and writing activities. For example, "Housekeeping" is a familiar play center in which children pretend they are family members taking care of household responsibilities. You might then read aloud *No Room for Sarah* (Greenleaf, 1983) or *The Boy in the Drawer* (Munsch, 1986), stories about children and their messy rooms. Later the children would tell or write stories about their own experiences with household chores. Other dramatic plays could involve the children in role-playing favorite storybook characters.

Play of all kinds is fundamental to language development (Piaget, 1952) and in general helps to make the transition between home and school easier. Roskos (1988) contends that "children who actively and frequently participate in pretend play episodes as a kind of story making may have a 'leg up' on literacy learning as they enter the school doors" (p. 563). Pretend play is easily incorporated into the kindergarten curriculum through creative dramatics. The social interaction that occurs during play and creative dramatics encourages children's emergent reading and writing behaviors.

***Lap Techniques.***     One-on-one, "lap" reading techniques are not always possible because of the large number of children in an average kindergarten classroom. However, more and more kindergarten teachers are eliciting the help of parents, paraprofessionals, and older children. One kindergarten classroom teacher initiated a volunteer storybook read-aloud program in which every day at least one parent, paraprofessional, school administrator, or student reads to children individually. The most successful read-aloud time is the fifteen minutes before school starts as children begin to arrive in the classroom. The kindergartners either sit in the volunteer's lap or alongside the person reading. Lap reading takes place in a quiet, partitioned corner of the room, which looks very much like a child's bedroom, complete with rocking chair, day bed, and antique bathtub—"Rub-a-dub-dub-let's read in the tub!" By the end of the week, all children have had a chance to participate in the activity. The lap technique can also be used successfully for storytelling and retelling. It is a valuable method that encourages talk about books, which is so very important to the development of literacy.

***The Kindergarten Classroom Library.***     The books that we choose to read or tell to kindergartners influence their love of books and their desire to become independent readers themselves. A well-stocked classroom library is a key factor in the literacy development of five- and six-year-old children. Martinez and Teale (1988) studied kindergartners' independent library book selections and identified three factors that influence them: book familiarity, degree of familiarity, and the structure of stories. Martinez and Teale recommend including in classroom libraries not only storybooks, picture books, alphabet and counting books, and concept and nonfiction books but also numerous books with predictable texts, big books, and conventionally sized books. Nursery rhymes and rhymed and unrhymed poetry of all kinds are also highly recommended.

Ideally a kindergarten classroom library ought to have somewhere between 100 and 200 books, with an additional 50 books or so from the school library that are frequently rotated. These books are accessible to the children at all times, beckoning them to escape into fantasy and adventure, to develop a love of literature. Bibliographies of books appropriate for kindergarten classroom libraries are included at the end of this chapter.

## Oral Language and Writing

"Writing is drawing pictures," says five-year-old Kirk in response to his teacher's question, "What is writing?" Kirk's response is typical of an emergent writer's view of the writing process. He equates writing with drawing that represents his intended meaning—a Vygotskian (1962, 1979) notion. Picture drawing is a child's early attempt at symbolizing his or her world and in the beginning is preferable to printing words. Picture drawing is much more satisfying to beginning writers, primarily because the process is less tiring than putting together sounds and alphabet symbols to make words. Drawing pictures, scribbling, combining scribbles and pictures, writing with invented spellings, and ultimately conventional spelling constitute the basic developmental stages that emergent writers exhibit throughout the kindergarten year (Sulzby, 1986). Figure 2.3 is an example of Kirk's early kindergarten writing. His work is dominated by the picture. His message, "space," appears along with his name. When asked to talk about his picture, Kirk's oral language flows as he elaborates on his creation: "The spaceship launched the other spaceship up in outer space. It's trying to get back to earth. The astronaut is going to fix the spaceship that got broke. He has space equipment." For now it is much easier for Kirk to talk about his picture than to write about it.

*Oral Composition.*      Talk is very important in making the transition from picture drawing to printed message. When teachers talk with kindergartners about their pictures, it helps children to think about the expressive power of written language (Dyson, 1982). Making the connection between oral and written language lays the foundation for reading and reading and writing connections. We often elicit children's oral compositions through individual or group dictations traditionally called *language experience stories.* The language experience approach was originally developed as an alternative method of teaching beginning reading, using a child's

**FIGURE 2.3**   "Space," by Kirk, age 5

oral language as the basis for the day's reading lesson (Stauffer, 1980). Integrated, or whole-language, methods of teaching reading and writing concurrently take language experience a step further by utilizing the child's oral *and* written language as a primary text for developing word recognition skills, reading comprehension, and written composition.

Language experience lessons are theoretically and pedagogically appropriate in kindergarten. Seeing their own language in print enables young children to better understand the relationships between speech and print and to internalize the concept of word. Further, a direct or concrete experience of some kind, such as a field trip, is integral to language experience activities. Language is rooted in concrete behavior and flourishes in social settings (Vygotsky, 1978) afforded through language experience approach. The following instructional guidelines detail the steps in an effective kindergarten language experience lesson.

As Andrew dictates a story to his teacher, he is beginning to realize the relationships among talking, writing, and reading.

## INSTRUCTIONAL GUIDELINES
### Implementing the Language Experience Approach

The steps of a language experience lesson highlight the relationships among listening, speaking, writing, and reading.

#### EXPERIENCING

**1.** Begin with a direct experience in which all of the children have an opportunity to participate. Numerous opportunities occur throughout the day and lend themselves to experience stories.

#### Example Experiences

Process activity during which the children make things
to eat—peanut butter and jelly sandwiches, popcorn, no-bake cookies, banana bread, butter

*(continued)*

**Instructional Guidelines (continued)**

> to drink—juice, blender milkshakes
>
> to touch—paper snowflakes, tie-dyed material, velcro or sandpaper shapes and alphabet letters, finger paintings
>
> to hear—kazoos, drums, water glass chimes, rain sticks
>
> to see—kaleidoscopes, wax paper "stained glass" pictures, aquariums, terrariums, potted plants

Dramatic theme plays (or role playing), such as Post Office, Restaurant, Style Shop, Grocery Store, Shopping Mall, Jungle Safari, Junk-Food Restaurant, Doctor's Office

Nature walks (during all seasons) around the school building and nearby natural areas

Field trips of all kinds, including visits to the fire station, police station, young people's concerts, planetarium, movies, plays, zoo, nursing home

Holiday or special-occasion picture or poster drawing or painting; valentines; Christmas, Hanukkah, or Easter cards; birthday cards

Children's literature-based activities: For example, after reading Ina Friedman's (1984) *How My Parent's Learned to Eat,* prepare rice in a steamer and teach the children to use chopsticks. Asian American children in the class who are already proficient users would serve as models for everyone.

Multicultural activities: Take a field trip to a neighborhood restaurant or grocery store that features authentic ethnic foods; invite guest speakers to talk about their customs and culture; visit a nearby cultural exhibit, an Indian reservation, or an ethnic neighborhood; talk to the people about their world.

**DISCUSSING**

2. Talk with the children about the experience to elaborate and extend their knowledge and understanding of new and old concepts: "What is the most interesting new thing you learned at the fire station?" or "I like your holiday cards. Do you remember your very favorite Christmas or Hanukkah?"

3. Draw pictures of the experience to stimulate memory and cognition about what has just happened. Talk about the pictures with the children as they are being drawn.

4. Talk about purposes for telling a story (or simple nonfiction) about the experience. Encourage the children to establish a reason to dictate: "Shall we write the steps for making no-bake cookies so we can give Mom our

recipe?" or "Shall we write a story about our field trip to the zoo? For whom shall we write our story?

### TELLING AND WRITING

5. Write the children's oral contributions to the experience story exactly as dictated. Writing exactly what the children say encourages risk taking during storytelling. In so doing we demonstrate respect for children's ideas and create an environment where they are not fearful of doing something "wrong" during a dictation. Simultaneously, the teacher takes every opportunity to model standard English grammar and syntax, by discussing the work in progress and encouraging the children to use complete sentences and correct grammar in their oral language.

   The structure of a language experience lesson naturally highlights the recursive nature of the composing process. We can pause, reflect on what the children have contributed, and encourage reacting to as well as rewriting the work in progress. Sensitive teachers are able to guide the children's writing in a nonthreatening manner without taking away ownership.

   When taking dictation in large or small groups, make sure that each child can easily observe while you print in manuscript (see Appendix C for handwriting models). For best results, use large, unlined white paper that is securely situated on an easel and easily seen by all children. A glare-free chalkboard or overhead transparency are alternatives to an easel.

   When taking dictation from children one on one, situate yourself alongside the child. Use two sheets of unlined white paper with a carbon in between. When you are through both you and the child will have a copy of the story to share.

   Computers are valuable tools when taking dictation from a single child or from small groups of children. Use a good word-processing program that utilizes primary type especially designed for children, such as *The Children's Writing and Publishing Center* (1989). As the children gather around the computer, they dictate and observe their story unfold (Figure 2.4). Liquid crystal displays (LCDs) are also available for overhead projectors. LCDs enable you to project a computer image onto a screen for the whole class to see.

### READING

6. Read the contributions aloud throughout the dictation, pointing to individual words; modeling fluent, expressive oral reading; and at the same time reflecting on the children's work in progress. When the

*(continued)*

**Instructional Guidelines (continued)**

children have finished dictating, reread their work, again pointing to each word and encouraging the children to read aloud with you. The read/reread sequence that you use during language experience lessons reinforces the children's understanding of the connections among oral language, listening, writing, and reading.

# Halloween

## By

## Alecia, Sarah, T.J., Greg, Paul, Daniel, Charlie, & Jordan

The old, old witch ran. She found a pumpkin, and she carved it. She jumped on a broom. She crashed through a window.

She ran into a friend. The witch flew on her broom, and she crashed off her broom. The witch found a friend to give a valentine to.

The witch played with the computer. The witch wrote all of this story.

## The End

**FIGURE 2.4** "Halloween," a small-group dictation

**PUBLISHING**

7. Display the children's finished work prominently in the room so that they can reread the story by themselves and to others. Traditional LEA procedures recommend that the children copy the experience story, then underline known sight words. Emergent kindergarten readers and writers do not yet have the eye-hand coordination to copy from chart paper. Some do not yet know how to form all the letters. But sometime during the year many kindergartners may be able to copy their stories into their journals or writing folders. In the meantime, if you have access to a word processor or typewriter, you may wish to make a collection of experience stories in little-book form for the classroom library. The kindergartners could illustrate each book, which is a coveted addition to classroom reading resources.

***Written Composition.*** Gradually, kindergartners gain control over written language and are less reluctant to express themselves in ways other than picture drawing. The physical act of printing letters is hard work for young children whose oral language exceeds their ability to compose in writing. Formal handwriting instruction is normally reserved for the first-grade year. Suggestions for fostering the emergence of handwriting skills in kindergarten are contained in "For Your Handwriting Notebook," at the end of this chapter.

Although oral composition remains a very important part of the overall curriculum, the children should be encouraged from the first day to write simple stories and nonfictions, which may evolve from concrete experiences (D. H. Graves, 1983). Figure 2.5 is a story by Philip, a six-year-old who entered his kindergarten year

**FIGURE 2.5** "How I Spent My $100," by Philip, age 6

already reading. His narrative is based on a weekend trip to the mall that he took with his parents: "I had 100 dollars. I went to the mall with my 100 dollars. I took the super friends play dough. It cost $7.50. I had $92.50. I bought a GoBot. His name was Scooter."

Philip uses a combination of invented and conventional spellings to convey his message. He does not consistently put spaces between words in his writing, which might suggest that he has an unstable concept of what a word is. In contrast, Sarah also uses invented and conventional spellings as well as spaces between words (Figure 2.6). But she does not read independently as well as Philip. Her story is a work of fiction: "Once there was a donut, and he liked to play with other donuts."

Sulzby (1986) observed inconsistencies between oral-language-proficient children and their reading and writing behaviors. Just because a kindergartner is already reading does not mean that his or her written language will reflect mature, conventional form and content. Such ambiguities seem to be prevalent in kindergarten classrooms and should be kept in mind when designing a language arts curriculum that fosters the interrelationships among listening, speaking, reading, and writing.

### The Kindergarten Language Arts Curriculum

A kindergarten language arts curriculum is guided by goals basic to literacy development. Recommendations made in a joint statement prepared by the Early Childhood and Literacy Development Committee of the International Reading Association

**FIGURE 2.6**   "The Donut," by Sarah, age 5

(1986) urge us to "Encourage children's first attempts at writing without concern for the proper formation of letters or correct conventional spellings; encourage risk-taking in first attempts at reading and writing and accept what appear to be errors as part of children's natural patterns of growth and development; provide time regularly for children's independent reading and writing" (p. 111). With basic goals clearly in mind, we can begin to organize a curriculum that is developmentally appropriate for all children, starting with the first day of school.

***Getting Started the First Day.*** "I know how to get my kindergartners to listen to stories and to talk about stories and about themselves. But how can I expect them to write? Some of them don't even know the proper way to hold a pencil on the first day of school." These are legitimate concerns of even the most veteran kindergarten teachers, especially if writing has not been an integral part of the first year of formal schooling. One suggestion is to nurture the children's natural curiosity about and enthusiasm for print starting on the very first day of school when they are eager to learn. From the beginning children should realize that print is important, for without it we could not read our storybooks or write notes to our friends or know where we are in an unfamiliar environment.

The classroom should abound with print of all shapes and sizes, communicating to the children that the written word is of great value to us. Traditional classrooms include the alphabet, numbers, calendar and seasonal bulletin boards, classroom libraries, and the children's names neatly taped to the tables. Going beyond the traditional involves the creative use of print to help instill its value.

As mentioned earlier in the chapter, five- and six-year-olds enter school knowing a great deal about the forms and functions of print. They expect print to make sense and to fulfill a variety of social purposes. Their knowledge of environmental print in particular is well documented in the research literature. Easily recognized signs about town include "McDonalds," "Stop," "No Parking," "Handicapped," "Wal-Mart," "Putt-Putt," "Zoo," "School Zone," "Exit," "Swimming Pool," and "U.S. Post Office." Bringing environmental print into the classroom helps to bridge the gap between home and school. A deep sense of satisfaction goes along with kindergartners' realization that they can read their names as well as the signs around the classroom. Not only can they read them, they can write the words in nonthreatening, social contexts that are set up by the teacher.

First-day kindergarten writing activities should be closely aligned with the children's prior knowledge of environmental print and home and leisure-time reading and writing experiences. Our ultimate goal is to foster independent reading and writing, and first experiences are crucial to this outcome. Open-ended assignments, such as "Write about anything you want," can be just as frustrating for children as teacher-directed topics such as "Write a story called 'How I Spent My Summer Vacation.'" It is far easier to get kindergartners to put pencil or crayon to paper if gentle guidance is given within a risk-free environment that fosters a love of reading books and writing.

First writing experiences should take advantage of what the children already know about print, in the context of children's literature and direct experiences. Consider the following real-world model.

INSIDE THE CLASSROOM
## Going to the Post Office: A First-Day Kindergarten Experience

Ms. Collins is an experienced kindergarten teacher who wants the children to begin writing on the first day of school. Her lesson plans for day 1 include a variety of "getting to know you" activities designed to fulfill several objectives: (1) to learn each child's name and something about the child; (2) to help the children feel at ease in their new learning environment; (3) to give the children the opportunity to know one another; (4) to encourage communication through talking and writing; and (5) to observe and assess informally the children's facility with listening, oral, and written language, including reading and writing.

The room is filled with print. Upon entering the room, one is struck by the fact that books and words seem to be everywhere. Ms. Collins uses bulletin boards, flannel boards, and easel pads to exhibit concepts that are familiar to the children: their names; the days of the week and months of the year; the primary colors; numbers; animals; family members; and environmental print such as a stop sign, fast-food restaurant logos, and exit and enter signs. Colorful picture posters of familiar city and country scenes dominate each wall and contribute to an orderly atmosphere. The room is divided into five practical, often thematic, areas for play and direct instruction: The Writing Center, Dramatic Play Area, Lap Reading Space, Math-Magic Table, and The Blue Rug Read-Aloud Area.

Ms. Collins begins the day with a "Morning Message," a teaching strategy described by Crowell, Kawakami, and Wong (1986) at the Kamehameha Schools in Honolulu, Hawaii. The morning (or afternoon) message is written on chart paper or chalkboard and is read aloud by the group. It always has something to do with the daily events of the classroom.

*Today is Monday, August 23, 1993*
*It is the first day of school.*
*Welcome Kindergartners!*

After reading and talking about the message and making introductions, Ms. Collins takes the children on a "tour" of the room so that they know where things are and what kind of behavior is expected of them in each area. She shows them their cubbies, where they put coats and backpacks. She shows them the tables, where for now they have assigned places. She also reviews the sequence of events for the day, which is written on a large easel pad and is easily seen by all of the children.

*First we read the Morning Message.*

*Next we'll listen to a story called* The Jolly Postman or Other People's Letters *(Ahlberg & Ahlberg, 1986).*

*Then we'll draw some pictures and write a letter to a new kindergarten friend.*

*After recess we'll share our letters and have a snack.*

*Next we'll listen to poetry and play a rhyme game.*

*Then we get to visit the library and check out books.*

*Finally, we'll play a game about numbers.*

*After that we'll get ready to go home for lunch.*

The dramatic theme play for the week is "Going to the Post Office." Themes are changed weekly to keep boredom in check and to maximize the influence familiar ideas have on children's emerging concept development. When they arrive at the dramatic play area, Ms. Collins carefully describes the purpose of the milk carton mailboxes, each with a child's name carefully printed on it.

> **Ms. COLLINS:** These milk carton mailboxes are for the pictures and messages that each of you will be drawing and writing. What does this area remind you of?
>
> **TYLER** (excitedly pointing to the sign on the wall over the milk cartons)**:** That says Post Office. My mom works at the post office. She's a postal worker!

Ms. Collins compliments him for reading the sign and suggests that Tyler's mom might like to visit the class and tell them what it's like to be a postal worker. Tyler says he'll ask his mom tonight. Ms. Collins goes on to explain that the children are going to get a chance to write messages to each other later in the morning. They seem very excited about this idea. Some want to get started right away; others look nervous.

After the tour, Ms. Collins and the children settle down in the "Blue Rug" reading area. Her first activity is to read aloud Janet and Allan Ahlberg's (1986) *The Jolly Postman or Other People's Letters,* a cleverly written book about a postman delivering letters to fairy-tale characters. The letters, also included in pocket envelopes within the book, are written from the point of view of other characters in the same fairy tale. For example, the big, bad wolf gets a letter from the three little pigs' lawyer regarding the destruction of the pigs' property. Jack, of Jack and the Beanstock fame, sends a picture postcard to the Giant thanking him for providing the gold to fund his vacation. The main text of the story is rhymed and predictable as the postman makes his rounds to all of the characters' houses.

*(continued)*

**Inside the Classroom (continued)**

> **Ms. COLLINS:** While you are listening to the story about the postman delivering his letters, I want you to listen to the message that each fairy tale character sends.

From the first day she wishes to encourage her kindergartners to listen purposefully.

Ms. Collins reads the story aloud, stopping frequently to point to pictures and words, to ask questions about content and rhyme, and to respond to the children's enthusiastic statements and questions. As she pulls each letter from its envelope, she opens it with a flourish, reads it, and passes it to the children, who giggle as they look at the words and touch the parts of this special book. Most of the children are very familiar with the fairy tale characters. Their prior knowledge contributes to their understanding of the unfolding story.

Throughout the story-reading activity, Ms. Collins relates the concept of communicating through letter writing to the children's experiences. "Have you ever received a letter? Have you ever written a letter?" When the story is over, she models letter writing for the children by *telling* about a letter she once wrote to her own little girl who just happened to be a kindergartner:

> *Dear Melissa,*
>
> *Today is your very first day of kindergarten. I hope that you have a wonderful time. Soon you will be reading and writing. I am very proud of you.*
>
> > *Love, Mommy.*

She then displays the letter on chart paper and reads the letter aloud while pointing to each word. At the bottom of the letter, she has drawn a picture of Mommy waving goodbye to Melissa as she gets on the bus to go to school. Their interest aroused, the children seem very anxious to write their own letters. A few appear hesitant. Jeremy announces loudly, "But I can't write."

> **Ms. COLLINS:** Jeremy, what is writing?
>
> **JEREMY:** It means you put words on a piece of paper. I can't make the letters. The pencil's too skinny.
>
> **Ms. COLLINS:** Jeremy, I don't expect your writing or any of the other kindergartners' writing to look exactly like mine. You could start by just drawing a picture of anything you want, then maybe try writing what's in the picture. What do you think?
>
> **JEREMY:** OK. Where's the colors?

Ms. Collins's instructions about what the children write on this first day of school are both structured and open-ended. She wants them to try writing letters (or messages) to an immediate audience, their peers. However, she is an experienced teacher who realizes that not all of the children will feel comfortable playing with written language or even communicating with children they do not know. She decides to encourage the children to write a letter to or draw a picture for a classmate, perhaps describing something about themselves or their feelings about going to school. The letter or picture is then to be delivered to the children's individual mailboxes. Ms. Collins randomly pairs the children so that they each have a writing buddy to send a letter or picture message to.

Another option that she suggests is to write a letter to or draw a picture for the teacher, who also has a mailbox; the principal; or a family member. A "general delivery" box is also located in the center. Ms. Collins is open to suggestions for audiences as well as letter and picture content from the children. Some children want to write "story" letters; others want to write poetry. Anything goes, as long as a message or picture is sent to someone.

Writing materials are in the "writing center" area, where all children go to retrieve folders that have been spread out on a table and have their names clearly printed on them. Many of the children recognize their names. Several do not. Ms. Collins makes a note of Sam, Kelly, Christopher, Jeremy, and Cynthia, who get lost in the shuffle of trying to find their folders. They do not yet recognize their names and appear to be frustrated.

The children will keep their writing folders in the center but bring them to their tables for large-group work. Initially, the children use unlined white paper and have the option of writing with any size pencil, crayon, or marker that they wish. They are encouraged to date each paper (although Ms. Collins must do this for months) and always keep their work in a folder for use much later during parent conferences.

While the children are working, Ms. Collins moves about the three main tables, responding to the children's questions and concerns. Terry is a reluctant writer who puts his head down on the table and cries.

**Ms. Collins:** Terry, what's wrong?

**Terry:** I want to go home.

**Ms. Collins:** You want to go home? Tell me about your home. I know you have a new baby brother. What's his name?

**Terry:** Tommy.

**Ms. Collins:** And what do you suppose he's doing right now?

*(continued)*

**Inside the Classroom (continued)**

> TERRY: Probly sleeping. He sleeps all the time.
>
> Ms. COLLINS: How about your mommy? What's she doing?
>
> TERRY: She's at work. At K-Mart.
>
> Ms. COLLINS: Do you think you might like to draw a picture for me of your little brother sleeping or of your mommy working at K-Mart? Or maybe something else?
>
> TERRY: OK. Can I use those markers?
>
> Ms. COLLINS: Absolutely.

Terry perks up and begins his creation as soon as Ms. Collins has moved to another table. Most of the children in the room engage in picture drawing. A few children quickly begin writing but at the same time wave their hands in the air for help with spelling. They want words spelled correctly for them. "How do you spell *kindergarten?*" says Jill. Ms. Collins encourages invented spelling. Her general response is "Spell the words the way you think they're spelled. Think about the sounds in the word. Spell them as they sound to you." If the children persist in wanting to know how to spell a word, she spells it for them in order to keep the composing process flowing. Sometimes the questions are more difficult to answer, as demonstrated in the following dialogue:

"How do you spell *W?*" asks Michael.

*"W* is just a letter in the alphabet, Michael," says Ms. Collins with a smile.

"I know that. But how do you *spell* it. It's got a /d/ in it somewhere, I just know it. Listen, *duh, duh, W."*

Ms. Collins then asks Michael the word he's trying to spell, which happens to be *rock.* She spells *rock* for him, but at the same time encourages him to keep trying and asking for help when he needs it.

Encouraging risk taking with spelling is important but should not be forced at the expense of writing fluency. Kindergartners naturally want their writing to look like conventional print, and they know that words are spelled in conventional ways (Dyson, 1982). They eventually learn that invented spelling is a kind of written language play that will help them to become better writers. They also learn that the more they write and the more they read, the better they spell. As their sight-word vocabulary increases, so does their conventional spelling. Chapter 3 elaborates on the stages of spelling development through which children progress during kindergarten and primary grades.

Ms. Collins carries with her an anecdotal journal in which she writes observations about the children as they are composing. Her purpose is to assess informally the children's writing attitudes and abilities. She also asks the children to read or talk about their work so that she has a record of each child's work. This activity is very important because she wants to be able to respond to what the children have written during sharing time. If the child has forgotten what he or she wrote, Ms. Collins has a record and can help. A comparison of the child's oral rendition of his or her written work is also useful in assessing oral and written language and the child's ability to spell inventively. These brief anecdotal records of what the children wrote are then placed in their assessment portfolios for future reference.

Throughout the composing process, the children may collaborate, ask each other for help, respond to one another's work, and finally share their letters with the other children at their tables. Ms. Collins frequently models appropriate reader responses in this way: "Kerry, your letter is very interesting. I didn't know that you were a ballerina. Can you tell Sheila more about your ballet classes? What's this word [spelled *dr*] right here? Oh, *barre*. That's what you hold on to when you're taking lessons, right? Very good. I see you've drawn a picture of a barre. Keep going, you're doing a great job!"

Upon completing their letter or picture, each child gets a sticker to place on the envelope as the "stamp." Then the children deliver their creations to the appropriate mailboxes with the help of Ms. Collins. It is now time for recess. They will have more time for sharing their writing during snack time.

During snack time the children sit next to their peers and read aloud or discuss their message or picture.

> RENAE (reading to Sally): Dear Sally. I like you. You are pretty. The end.
> SALLY (reading to Renae): This is my cat, Pauline. [Shows picture of a cat. The cat has a head and three lines for its body.]

Shared reading and telling of messages is another way to develop a sense of community within the kindergarten classroom. The children exhibit a wide range of written language capabilities, from scribble writing and tentative line drawings to more elaborate messages written in invented spelling and carefully illustrated. Karla has drawn a thin yellow line in the middle of her paper ("My fish"), and Micky has penciled an elaborate blue dinosaur complete with horns and bony plates ("Stegosaur"). Joey's drawing is white crayon scribbles on white paper ("Snow"). The range is typical of kindergarten classrooms made up of children from diverse family backgrounds.

Ms. Collins next announces to the children that tomorrow they will draw "secret pal" names and write secret messages to their kindergarten friends. Tomorrow *everyone* will get a special message in their mailboxes. Messages to friends and family would be an ongoing activity throughout the kindergarten year.

Kelly talks over a writing topic with her sixth-grade writing mate.

***After Day 1.***     Structuring regular times to write and to read and to talk about reading and writing is crucial to kindergarten curriculums. Writing and reading connected text is critical to the success of any program, be it in kindergarten or grade 12 (B. T. Peterson, 1986). Connected text refers to texts that go beyond the sentence level—whole paragraphs, stories, and poems. The length of connected text that children are able to tolerate varies within and across all grade levels. For instance, in kindergarten most children should not be expected to compose more than a one- or two-sentence story: however, they are fully capable of listening to ten to fifteen minutes' of a story.

Scheduling writing and reading time is the easy part. We can determine when the children will write and when they will read and be read to. The question posed most often by teachers developing early literacy programs is what to write day after day.

## INSTRUCTIONAL GUIDELINES
### Helping Kindergartners Compose

When deciding on daily writing activities that encourage a love of print, keep in mind that kindergarten children should:

### 1. Write about activities that matter to them personally.

Five- and six-year-old children are still very ego-involved. They are struggling to make sense of their personal world and to gain control over print. How do you know what matters personally to a kindergartner? Simply put, you ask them. You can organize your inquiries by using interest inventories that are administered orally (See Chapter 8 for examples of interest inventories). "Tell me what you like to do for fun" is a typical question that will yield an abundance of information about the children in your class.

Records of the children's responses are kept in portfolios and used in planning individual and group writing and reading activities. You may also wish to model for the children what you enjoy reading, writing, or doing to give them a better idea of what is meant by the concept of interest (D. H. Graves, 1983). You might say something like this: "I'm interested in all kinds of things, like biking, cooking, and reading. These are the things that make me feel good about myself." Then present an oral or written narrative about something you're interested in.

### 2. Write about things that they have experienced.

Child-centered, experience-based lesson plans give children ideas to think, talk, and write about. Earlier in this chapter, I described the language experience approach traditionally associated with oral composing. Active, hands-on involvement in a variety of activities ranging from field trips to finger painting to making no-bake cookies gives children knowledge and incentive for writing, for reading what they have written, and for reading published books on topics stimulated by the experience.

### 3. Write about familiar persons, places, or things, such as themselves, friends, families, teachers, famous individuals, home, school, toys, pets.

Young children like to talk and write about things that are familiar and comfortable: friends and family, home and school, toys and pets. The personal narrative is a popular form frequently chosen by children or assigned by their teachers (M. F. Heller, 1987). Personal narratives are stories about events that really happened to the children. Philip's narrative in Figure 2.5 is a true story about his going to a shopping mall with his parents to spend $100.

*(continued)*

**Instructional Guidelines (continued)**

Kindergartners will attempt fictional narratives, but they may be less successful in terms of producing true fiction. The fictionalization of self is a developmental step toward literacy that kindergartners must take. It is the ability to distance oneself from an event and then to write or tell about it as if it had happened to someone else (Teale, 1982). Teachers should realize that stories in kindergarten will gradually become fiction when children begin to distance themselves from events that have actually happened to them.

Figure 2.7 is an example of a kindergarten fiction. "Once upon a time David was on a rock" is David's early attempt at fictionalizing an event. David also put the short *o* symbol above the words with short *o* sounds. David's teacher had been drilling the children on the sounds of the short vowels, and he felt that he should indicate the short sounds, thus making a metalinguistic statement. David is able to articulate the short *o* sound and relate the sound to symbol in his own writing.

**FIGURE 2.7**    "Once Upon a Rock," by David, age 6

### 4. Write in response to children's literature.

A literature-based kindergarten program incorporates all genres, including narration, exposition, and poetry. As children are exposed to listening to and reading a variety of literary forms, they begin to internalize the structure and are more able to imitate the form through their own writing (Pearce, 1984). "Did the book give you any ideas for writing?" is a typical response question designed to stimulate ideas for composing. Writing in response to children's literature reflects the developmental stages of kindergarten composition discussed earlier in this chapter. For example, a child may simply draw a picture of a house in response to Ellen Raskin's (1966) *Nothing Ever Happens on My Block*. A more elaborate response might be a personal narrative about the child's own house or neighborhood, a fictional tale about pirates and buried treasure, or a poem about the ideal neighborhood.

Listening to, reading, responding to, and writing rhymed and unrhymed poetry are very important to the emergence of literacy. Verbal word play research tells us that children spontaneously explore the sound segments of speech characterized by experimentation with rhyme, rhythm, and repetition of sound units (Geller, 1984). Language play kindergartners especially love includes tongue twisters ("Rubber Baby Buggy Bumper"), teases and taunts ("Jimmy and Susie sittin' in a tree. K-I-S-S-I-N-G"), jump-rope songs ("Cinderella dressed in yella"), and rhyme games of all kinds ("Name all the words you can think of that rhyme with school").

Exposure to all kinds of poetry enhances a child's ability to segment language. In turn, the ability to segment sounds directly affects a child's emerging writing and reading behaviors. A kindergartner's knowledge and understanding of the sound system of our language helps him or her to figure out how to spell a word while composing or to pronounce a word while reading.

Prose and poetry written for young children are listed in the bibliography at the end of this chapter. Reading and reciting, drawing pictures and writing their own fiction, nonfiction, and poetry help children to appreciate literature as an art form that enhances the quality of our lives.

## Curricular Decision Making

District-level decisions about school curricula are sometimes made without regard to the developmental nature of learning (Elkind, 1988). The lag between theory and practice is well documented in the literature on reading and writing instruction (Otto, 1988). The kindergarten language arts curriculum is no exception. Teachers are frequently faced with mandates to use the adopted basal readiness books and worksheets in their classes, progressing through a prescribed scope and sequence of skills, all for the purpose of preparing children for beginning reading (Gentile & Hoot, 1983).

Working through a series of workbook exercises designed to promote letter naming, visual and auditory discrimination, or handwriting practice does not guarantee that children will be ready to read and write once the workbook is completed. The activities may be developmentally inappropriate for some children, as in copying from a chalkboard (Mavrogenes, 1986). Bondy (1984) discovered that children often develop inaccurate concepts about reading and writing because of a focus in kindergarten on letter drill and workbooks. Dyson (1982) found that worksheet practice with sound and symbol correspondence did not appear to positively influence children's compositions. Connections between isolated writing skills and skillful writing were never brought to the children's attention by the teacher.

***Teaching Skills in Context.***    Children need to understand the relationship between isolated segments of language, as presented on a skills worksheet, and the application of the skill during comprehending and composing connected text. A misuse of worksheets can occur, especially when children become involved in the mechanical task of copying or tracing letters and words that have no intrinsic meaning to them. For example, the following directions appeared on a teacher-made kindergarten worksheet designed to reinforce the short vowel sounds *o, i,* and *a* and the *consonant letter d* sound:

Sound out each word. Trace over dotted letters and fill in missing letters. *Pictures of a dog, a sad face, a bat, and a bib accompanied the words with missing letters:* **D—g, sa—, —at,** and **—ib.**

Five-year-old Dustin filled out his worksheet in this manner: dug, sat, cat, and rib. He ignored the picture clues, opting for what he later described as "words that I like to write." Sue found the exercises tiring and resorted simply to coloring the pictures. Larry made a paper airplane out of his and retired to the lap reading area, where he independently began reading *In the Night Kitchen* (Sendak, 1970), a story filled with rhyme, rhythm, meter, and repetition of sounds. When left to their own designs, children will very often impose their own meaning onto an otherwise meaningless exercise.

Conversely, creative applications of worksheet objectives can promote literacy in an interesting and more efficient manner. An alternative to the previously described worksheet exercise that segments language is to incorporate instruction in sound and symbol correspondences directly into a language arts lesson plan. When studying the sound of the letter *D,* for example, you could begin by asking the children to tell you all the words they know that begin with the letter *D.* Next, read aloud a book like Robert McCloskey's *Make Way For Ducklings* (1988) and suggest that the children listen for words that have the letter *D* in them. After responding to the book, the children could write a narrative about their favorite thing that begins with the letter *D.* While brainstorming favorite *d* words—*donut, dollar, duck, dog, Dad*—you could print them on an easel, simultaneously pointing out the short vowel sounds that the children (and you) generate. The children would then refer to the words when writing their stories, choosing to copy concepts that have personal meaning to them.

Pam's favorite *d* word, *duck,* inspired her original narrative "The Ducks Don't Like the Fat Duck" (Figure 2.8). Integrating direct instruction in phonics with reading children's literature and independent writing accomplishes the same objectives as the worksheet: to reinforce the sound of the letter *d,* the short *u* and *a* sounds, and to write *d* words. However, the lesson goes beyond what a worksheet does, as it encourages children to communicate ideas through listening to, talking about, writing, and reading connected text.

***Setting Realistic Expectations.*** The physical act of writing is hard work for five- and six-year-olds, who may still be gaining control of the pencil, not to mention developing control over their printed message. By the end of the kindergarten year, one- or two-sentence stories, poems, or nonfiction may be all we can expect from even the most astute kindergartner. What matters most is not length but that writing does not become a tiring physical effort that makes the children dislike the process altogether. Kindergartners should not be expected to revise their work in the same way that older children do. Revision requires objectivity and self-monitoring that children will develop later in the primary and intermediate grades. For now, kindergarten children may recreate or "redo" their picture or story if they want to and especially if it gives them a sense of self-satisfaction in perfecting their work.

Both reading and writing are interactive, social events. While writing at their

**FIGURE 2.8** "My Favorite 'D' Words," by Pam, age 5

tables, the children should be encouraged to talk among themselves about their work in progress, give recommendations concerning the form and content of one another's stories, attempt to spell words for anyone who needs help, react to their own writing and the writing of their peers, and read one another's work in progress (Piazza & Tomlinson, 1985). During sharing time children read their creation aloud, show their pictures, and verbally elaborate on their creation. Their peers listen and react, following the teacher's lead as he or she models appropriate responses to the writing. Typical kindergarten responses focus on what has interested the listeners, what they liked best about the story, or perhaps what might have been unclear or confusing. It is important to model positive comments so that the children will learn to encourage one another as they become authors themselves.

In subsequent chapters of the book I emphasize the recursive stages of the composing process—prewriting, writing, rewriting, and editing. For a number of reasons during the kindergarten year, you will be spending a far greater amount of time on prewriting and writing stages. Having something to think, talk, and write about in a risk-free environment is critical to a child's first writing experiences in school. Although rewriting and editing skills are always valued, they nevertheless will come later, after the child has internalized a deep sense of self-satisfaction from composing his or her own work.

***Managing and Publishing Kindergartners' Work.***    When kindergartners write every day, happily many papers will evolve. Writing portfolios, described in detail in Chapter 7, are one way to manage children's daily writing. Normally, portfolios are file folders kept in the writing center and are accessible. Kindergartners learn that their work is to be kept in the folder. Together the children and their teacher decide which papers go home at the end of the day, week, or grading period.

Another organizational tool is a daily writing journal. Kindergarten journals may be as simple as a few pieces of unlined paper stapled together. Each child personalizes the journal by illustrating the cover. The journal remains at the child's desk or table for easy retrieval.

Like the writing portfolio, a daily journal is a valuable record of each child's progress in writing and responding to literature. Hipple (1985) describes a kindergarten journal-writing project in which the children wrote freely for thirty minutes a day on unlined duplicating paper that had been stapled together. As the year progressed, the form and content of their writing became more sophisticated. From scribble writing, to random letters, to invented spellings, the children played with print on paper and communicated feelings and ideas for self-enjoyment and for others. Two children per week orally shared excerpts from their journals, and their peers responded to the authors' work. Each day Hipple and paraprofessional volunteers asked the children, "Tell me what you have written," recorded the entries, and stapled them directly to the children's journals for future reference.

Kindergarten writing becomes public throughout the composing process through sharing pictures and stories in progress, responding to one another's writing, and reading original prose and poetry aloud. A more formal way of publicizing the children's work is to create a class collection of stories, poems, and nonfiction. Individual children's work may also be published. Appendix B contains several ideas for making a big or little class book. Published books are ordinarily typed on a typewriter or word processor, illustrated by the children, bound, and then placed in the classroom or school library. Conventional spellings are used in the children's published work because every child then has a chance of independently reading his or her peer's message.

## Paraprofessionals in the Kindergarten Classroom

Paid paraprofessionals and parent volunteers are a luxury in the typical elementary school classroom. Under your guidance and influenced by your model teaching behavior, volunteers can make a significant difference in the quality of instruction because you are freed to attend to the individual needs of the children. If you have the opportunity to employ others to help you on a daily basis, a few commonsense guidelines should be kept in mind when organizing reading and writing instructional help.

Always actively engage parents and paraprofessionals in the children's reading and writing lessons. Adult-child interaction is crucial to both processes, and the more help you have, the better. Examples of interactive situations are lap reading; taking dictation; recording children's oral story tellings, retellings, or writing; helping children while they are composing; and reacting to children's oral or written work and reading. Also, a classroom volunteer can be invaluable in helping you to keep track of the children's daily progress in reading and writing. Chapter 8 contains examples of organizational data systems and observation checklists appropriate in kindergarten classrooms.

Rarely use a parent or paraprofessional's time for menial tasks such as running off ditto masters, making instructional materials, or simply sitting and "watching" children while you are out of the room. If possible, work with your principal to organize an after-school student volunteer program to help with the more secretarial side of classroom organization and management.

## FROM HOME TO SCHOOL AND BACK AGAIN

This chapter begins and ends with the influences of the home environment on children's emergent literacy behaviors. The value of reading and writing begins at home and is influenced there throughout a child's formative years. American schools are becoming increasingly diverse, and our classrooms are often filled with children from many different cultural backgrounds. Research into the literacy child-rearing practices of poverty-level, middle class, and disabled children's families reveals that "parents of various cultural groups in the United States provide the values and parental support necessary for school success of their children" (Crawford, 1993, p. 11). For example, Lynch (1989) found that the quality of home literacy experiences was not necessarily contingent upon socioeconomic status. In his study, children in single-parent households often had books and were read to, while children in more affluent homes sometimes experienced sterile literacy environments devoid of books altogether. Other studies of culturally diverse families reveal that parents and extended family members are concerned about the education of their children. Crawford reports the following observation made by a teacher during a home visit:

> In a home visit to an extended family of one of his students in the southwest United States, a teacher found a very small two-room house, sparsely furnished with only one bed, books, a framed art print, and records on loan from the local library. An older female child assisted younger children with homework during his visit and later read with one of the children. She cross-switched between the English of the book and her Spanish language in discussing and sharing the book. An apparently bright first grader played school outside the door, teaching her younger siblings and neighbor children the alphabet. (p. 12)

It is important to avoid adopting stereotypic assumptions that children from households other than mainstream America should be automatically labeled "at risk." Conversely, teachers should not speculate that a child will value literacy because of living in a two-parent, middle-class home. All children bring with them a unique cultural heritage, which should be respected and utilized in the process of nurturing life-long reading and writing.

Collaborative efforts between home and school are to be encouraged. Getting parents involved in their children's schooling is extremely important yet often difficult to accomplish. Parent-teacher conferences are occasions in which teachers ordinarily try to elicit more parental help at home, especially if a problem is developing. However, the perennial request, "Read more to your children," is often followed by "When? I don't have time." Rasinski and Fredericks (1988) suggest that teacher-recommended activities for parents must make sense, be reasonable and workable, and pay off in a tangible way. Further, parents must be informed about what really helps in the home and school collaborative effort. At home and at school, children become skilled enthusiastic readers and writers through varied, ongoing positive experiences with print (Ross & Bondy, 1987). Research-based ideas for parent involvement include setting aside regular daily time for parents to interact with their children through talking, reading, and writing. Bedtime storybook reading has a significant influence on children's emerging literacy, especially when it is consistently accomplished. Making parents aware of the positive effects of bedtime reading is helpful in encouraging daily read-aloud sessions at home.

The concept of quality time for most parents who work is something to aspire to but in reality may not happen because of the complicated lives that we live. It is far easier to convince a working parent that every minute spent with their children should be thought of as quality time, from the daily car trip to school, to thirty minutes of meal preparation, to the weekly trip to the grocery store, to the carefully planned family outing. It is during the mundane, everyday activities that parents can respond to their children's curiosity about language; encourage the reading of environmental print, books, newspapers, and magazines; and encourage writing with always accessible pencil and paper. When working with parents, the teacher should provide simple, realistic guidelines that they can comfortably fit into daily routines.

## INSTRUCTIONAL GUIDELINES
### Encouraging Literate Behaviors at Home

SUGGESTIONS FOR PARENTS, GRANDPARENTS, SIBLINGS, GUARDIANS, AND CHILD CARE PROVIDERS

### Take Time to Listen and Talk

1. Oral language is the foundation of literacy. Take time to listen to your child and respond to your child's daily questions and observations.
2. Tell stories to your child, and encourage him or her to tell you real or imagined stories.
3. Talk with your child about the books he or she's been reading and writing about.
4. Tell your child about the reading and writing that you do every day.
5. Tell your child again and again that his or her reading and writing is getting better, every day. Genuine encouragement (not empty praise) is needed in order to build children's self-esteem.

### Read-Aloud Time Can Be Anytime

1. Set aside five to fifteen minutes every day to read to your child. Although bedtime read-aloud routines are highly recommended, there may be other times during your busy day when you could spend a few minutes of quiet reading time with your child.
2. Choose good children's literature to read—stories with good plot and character development; nonfiction that interests your child; poetry that appeals to children; children's magazines.
3. Take your child to the public library as often as you can. Ask teachers and librarians to guide you to good materials. A list of recommended children's books by grade level is attached.
4. Read favorite books again and again, as often as your child begs for them to be read.
5. Take every opportunity to draw attention to print in the environment, and have your child read it to you. Examples: signs, newspaper headlines, labels, grocery ads, bill boards, marquees, and print that appears in movies and on television.

*(continued)*

**Instructional Guidelines (continued)**

6. Encourage your child to respond to what's been read. Ask your child to tell you (or write) some thoughts or feelings about the book and about his or her favorite part.
7. Read alongside your child. Being a model reader is important in encouraging a love of reading.

**Take Time to Write**

1. Make available a variety of paper (lined & unlined), pencils, crayons, markers, scissors, paste, scotch tape, as well as the home computer.
2. Encourage scribbling, drawing pictures, labeling pictures, writing letters or messages, and composing stories and poems. Say to your primary grade child, "Spell the word the way you think it should be spelled," in order to encourage writing. Spell the word for your child, if he or she insists on the correct spelling.
3. Older children will still invent spelling when writing a first draft. Encourage your child to use a dictionary to solve spelling problems while revising and editing.
4. Try journal or diary writing with your child. Respond to the journal entries, either verbally or in writing.
5. If you have a computer, have your child either dictate or compose stories. Print/publish your child's work, and have the child read it to you.
6. With your child's permission, post written work on the refrigerator for all to admire. Keep drawings and writing in a portfolio or folder. It's lots of fun and also motivating to look back in time and see how writing skills have progressed.
7. Write alongside your child. Like modeling reading, being a model writer helps promote lifelong writers.

**YOUR HANDWRITING NOTEBOOK**

### The Emergence of Handwriting Skills

Until about age three, young children explore the world of print through scribble-writing. Sometime between ages three and six, preschoolers and kindergartners will gain control over their scribbles, which eventually become recognizable letters and numbers (Dyson, 1986). The process of moving from scribbles to fully formed letters is not necessarily linear, as children move back and forth during their play with scribbles, lines and circles, pictures, and fully formed alphabet letters.

The emergence of handwriting during preschool and the kindergarten year frequently occurs in the context of communicating ideas. Michelle's scribbled note (Figure 2.1) said that she wanted to let her mother know where she would be, "I'll be in my room if you need me." Other children may simply draw a picture that tells a story, as did Kirk in Figure 2.3. Sulzby (1985) described the early writing behaviors of kindergartners according to six general categories, each of which may overlap onto the other.

1. **Picture drawing.** Here the picture contains the message. A child will draw pictures for a variety of reasons as she works through the difference between pictures and print as a medium for communicating ideas. Encourage kindergartners to "read" their pictures to you and peers. Pictures are sometimes accompanied by scribble-writing.
2. **Scribbling.** When a child scribbles, she often uses lines and circles, loops and half-moons, dots and dashes. She will move the pencil or crayon all over the page, top to bottom, and sometimes left to right in a adultlike manner. The purpose is again to convey a message through "writing." Scribbles eventually start to look like letters.
3. **Letterlike forms.** Letterlike forms at first glance seem not to be scribbles at all but, rather, real letters—the emergence of an "o" or a "t." On closer examination these early attempts at manuscript writing are not yet fully formed. Nevertheless, the child is still using print to communicate her ideas, and fully formed letters are soon to follow.
4. **Fully formed letters.** The very first fully formed letters and letter sequences are usually the child's name. For a while, many children will play with the arrangement of letters in their name, transposing or even replacing a letter or two. During this stage of handwriting development, some children will begin to string letters together in random order to convey a message. These early attempts at spelling are termed "prephonemic" because there is no logical sound/symbol correspondence between letter and word. Prephonemic strings of letters are soon accompanied by invented spellings.
5. **Invented spelling.** When children create their own spelling, they engage in the problem-solving task of matching speech to print. Invented spellings will range from a single letter representing an entire word, as in "B" for "ball," to more elaborate spellings, as in "wstjrgztwr," "The soldier guards the tower," (Figure 8.5). Invented spellings are often accompanied by conventionally spelled words.
6. **Conventional spelling.** The child spells words correctly. Children will spell words conventionally as they simultaneously learn to read and write and begin to internalize correct spelling patterns. (A comprehensive explanation of the stages of spelling development is described in Chapter 3).

*The Writing Center.*     Early writing attempts are important forms of language play that are critical to literacy development. Writing implements and paper should be easily accessible through the classroom. When setting up an environment that encourages written language play, developmentally appropriate materials could also be organized in a special "Writing Center." As children develop their communication skills and fine-motor coordination during the kindergarten year, the following materials are of value.

### Writing Implements and Aids

1. Provide a variety of pencils, crayons, markers, and chalk in wide-ranging sizes and shapes. Allow the children to choose the size that is most comfortable. Modern handwriting instruction no longer insists that children progress from fat to skinny pencil.
2. Fingerpaints, tempera, and water colors are also essential tools for communication through picture drawing and writing.
3. Introduce children to pencil guards as a aid in gaining control of their handwriting. The rounded pencil guard that has indentations for thumb and fingers is the best for small hands. Triangular-shaped guards are less popular among young children with tiny hands and fingers. Children will naturally abandon the guard as they become more comfortable manipulating a pencil.

*Handedness*.    Upon entering kindergarten, most children will have developed handedness. If you observe a child switching from right to left hand during the writing process, encourage her to choose the hand that feels best and to use it consistently. Some children may indeed be ambidextrous, cutting paper with right-handed scissors yet drawing pictures with the left hand. Regardless of a child's preference, right- and left-handed children's preferences should be respected, as all children have the potential to achieve.

*Paper*.    Help children begin to work with their position in space by letting them experiment with many different sizes of unlined, white paper or newsprint—from tablets of small stick-on tags to large chart paper. Morrow (1989) cautions teachers not to use "manuscript practice paper that is lined with different colored and dotted lines specifically to encourage proper size of letters and spacing between lines" (p. 158). Most kindergartners are not ready for the discipline of forming perfectly shaped letters on straight lines.

*Language Arts Aids and Manipulatives*.    Every kindergarten room should be surrounded with print. Bulletin boards display the children's work along with interesting pictures and environmental print. An alphabet chart that clearly shows upper- and lower-case letters helps children begin to identify and remember letter shapes (see Appendix C for model handwriting charts). It is also important to take advantage of the sense of touch, for it is a powerful mode to help children internalize letter formation. Tactile/kinesthetic materials for kindergarten include the following: plastic, wooden, or styrofoam alphabet blocks; sandpaper letters; flannel or magnetic alphabet letters and flannel or magnetic boards; and shape stencils.

Other materials that will facilitate communication through skillful writing include the following:

scissors (left- and right-handed)

stapler and staples

scotch tape in a sturdy dispenser

glue and paste

paper hole punch

a variety of colored construction paper

yarn (for hand-sewn book bindings)

typewriter and/or computer terminal and printer

For young children emerging into literacy, the physical act of handwriting is hard work. In an atmosphere of patience and understanding, every child is capable of the joys of communicating through print.

***Bookmaking***.      Appendix B contains ideas for making books.

## FOR YOUR JOURNAL

1. Observe a kindergarten class and take special note of the emergence of reading and writing. Talk to some children. What do they already know about reading and writing?

2. Ask a kindergartner (or preschooler) to draw a picture and then write or tell about the drawing. Observe the process and describe what happens.

3. Read an appropriate piece of children's literature to one or more kindergartners (or preschoolers). Ask the children to respond to the story: "What did you think about the story?" Ask, "If you were to write a story now, what would it be about?" What did they say? What did they write?

4. Interview the parents of a preschooler or kindergarten-age child. Ask them to describe the routine home reading, writing, and talking experiences with their children. What insights do you gain from talking with parents about home literacy events?

## SELECTED BOOKS FOR PRESCHOOL CHILDREN

### Picture Books

Arnosky, Jim (1987), *Raccoons and Ripe Corn,* Lothrop.
Atlas, Ron (1987), *A Room for Benny,* Simon & Schuster.
Bond, Felicia (1987), *Wake Up Vladimir,* Dial Press.

Brimmer, Larry Dane (1988), *Country Bear's Good Neighbor,* Orchard.
Brown, Margaret Wise (1947, 1977), *Goodnight Moon,* Harper & Row.
Cecil, Laura (1988), *Listen to This,* Greenwillow.
Chalmers, Mary (1988), *Easter Parade,* Harper & Row.
Chorao, Kay (1987), *George Told Kate,* Dutton.
Crowe, Robert (1976, 1987), *Clyde Monster,* Dutton/Unicorn.
de Lynam, Alicia Garcia (1988), *It's Mine,* Dial Press.
Egan, Louise (1987), *The Farmer in the Dell,* Whitman.
Fox, Mem (1987), *Hattie and the Fox,* Bradbury.
Ginsburg, Mirra (1987), *Four Brave Sailors,* Greenwillow.
Grindley, Sally (1987), *Four Black Puppies,* Lothrop.
Hogrogian, Nonny (1988), *The Cat Who Loved to Sing,* Knopf.
Kitamura, Satoshi (1987), *Lily Takes a Walk,* Dutton.
Kraus, Robert (1986), *Where Are You Going, Little Mouse?* Greenwillow.
Levinson, Riki (1987), *Touch! Touch!* Dutton.
McCully, Emily Arnold (1987), *School,* Harper & Row.
Mayer, Mercer (1987), *There's an Alligator under My Bed,* Dial Press.
O'Conner, Jane (1986), *The Teeny Tiny Woman,* Random House.
Phillips, Joan (1986), *Tiger Is a Scaredy Cat,* Random House.
Rayner, Mary (1987), *Mrs. Pig Gets Cross and Other Stories,* Dutton.
Stadler, John (1987), *Three Cheers for Hippo,* Crowell.
Steig, William (1987), *Solomon the Rusty Nail,* Farrar, Straus & Giroux.
Steptoe, John (1988), *Baby Says,* Lothrop.
Stevenson, James (1980), *That Terrible Halloween Night,* Greenwillow.
Stock, Catherine (1988), *Sophie's Knapsack,* Lothrop.
Tejima, Keizaburo (1987), *Fox's Dream,* Philomel.
Titherington, Jeanne (1986), *Pumpkin, Pumpkin,* Greenwillow.
Titherington, Jeanne (1987), *A Place for Ben,* Greenwillow.
Wadsworth, Olive (1987), *Over in the Meadow,* Bantam Books.
Williams, Vera (1986), *Cherries and Cherry Pits,* Greenwillow.
Winthrop, Elizabeth (1987), *Maggie and the Monster,* Holiday.
Yamashita, Hauro (1987), *Mice at the Beach,* Morrow.
Yoshi (1987), *Who's Hiding Here?* Picture Book Studios.
Ziefert, Harriet (1987), *So Hungry,* Random House.

## Wordless

Alexander, M. (1968), *Out! Out! Out!,* Dial Press.
Amoss, Berthe (1987), *What Did You Lose, Santa?* Harper & Row.
Bollinger-Savelli, A. (1971), *The Knitted Cat,* Macmillan.
Briggs, Raymond (1978), *The Snowman,* Random House.
Carle, Eric (1973), *I See a Song,* Crowell.
Crews, Donald (1980), *Truck,* Greenwillow.
Daughtry, D. (1984), *What's Inside,* Knopf.
de Paola, Tomie (1978), *Pancakes for Breakfast,* Harcourt Brace Jovanovich.
Goodall, J. (1977), *The Surprise Picnic,* Atheneum.
Hutchins, Pat (1971), *Changes, Changes,* Macmillan.
Krahn, F. (1979), *Robot-bot-bot,* Dutton.

McCully, Emily Arnold (1984), *Picnic,* Harper & Row.
McCully, Emily Arnold (1988), *New Baby,* Harper & Row.
Mari, I., & Mari, E. (1969), *The Apple and the Moth,* Pantheon Books.
Mari, I., & Mari, E. (1969). *The Chicken and the Egg,* Pantheon Books.
Mayer, Mercer (1977), *Oops,* Dial Press.
Zemach, Margaret (1987), *Hush Little Baby,* Dutton.

## Concept—Alphabet

Burningham, John (1967), *John Burningham's ABC,* Bobbs-Merrill.
Crowther, Robert (1978), *The Most Amazing Hide and Seek Alphabet Book,* Viking Press.
Fletcher, Helen Jill (1978), *Picture Book ABC,* Platt & Munk.
Isadora, Rachel (1983), *City Seen from A to Z,* Greenwillow.
Johnson, Laura (1982), *The Teddy Bear ABC,* Green Tiger Press.
Merriam, Eve (1980), *Good Night to Annie,* Four Winds Press.
Piers, Helen (1987), *Puppy's ABC,* University Press.
Pragoff, Fiona (1987), *Alphabet,* Doubleday.

## Concept—Counting

Bang, Molly (1983), *Ten, Nine, Eight,* Greenwillow.
Bridgeman, Elizabeth (1977), *All the Little Bunnies: A Counting Book,* Atheneum.
Carle, Eric (1968, 1987), *1, 2, 3, to the Zoo: A Counting Book,* Philomel.
Carle, Eric (1969), *The Very Hungry Caterpillar,* Collins.
Gardner, Beau (1987), *Can You Imagine . . . ? A Counting Book,* Dodd, Mead.
Hoban, Tana (1987), *26 Letters and 99 Cents,* Greenwillow.
Lindbergh, Reeve (1987), *The Midnight Farm,* Dial Press.
Pragoff, Fiona (1987), *How Many?* Doubleday.

## Other Concepts—Miscellaneous

Hoban, Tana (1978), *Is It Red? Is It Yellow? Is It Blue?* Greenwillow.
MacMillan, Bruce (1988), *Dry or Wet,* Lothrop.
MacMillan, Bruce (1988), *Step by Step,* Lothrop.
Martin, Bill Jr., & Archambault, John (1985, 1987), *Here Are My Hands,* Holt, Rinehart & Winston.
Messenger, Jannat (Illus.) (1986), *Twinkle, Twinkle Little Star,* Macmillan.
Potter, Beatrix (1904, 1986), *The Two Bad Mice,* Warner.
Pragoff, Fiona (1987), *Growing,* Doubleday.
Pragoff, Fiona (1987), *What Color,* Doubleday.
Rockwell, Anne (1986), *Things That Go,* Dutton.
Wallner, John (Illus.) (1987), *The Three Little Pigs,* Viking Press.

## Poetry—Rhymes

Allen, Steve, & Meadows, Jayne (1987), *Shakin' Loose with Mother Goose,* Kids Matter.
Conover, Chris (1987), *The Adventures of Simple Simon,* Farrar, Straus & Giroux.
Emberley, Barbara (1967), *Drummer Hoff,* Treehouse.

Fujikawa, Gyo (1968, 1987), *Mother Goose,* Grosset & Dunlap.

Hayes, Sarah (1988), *Clap Your Hands: Finger Rhymes,* Lothrop.

Hughes, Shirley (1988), *Out and About,* Lothrop.

Josefowitz, Natasha (1988), *A Hundred Scoops of Ice Cream,* St. Martin's Press.

Marshall, James (Illus.) (1979), *James Marshall's Mother Goose,* Farrar, Straus & Giroux.

Tarant, Margaret, (Illus.) (1978), *Nursery Rhymes,* Crowell.

Zolotow, Charlotte (1958, 1988), *Sleepy Book,* Harper & Row.

Zolotow, Charlotte (1987), *Everything Glistens and Everything Sings,* Harcourt Brace Jovanovich.

## SELECTED BOOKS FOR KINDERGARTEN CHILDREN

### Big Books (with accompanying little-book version)

From DLM Teaching Resources
   P.O. Box 4000
   One DLM Park
   Allen, TX 75002
   (800) 527-4747

The Bill Martin, Jr., Library

*Argyle Turkey Goes to Ganderland*
*Argyle Turkey Goes to Sea*
*The Braggin Dragon*
*The Color of Poetry*
*Counting Sheep*
*Don't Be the Leaf*
*The Magic Pumpkin*
*The Merry Months of Birds*
*Rhymes about Fun Times*
*There's a Moose and a Goose in the Caboose*
*They Tell Me That I Shouldn't Stare*

The Bobber Books (Bill Martin, Jr.)

*Allafred the Anteater*
*Captain Tom Cat*
*The Goats, the Bugs, and the Little Pink Pigs*
*Good Night Mr. Beetle*
*Here Are My Hands*
*I Am Freedom's Child*
*Listen to the Rain*

*Old Old Witch*
*Susie Moriar*
*Wordsong*

From Resources for Creative Teaching
  P.O. Box 12399
  Department R
  Salem, OR 97309-0399

*Down by the Bay*
*I Can Read Colors*
*I've Got a Cat*
*Oh, a Hunting We Will Go*
*Opposite Song*
*Teddy Bear, Teddy Bear*

From Scholastic Inc.
  P.O. Box 7501
  Jefferson City, MO 65102

*Caps for Sale*
*Chicken Soup with Rice*
*Clifford's Family*
*The Little Red Hen*
*Madeline*
*Noisy Nora*
*The Owl and the Pussycat*
*Rosie's Walk*
*The Three Billy Goats Gruff*
*What Do You Do with a Kangaroo?*
*Wynken, Blynken and Nod*

## Picture Books

Aardema, Verna (1976), *Why Mosquitoes Buzz in People's Ears,* Dial Press.
Abolafia, Yossi (1987), *Yanoshi's Island,* Greenwillow.
Aliki. (1984), *Feelings,* Greenwillow
Aliki (1987), *Feelings,* Morrow.
Aliki (1987), *The Two of Them,* Morrow.
Allard, Harry (1983), *Miss Nelson Is Back,* Houghton Mifflin/Sandpiper.
Arnold, Tedd (1987), *No Jumping on the Bed,* Dial Press.
Asch, Frank (1983), *Mooncake,* Prentice-Hall/Treehouse.
Baker, Leslie (1987), *The Third Story Cat,* Little, Brown.
Barbaresi, Nina (1987), *Firemouse,* Crown.
Bassett, Lisa (1987), *Beany and Scamp,* Dodd, Mead.
Bauer, Carline Feller (1987), *Midnight Snowman,* Atheneum.

Bemelmans, Ludwig (1962), *Madeline*, Viking Press.

Birdseye, Tom (1988), *Airmail to the Moon*, Holiday.

Blos, Joan (1987), *Old Henry*, Morrow.

Brett, Jan (1988), *Goldilocks and the Three Bears*, Dodd, Mead.

Bunting, Eve (1986), *The Mother's Day Mice*, Clarion.

Bunting, Eve (1989), *Ghost's Hour, Spook's Hour*, Clarion.

Burningham, John (1977), *Come Away From the Water, Shirley*, Harper & Row Junior Books Group.

Carle, Eric (1969, 1987), *The Very Hungry Caterpillar*, Putnam.

Caseley, Judith (1987), *Apple Pie and Onions*, Greenwillow.

Cazet, Denys (1986), *December 24th*, Bradbury.

Cleary, Beverly (1986), *Two Dog Biscuits*, Morrow.

Cleary, Beverly (1987), *The Growing Up Feet*, Morrow.

Cohen, Miriam (1987), *Don't Eat Too Much Turkey*, Greenwillow.

Cohen, Miriam (1988), *It's George!* Greenwillow.

Cohn, Janice (1987), *I Had a Friend Named Peter*, Morrow.

Cole, Joanna (1983), *Bony-Leggs*, Macmillan.

Cole, Joanna (1987), *Evolution*, Crowell.

Collington, Peter (1987), *The Angel and the Soldier Boy*, Knopf.

Craig, Helen (1987), *A Welcome for Annie*, Knopf.

Damjan, Mischa (1987), *The Fake Flamingos*, Holt, Rinehart & Winston.

Davison, Brian (1987), *Looking at a Castle*, Random House.

de Beer, Hans (1987), *Little Polar Bear*, North & South.

Dubanevich, Arlene (1983), *Pigs in Hiding*, Macmillan.

Dupasquier, Philipe (1988), *Our House on the Hill*, Viking/Kestrel.

Eastman, P. D. (1960), *Are You My Mother?* Random House.

Forrester, Victoria (1986), *Poor Gabriella: A Christmas Story*, Atheneum.

Freeman, Don (1968), *Corduroy*, Viking Press.

G'ag, Wanda (1928), *Millions of Cats*, Coward, McCann & Geoghegan.

George, Lindsey (1987), *William and Boomer*, Greenwillow.

Gibbons, Gail (1987), *Trains*, Holiday.

Gibbons, Gail (1987), *Zoo*, Crowell.

Girard, Linda W. (1984), *My Body Is Private*, Albert Whitman.

Graham, Thomas (1987), *Mr. Bear's Chair*, Dutton.

Greenleaf, Ann (1983), *No Room for Sarah*, Putnam.

Gretz, Suzanna (1987), *Roger Takes Charge*, Dial Press.

Grifalconi, Ann (1987), *Darkness and the Butterfly*, Little, Brown.

Griffith, Helen (1986), *Georgia Music*, Greenwillow.

Hadithi, Mwenge (1987), *Crafty Chameleon*, Little, Brown.

Hayes, Sarah (1986), *A Bad Start for Santa*, Atlantic Monthly Press.

Haywood, Carolyn (1986), *How the Reindeer Saved Santa*, Morrow.

Henkes, Kevin (1987), *Once Around the Block*, Greenwillow.

Henkes, Kevin (1987), *Sheila Rae, the Brave*, Greenwillow.

Hirschi, Ron (1987), *Who Lives in . . . Alligator Swamp*, Dodd, Mead.

Hoban, Lillian (1978), *Arthur's Prize Reader*, Harper & Row.

Howe, James (1987), *I Wish I Were a Butterfly*, Harcourt Brace Jovanovich.

Hurd, Thacher (1986), *The Pea Patch Jig*, Crown.

Hutchins, Pat (1968), *Rosie's Walk*, Macmillan.

Hutchins, Pat (1985), *The Very Worst Monster,* Macmillan.

Hutchins, Pat (1986), *The Doorbell Rang,* Greenwillow.

Hutchins, Pat (1988), *Where's the Baby?* Greenwillow.

Jonas, Ann (1983), *Round Trip,* Greenwillow.

Keats, Ezra Jack (1962), *The Snowy Day,* Viking Press.

Keller, Holly (1987), *Lizzie's Invitation,* Greenwillow.

Kellogg, Steven (1986), *Pecos Bill,* Morrow.

Khalsa, Dayal Kaur (1987), *I Want a Dog,* Tundra.

Khalsa, Dayal K. (1990), *Cowboy Dreams,* Clarkson N. Potter.

King, P. E. (1986), *Down on the Funny Farm,* Random House.

King-Smith, Dick (1987), *Farmer Bungle Forgets,* Atheneum.

Kraus, Robert (1987), *Spider's First Day at School,* Scholastic Books.

Krementz, Jill (1987), *A Visit to Washington D.C.,* Scholastic Books.

Kunhardt, Edith (1986), *Danny's Birthday,* Greenwillow.

Lakin, Patricia (1987), *Oh Brother!* Little, Brown.

Leaf, Margaret (1987), *Eves of the Dragon,* Lothrop.

Leedy, Loreen (1986), *The Dragon Halloween Party,* Holiday.

Levy, Elizabeth (1987), *Something Queer in Rock n' Roll,* Delacorte Press.

Lionni, Leo (1987), *Nicholas, Where Have You Been?* Knopf.

Lobel, Arnold (1970, 1979), *Frog and Toad Are Friends,* Harper & Row.

Lobel, Arnold (1972), *Frog and Toad Together,* Harper & Row.

McCaulay, David (1987), *Why the Chicken Crossed the Road,* Houghton Mifflin.

McCloskey, Robert (1988), *Make Way for Ducklings,* Putnam.

McGovern, Ann (1986), *Stone Soup,* Scholastic Books.

McPhail, Davide (1988), *First Flight,* Joy Street.

Mahy, Margaret (1987), *17 Kings and 42 Elephants,* Dial Press.

Marshall, James (1972), *George & Martha,* Houghton Mifflin.

Marshall, James (1986), *Yummers Too,* Houghton Mifflin.

Marshall, James (1987), *Red Riding Hood,* Dial Press.

Mayer, Mercer (1988), *There's Something in My Attic,* Dial Press.

Mayper, Monica (1987), *After Goodnight,* Harper & Row.

Minarik, Else Holmelund (1978), *Little Bear,* Harper & Row Junior Books Group.

Munsch, Robert (1985), *Thomas' Snowsuit,* Annick Press.

Munsch, Robert (1986), *The Boy in the Drawer,* Annick Press.

Munsch, Robert (1987), *Moira's Birthday,* Annick Press.

Nicoll, Helen (1976), *Meg & Meg,* Penguin Books.

Nordquist, Sven (1988), *The Fox Hunt,* Morrow.

Parish, Peggy (1988), *Scruffy,* Harper & Row.

Pearson, Susan (1987), *Happy Birthday Grampie,* Dial Press.

Pearson, Susan (1988), *My Favorite Time of Year,* Harper & Row.

Pizer, Abigail (1987), *Harry's Night Out,* Dial Press.

Polushkin, Maria (1987), *Baby Brother Blue,* Bradbury.

Potter, Beatrix (1929, 1987), *Country Tales,* Warner.

Rey, H. A. (1973), *Curious George,* Houghton Mifflin.

Rogers, Paul (1988), *From Me to You,* Orchard/Watts.

Rylant, Cynthia (1985), *The Relatives Came,* Bradbury.

Rylant, Cynthia (1986), *Night in the Country,* Bradbury.

Rylant, Cynthia (1987), *Birthday Presents,* Orchard.

Samuels, Barbara (1986), *Duncan and Dolores,* Bradbury.

Schertle, Alice (1987), *Jeremy Bean's St. Patrick's Day,* Morrow.

Seuss, Dr. (1987), *I Am Not Going to Get Up Today,* Random House.

Shulevitz, Uri (1986), *One Monday Morning,* Macmillan.

Simmonds, Posy (1987), *Fred,* Knopf.

Small, David (1985), *Imogene's Antlers,* Crown.

Stanley, Diane (1987), *Captain Whiz-Bang,* Morrow.

Stevens, Janet (1987), *The Three Billy Goats Gruff,* Harcourt Brace Jovanovich.

Tafuri, Nancy (1987), *Do Not Disturb,* Greenwillow.

Tusa, Tricia (1987), *Maybelle's Suitcase,* Macmillan.

Vigna, Judith (1993), *I Wish Daddy Didn't Drink So Much,* Albert Whitman.

Viorst, Judith (1972), *Alexander and the Terrible, Horrible, No Good, Very Bad Day,* Atheneum.

Wahl, Jan (1986), *Rabbits on Roller Skates,* Crown.

Wells, Rosemary (1986), *Max's Christmas,* Dial Press.

Willard, Nancy (1987), *The Mountains of Quilt,* Harcourt Brace Jovanovich.

Wood, Audrey (1987), *Detective Valentine,* Harper & Row.

Yeoman, John (1986), *The Wild Washerwomen: A New Folktale,* Crown.

Ziefert, Harriet (1987), *Harry Takes a Bath,* Viking Press.

Zion, Gene (1976), *Harry the Dirty Dog,* Harper & Row Junior Books Group.

## Concept Books—Alphabet

Anno, Mistumasa (1975), *Anno's Alphabet: An Adventure in Imagination,* Crowell.

Base, Graeme (1987), *Animalia,* Abrams.

Bayer, Jane (1984), *My Name Is Alice,* Dial Press.

Brown, Marcia (1974), *All Butterflies: An ABC,* Scribner.

Chouinard, Roger, & Chouinard, Mariko (1988), *The Amazing Animal Alphabet Book,* Doubleday.

Duke, Kate (1983), *The Guina Pig ABC,* Dutton.

Fujikawa, Gyo (1974), *Gyo Fujikawa's A to Z Picture Book,* Grosset & Dunlap.

Lobel, Arnold (1990), *Alison's Zinnia,* Greenwillow.

McPhail, David (1988), *David McPhail's Animals A–Z,* Scholastic Books.

Musgrove, Margaret (1976), *Ashanti to Zula,* Dial Press.

Oechshi, Kelly (1982), *The Monkey's ABC Word Book,* Golden Books.

Pallotta, Jerry (1986), *The Icky Bug Alphabet Book,*

Rockwell, Anne (1987), *Albert B. Cub & Zebra: An Alphabet Story Book,* Harper Junior Books Group.

Stevenson, James (1983), *Grandpa's Great City Tour,* Greenwillow.

Watson, Clyde (1982), *Applebet, an ABC,* Farrar, Straus & Giroux.

## Concept—Counting

Anno, Mitsumasa (1977), *Anno's Counting Book,* Crowell.

Farber, Norma (1979), *Up the Down Elevator,* Addison-Wesley.

Sis, Peter (1988), *Waving: A Counting Book,* Greenwillow.

## Wordless Picture Books

Briggs, Raymond (1978), *The Snowman,* Random House.

de Paola, Tomie (1981), *The Hunter and the Animals,* Holiday.

Goodall, John S. (1969), *The Ballooning Adventure of Paddy Pork,* Harcourt Brace Jovanovich.

Goodall, John S. (1970), *Shrewbettina's Birthday,* Harcourt Brace Jovanovich.

Goodall, John S. (1975), *Creepy Castle,* Atheneum.

Mayer, Mercer (1967), *A Boy, a Dog, and a Frog,* Dial Press.

Mayer, Mercer (1969), *Frog, Where Are You?* Dial Press.

Mayer, Mercer (1974), *Frog Goes to Dinner,* Dial Press.

Mayer, Mercer (1976), *Abchoo!* Dial Press.

Spier, Peter (1977), *Noah's Ark,* Doubleday.

Turkle, Brinton (1976), *Deep in the Forest,* Dutton.

## Poetry—Songs

Brown, Marc (1987), *Play Rhymes,* Dutton.

Clifton, Lucielle (1970), *Some of the Days of Everett Anderson,* Holt, Rinehart & Winston.

Cole, William (Ed.) (1978), *An Arkful of Animals,* Houghton Mifflin.

Hopkins, Lee Bennett (1987), *More Surprises,* Harper & Row.

Ivimey, John W. (1987), *Three Blind Mice,* Clarion.

Lewis, Richard (1988), *In the Night, Still Dark,* Atheneum.

Martin, Bill, & Archambault, John (1985, 1988), *Up and Down the Merry-Go-Round,* Holt, Rinehart & Winston.

O'Neill, Mary (1961, 1973), *Hailstones and Halibut Bones,* Doubleday.

Platz, Helen (1988), *A Week of Lullabies,* Greenwillow.

Prelutsky, Jack (1986), *Read Aloud Rhymes for the Very Young,* Knopf.

Raffi Songs to Read (1987), *Shake My Sillies Out,* Crown.

Stevenson, Robert Louis (1986), *The Moon,* Harper & Row.

Swann, Brian (1988), *A Basket Full of White Eggs,* Orchard.

Weiss, Nicki (1987), *If You're Happy and You Know It,* Greenwillow.

## Multicultural Books for Preschool and Kindergarten Children

Ahlberg, Janet, & Ahlberg, Allan (1988), *Starting School,* Viking.

Baden, Robert (1990), *And Sunday Makes Seven,* Whitman.

Bang, Molly (1985), *Ten, Nine, Eight* (counting), Greenwillow.

Bogart, Jo-El (1990), *Daniel's Dog,* Scholastic.

Brusca, Maria C. (1991), *On the Pampas,* Holt.

Caines, Jeann (1988), *I Need a Lunch Box,* Harper & Row.

Cummings, Pat (1986), *C.L.O.U.D.S.,* Lothrop, Lee & Shepard.

Delacre, Lulu (Ed.) (1989), *Arroz con Leche: Popular Songs and Rhymes from Latin America,* Scholastic.

Dragonwagon, Crescent (1986), *Half a Moon and One Whole Star,* Macmillan.

Daly, Niki (1986), *Not So Fast, Songolo,* McElderry.

Fields, Julia (1988), *The Green Lion of Zion Street* (poetry), McElderry.

Flournoy, Valerie (1985), *The Patchwork Quilt,* Dial.

Gray, Nigel (1988), *A Country Far Away,* Orchard Books.

Hall, Mahji (1989), *T is for Terrific/T es por Terrifico* (Alphabet), Open Hand.

Heide, Floren P. (1990), *The Day of Ahmed's Secret,* Lothrop.

Johnson, Angela (1991), *One of Three,* Orchard Books.

Johnson, Angela (1989), *Tell Me a Story, Mama,* Orchard Books.

Lee, Holme M. (1985), *My Grandfather and Me* (wordless), Wah Mei School.

Loh, Morag (1988), *Tucking Mommy In,* Orchard Books.

Lyon, George E. (1989), *Together* (poetry), Orchard Books.

McKissack, Patricia (1986), *Flossie and the Fox,* Dial.

Mendez, Phil (1989), *The Black Snowman,* Scholastic.

Miller, Moira (1989), *Moon Dragon,* Dial.

Munsch, Robert & Kusugak, Michael (1989), *A Promise Is a Promise,* Annick Press.

Musgrove, Margaret W. (1976), *Ashanti to Zulu: African Traditions* (alphabet book), Dial.

Narahashi, Keiko (1987), *I Have a Friend,* Margaret K. McElderry Books.

Pomerantz, Charlotte (1982), *If I Had a Paka: Poems in Eleven Languages,* Greenwillow.

Soya, Kiyoshi (1987), *A House of Leaves,* Philomel.

Steptoe, John (1980), *Daddy Is a Monster . . . Sometimes,* Lippincott.

Stewart, Dianne (1993), *The Dove,* Greenwillow.

Tord, Bijou L. (1993), *Elephant Moon,* Doubleday.

Williams, Karen L. (1990), *Galimoto,* Mulberry Books.

Williams, Vera B. (1982), *A Chair for My Mother,* Greenwillow.

# 3 READERS AND WRITERS IN THE PRIMARY GRADES

*Writing is when you write a note to somebody so they can read it and then write back to you and say something nice like "I wish you were here" and then you read their note and write back to them.*

*Shannon, age 7, on the social nature of writing and reading.*

## CHAPTER CONCEPTS

Reading and writing connected text on a daily basis promotes the development of literacy.

Listening and talking are essential in the process of learning to read and to write.

The processes of reading and writing provide structure for integrating the language arts across the curriculum.

The recursive nature of reading and writing supports the development of comprehension and composition in all subject areas.

---

Reading and writing in the primary grades are essential processes through which children develop and refine their kindergarten emergent literacy skills. Additionally, listening and speaking are very prominent throughout the longer, more complicated school day, as oral language remains the foundation for promoting reading and writing connections across a more diversified curriculum. Many of the basic tenets of kindergarten language arts instruction apply to grades 1–3 as well. Indeed, first-graders are still emergent readers and writers. It is therefore desirable to create an environment rich in opportunities for listening and oral language development through play, children's literature, environmental print, and direct learning experiences involving a wide range of topics.

The primary purpose of this chapter is to discuss how the composing and comprehending processes can be used to structure an integrated language arts curriculum that takes advantage of the relationships among listening, speaking, reading, and writing. Efficient lesson planning is fundamental to quality language arts instruction, especially in a school day filled with the growing demands of a variety of subjects and extracurricular activities. The child-centered and direct instructional methods described herein enable us to make better use of available time, as we create an environment where all children can become literate.

## READING AND WRITING CONNECTED TEXT

Children need to write and to read connected text *every day* in order to achieve literacy. Connected text refers to reading or writing texts that go well beyond the sentence level—in other words, reading and writing whole stories, nonfiction, or poetry that could be found in or inspired by any piece of children's literature or subject area textbook. Activities that do not involve connected texts include filling out worksheets, answering comprehension questions at the end of a reading lesson, and completing sentence-level grammar exercises in a language arts textbook. Recent research cautions us that far too much time is spent on worksheet lessons that fragment language and fail to demonstrate to children the relationship between subskill and reading or writing (Shannon, 1989). Shannon's admonition is directly observed in a second-grade child's remark to his teacher: "Whew. I don't know what I just did, but I'm through with all my five papers (worksheets) for today. Now may I please read?"

The somewhat "revolutionary" stance of giving children time to read and write connected text every day is "the most crucial of the newer insights into beginning literacy" (Templeton, 1986, p. 407). Acquiring more time for literacy development is a continuous, joint effort by teachers, administrators, parents, paraprofessionals, and volunteers working together to create a literate classroom environment. (See Chapter 8 for further discussion on classroom management.) Fully integrated language arts lessons help to rearrange instructional time efficiently, giving children extended experience with connected text throughout the day.

When, what, how, and where children should read and write are major decisions we must make every day when planning for instruction. As discussed in Chapter 1, our teaching is influenced by our definitions of reading and writing. If we take an integrated approach, which emphasizes reading-writing connections, we are primarily concerned with an interactive viewpoint: Reading and writing are the processes of constructing meaning from and with print, respectively. This view gives us flexibility in designing a program that maintains a balance of child-centered and teacher-directed instruction.

The stages of the reading and writing process provide a framework that supports a fully integrated language arts curriculum. Prereading and prewriting, reading and writing, rereading and rewriting, and postreading and editing stages are recursive in nature. That is, each stage of the process overlaps onto another again and again as the reader/writer actively constructs meaning through print. For pedagogical reasons, it is useful first to discuss each stage separately and then to demonstrate how reading and writing processes can be orchestrated during individual lessons and throughout the day.

## THE STAGES OF READING AND WRITING

### Prereading/Prewriting

The initial stage of reading and writing is characterized as a period of getting ready to comprehend or to compose, respectively. Time spent in preparation for constructing meaning from print is well worthwhile. During this phase of a lesson, we can discuss what we already know about a topic, think about what new information we might acquire, and determine our purposes for reading or writing.

A good deal of research during the 1980s focuses on the concept of prior knowledge and its influences on comprehending and composing (Anderson, 1977; Rumelhart, 1980; Stein & Trabasso, 1982). Research findings indicate that comprehension and composition are impaired if a reader or writer lacks sufficient background knowledge about text structure, topics, and ideas. In other words, a reader cannot construct meaning from text without calling to mind a host of print and non-print-related experiences. Similarly, a writer cannot construct a meaningful text without a sufficient knowledge base from which to draw. For example, if a child has never been to a museum, as is the case with many primary school children in small towns, a story called "Going to the Museum" may be difficult to understand without initial discussion of the related concepts. Going to a museum is even better, though not always practical. Further, it is ludicrous to expect children to write about things that are outside of their real world, unless you have provided a variety of prereading/prewriting experiences that will help them to construct a meaningful text.

What children think, talk about, and experience before reading and writing influences their comprehension and composition. When planning integrated language arts lessons, consider the following methods of developing concepts prior to reading and writing.

***Providing Direct Experiences.***   Children bring to school a wide array of experiences, most of which have taken place amidst diverse backgrounds and cultural settings. Our goal is to help children use the experiences they've had to enhance their facility with oral and written language. At the same time, it is important to provide additional direct experiences that will improve the quality of the children's school lives and at the same time promote literacy. For example, a child from Central America might bring a rain stick to school and explain the cultural context for making and using this tube-shaped object that—when shaken—sounds like falling rain. A Native American child could explain how the delicately woven web of a dream catcher keeps bad dreams away at night. Children from Jewish and Christian homes could compare family holiday traditions. At every opportunity teachers should

A whole-class language experience activity stimulates a written invitation to parents.

encourage children to share their worlds with us. Simply told multicultural and multiethnic experiences of all kinds enrich everyone's lives. With the help of classmates, we learn to be appreciative of the diverse world in which we live, work, and play.

Direct experiences need not be complex to introduce important concepts and to motivate children to learn. Prereading/prewriting experiences can be as simple as making angels in the snow before reading *The Snowy Day* (Keats, 1962) or preparing peanut butter and jelly sandwiches before learning to write a process paragraph. A familiar topic in the primary grades is "pets." In preparation for the study of the concepts of habitat and ecology, field trips to the zoo or nearby farms are desirable but not often practical. Parents, grandparents, and siblings are wonderful resources to provide new experiences. For example, parents could bring the family parakeet or pet turtle. Their child could then talk about the responsibilities involved in taking care of a pet. Additionally, experiences with animals can be provided in the classroom through science-related activities such as building aquariums, making ant farms, hatching baby chicks in an incubator, or conducting humane nutrition experiments with white rats.

Much classroom talk in the form of reaction, conversation, and discussion is fundamental to language experiences and promotes thinking and concept formation. It is desirable to incorporate tangible learning experiences into the primary grade curriculum whenever possible because these experiences provide a natural social setting through which children can organize and internalize their new world knowledge (Vygotsky, 1978).

***Listening and Responding to Literature.***     Talk is essential to learning through experience in print and nonprint environments. Therefore, listening experiences that actively involve children in constructing meaning from speech are important in preparing children to read and write. Children's literature is an important resource for prereading/prewriting acitivies designed to introduce students to difficult content area concepts. For example, before a science unit on lizards and amphibians, one third-grade teacher introduced her class to a puppet named Hillary Gila Monster. The teacher then let Hillary read aloud Marjorie Weinman Sharmat's (1983) book, *Gila Monsters Meet You at the Airport.* Next the children viewed an animated version of Sharmat's book on a videotaped "Reading Rainbow" program, which also featured nonfiction segments on desert animals. During the video session, the teacher modeled good listening behavior by remaining silent and watching the program with the children. A discussion followed, which highlighted the similarities and differences among the storybook, animated, and nonfiction versions of gila monsters. Through discussion and reaction to the book and video, the teacher was able to praise the children who had been active listeners and good models for their peers. With their interest and enthusiasm aroused, the children were ready to read and respond to the first chapter in the science unit.

Abstract ideas contained in language arts or content area texts can also be introduced through children's literature. Concepts familiar to primary grade curricula

Andrea role-plays a TV anchorwoman as she delivers the morning's announcements.

Wide reading inspires writing among primary grade children.

include friendship, family, love, compassion, fantasy versus reality, and fact versus fiction. A well-chosen children's literature book read aloud is an excellent source for building a background of information relative to an abstract idea. Additionally, read-aloud sessions expose children to a variety of genres, thus expanding their growing understanding of text structure. For example, Seymour Simon's (1979) nonfiction picture book, *Animal Fact/Animal Fable,* is a wonderful way to introduce the difference between fact and fable, since the fable form is prevalent in primary grade language arts programs.

***Directed Listening and Thinking.***    The directed listening/thinking activity (DLTA) is another approach that encourages active listening and critical thinking during read-aloud time. The DLTA, patterned after Stauffer's (1981) Directed Reading/Thinking Activity, teaches children to be actively involved in constructing meaning *while* listening. Setting purposes for listening, making predictions before and during the read-aloud session, and finally verifying predictions when the story is over are all part of this method. As in reader response lessons, children soon learn that listening helps us to become better readers, writers, and thinkers.

## INSTRUCTIONAL GUIDELINES
### Encouraging Active Listening and Thinking

**Before We Listen**

1. Teach children the value of purposeful listening by helping them establish a reason to listen to a story or textbook chapter.

   *Today I'm going to read a book to you about what some animals do when it begins to rain. This is also a book that rhymes. Can you tell me a word that rhymes with kitten? As you listen to the story, think about where the animals go when it rains and also the words that rhyme.*

2. Ask questions that encourage predictions from as many children as possible.

   *The name of this book is* Where Does the Butterfly Go When It Rains *[Garelick, 1961]. What do you think it is going to be about? How do you know? Have you ever seen a butterfly flying in the rain? Here's a picture of a butterfly trying to get out of the rain. What do you think will happen in the story?*

**While We Listen**

1. As you are reading the story aloud, stop periodically to talk about the pictures, elaborate on important details, or clarify difficult vocabulary words or concepts.

   *The narrator of the story tells us that a mole stays in its hole when it rains. What is a mole? Does a butterfly go into a hole when it rains? How do you know? Can you prove it by rereading or retelling part of the story?*

2. Continue reading the story, stopping at appropriate points to verify the children's predictions. It is not necessary to stop after every page, especially if this would interfere with the flow of the story and thus impair comprehension.

   *Did you like this story? What did you like best? How do you know what a bird does when it rains? Retell the part of the story that gives you that information. Did we learn where the butterfly goes?*

   *(continued)*

**Instructional Guidelines (continued)**

3. Repeat the cycle of reading, discussing pictures and content, and rereading or retelling to confirm the children's predictions. Encourage the children to adjust their initial predictions or to make new ones.

*Where does a turtle hide when it rains? Do you think we're ever going to find out where the butterfly goes when it rains?*

4. Throughout the lesson encourage active involvement in the listening process. Model metacognitive strategies to teach the children how to reflect critically on the story.

*While I'm reading the story aloud I'm noticing lots of rhyming words, such as* mole/hole, heard/bird, scat/that, back/quack. *This makes the story fun to read, don't you think? What rhyming words have you heard?*

*I'm also noticing that the author makes some jokes about where some animals might go when it rains. For instance, where do fish go when it rains? Why is that a silly question?*

*What did you notice while you were listening?*

**After We Listen**

1. After the children have listened to the story, have them orally summarize or retell it. Oral retellings help children internalize the basic story structure and reinforce the concept of rhyme.
2. Confirm predictions that are associated with the purpose for listening.

*Can anyone tell me where butterflies go when it rains? How do you know? Does the narrator know where butterflies go when it rains? If necessary, reread the part of the story that answers the question.*

3. Follow up the DLTA with a reading and writing lesson that extends the major concepts in the original story. Encourage the children to develop their own ideas for writing fiction, nonfiction, or poetry. Talk about possible writing topics as a whole class. Provide models whenever possible.

**Example Writing Topics**

*Draw a picture of where you think butterflies go when it rains. Then write a rhymed or unrhymed poem about your picture. Share your poem with a friend. Here's my poem:*

*My butterfly*
*Likes to keep dry*
*When it rains outside.*
*So she hides in a tree*
*And there she will be*
*When it rains outside, no more.*

*Write a paragraph about the importance of staying inside when it's raining outside. Illustrate your paragraph. Read your paragraph to Mom or Dad.*

*Write a story about a little boy or girl who always wanted to play in the rain. Read your story to a younger child.*

***Brainstorming.***     "Tell me everything you know about . . ." is a frequently used concept formation (or brainstorming) activity that can be applied to numerous pre-reading and writing instructional settings. In a first-grade classroom you could ask the children, as Mr. Dodd did, to tell you everything they know about the letters *A, B, C,* and so on. While listing on the chart paper what they already know, you will also learn what they don't know. Valuable time is saved when reteaching known concepts is bypassed in favor of new knowledge to be learned. Further, much classroom talking and writing communicates to children the value of language as a means of stimulating ideas before we read or write.

Every primary grade classroom should be equipped with large chart paper, an easel, and colored markers. Writing on lined or unlined chart paper is easier for children to see than writing on a chalkboard. There are opportunities for spontaneously dictated or written lists, fiction, and nonfiction throughout the day that reinforce a variety of print-related concepts, ranging from individual sound and symbol correspondences to whole words, sentences, paragraphs, stories, poetry, and nonfiction.

## INSIDE THE CLASSROOM
### Today Is Tuesday, the First Day of School

"Tell me everything you know about the letter *T*," said Mr. Dodd the first-grade teacher, as he pointed to a carefully formed uppercase *T* that he had written on chart paper.

"It's a letter," said Ryan.

"It's in my name," said Tiffany.

"*T* is for *Taffey,* my dog," said Billy.

*(continued)*

**Inside the Classroom (continued)**

"*T* is for *turtle*," said Mindy.

"*T* is for *ticky-tacky-tucky trouble trucks!*" said Marcel.

"What is the *T* shaped like? asked Mr. Dodd.

"It's shaped like the letter *T*," said Daniel.

"It's shaped like a tree. *T* is for *tree!*" said Gregory.

"It looks like it gots lines and they connect," said Cynthia.

"When do you use the letter *T?*" asked Mr. Dodd.

"When we write *T* words," said Kathy.

"I use the letter *T* when I write my name," said Timmy.

"I make a *T* when I write *teeth*," said Kevin.

"What is the sound of the letter *T?* asked Mr. Dodd.

"/T/," exclaimed the entire class.

"Is this also the letter *t?* asked Mr. Dodd, pointing to a lowercase letter on the chart.

"Yes," shouted the entire class, laughing and smiling.

"Tell me your very favorite word that begins with the letter *T*," said Mr. Dodd.

"*T-ball*," said Jeremy.

"*Touch football*," said Courtney.

"*Taco*," said Barbara.

"*Truck*," said Brian.

"My favorite *T* word is *travel*," said Mr. Dodd. "*Travel* means to go some-where for a special reason—as you do when you're on a vacation or when you're taking a trip. Listen to a story I wrote about a day when I decided to travel to Topeka. Listen for all of the *T* words in my story. Also, listen for why I traveled to Topeka." Mr. Dodd tells his story.

**Traveling to Topeka**

*One day I decided to take a trip to Topeka and visit the Topeka City Zoo. I got into my tan Toyota and traveled down Highway 70 toward the capitol of Kansas. Along the way I saw trees and telephone poles. A timid turtle trudged slowly across the road, and I almost ran over it. That would have been a terrible tragedy! As I traveled closer into town, I saw the tall buildings towering above the horizon. I knew I was almost to the zoo! And I began to think about all of my favorite animals that begin with the letter* T: *tigers, turtles, tarantulas, and tadpoles. My trip to the zoo was going to be terrific!*

After a discussion of the *T* words that the children heard in the story, Mr. Dodd showed the children his story written on chart paper and read it aloud, pointing to each word and highlighting the *T* words. He then said, "Now I want each of you to write a story about your favorite *T* word. Draw a picture to go with your story. Be sure to give it a title. You may ask your buddy if you need help while you're writing. I'll be around to see how each of you is doing. When you're finished with your first drafts we'll be sharing them with one another."

***Writing before Reading.***    Writing or dictating before reading is a method that simultaneously supports comprehension and composition. The Directed Reading and Writing Lesson (DRWL) (M. F. Heller, 1986a) is a planning model based upon the Directed Reading Activity (Durkin, 1984), which for years has been the mainstay of traditional reading lessons. Originally designed for intermediate-level content area reading and writing, the initial stage of the DRWL prepares children to comprehend via listening, talking, and writing about concepts central to the text. As the name implies, composing is incorporated into the reading lesson from the very beginning. The teacher encourages writing before, during, and after reading. In this way, vocabulary and concepts are reinforced through talk and written language early and throughout the lesson. The following instructional guidelines illustrate the prereading/prewriting stage of the DRWL.

## INSTRUCTIONAL GUIDELINES
### Activating Prior Knowledge of Concepts*

The procedures during the prereading/prewriting stages of the DRWL are:

1. *Activate the students' prior knowledge of vocabulary and concepts relevant to a story or nonfiction.* For example, "Getting the Facts" (*Heath American Readers, Level 2-2,* 1986, pp. 40–48) is the story of Terry Rich, a child reporter who forgets to get some important facts while interviewing a female auto mechanic. List on the chalkboard or overhead the vocabulary words (from the teacher's manual) that are important for understanding the story: *career, writer, edit, editor, notes, note taker,*

*(continued)*

*Adapted from M. F. Heller (1986a).

### Instructional Guidelines (continued)

*fact, idea, care, strict.* Also list concepts (also in the teacher's manual) related to the story's main ideas: Other occupations—magician/magic, actor/act, movie, disc jockey/radio, airplane pilot, cowboy/prairie, painter, sailor/sail, hunter/hunt, mechanic (often get so dirty they have to rub dirt and oil off their hands), gardener/grew. (These are the same words that the children learn through worksheet drill and practice.)

2. *Use a direct learning experience to help motivate both reading and writing.* Ask, "What do you want to be when you grow up?" In the context of a discussion about careers and career choices, elaborate on the vocabulary and concepts relative to being a reporter, frequently pointing to the words as you use them. Conduct a model mock interview in which you (the teacher) are a reporter interviewing a second-grader who role-plays himself or herself as an adult engaged in the occupation he or she always wanted. For example, if a child says she wants to be a ballerina when she grows up, she pretends she's a grownup ballet star being interviewed by a reporter. After the model interview, the children pair off and interview each other, using the same format.

3. *Write before you read.* During the interview, the children take notes to be used afterward in a descriptive paragraph about the person they interviewed. They then exchange paragraphs, read, and react to one another's work. Reaction questions include What did you like best? What did the author do best? What confused you? What advice do you have for the author?

4. *Model prediction strategies for the students.* After the role-playing and writing activities, introduce the story, "Getting the Facts." Ask questions that encourage predictions about the narrative. Design prereading questions that stimulate critical and creative thought. "What do you think, How do you know, and Can you prove it" are Stauffer's (1981) recommendations for questions that lead to active involvement throughout the reading process. An example sequence of questions for "Getting the Facts" might be this:

*From the pictures, can anyone tell me what this story is going to be about? The picture tells me it's probably going to be about a little girl who's asking somebody who's working under a car some questions. What else do you think the story is going to be about?*

*How do you know when something is a fact? Did you get some facts in your interview? What do you think we'll learn about reporters and careers as we read this story? What would be a good reason to read this story? Maybe we'll find out how important the facts are, just like we did during our mock interviews. And by reading the story, we'll learn if our predictions were correct.*

5. *Set a purpose for reading.* Say, for example, "Let's read to find out how important questions are during an interview. As you learn new things about interviewing, take some notes, just as Terry Rich does in the story, to help you remember important facts in the story. As I read the story, I learned that reporters must find out who, what, where, when, why, and how. I wrote those words here on my chart paper."

   *Set a purpose for writing.* Say, "After we've learned how important questions are during an interview, what do you think would be a good thing to write about? We could write a paragraph about what a reporter does in an interview. You'll be able to use your role-playing experience and the new things that you learn about reporters in our story for today."

   Alternative assignments are these: "Write a paragraph describing what Terry Rich did during her interview" or "Write a definition paragraph in which you define what facts are." Whenever possible, the purposes for reading and writing should be generated through discussion by both teacher and students. In this way, ownership of the ultimate written work is established early in the lesson.

6. *Describe the intended reader/writer audience.* Developing a sense of audience is important to both reading and writing. Write not only for a purpose but for an intended group of readers. Young children learn to appreciate literature by knowing that a real person wrote the story or poem or nonfiction for them to read. Brief author profiles are interesting ways to introduce the children to the concept of authorship. It is a good idea always to clearly state the author's name and perhaps allude to other works by the same author whenever you read a book aloud or make an assignment.

   The child author most often has an audience of peers and a teacher to respond to his or her work. Other audiences outside the classroom are also possible, depending on the purpose for writing. Other possibilities include parents; siblings; school personnel; the principal; guest speakers; or fictitious audiences such as animals, aliens, or inanimate toys. Sometimes child authors may write only for themselves, as in journal writing that is never shared with peers or teacher.

***Note Taking.***    "What I Know" (M. F. Heller, 1986b) is a strategy that encourages children to think about what they already know or don't know about an assigned reading or writing topic and then to articulate that knowledge in writing. By talking about and then writing all the facts and opinions that they already possess, the children simultaneously activate important prior knowledge that will enhance comprehension and composition. The children can then refer to their list of prior understandings both during and after reading and writing to reinforce comprehension and composition. Articulating what they don't know is also important because it gives the children direction for reading and research before composing a meaningful text. "What I Know" can be retitled "What We Know" if you use it with small or large groups. The first example uses a story about dinosaurs (Gibbons, 1987).

Hennings (1990) recommends a variety of data-gathering charts that help children to organize new information gained from either sensory language experiences or library research prior to composing. Among her recommendations for information gathering and recording are sensory impression charts ("Our Impressions of Popcorn"); observation charts ("This Is the Way It Is"); and data charts containing information from a variety of sources, such as a text, trade book, or encyclopedia, on a particular topic ("Data Chart on Endangered Species").

## Dinosaurs

by Gail Gibbons (1987)

*Purpose for reading or listening: Read (or listen to) the story about dinosaurs and discover where and how dinosaurs lived millions of years ago.*

| *What We Already Know* | *What We Now Know* | *What We Still Don't Know* |
|---|---|---|
| *Dinosaurs are big.* | *Their bones are.* | *Scientists think that the* |
| *They lived a long time* | *underground.* | *dinosaur died because* |
| *ago.* | *They ate either plants* | *the earth got too* |
| *They are scary.* | *or meat.* | *cold. But they're not* |
| | *Dinosaurs hatched* | *sure.* |
| | *from eggs.* | *Did dinosaurs live in* |
| | *Brontosaurus means* | *Kansas?* |
| | *"thunder lizard."* | |
| | *It lived in the swamps.* | |
| | *Tyrannosaurus rex was* | |
| | *taller than a house.* | |
| | *Dinosaurs fought each* | |
| | *other to survive.* | |

Organizing and writing opinions, impressions, observations, and factual information is a powerful prereading/prewriting activity that activates and reinforces children's prior knowledge. The example gives a sensory impression chart dictated by a group of second-graders who had participated in a "hidden object" prereading activity. The object hidden in a shoe box was a peeled grape. After passing the box around and letting each child reach in and feel the grape, the teacher wrote their impressions on a chart. The next step was for the children to write their own

"Gooey Grape" descriptions and share them with their peers. A story about a haunt-ed house then naturally followed the concrete motivation and writing activity.

### THE GOOEY GRAPE

| *What It Felt Like* | *What It Looks Like* | *Our Description* |
|---|---|---|
| Gooey | A small round thing | The thing in the box |
| Yucky | An itty-bitty ball | feels gooey and |
| Wet glass | A bug | yucky. It might be a |
| Soggy | A circle | small ball or a bug. |
| Round | A pea | It's probably yellow |
| Soft and squishy | A grape | or green. It might be |
| | | a pea or a grape. |

***Drawing.***     Like composing, drawing pictures that represent major concepts in a lesson is a motivating prereading/prewriting activity. Students can draw pictures of ideas talked about during class discussions, sketch the plot episodes of a story they are about to write, or simply plan some illustrations for prose or poetry to be com-posed. For example, before a science lesson on the weather, a second-grade teacher read aloud Tomie De Paola's nonfictional picture book, *The Cloud Book* (1972). Inspired by the read-aloud session, eight-year-old Daniel drew pictures of clouds (Figure 3.1) in his journal and then labeled them. Later during the science lesson he referred to his illustrations while composing a descriptive paragraph on cloud for-mations.

Drawing pictures to represent the parts of a story is an excellent way to help children internalize the structure of narrative texts. Conventional stories have a set-ting, characters, plot, conflict, resolution, and ending. Direct instruction in narrative structure appears to improve skill in comprehending and composing stories (Spiegel & Fitzgerald, 1986). Circle stories (Smith & Bean, 1983) are a prereading/prewriting picture-drawing activity that helps children to visualize the sequence of events in a narrative that they are about to read or write. The method can also be used when making predictions about the sequence of events in a narrative.

To create a circle story, draw a circular diagram on a chalkboard, chart paper, or overhead transparency. Divide the circle into as many pie-shaped sections as there are episodes in the story. Model a circle story for the children by drawing the first picture that depicts a familiar setting, such as Goldilocks walking through the woods to Grandmother's house. Subsequent pictures in the circle tell the tale of Goldilocks and the three bears. Once the children understand the concept, they can indepen-dently create circle stories before writing their own narratives.

When using circle stories as a preceding prediction activity, draw pictures as you and the children describe what they think is going to happen in a story, such as *Alexander and the Terrible, Horrible, No Good, Very Bad Day* (Viorst, 1972). Both during and after reading, you can then revise the circle story to make it compatible with the actual narrative (Figure 3.2).

**FIGURE 3.1**    "Clouds," by Daniel, age 8

***Developing Writing Topics.***    "But I can't think of anything to write about" is a statement familiar to elementary and middle school teachers. And it is during the prewriting phase of the composing process that concerns about writing topic emerge, especially if the topic is not teacher-directed. Modeling topic selection is the best way to help children develop independent thinking and decision-making skills for composing (D. H. Graves, 1983). There are many opportunities throughout the days and weeks to model topic selection.

List making is a practical way to generate and organize potential writing topics. Making lists also encourages concept formation through the process of categorizing ideas. General writing topic categories may include expert lists, curiosity lists, literature-based ideas, and content area writing. Initially the teacher models how one goes about generating a list of ideas for composing. The children keep personal lists of topics in their writing folders or journals for future reference. The lists grow and develop throughout the year as the children become experienced and independent readers, writers, and thinkers. The following illustrates the process of teaching children to discover topics for writing.

*Expert Lists*.    Write on the chalkboard, overhead, or chart paper three things that you think that you do better than anyone else. Explain that this is your personal "expert list" of things you know a lot about and feel comfortable writing about, for

**FIGURE 3.2**    Circle story for *Alexander and the Terrible, Horrible, No Good, Very Bad Day,* by Judith Viorst

example, making pizza, watercoloring, or planting a garden. Then model how you came up with each item on your list: "Making pizza is on my list because I think that I make the best homemade pizza in town! Know how I know that? Because my spouse and children and friends have told me so. What's more, I also have a secret sauce recipe that my Italian grandmother gave me. It makes the pizza taste better than any pizza you could buy! Want me to make the class some pizza sometime?"

We list some examples from grades 1–3:

| *John, Grade 1* | *Katherine, Grade 2* | *Peter, Grade 3* |
|---|---|---|
| Playing marbles | Skipping rope | Playing T-ball |
| Climbing trees | Playing dolls | Making paper airplanes |
| Washing my dog | Helping my Mommy | Building snowmen |

It is always to our benefit as teachers to know the children in our classrooms because it enables us to help them think of things they are interested in—what they already know a great deal about as well as what they are curious about.

*Curiosity Lists.*      Curiosity lists contain items that we know a little bit about but always wanted to know more than we know. These lists are especially useful when deciding on a research topic that is child-centered and not teacher-directed. You can model your own curiosities on chart paper by first listing topics such as: "Snorkeling, Origami, and Bird Watching," and then describing why the items are on your list.

> *I'm curious about snorkeling because I'm going to Hawaii on vacation, and I've read in the brochures that snorkeling is something fun to do in the shallow waters near coral reefs. All I know about it so far is that you wear a swimmer's mask so you can see the beautiful fish and a snorkel so you can put your head in the water and still breathe!*

You will find that children are curious about myriad things, ranging from the mundane, such as pet turtles (Kimberly, grade 1), to the more unusual, such as punk rock (Ryan, grade 3) (Figure 3.3). What teachers and children are curious about may

**FIGURE 3.3**     "The Punk Snake," by Ryan, age 9

**FIGURE 3.4** "Where the Moon Goes," by Jill, age 7

stem from day-to-day experiences both in and out of school. Whenever possible, model items of interest that are stimulated by reading and writing activities. Oriagmi, for example, is on the teacher's list because she happened to read the book *Easy Origami* (Nakano, 1986) while browsing in a bookstore.

*Literature-Inspired Topics.*    Children's literature frequently inspires topics to think about, discuss, and write about. Jill wrote the story in Figure 3.4 after having read *Where Does the Sun Go at Night?* (Ginsburg, 1980). Because children may not automatically think of writing topics related to books they read or listen to, it is a good idea to model topic generation once again. For example:

## AFRICA DREAM

by Eloise Greenfield (1977)

*I feel good when I read this lovely illustrated poem about living in long ago, far away Africa. It makes me want to close my eyes and dream. I could dream about when I was a little girl and my grandmother would tell me stories about growing up in a small Irish neighborhood New York City. Grandma always want-*

*ed to move west. That was her dream. We can write stories and poems about our dreams, just like Eloise Greenfield did. What do you dream about? What would you write about?*

## PUEBLO STORYTELLER

by Diane Hoyt-Goldsmith (1991)

*I love this book. It's filled with many beautiful pictures and interesting facts about the Pueblo Indian culture. My favorite sections are "Making the Pottery" and "Making the Cochiti Drum." The picture of the clay storyteller figure looks so delicate and so real. I can imagine the storyteller telling a tale about the Cochiti people who are famous for their drums made from tree bark and cowhide. I could make a storyteller puppet and retell the Pueblo legend "How the People Came to Earth." Would you like to be a storyteller too? What story would you tell?*

## ANGEL CHILD, DRAGON CHILD

by Michelle Maria Surat (1983)

*This story makes me sad and happy at the same time. I felt badly when the first graders teased Ngugen Hoa. They called her "pajamas" and made fun of her Vietnamese language. She really missed her mother who had to stay behind in Vietnam. If Hoa were in our class, how would you be her friend? I might write a story about Hoa or another friend from a different culture. Some of you might like to write about how you felt when you moved to a new school and had to make new friends all over again.*

*Content Area Ideas.*    Reading in any of the school subjects, such as math, science, and social studies, also suggests a multitude of interesting topics for writing and further reading. Wide reading and writing in the  content areas helps children to think like a scientist, mathematician, or sociologist because it gives them the opportunity to internalize the vocabulary and concepts important to a particular discipline (Squire, 1983). The primary grades are not too early to begin writing simple scientific observations, math problems, poetry, or personal narratives related to the child's social environment. It is a good idea to peruse the contents of your science, math, and social studies textbooks to be ready when the opportunity arises to model content area topic generation. Some examples of topics include science poems, math-magic mystery stories, and secret pal message writing.

The following poems were written before a third-grade lesson on animal adaptive behaviors. The poetry addresses the concepts of adaptation and survival in the animal world.

*Teacher's Model Poem: "If I Saw a Panda" by Mr. Carter*

*Third-Grader's Poem: "If I Saw a Raccoon" by Mary*

*If I saw a Panda,*
  *he'd climb a tree.*
*If I saw a Panda,*
  *would he see me?*
  *If I saw a raccoon,*
    *he'd hide from me.*

*If I saw a raccoon,*
  *he'd climb a tree.*
*If I saw a raccoon,*
  *would he be scared of me?*

*Skills in Context.*     During all stages of the composing and comprehending process, language arts skills ought to be taught in the context of connected text. Determining the essential skills to be taught or reviewed is prerequisite to designing activities that prepare children to internalize the connection between isolated skill and comprehending and composing. Once you have decided which language arts skills are essential, then you can begin planning lessons that demonstrate the connections between reading and writing across all content areas.

"Short Cuts" is a prereading/prewriting lesson on contractions, a skill normally introduced in third grade and reinforced thereafter in the intermediate and middle school curricula. The standard procedure in a language arts workbook would be for the children to identify contractions in a list of sentences and then create original contractions from a list of base words. This lesson, however, introduces the concept in the context of an original narrative in which the teacher and her family once took a shortcut to save time.

### A SHORT CUT WE SHOULDN'T HAVE TAKEN

*It was the summer of 1984, and my family and I were on vacation in Rocky Mountain National Park. "We're going to try to get to our camp ground before dark," said my husband, who decided to take a short cut off the main highway. "This is a short cut that I know real well," he said. We're driving on dirt roads that look like no one's traveled in centuries, I thought to myself.*

*The road got bumpier and bumpier. "We'd better not go this way," I said. "We'll get lost," said Daniel, my youngest son. "There are probably lions and tigers and bears in those woods," said Michael, the four-year-old. David, who'd just turned seven, sat quietly thinking through the situation. "Dad, just stick to the main road. We'll get there soon enough. Isn't it about four miles from here anyway?"*

*In spite of our pleas, the children's father drove on up the steep hill. Suddenly a grizzly bear and two baby cubs shot out of the woods toward our car. "Look, she's coming straight for us," cried the children. My husband stopped the car as the mother bear stood tall and growled at us. Just as she was about to lunge toward the car, we heard three loud shots. The bear and cubs bolted for the woods.*

*"What're you folks doing off the main road," said a park ranger who'd pulled up behind our car. "This road's too dangerous for tourists. Where're you headed?"*

*We told him the name of our campground, and he got us back on the main road. "It's only two miles down the road. Keep to the highway!"*

*"That's the last time I'll ever try to save time without knowing what I'm doing," admitted my husband as we drove safely into camp a few minutes later.*

The children listen for the message in the story and then discuss the concept of short cuts in relation to contractions. You would then display your short cut story on chart paper, showing all of the contractions in the narrative. After rereading and discussion, the children then write their own shortcut stories, using as many contractions as they already know. Shortcut stories are shared in small groups before the main lesson begins.

The language arts lesson on contractions then *follows* the writing activity. The children learn new contractions, rewrite their original stories to include newly learned contractions, and then share their shortcut narratives with the whole class. The worksheets serve only as a resource for contractions to be used in the childrens' narratives. You may choose to have the children underline the contractions in their stories, list them on a separate page, and then write the two words that form the contraction. "Short Cuts" fulfills the same objective as the language arts workbook lesson, but in a different, more efficient manner, which includes reading and writing connected text.

## Reading/Writing

***Monitoring Reading and Writing.***     Comprehension and composition depend on what we think about *while* we are constructing meaning from and with print, respectively. To be actively involved in either process requires adequate preparation, motivation, and concentration. Good readers and writers consciously monitor what they are doing, checking and rechecking to ensure that their purposes and intent are fulfilled.

Modeling what we do while comprehending and composing is a powerful way to demonstrate fluency in reading and writing. Children need to see that teachers also read books and write for genuine purposes. A second-grade teacher's retelling of the first two pages of Slobdkina's (1968) classic tale *Caps for Sale* illustrates the process of comprehension monitoring and metacognition, or knowing what one knows or does not know (Flavelle, 1976) while reading.

*While I was reading* Caps for Sale, *I learned on the first page that it was going to be a story about a peddler. A peddler must be like a salesperson, I thought, because the narrator of the story told me that the main character sold caps. The picture on page one also gave me some clues about the story. The peddler was a man shown with stacks of hats on his head! They were checked, gray, brown, blue, and red, just like the story said. Those hats must be his "wares," I thought, because I also learned that most peddlers carry what they sell on their back rather than on their heads, like this peddler does. I wondered, "How can the peddler walk around selling hats that are balanced on his head without them falling off!" Then on the very next page I found out why the hats didn't fall off. The peddler stood up straight and tall as he walked down the street trying to get people to buy his caps for fifty cents apiece.*

During a modeling lesson you can also take the opportunity to connect reading to writing by describing writing topics stimulated by the text: For example, "The peddler in *Caps for Sale* reminded me of my grandfather, who collected hats. So I wrote the title 'Grandpa Collects Hats' on my writing folder so I wouldn't forget. That will make a great story to tell." You would later model what you were thinking about while composing a descriptive paragraph such as the following.

## GRANDPA COLLECTS HATS

*My grandpa is ninety-three years old, and he collects hats. He has 102 different hats that he has collected since he was a little boy in first grade. Grandpa has baseball caps, cowboy hats, straw hats, and felt hats. His hats come in all different colors, too—red, blue, green, even purple! Some of his hats have either bills or wide brims to keep the sun out of his eyes. Others are made of heavy cotton or wool and have flaps to cover his ears when the cold winter wind blows. One special kind of hat is called a fedora, which is a felt hat that Grandpa likes to wear when he goes shopping downtown. My grandpa says it's fun to collect things, especially hats. "Hats won't ever go out of style," he says with a twinkle in his eye, "as long as we've got our heads to keep warm and dry."*

*While I was writing "Grandpa Collects Hats," I thought about all of the details that you [the reader] would want to know about my grandpa's special collection. To make my paragraph as interesting as I could, I decided to include how old my grandpa is, how many hats he has in his collection, and the kinds and colors of hats he has. I also decided to mention the fedora because I thought that might be a new kind of hat that you've probably never heard of before. Finally, as I was coming to the end of my paragraph, I decided to add something my grandpa always says about his hat collection because I thought that this would make my description even more real and fun for you to read.*

## INSTRUCTIONAL GUIDELINES
### Modeling the Reading/Writing Process

It is a good idea to plan your modeling scenario and practice "thinking out loud" before demonstrating what you think about while reading or writing. Here are a few points to keep in mind when preparing your lesson.

1. Choose a relatively short narrative or nonfiction to model. Thus, you will maximize the chance of keeping the children's attention while you are explaining the process of constructing meaning through print.

2. Tape-record your modeling scenario and listen to yourself "thinking aloud." Is what you are saying clear? Are you attending to aspects of print that are appropriate for your specific audience? For example, primary grade children still make extensive use of picture clues to decode words and comprehend the meanings of new concepts.

3. Provide young children with the vocabulary they need to become aware of their own metacognitive abilities. For example, primary grade children may not realize that concepts like *describe, detail,* and *interesting,* are important when planning to write a descriptive paragraph for an audience of peers.

4. Give the children a reason to listen to your oral model. Explain to them that you are going to teach them how to be better readers and writers by using their thinking skills.

5. Provide numerous opportunities for children to model their own metacognitive strategies. One-to-one or small-group settings work best when children must call to mind and articulate what it is they did while comprehending and composing.

6. Use language experience lessons to teach reflective thinking (Birnbaum, 1986), reading, and rereading while writing. You will want to position the experience chart or overhead projection so that all children can easily read your writing as they dictate. While taking dictation, read and reread the narrative or nonfiction as it unfolds, calling attention to the structure of the text as well as content and meaning.

   Encourage the children to become actively involved as the prose develops. Ask questions that stimulate thinking about matters of form and content that may need clarification to communicate ideas more effectively. Talk about the children's oral composition to demonstrate the importance of reflective thought in relation to constructing meaning.

   An alternative to taking children's dictation would be for you to write a first draft of your own on an overhead, demonstrating to the children that we all make changes *while* we write (D. H. Graves, 1983).

Whereas composing requires reading to construct meaning, comprehension does not necessarily require writing. However, note taking is a familiar aid to reading comprehension that is accomplished during the process of reading. You can show young children how to get the most out of their reading selection by teaching them how to take *key word notes* that can be used later during writing assignments (Bromley, 1988). Bromley's key word notation system calls for a sheet of paper divided into two sections, one narrow part for key words and a wide section for phrases and sentences that elaborate on the key words. Model the process of taking key word notes as you read aloud a familiar story or short nonfiction, simultaneously writing notes on an overhead projector. The children listen to the story, read your notes, and then write their own notes in their journals. Figure 3.5 shows eight-year-old Joey's list of key words, which he identified while listening to *Gila Monsters Meet You at the Airport* (Sharmat, 1983). He then retold the story to the class.

Teacher modeling is a time-honored method that makes effective use of oral language and listening to bring together the relationship between reading and writing. It should be used often.

**FIGURE 3.5**   Key word notes, by Joey, age 8

*A second-grader's notes taken while listening to Gila Monsters Meet You at the Airport (Sharmat, 1983).*

Retelling:
   The boy lives in New York. His parents decided to move. The boy wanted to stay at the house that they are leaving. But his mother and father said that he would have to come with them. And then they got on the airplane and flew away. Chapter 2. The boy was on his way. They saw lots of clouds. The boy looked at a map. His new house was at the right, but the boy kept yelling, "Left, left." When they finally got to the airport, he saw Gila Monsters. But they were only Halloween stuff. The boy wondered why they wear the Gila Monster halloween costumes. When they finally got a taxi, he drove across town. The boy saw no horses yet. But he saw a restaurant just like in New York. He saw kids playing baseball. Then when they were almost to the house, he saw a red horse. And he saw some kids by their new house. And they were riding their bicycles. The boy wondered what names they had. The boy liked his new house, and he said to himself that he wanted to write a letter to his friend.

***Talking While Writing.***     Reading and writing are interactive processes that flourish in social contexts where much talk surrounds comprehending and composing. In Chapter 2, I discussed the importance of mediated storybook reading, in which talking about stories during read-aloud time is beneficial to children's comprehension in general and the emerging concept of word in particular. With regard to talking while writing, Britton (1970) has perhaps said it best: "writing floats on a sea of talk" (p. 164). Research into children's classroom talk during writing reveals the value of social interactions during the composing process. A child's verbal interactions with peers and adults promote intellectual growth and literacy. Further, talk promotes intellectual activity that goes far beyond what we normally expect of primary-age children learning to read and write. When allowed to think out loud during writing, children help one another clarify meaning by asking challenging questions and offering suggestions or explanations about the ideas being presented (Cazden, 1981).

In a two-year observational study of kindergarten and first-grade children's spontaneous speech during journal writing, Dyson (1987) found that talk enabled children "to create and critique imaginary worlds." When given "the right to talk," children were better able to extend story boundaries, critique the logic of texts, and accomplish tasks that were frequently considered to be "over their heads" (p. 415). In an earlier case study, Dyson and Genishi (1982) described the self-directed and peer-directed speech of two first-grade children when they composed alone and when they were seated at a table of other children who were also writing. Their findings demonstrated that young children are capable of taking responsibility for their own learning by seeking out information from others as well as contributing to their peers' learning.

Piazza and Tomlinson (1985) found that when kindergartners collaborate while they are completing individual writing assignments, they reveal an awareness of the purposes of writing for an intended audience. The decisions they made about their work in progress centered on getting started; clarifying story information; rereading and then elaborating on the emerging story; and negotiating writing conventions such as spelling, punctuation, and capitalization. After writing their first drafts, the children read their work to one another, therefore bringing a sense of closure to the social setting in which peers helped create meaning.

Another line of research describes the verbal negotiations that take place during group writing, or collaborative efforts by two or more children that result in a single piece of prose or poetry. Long and Bulgarella (1985) analyzed the talk that accompanied group-written stories in the first grade. They found that young children working together on a single composition will focus on matters of both form and content. The children made decisions about planning the story, handwriting, pronoun usage, maintaining story coherence, and proper verb tense. Although varying points of view often clashed during the children's interactions, the collaborative process helped them to think creatively and critically.

It is important to give children many opportunities to talk about worthwhile things, especially in conjunction with what they are reading and writing both in and out of school. We often associate talk with the prewriting phase of the process. However, talking while writing is an important avenue to pursue when encouraging primary-age children to think critically about their own work in relation to an intended audience. By interacting while composing, children will more readily understand the recursive nature of the writing process as they create, clarify, and refine their ideas. Chapter 8 discusses cooperative/collaborative classroom management systems.

***Spelling.***     "Tell me how to spell . . ." is a frequent request by child authors who are emerging into literacy. Concerns about spelling words correctly arise throughout the composing process and must be dealt with judiciously. It is natural for young children to want their spelling to be conventional. Like kindergartners, primary-level children know that words are spelled in certain ways in order for us to understand what they mean. But the inability to spell every word correctly can interfere with the process of writing, sometimes causing children to forget what they were going to write or to become completely discouraged.

During the early years of schooling, when children's impressions about composing are being formed, it is important to emphasize meaning over standard conventions, but at the same time, to maintain high standards for written communication. Our ultimate goal is for children to become independent, skillful writers capable of effective communication. Setting up a risk-free classroom environment is the first step in helping children to enjoy writing without fear of having to spell every single word correctly on the first draft. By encouraging invented spelling, or spelling words the way children think they are spelled, you will be helping children to become fluent composers. Children's writing vocabularies will include more standard spellings as they gradually internalize the spelling patterns in our language through wide reading.

A great deal of research into children's early spelling attempts reveals that all children develop strategies that they use systematically and predictably when learning how to spell (Bissex, 1980; Chomsky, 1979; Marsh, Friedman, Welch, & Desberg, 1980; Read & Hodges, 1982). Gillet and Temple (1989) describe five research-based, natural stages of spelling development through which all children seem to progress during the primary grades. Knowledge of these stages will help you to understand how spelling develops during the primary grade reading and writing curriculum.

## INSTRUCTIONAL GUIDELINES
### Understanding Spelling Development*

**PREPHONEMIC**

In the prephonemic stage, there is no relationship between sounds and letters in how words are spelled. Random strings of letters and sometimes numbers characterize this stage. Prephonemic spellers are typically preschoolers, kindergartners, and first-graders who do not yet read. They have not developed the concept of word. Their writing cannot be read because these young children have not discovered the principle that words are divisible into phonemes and that letters correspond to some sounds in words.

*Example:* rwpsm8tf = I am going to town today.

**EARLY PHONEMIC**

In the early phonemic stage, the child will write one or two letters per word before giving up, thus producing a spelling with limited representation of sounds. This stage is typical of most beginning readers, who may be kindergartners, first-graders, or older children just learning to read. They have not yet developed a stable concept of "word," although they are beginning to understand the alphabetic principle that is crucial when learning to spell; that is, letters stand for sounds in words. Early phonemic writing is easier to read, although the spellings still do not look like adult conventional spelling.

*Examples:* el = fell, nd = send, dss = dish

**LETTER NAME**

In this stage, a letter name represents most of the sounds in a word. To spell a word, the child will choose the letter name that most closely resembles the sound that he or she hears. Common short vowel substitutions are *a/e: pet = pat; e/i: nit = net; i/o: lot = lit; o/u: run = ron.* Letter-name spellers are beginning readers in first and second grade. They have developed a stable concept of "word." Most of the writing is readable and is often referred to as *phonetic spelling.*

*Examples:* liks = likes, batm = bottom, hruk = truck

---

*Adapted from Gillet and Temple (1989, pp. 385–407).

## TRANSITIONAL

Transitional spellers no longer use invented spellings but rather attempt to incorporate features of standard spelling. Spellings are much more wordlike, although the transitional speller will forget to double consonants (spelling = speling) or will spell grammatical endings the way they sound (dropped = dropt). Transitional spellers may also experience difficulties with Latin-based words that are no longer spelled the way they were once pronounced (nature = nacher), words with unstressed vowels resulting in the schwa /∂/ sound (*lit-tle = littul*), and words with no logical rule governing their spelling because of historic scribal traditions (*love = luv*).

Transitional spellers are typically late first- or early second-grade children who have become fluent readers and who now realize the sense in some spelling rules they have been taught. Children often remain in the transitional phase through second and third grade. Older remedial readers and some adults persist in their use of transitional spellings.

## CORRECT

The entire word is spelled correctly in the correct stage.

An important point to remember with regard to spelling in the primary grades is that children's spelling improves as a direct result of wide reading and copious writing coupled with some direct instruction in the more reliable spelling rules of our language (Gillet & Temple, 1989). In other words, children do not learn how to spell correctly through rote memorization of lists of words. It is crucial to have numerous opportunities to read and write connected text *every day* for the children to internalize the many spelling patterns that govern written language.

*Personal Dictionaries.*    The personal dictionary (Figure 3.6) is a practical and effective way to manage the emergence of spelling in kindergarten and the primary grades. Personal dictionaries are stapled or sewn books of unlined paper, approximately 4″ by 6″. At the top of each page are upper and lower case alphabet letters written in manuscript. A few sight words or words most frequently used in written language are also printed on each page. For example, on the "A a" page you could print the words *a, an, and.*

During the composing process, children refer to their personal dictionaries, which contain word lists that grow as the year progresses. When a child insists on the correct spelling of a word, either you or the child writes in the booklet for future reference. Personal dictionaries reinforce the concept of "word" and correct spellings. They can also be used when teaching alphabetizing, skimming, and scanning skills needed to use commercial children's dictionaries and thesauri.

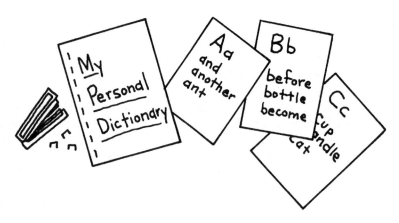

**FIGURE 3.6**   My personal dictionary

## Rereading/Rewriting

Readers and writers are concerned about similar kinds of things *after* they have completed their respective tasks. Readers consider whether or not they have achieved their purpose for reading and have reconstructed the author's intended meaning. Writers check to make sure that what they have constructed is meaningful and whether or not they have achieved their purpose for writing.

Rereading is a frequently used strategy for checking text comprehension, whether we are engaged in another author's work or in our own work in progress. Teacher's manual recommendations for basal readers often involve "purposeful reading" of text parts to clarify meaning and confirm predictions that were made before reading. Rereading portions of a text augments class discussions and helps children to answer comprehension questions or write paragraphs or multiparagraph papers that demonstrate an understanding of the whole text.

We also reread while writing. The rewriting phase of the composing process best illustrates the recursive nature of writing. As we write, we are continuously reading and rereading our work to ensure that what we are communicating makes sense to our intended audience. As we reread what we write, we very often rewrite our ideas, making additions, substitutions, deletions, and rearrangements in order to construct meaning. (Note: Rewriting does not mean recopying to produce a "neater" paper.) The rewriting phase of the composing process, therefore, occurs both *during* and *after* we have completed a first draft. The writer's concerns while rewriting center on matters of form and content. To encourage critical thinking about work in progress, you can suggest questions for young children to ask themselves while revising.

> ***When I read and reread my writing, these are some questions I will think about:***
> 1. Have I included everything I want to say?
> 2. What words or sentences do I need to change?

3. How can I make my writing more interesting?
4. Will my teacher and my friends understand me?

***Readers Respond.***    Children's writing should be responded to at all levels of the composing process and especially when revisions are about to be undertaken. Reaction, which is only one form of assessing children's writing, means responding to the work as a reader, not as an expert writer (Temple & Gillet, 1989). Both peer and teacher responses are helpful during the initial stages of revising a paper. You should model for the whole class appropriate responses when reading a peer's work in progress, in order to head off unnecessarily critical or hurtful comments. Three basic questions helpful to the primary-level peer reviewer are these: (1) What did you like best? (2) What confused you? (3) What advice do you have for the author? Responses can be put in writing for the child author to read or presented orally in one-to-one or small-group settings.

***Writers Rewrite.***    Rewriting a paper takes time and effort and as a result may be resisted by some children. It is important to remember that not everything that children write needs to be rewritten, and children need to have a voice in what is to receive extended attention through revision. The younger the children, the less likely they will be to revise very many things to the point of publication. *Publication* refers to readying a piece of prose or poetry for a literate audience to read. A published work is as perfect as a child can make it; it is free of errors that could result in the inadequate communication of ideas. Depending on your short- and long-term goals for the school year, you may want to set up some objectives to follow when making decisions about requiring revisions of young children's work.

*Revision Goals.*    The following examples represent realistic goals for primary grade children.

> *First grade.* After writing a variety of narratives, poems, and nonfiction, the students will choose from their portfolios one piece of prose or poetry to revise each semester. The prose and poetry will be illustrated and included in a classroom publication to be placed in the school library.
>
> *Second grade.* The students will choose and revise at least one fictional story, nonfiction piece, and poem during each semester. The revised works will be illustrated and published as an individual collection by each child.
>
> *Third grade.* During the semester of daily writing, the students will revise one or more papers in each of the following genres: personal narratives, short fictional stories, nonfiction descriptive paragraphs, and poetry. The revisions will receive a grade (S/E) based on a checklist developed for each assignment. The revisions will be illustrated and placed in four separate classroom publications. (See Chapter 7 for a further discussion of writing assessment checklists.)

## Editing

Editing, or the process of readying the paper for an audience of readers, often occurs in unison with writing and revising. During this final phase, the writer is concerned with proofreading for grammar, mechanics, and spelling. An important concept to instill in young children is that to communicate our ideas effectively to readers, our papers must contain clearly written content and be relatively free of errors that would interfere with comprehension. Children will ultimately understand that editing is the final stage before publishing, or making our work accessible to peers, parents, and teachers. Editing is a skill that can be directly taught in conjunction with traditional language arts lessons. Primary grade children are not too young to learn how to proofread their papers both during and after writing, although it is best to work on only one editorial concern at a time. For example, when a language arts lesson on capitalization is coming up, you will want to relate that lesson (as well as all lessons) directly to your daily composition curriculum. Instead of having the children capitalize words on a worksheet, isolated from connected text, they should capitalize sentence beginnings or proper nouns in their own writing. When capitalization is no longer a problem in a child's work, both you and the child should make a notation on the writing folder, such as "√ James correctly uses capitalization. Hurrah!"

When teaching proofreading skills in the primary grades, teacher modeling is again important. It is a good idea to introduce, one at a time, simple proofreading

Primary grade children make their writing public in a hallway bulletin board display.

marks (Figure 3.7) that give children the tools that will make their final editing job easier. Editorial partners are also an excellent way for children to develop an eye for proofreading, especially when they may be too close to their own work to see a problem. When partners exchange papers and respond to both form and content, they are helping one another to be effective communicators of ideas. A simple checklist of editorial matters helps to structure the editing job for an individual child.

Handwriting legibility is also a concern during the editing phase of the composing process. Direct instruction in manuscript and cursive handwriting provides opportunities for handwriting practice in meaningful contexts. The "Your Handwriting Notebook" section at the end of this chapter contains helpful suggestions for teaching handwriting in the primary grades.

***The Editor's Desk.***    An enjoyable way to teach children the value of communicating our ideas through carefully edited final drafts is the "Editor's Desk" concept. Based on the same principle that governs a newspaper office, the Editor's Desk activity encourages interaction among all children in the class. Each child is given the chance to be an editor of the week, the role alternating throughout the year. After

**FIGURE 3.7**    Editing checklist

## Editing My (or My Partner's) Work

| | | |
|---|---|---|
| 1. Is each sentence beginning capitalized? | + | − |
| 2. Does each sentence have the correct end mark? | + | − |
| 3. Are the paragraphs indented? | + | − |
| 4. Is each word spelled correctly? | + | − |
| 5. Does each sentence make sense? | + | − |
| 6. Is the handwriting readable? | + | − |

**This is my best advice for me (or my partner):**

## Proofreader's Marks

| | |
|---|---|
| ≡ | Capital letter |
| ⊙ | Add a period |
| ⋀ | Add a comma |
| ✓sp. | Check spelling |
| ∧ | Add a word or words |
| ℘ | Take out |
| ¶ | New paragraph |

you have taught the basic principles and skills associated with editing final drafts, use the following procedures to organize the activity.

1. Choose a different guest editor each week for every four children in your class. For example, if there are thirty students, there would be six designated editors.
2. Using the preceding example, arrange six writing areas (tables or clusters of desks), labeling each "The Editor's Desk."
3. The editor, who usually wears a hat of some kind, gathers the authors around his or her desk and works with individuals or small groups. The editor uses checklists to aid in the conference.
4. While the editor is working individually with an author, the other children at the table continue to revise and edit their work, write questions that they will ask the editor when it is their turn, or seek information from peers at their table.
5. The teacher circulates among the writing areas to lend encouragement and advice.

Although the Editor's Desk activity is primarily designed for the final draft phase, an alternative would be to have a single designated editor who helps with editing throughout the composing process. The same rotation system would occur, with a different child each week taking a seat at the Editor's Desk and assuming the responsibility of helping with matters of editorial concern as they arise.

Ironically, editing means putting the finishing touches on a piece of writing, yet it is often overemphasized at the beginning of the composing process. If a child is inundated year after year with assignments that emphasize spelling, grammar, and punctuation *first,* and the child does not see the form of his or her writing getting any better, composing becomes drudgery. Intermediate-level children especially may resist writing because of the depression that accompanies the thought of producing a perfect paper on the first draft. Emphasizing the process of writing early in the primary grades helps to eliminate the fears traditionally associated with writing.

***The Sharing Process.***    Children share their written work at many times throughout the composing process and in a number of social settings within the classroom. Sharing can take the form of an individual child author seated in "the author's chair" (Graves & Hansen, 1983) in front of the whole class, reading his or her creation aloud for all to enjoy. The author's chair is rotated, to ensure that every child gets a chance to read to the whole class. Other sharing situations include peer partners, small-group read-alouds, and cross-grade-level buddies.

Peer partners is a way of pairing children in your class to help achieve several composition objectives. Partners are the first to respond to works in progress. Talk between partners is focused on helping one another produce the best possible composition. Cooperative efforts teach children the value of collaboration throughout the composing process. It is also the best way to make sure that each child's work is

A small group of first-graders listen to and talk about good children's literature.

responded to frequently and appropriately. Partners should be rotated frequently to allow for individual differences in the classroom.

Small-group read-alouds may be more conducive to certain classrooms, where attention spans are short or children are reluctant to read their work before the whole class. Working in groups of three or four, each child takes a turn reading his or her paper aloud while other members of the group listen and respond orally or in writing.

Cross-grade-level buddies are pairs of children from different grades. For example, a kindergartner or first-grader may be paired with a sixth-grader. The children develop a relationship with one another throughout the year by writing and reading to each other. One-to-one language experience stories can be implemented more easily when buddies from sixth grade are in the room to help. This approach is also an excellent way to introduce older children to the concept of writing for a younger audience as well as to the idea of collaborating on writing efforts. A variety of grade-level pairings are possible, depending on your goals for the year. Adjacent grade pairings, such as kindergarten and first grade or first grade and second grade are useful when you want children to be exposed to appropriate reading and writing behaviors that will be expected in the coming year.

## Postreading/Publishing

***Readers Responding.***     After readers and writers complete the processes of comprehending and composing, they frequently engage in reader response activities. As discussed in Chapters 1 and 2, reader response refers to children responding on a personal level to children's literature, content-area textbooks, or another child's writing, telling what they thought about the prose or poetry and/or articulating what they learned from the text.

Open-ended reader response questions, as modeled in "Inside the Classroom: Listening and Responding to Literature" (on pages 107-110) give children the opportunity to respond aesthetically, or to express their feelings and attitudes about what they have read. Reader response questioning appears to promote critical thinking about literature (Many, 1991) and does not necessarily preclude direct instruction in literary skills (Heller, 1993; Spiegel, 1992). For example, the responses of students to open-ended questions such as "What did you think about the story?" may be followed up with a line of questioning that focuses attention on the structure of a narrative, such as setting, character, or plot.

A simple procedure for incorporating reader response into the primary grade curriculum would be first to read aloud a piece of prose or poetry. Next, ask the children to write in their literature logs or journals what they thought about the piece. The teacher also writes a response and later reads the model reaction to the children. Students can also respond in their journals after independent reading. Personal expressive writing in journals is an excellent vehicle for responding to a variety of literary forms. Focused class discussions and journal entries that encourage reader response create an environment in which children are free to express their ideas within a community of readers and writers.

The following glimpse inside a first-grade classroom allows us to visualize the process of children responding to literature before, during, and after a read-aloud session. The purpose of read-aloud session was to prepare the children for a social studies unit on worldwide diversity: "People and Places." One of the major ideas to be explored in the unit was that we are all unique individuals. Mrs. Wallace, the first-grade teacher, chose Daniel Pinkwater's (1977) *The Big Orange Splot* because of its engaging story about a man who expressed his individuality and his dreams through his house, which is initially located in a bland neighborhood where all houses look the same, and everybody likes it that way.

## INSIDE THE CLASSROOM
### Listening and Responding to Literature*

**VISIONS FROM MRS. WALLACE'S FIRST-GRADE CLASS**

"What does it mean to be an individual?" I ask my 21 first-graders before reading them my favorite picture book, *The Big Orange Splot* (Pinkwater, 1977). It's a lovely story about the human need to be an individual and the need to seek out and fulfill our dreams. The main character, Mr. Plumbean, decides one day to paint his house different from his neighbors, since a passing seagull just happened to drop a "splot" of orange paint on his roof. The neighbors are upset by what he has done to his house, for the image of the neighborhood is totally ruined, according to them.

The children respond with enthusiasm:

"If you're an individual, it means you get to do whatever you want," responded Mark.

"I think it means you're you and nobody else but you," replied Sarah.

We talk for awhile about what it means to be an individual. Eventually our discussion centers on the topic of dreams and how each of us has unique dreams that we hope will someday come true. Together we establish a reason for listening to the book: to think about the importance of being ourselves, no matter what others might think.

Next, I read the story straight through, pausing only to acknowledge the children's spontaneous comments about the unfolding narrative: "I wish I had a house like Cinderella," says Mary. "This is a lovely house," I say, pausing to admire the colorful illustration that looks like a medieval castle. After reading the story aloud, I ask the children, **"What did you think about *The Big Orange Splot?*"** A sea of hands wave in the air. While not all children volunteer an answer, the typical response is a single, descriptive adjective: "awesome, cool, wacko, nabular, crazy, and unusual," the last being the most conventional word choice.

**"How did the story make you feel?"** is my next question. It is not often that children are asked how literature makes them feel. I have learned that first-graders often find it difficult to express their feelings, as an initial silence fills the room after the second question. However, their thoughts and feelings

*(continued)*

---

*Adapted from Heller, M. F. (1992). " 'What'd you think about that story?' Children Responding to Literature." Paper presented at the 37th annual convention of the International Reading Association, May 3–8, Orlando, Florida.

### Inside the Classroom (continued)

about the narrative soon merge, as illustrated by the vocabulary used to express how the story made some of them feel: "[The story made me feel] . . . good, stupid, funny, rad, funky, cool, happy, sad."

I do not proceed down the list of response questions without first engaging the children in "Why/because" exchanges. "Why do you think the book is nabular?" . . . "Because the houses are cool," and "Why does the story make you feel stupid?" Carl chooses to answer: "I felt stupid because the people in the book thought it was stupid to change your house. I wouldn't change my house because people would yell at me if I did." I and the children acknowledge Carl's right to identify with the people in the neighborhood. I note that Carl does not recognize that the neighbors also changed in the story and became accepting individuals themselves. Throughout our discussion, I try to focus attention on the individual child and his or her emerging understanding of the text. There are no right or wrong answers, yet the responses are a reflection of not only the children's personal involvement in the story but also their skill in critical thinking and strategic reading abilities. Each response is treated with respect, as any child may volunteer to elaborate upon his or her contribution. Carl is having a hard time with reading this year and often says he feels "stupid."

**"What was your favorite part of the story?"** This question is easier for the children, more comfortable and familiar than expressing one's feelings to the teacher. It is a question that simply calls for a literal response, and one would expect the children to name a specific event or episode in the story. Everyone seems to have an answer: "I liked the way the first house was painted; [My favorite part was] . . . when we saw the houses when they were different; when he has a crocodile and palm tree; when they yell at him; when they got to drink lemonade; when he changed the house to a boat." Many of the responses are linked to Pinkwater's illustrations, which are colorful portrayals of exotic-looking dwellings where dreams must surely come true.

The children's feelings about the story again emerge as I ask more why/because questions: "Why did you like it when one of the characters changed his house into a boat?" "Because it made me feel like going fishing with my dad," says Daniel. "Why is the part about people yelling at him your favorite part?" "Because the words made me feel funny," says Jayme. "What words were funny?" I ask. "Knots in his noodle" and "Gushed his mush." The children and I laugh hysterically, recalling Pinkwater's language play that so vividly characterizes the rigid attitudes of the neighbors. I reread some of the sillier phrases aloud. "Why do you think the neighbors said those silly things about Mr. Plumbean?" "Because they're all stuck up and think Plumbean's crazy. They all want to have boring houses," says Caroline. I am struck by the children's level of involvement in the text, the personal connections that many of them seem to have made with character and setting.

**"Did the story leave you with a special message?"** My purpose in asking about the special message is to elicit a personal response and to ascertain the children's level of understanding about the themes implied in the text. The children's responses are as varied as the houses on Mr. Plumbean's new street. "Don't change your house because people will say not to; it's boring to be all the same; if they [the houses] were all the same, we wouldn't know which is ours; don't listen to what the neighbors say; when others boss you around, do what you want to do; everybody is different. "Is it a good enough reason to keep things just the way they are, just because somebody tells you not to change?" I asked. Luke suggested: "Well, if you don't want to get yelled at you better not change." But what happened at the end of the story, Luke?" "Well, everybody changed their houses. I still don't like to be yelled at."

Luke is uncomfortable with the concept of change, especially if it means confrontation or conflict. There are others in the classroom who are of the same opinion, quite tentative children who know full well the impact of change in our lives: "I don't ever want to move again," replies Erica, the newest member of the class. "I'd miss all of my neighbors." Many children respond to the heart of the story and articulate messages about freedom and individuality that are clearly intended by the author. The prereading discussion about the concept of individuality prepared the children to make thematic responses.

**"Did the story give you any ideas for writing your own story, poem, or nonfiction?"** My final question gives the first-graders a chance to respond in writing. I let them know that their written responses can be as simple as answering the question, "What'd you think about that story?" to more elaborate compositions that were inspired by the listening or reading experience. The first-graders' ideas for writing are diverse: "I would have a story about a purple splot; mine would be a story about a man painting windows; I'd write about a boy or girl painting themselves; I would have a story about a big red splot; I'd write a poem about a big mud puddle; in my story a bird came and put a Z instead of a splot; how about a story where a bird put footprints on the house."

As I record their answers on chart paper, I think that I alone could never have designed such wonderful ideas for writing. Perhaps it is no accident that the children's writing topics are so imaginative. I've tried to immerse them in a classroom environment where everyone respects one another's feelings and opinions. My prereading discussion, sequence of questioning, and our subsequent discussions serve to stimulate their creative thinking, and ultimately their creative writing, which we published in a class collection entitled *My Dream House*. Figure 3.8, "My Imaginary House" is David's creation.

*(continued)*

**Inside the Classroom (continued)**

My umalhery hous
By David

I WiSh I had a hous that terned in to a
Spacship. and the Spacip had Many cintenolls
in it. it colud Fly 2000 MiLSe Ubuv the Erths
Serfis. I rely wolud Like to have a hous Like that
I have it in a teru Story at the firunt of My
bernoll. it auBot how derdy My housis.

**FIGURE 3.8**   "My Imaginary House," by David, age 7

## MY IMAGINARY HOUSE

By David

> *I wish I had a house that turned into a space ship. And the spaceship had many controls in it. It could fly two thousand miles above the earth's surface. I really would like to have a house like that. I have written a true story at the front of my journal. It's about how dirty my house is. **The end.***

September 1, 1994

Dear Parents and Guardians,

Welcome to the new school year! I'm so happy to have your child in my class. This first week we've spent a lot of time getting to know one another. This year's class is as excited as ever about learning.

Attached to this letter is a copy of your child's first experience writing. I asked the children to write or draw a picture about a recent experience and to share it with us. I've included what your child shared, so you'll appreciate fully the creation.

We'll be writing and reading every day in first grade. Ask your child to tell you about "Authors' Club." This the time set aside every day when the children write and share stories, poems, or nonfiction.

Most of the first-graders are not yet reading, so their ability to spell words is limited. We call these early attempts at spelling "invented spelling." For example, a child might write "uv" for the word "of," or simply put the first letter of a word, as in "b" for "boy." During Authors' Club I tell the children, "Spell the word the way you think it should be spelled." If they insist on having the correct spelling, I give it to them.

Your first-grader will learn it's important to get one's thoughts down on paper first and to be concerned with spelling during editing, especially if we intend to publish the writing for others to read.

Invented spelling makes children even more aware of the importance of phonics, or the relationships between sounds and letters in words. As your child learns to read and write, he or she will at the same time become a better speller as a result.

I've attached a list of suggestions [See Instructional Guidelines: Encouraging Literate Behaviors at Home] for helping your child's reading and writing develop. If there's anything I can do to make your child's first grade year even better, please give me a call. Thanks for your support.

Sincerely,

*Molly Green*

Mrs. Molly Green
First Grade Teacher

**FIGURE 3.9**   Letter to parents

***Writers Publishing.***   The ultimate stage of the composing process results in publication. Publishing refers to readying a piece of writing for a literate audience of readers. Here students have created final draft stories, poems, and nonfiction that are interesting, readable, and error-free. Kindergarten and first-grade teachers are frequently the primary editors during the publishing phase of the composing process. Gradually children in the primary grades become more independent in their ability to prepare a final draft for publication. As stated earlier in this chapter, not everything a child writes needs to be rewritten, edited, and published. Children should be free to choose a piece of writing that they wish to share publicly.

**FIGURE 3.10**   Merriam's first composition

Classroom and school libraries often house desktop published writing of individual children and whole classes. Chapter 8 contains information on word processing and paint programs that assist teachers in desktop publishing. Appendix B contains bookmaking ideas. Teachers may also submit their students' work to professional journals that publish children's writing.

## COMMUNICATING WITH PARENTS

Parents are important partners as we provide each child with total access to composing and comprehending processes. From time to time parents may question developmentally appropriate language arts activities. For instance, when a first grader's inventively spelled writing is sent home, parents may question why the paper was not "corrected." One way to diffuse potential misunderstandings about written language play is to write a letter to parents. In the letter (Figure 3.9—see p. 111) you could explain the daily reading and writing routines that will occur during the year. It is also helpful to attach a copy of the child's first piece of writing (Figure 3.10).

## YOUR HANDWRITING NOTEBOOK

## Manuscript and Cursive Handwriting

Manuscript writing, or printing, is taught in American schools beginning in kindergarten and first grade. Children continue to develop their printing skills through second grade. Cursive, or fluid connected writing, is normally introduced in third grade. Primary grade students learn manuscript first because it is easier to master than cursive writing. In addition, manuscript looks more like the print in books from which children are learning to read. Print is also easier for teachers and peers to read and respond to one another's work in progress.

The primary objective of handwriting instruction is legibility, which is achieved through well-formed letters, consistent slant, and proper spacing of letters and words. A variety of handwriting programs are available, and no one style or method has proved to be superior to another. (See Appendix C for example handwriting styles). Children learn to write best through practice in a meaningful context where communication of ideas is valued (Temple & Gillet, 1989).

***Modeling Handwriting Skills.***    Teacher modeling is crucial to direct instruction in proper letter formation, consistent slant, proper posture, and paper/pencil position. Furner (1969) described a structured procedure for teaching letter formation that takes advantage of basic principles of perceptual motor learning. The approach combines fine motor and sensory experiences with oral and written language, thus enabling children to internalize more readily the concept of a letter. The following are the steps in her procedure, which are appropriate for both manuscript and cursive handwriting instruction:

1. *Chalkboard modeling:* Draw lines on the chalkboard that correspond to the lines on the children's paper. Introduce letters in groups according to shape, such as lowercase circle letters *(o, a, c,* and *e),* and line letters *(l, k, i).*
2. *Observing and talking:* As you are modeling the correct letter formation, talk about how the letter looks. Describe each feature of the letter, telling where to begin each line or curve and where to end. Next, have the children orally tell the features of the letters as you continue to model on the chalkboard.
3. *Verbalizing and practicing:* Next, have the children describe aloud the features of the letters as they write them on their own paper or on the chalkboard. This procedure helps children to make the connection between verbalizing letter features and the physical act of writing. Teachers should carefully supervise children's formation of letters so that incorrect letter formations are not reinforced.
4. *Comparing:* Finally, have the children compare their handwriting with standard handwriting models. Encourage them to discover similarities and differences

and to make necessary corrections so that poor handwriting habits are quickly eliminated. Overhead transparencies of legible and illegible handwriting will also help children understand the importance of communication in relation to penmanship.

***Encouraging Written Communication.***    Modeling correct letter formation and copying activities are only a part of the overall process of developing handwriting skills. Practicing isolated letters and words is tiring and of little value if children are not also given ample time throughout the day for writing connected text. Daily practice in the context of meaningful communication contributes to legible penmanship and makes handwriting instruction more interesting. The composing process provides a valuable structure that encourages respect for the reader audience through legible, neat final drafts. Children focus on content while writing a first draft, sometimes called a sloppy copy. Here neatness is not overemphasized at the expense of getting ideas down. Once ideas are in place, children are freer to attend to final draft form, including spelling, grammar, punctuation, and handwriting. The process of writing, sharing, rewriting, and editing places handwriting legibility in perspective. It is a valuable skill that enables us to communicate ideas effectively to a community of readers.

***Using Handwriting Tools.***    The following materials facilitate direct instruction in manuscript and cursive handwriting instruction.

1. Provide a variety of pencils and pens in several sizes and shapes. Allow children to choose the size of a writing implement that gives them the best control while practicing penmanship skills.
2. Pencil guards, rounded and triangular, are valuable aids for gaining control of a pencil, especially in first grade. Holding a pencil improperly or too tightly can create fatigue. Another way to remind children of how to hold a pencil is by placing a piece of scotch tape just above the painted portion of the pencil to remind children of proper finger placement.
3. Unlined paper is still valuable for handwriting practice, as children explore the world of print. Direct instruction in manuscript and cursive handwriting normally involves practice writing on lined paper, such as Hytone or Big Chief brand tablets for first and third grades.

Penmanship is an important skill that facilitates communication throughout one's lifetime. When approached from this perspective, handwriting instruction becomes a worthy part of the overall language arts curriculum.

## FOR YOUR JOURNAL

1. Interview some primary grade children. Ask, "What is reading? What is writing?" Compare their answers. Are there obvious developmental differences within and across grades 1, 2, and 3?

2. Listen to the conversation that accompanies the composing process in any primary grade classroom. What did you hear? How does talk facilitate prewriting, writing, rewriting, and editing in the situations you observed?

3. Analyze the content of a primary grade basal reader and language arts book. Which theoretical viewpoints appear to dominate the texts? Describe how you might enhance the language arts curriculum by designing lessons that reflect other theoretical positions.

## SELECTED BOOKS FOR PRIMARY GRADE CHILDREN

### Picture Books and Illustrated Fiction

Adler, David A. (1987), *My Dog and the Birthday Mystery,* Holiday.

Aliki (1982), *We Are Best Friends,* Greenwillow.

Aliki (1988), *Dinosaur Bones,* Crowell.

Asch, Frank (1986), *Goodbye House,* Prentice-Hall.

Atkinson, Allen (1987), *Jack in the Green,* Crown.

Baker, Jeannie (1988), *Where the Forest Meets the Sea,* Greenwillow.

Barklem, Jill (1986), *The High Hills,* Philomel.

Bjork, Christina, & Anderson, Lena (1987), *Linnea in Monet's Garden,* Farrar, Straus & Giroux.

Bohdal, Susi (1987), *The Magic Honey Jar,* North & South.

Bonsall, Crosby (1986), *The Amazing the Incredible Super Dog,* Harper & Row.

Bridwell, Norman (1983), *Clifford's Christmas,* Scholastic Books.

Browne, Anthony (1986), *Piggybook,* Knopf.

Bulla, Clyde Robert (1987), *The Chalk Box Kid,* Random House.

Bunting, Eve (1984), *The Man Who Could Call Down Owls,* Macmillan.

Calhoun, Mary (1987), *Cross-Country Cat,* Morrow.

Cameron, Ann (1986), *More Stories Julian Tells,* Knopf.

Cameron, Ann (1987), *Julian's Glorious Summer,* Random House.

Canty, John (1987), *Shadows,* Harper & Row.

Carey, Valerie S. (1987), *The Devil and Mother Crump,* Harper & Row.

Carrick, Carol (1986), *What Happened to Patrick's Dinosaurs?* Clarion.

Cazet, Denys (1987), *Frosted Glass,* Bradbury.

Christelow, Eileen (1987), *Olive and the Magic Hat,* Clarion.

Cohen, Cron Lee (1987), *Renata, Whizbrain and the Ghost,* Atheneum.
Cole, Joanna (1986), *This Is a Place for Me,* Scholastic Books.
Cole, Joanna (1987), *The Magic School Bus Inside the Earth,* Scholastic Books.
Cole, Joanna (1987), *Norma Jean Jumping Bean,* Random House.
Cooper, Susan (1986), *The Seal Mother,* McElderry.
Craven, Carolyn (1987), *What the Mailman Brought,* Putnam.
Craven, Carolyn (1987), *Whiffle Squeek,* Dodd, Mead.
Cummings, E. E. (1987), *Little Tree,* Crown.
Daly, Niki (1986), *Not So Fast Songololo,* Atheneum.
de Brunhoff, Laurent (1986), *Babar and the Ghost: An Easy-to-Read Version,* Random House.
de Gerez, Toni (1986), *Louhi, Witch of North Farm,* Viking/Kestral.
Demi (1987), *Chen Ping and His Magic Axe,* Dodd, Mead.
Demi (1987), *The Hallowed Horse,* Dodd, Mead.
dePaola, Tomie (1991), *Bonjour, Mr. Satie,* Putnam.
Dragonwagon, Crescent (1987), *Diana Maybe,* Macmillan.
Drescher, Henrik (1983), *Simon's Book,* Lothrop.
Edwards, Patricia (1987), *Chester and Uncle Willoughby,* Little, Brown.
Erickson, Russell (1987), *Warton and the Contest,* Lothrop.
Faulkner, Matt (1987), *The Amazing Voyage of Jackie Grace,* Scholastic Books.
Girard, Linda W. (1992), *Who Is a Stranger and What Should I Do?* Albert Whitman & Company.
Girard, Linda W. (1993), *Alex, the Kid with AIDS,* Albert Whitman & Company.
Gould, Deborah (1987), *Grandpa's Slide Show,* Lothrop.
Griffith, Helen V. (1986), *Georgia Music,* Greenwillow.
Griffith, Helen V. (1987), *Grandaddy's Place,* Greenwillow.
Haley, Gail E. (1986), *Jack and the Bean Tree,* Crown.
Hall, Lynn (1987), *In Trouble Again Zelda Hammer Smith,* Harcourt Brace Jovanovich.
Harris, Joel Chandler (1987), *Jump Again! More Adventures of Brer Rabbit,* Harcourt Brace Jovanovich.
Harvy, Brett (1988), *Cassie's Journey: Going West in the 1860's,* Holiday.
Hasely, Dennis (1986), *Kite Flier,* Four Winds Press.
Haugaard, Erick (1987), *Prince Boghole,* Macmillan.
Hautzig, Deborah (1986), *Why Are You So Mean to Me?* Random House.
Heller, Ruth (1987), *A Cache of Jewels,* Grosset & Dunlap.
Hendershot, Judith (1987), *In Coal Country,* Knopf.
Hest, Amy (1986), *The Purple Coat,* Four Winds Press.
Hewett, Joan (1987), *Rosalie,* Lothrop.
Hiser, Berniece (1987), *The Adventures of Charlie and His Wheat Straw Hat,* Dodd, Mead.
Hoban, Lillian (1987), *Silly Silly and the Easter Bunny,* Harper & Row.
Hoban, Russell (1987), *The Rain Door,* Crowell.
Howard, Elizabeth Fitzgerald (1988), *The Train to Lulu's,* Bradbury.
Hurwitz, Johanna (1987), *Class Clown,* Morrow.
Hurwitz, Johanna (1987), *Russell Sprouts,* Morrow.
Hurwitz, Johanna (1988), *Teacher's Pet,* Morrow.
Ichikawa, Satomi (1986), *Nora's Castle,* Philomel.
Jonas, Ann (1987), *Reflections,* Greenwillow.
Jordan, MaryKate (1992), *Losing Uncle Tim,* Albert Whitman.
Jukes, Mavis (1984), *Like Jake and Me,* Knopf.

Keller, Holly (1987), *Goodbye, Max,* Greenwillow.

Kellogg, Steven (1987), *Prehistoric Pinkerton,* Dial Press.

Kenkes, Kevin (1987), *Two under Par,* Greenwillow.

Kline, Suzy (1987), *What's the Matter with Herbie Jones?* Putnam.

Knutson, Barbara (1987), *Why the Crab Has No Head,* Carolrhoda.

Korschunow, Irina (1986), *The Foundling Fox,* Scholastic Books.

Kraus, Robert (1974), *Herman the Helper,* Windmill Books.

Lent, Blair (1986), *Bayberry Bluff,* Houghton Mifflin.

Levinson, Nancy S. (1988), *Clara and the Bookwagon,* Harper & Row.

Littledale, Freya (1986), *The Magic Fish,* Scholastic Books.

Littledale, Freya (1987), *The Farmer in the Soup,* Scholastic Books.

Lobel, Arnold (1975), *Owl at Home,* Harper & Row.

Lobel, Arnold (1981), *Uncle Elephant,* Harper & Row.

MacClachlan, Patricia (1982), *Mama One, Mama Two,* Harper & Row.

MacDonald, George (1987), *Little Daylight,* North & South.

McKissack, Patricia C. (1986), *Flosie the Fox,* Dial Press.

MacLachlan, Patricia (1985), *Sarah, Plain and Tall,* HarperCollins.

McPhail, David (1986), *Pig Pig and the Magic Photo Album,* Dutton.

Maestro, Betsy, & Giulio (1987), *A More Perfect Union,* Lothrop.

Marshall, James (1984), *The Cut-ups,* Viking Press.

Martin, Bill, Jr., & Archambault, John (1986), *White Dynamite and Curly Kidd,* Holt, Rinehart & Winston.

Mauser, Pat Rhodes (1987), *Patti's Pet Gorilla,* Atheneum/Macmillan.

Morris, Winifred (1987), *The Magic Leaf,* Atheneum.

Muehlman, Mac (1986), *The Seagull Story,* J. M. Muehlman.

Munsch, Robert (1980), *The Paper Bag Princess,* Annick Press Ltd.

Murphy, Jim (1988), *The Last Dinosaur,* Scholastic Books.

Noble, Trinka Hakes (1980), *The Day Jimmy's Boa Ate the Wash,* Dial Press.

Noble, Trinka Hakes (1987), *Meanwhile Back at the Ranch,* Dial Press.

Nolan, Dennis (1987), *The Castle Builder,* Macmillan.

Nygren, Tord (1987), *Fiddler and His Brothers,* Morrow.

O'Conner, Jane (1987), *Lulu Goes to Witch School,* Harper & Row.

O'Donnel, Elizabeth Lee (1987), *Maggie Doesn't Want to Move,* Four Winds Press.

O'Kelly, Mattie Lou (1986), *Circus,* Atlantic Monthly Press.

Parker, Kristy (1987), *My Dad the Magnificent,* Dutton.

Patz, Nancy (1986), *Gina Farina and the Prince of Mintz,* Harcourt Brace Jovanovich.

Peavear, Richard (1987), *Our King Has Horns,* Macmillan.

Pinkwater, Daniel (1989), *Guys from Space,* Macmillan.

Pinkwater, Daniel Manus (1977), *The Big Orange Splot,* Hastings House Publishers.

Pizer, Abigail (1987), *Nosey Gilbert,* Dial Press.

Potter, Beatrix (1944, 1987), *Wag-by-Wall,* Warner.

Rappaport, Doreen (1988), *The Boston Coffee Party,* Harper & Row.

Ryder, Joanne (1985), *The Night Flight,* Macmillan.

Rylant, Cynthia (1981), *When I Was Young in the Mountains,* Dutton.

Rylant, Cynthia (1983), *Miss Maggie,* Dutton.

Rylant, Cynthia (1987), *Henry and Mudge,* Bradbury.

Rylant, Cynthia (1987), *Henry and Mudge in Puddle Trouble,* Bradbury.

Saltzburg, Barney (1986), *Cromwell,* Macmillan.

Schertle, Alice (1987), *Bill and the Goggle-Eyed Goblins,* Lothrop.

Schick, Eleanor (1987), *Art Lessons,* Greenwillow.

Scieska, John (1989), *The True Story of the 3 Little Pigs,* Viking Penguin.

Sharmat, Mitchell (1980), *Gregory the Terrible Eater,* Macmillan.

Shreve, Susan (1987), *Lily and the Runaway Baby,* Random House.

Siekkinen, Raija (1987), *Mister King,* Carolrhoda.

Small, David (1987), *Paper John,* Farrar, Straus & Giroux.

Smith, Jennifer (1987), *Grover and the New Kid,* Random House.

Stevens, Janet (1987), *The Town Mouse and the Country Mouse,* Holiday.

Stevenson, James (1987), *Will You Please Feed Our Cat,* Greenwillow.

Stolz, Mary (1988), *Storm in the Night,* Harper & Row.

Talbott, Hudson (1987), *We're Back! A Dinosaur's Story,* Crown.

Thomas, Jane R. (1988), *Saying Goodbye to Grandma,* Clarion.

Uchida, Yoshiko (1987), *The Two Foolish Cats,* McElderry.

Van Leeuwen, Jean (1987), *Oliver, Amanda and Grandmother Pig,* Dial Press.

Williams, Vera (1982), *A Chair for My Mother,* Greenwillow.

Williams, Vera B., & Williams, Jennifer (1988), *Stringbean's Trip to the Shining Sea,* Greenwillow.

Willoughby, Elaine Macmann (1980), *Boris and the Monsters,* Houghton Mifflin.

Wiseman, Bernard (1987), *Barber Bear,* Little, Brown.

Wood, Audrey (1987), *Heckedy Peg,* Harcourt Brace Jovanovich.

Wooding, Sharon L. (1986), *Arthur's Christmas Wish,* Atheneum.

Yeoman, John (1987), *The Bear's Water Picnic,* Atheneum.

Yep, Laurence (1987), *The Curse of the Squirrel,* Random House.

Yolen, Jane (1986), *The Sleeping Beauty,* Knopf.

Yolen, Jane (1987), *Owl Moon,* Philomel.

Zelinsky, Paul O. (1986), *Rumpelstiltskin,* Dutton.

Zemach, Margot (1979), *It Could Always Be Worse,* Scholastic Books.

Zolotow, Charlotte (1962, 1977), *Mister Rabbit and the Lovely Present,* Harper & Row.

Zolotow, Charlotte (1964, 1987), *The Poodle Who Barked at the Wind,* Harper & Row.

## Concept Books—Alphabet

Base, Graeme (1986), *Animalia,* Abrams.

Dragonwagon, Crescent (1987), *Alligator Arrived with Apples: A Potluck Alphabet Feast,* Macmillan.

Ryden, Hope (1988), *Wild Animals of America ABC,* Lodestar/Dutton.

Van Allsburg, Chris (1987), *The Z Was Zapped,* Houghton Mifflin.

## Concept Books—Counting

Kitchen, Bert (1987), *Animal Numbers,* Dial Press.

MacDonald, Suse (1986), *Alphabatics,* Bradbury.

Ryden, Hope (1988), *Wild Animals of America ABC,* Lodestar/Dutton.

## Poetry

Adolff, Arnold (1988), *Greens,* Lothrop.
DeRegniers, Beatrice Schenk (1988), *The Way I Feel . . . Sometimes,* Clarion.
Frost, Robert (1916, 1988), *Birches,* Holt, Rinehart & Winston.
Kumin, Maxine (1987), *The Microscope,* Harper/Trophy.
Livingston, Myra Cohn, & Fisher, Leonard Everett (1988), *Space Songs,* Holiday.
Lobel, Arnold (1986), *The Random House Book of Mother Goose,* Random House.
Milne, A. A. (1927, 1975), *Now We Are Six,* Dutton/Dell.
Norman, Charles (1988), *The Hornbeam Tree and Other Poems,* Holt, Rinehart & Winston.
Prelutsky, Jack (Ed.) (1983), *The Random House Book of Poetry for Children,* Random House.
Simmie, Lois (1988), *Auntie's Knitting Baby,* Orchard/Watts.

## Wordless Books

Alexander, Martha (1970), *Bobo's Dream,* Dial Press.
Aruego, Jose (1979), *We Hide, You Seek,* Greenwillow.
de Paola, Tomie (1983), *Sing, Pierrot, Sing,* Harcourt Brace Jovanovich.
Felix, Monique (1980), *The Story of a Little Mouse Trapped in a Book,* Green Tiger Press.
Fuchs, Erich (1969), *Journey to the Moon,* Delacorte Press.
Stevens, Kathleen (1985), *The Beast in the Bathtub,* Gareth Stevens.
Ward, Lynd (1973), *The Silver Pony,* Houghton Mifflin.
Wiesner, David (1991), *Tuesday,* Clarion.

## Folk Tales

Bang, Molly Garrett (1976), *Wiley and the Hairy Man,* Macmillan.
Helgadottir, Gudrin (1986), *Flumbra: An Icelandic Folktale,* Carolrhoda.
Ishii, Momoko (1987), *The Tongue-Cut Sparrow,* Lodestar.
Lattimore, Deborah Nourse (1987), *The Flame of Peace: A Tale of the Aztecs,* Harper & Row.
Mikolaycak, Charles (1984), *Baboushka,* Holiday.
Porazinska, Janina (1987), *The Enchanted Book: A Tale from Krakow,* Harcourt Brace Jovanovich.
Rogasky, Barbara (1986), *The Water of Life,* Holiday.
Steptoe, John (1987), *Mufaro's Beautiful Daughters,* Lothrop.

## Nonfiction

Arnold, Caroline (1987), *Kangaroo,* Morrow.
Arnold, Caroline (1987), *Koala,* Morrow.
Brown, Laurene Krasny, & Brown, Marc (1986), *Dinosaurs Divorce: A Guide for Changing Families,* Little, Brown.
Brown, Laurene Krasny, & Brown, Marc (1986), *Visiting the Art Museum,* Dutton.
Clement, Claude (1986), *The Painter and the Swans,* Dial Press.
Cole, Joanna (1987), *The Magic School Bus Ride Inside the Earth,* Scholastic Books.
Dayee, Frances S. (1982), *Private Zone,* Warner Books.
de Paola, Tomie (1972), *The Cloud Book,* Scholastic Books.
de Paola, Tomie (1978), *Popcorn Book,* Scholastic Books.

Dorros, Arthur (1987), *Ant Cities,* Crowell.

Gibbons, Gail (1987), *Weather Forecasting,* Four Winds Press.

Hausherr, Rosmarie (1992), *Children and the AIDS Virus: A Book for Children, Parents, and Teachers,* Clarion.

Kitzinger, Sheila (1986), *Being Born,* Grosset & Dunlap.

Kuklin, Susan (1986), *Thinking Big: The Story of a Young Dwarf,* Lothrop.

Munroe, Roxie (1987), *The Inside Outside Book of Washington, D.C.,* Dutton.

Parker, Nancy W., & Wright, Joan Richard (1987), *Bugs,* Greenwillow.

Patterson, Francine (1987), *Koko's Story,* Scholastic Books.

Ride, Sally, & Okie, Susan (1986), *To Space and Back,* Lothrop.

Schwartz, Amy (1987), *Oma and Bobo,* Bradbury.

Siebert, Diane (1988), *Mojave,* Crowell.

Simon, Seymour (1988), *Galaxies,* Morrow.

Wescott, Nadine B. (1987), *Peanutbutter and Jelly: A Play Rhyme,* Dutton.

## Multicultural Books

Bang, Molly (1987), *The Paper Crane,* Morrow.

Barrett, Joyce D. (1989), *Willie's Not the Hugging Kind,* Harper & Row.

Berry, James (1988), *A Thief in the Village, and Other Stories,* Orchard.

Cameron, Ann (1987), *Julian's Glorious Summer,* Random House.

Chang, Heidi (1988), *Elaine, Mary Lewis and the Frogs,* Crown.

Delacre, Lulu (1990), *Las Navides: Popular Christmas Songs from Latin America,* Scholastic.

dePaola, Tomie (1988), *The Legend of the Indian Painbrush,* Putnam.

Fisher, Leona E. (1986), *The Great Wall of China,* Macmillan.

Flournoy, Valerie (1985), *The Patchwork Quilt,* Dial.

Friedman, Ina R. (1984), *How My Parents Learned to Eat,* Houghton Mifflin.

Ginsburg, Mirra (1988), *The Chinese Mirror: A Korean Folktale,* Harcourt Brace & Company.

Giovanni, Nikki (1985), *Spin a Soft Black Song: Poems for Children,* Farrar, Straus, and Giroux.

Goble, Paul. (1982). *The Girl Who Loved Wild Horses.* Macmillan.

Greenfield, Eloise (1977), *Africa Dream,* HarperTrophy.

Hamilton, Virginia (1993), *Many Thousand Gone: African-Americans from Slavery to Freedom,* Knopf.

Hearn, Michael P. (1987), *The Porcelain Cat,* Little, Brown.

Hedlund, Irene (1990), *Mighty Mountain and the Three Strong Women,* Volcano, CA: Volcano Press.

Hopkins, Lee B., ed. (1983), *The Sky Is Full of Song,* Harper and Row.

Hoyt-Goldsmith, Diane (1991), *Pueblo Storyteller,* Holiday House.

Hru, Dakari (1993), *Joshua's Masai Mask,* Lee & Low Books.

Jones, Hettie (Ed.). (1993), *The Trees Stand Shining: Poetry of the North American Indians,* Macmillan.

Jordan, June (1981), *Kimako's Story,* Houghton Mifflin.

Joseph, Lynn (1991), *A Wave in Her Pocket,* Clarion.

Lewis, Richard (1988), *In the Night, Still Dark,* Atheneum.

Livingston, Myra C., ed. (1988), *Poems for Mothers,* Holiday House.

McDermott, Gerald (1972), *Anansi The Spider: A Tale from The Ashanti,* Henry Holt.

McKissack, Patricia C. (1988), *Mirandy and Brother Wind,* Alfred A. Knopf.

Maruki, Toshi (1982), *Hiroshima No Pika,* Lothrop.

Markun, Patricia M. (1993), *The Little Painter of Sabana Grande,* Bradbury.

Mochizuki, Ken (1993), *Baseball Saved Us,* Lee & Low Books.

Medearis, Angela S. (1993), *Dancing with the Indians,* Holiday House.

Ortiz, Simon (1988), *The People Shall Continue,* San Francisco: Children's Book Press.

Pomerantz, Charlotte (1989), *The Chalk Doll,* New York: Lippincott.

Ringgold, Faith (1991), *Tar Beach,* New York: Crown.

Rohmer, Harriet, Chow, Octavio, & Vidaure, Morris (1987), *The Invisible Hunters,* Children's Book Press.

Seeger, Pete (1986), *Abiyoyo: A South African Lullaby and Folk Story,* Macmillan.

Snyder, Diane (1988), *The Boy of the Three-Year Nap,* Houghton Mifflin.

Surat, Maria M. (1983), *Angel Child, Dragon Child,* Scholastic.

Young, Ed (1989), *Lon Po Po: A Red Riding Hood Story from China,* Philomel.

# 4 COMPREHENDING AND COMPOSING IN THE INTERMEDIATE GRADES

*The* Little House on the Prairie *books are the ones I like to read over and over. Then I like to pretend I'm Laura, and I write in my diary about my life. It's a happy life being Laura, reading and writing.*

*Constance, age 11, grade 5*

## CHAPTER CONCEPTS

The intermediate grades are often characterized by increased reading and writing in the content areas.

Prior knowledge and understanding of text structures facilitate comprehension and composition.

The basic forms of oral and written discourse are narration, exposition, and poetry.

Summary writing is an often-neglected but nevertheless important skill.

The intermediate grades (4–6) are a time of wondrous transition into adolescence. It is a time when child readers and writers begin to explore ideas through a variety of genres. And it is a time when children begin to discover who they are through reading and writing. Upon entering upper elementary school, children must also deal with the increasing demands of reading and writing across the curriculum. Along with those demands come the pressures to achieve, to attain grades and academic status, and at the same time to develop and maintain social relationships with peers in the classroom environment. It is a crucial time for children achieving literacy.

All too often, children who have until now progressed normally may develop difficulties with comprehension and composition. The classic remedial reader in middle school, for example, is often suspended at about a fourth-grade language level. The reading level of a "functionally illiterate" adult is frequently about fourth grade, and the writing ability of such an individual is virtually nonexistent (Anderson, Hiebert, Scott, & Wilkinson, 1984). These phenomena are blamed in part on the dramatic increase in content area reading and writing during grades 4, 5, and 6. For some children, a sudden increase in expository text structures not previously encountered appears to result in an interruption in the process of learning to comprehend and to compose. Suspended at the intermediate reading and writing level, some children may never recover, especially if adequate instructional support is consistently absent.

The challenges of teaching reading and writing in the intermediate grades may be directly associated with the many subject areas, technical vocabulary, and expository texts with which children are faced. Viewed as a whole, the structure of texts, or the form authors use to convey their ideas, is a primary influence on comprehending and composing as children read and write about a wide array of topics. Research during the 1980s demonstrates that an individual's knowledge of and experience with a variety of genres enables him or her to better understand and remember the prose (Meyer, 1984; Squire, 1983; B. M. Taylor, 1982).

Intermediate-grade reading instruction frequently emphasizes structural analysis of words in isolation and the use of sentence-level context clues. Reading comprehension beyond the literal level is often a curricular objective in the upper-elementary grades. Yet direct instruction in how to think inferentially and to read text structures other than narratives is at best inconsistent in basal programs and at worst nonexistent during the rest of the school day. In a study of eight basal-reader programs, Flood and Lapp (1987) found that narratives are most frequently used at each grade level, preprimer through grade 6. Poetic forms (rhymed and unrhymed verse) occur with about the same frequency across all grade levels, but with significantly less poetry than prose. In intermediate grade basal readers, expository reading is often treated like narrative reading, even though research indicates that the two forms should be taught differently. Added to these pedagogical dilemmas is the fact that expository text structures dominate all content areas in the daily reading and writing curriculum.

In contrast to the basal readers, language arts texts contain a better balance of narrative, poetic, and expository writing lessons. Although narrative and poetic writing are often assigned, they are accompanied by little instruction. Formal expository writing instruction may begin in earnest, but with the traditional matters of spelling, grammar, and punctuation controlling curricular objectives (M. F. Heller, 1988c). Clearly there is a need to resolve the problems associated with providing intermediate grade children experiences that will enable them to develop as readers and writers of many different kinds of texts.

The purpose of this chapter is to present a description of the nature of text structures followed by research-based instructional guidelines. A continuing theme throughout this text will again emerge, that of making efficient use of time by connecting reading and writing instruction. The process of writing and reading is still central to intermediate grade instruction and will form the theoretical basis of many

Fifth-graders read and respond to their collaborative writing project.

of the strategies and lessons described in this chapter. As in kindergarten and the primary grades, what fourth-, fifth-, and sixth-grade children experience and think about before, during, and after reading and writing is of particular importance.

## THE STRUCTURE OF TEXTS

Text structure refers to the basic organizational pattern or form that an author uses to convey his or her message. The classic forms of discourse are narration, exposition, and poetry. Discourse is the formal, orderly expression of thought through oral or written language. The form denotes the overall purpose or reason underlying the prose and poetry. Although for pedagogical reasons we can discuss them separately, prose forms often overlap onto and support each other as an author constructs a meaningful text. For example, narratives may include clear explanations of settings and characters. Expository prose sometimes calls for narration, especially if the author is explaining a sequence of events or describing a step-by-step procedure or process. Narratives are sometimes used in the content areas to teach difficult science or social concepts. Narrative poems tell a story. Research in the 1970s demonstrated differences in syntactic complexity among the prose forms of discourse (Crowhurst, 1977; Perron, 1977). Generally speaking, the complexity of both oral and written language increases as one moves from narrative to expository prose.

Readers expect a text to have clear, logical form. Internalized knowledge of text structure facilitates memory and cognition. In the following sections of this chapter, I will discuss narrative, expository, and poetic forms in relation to comprehending and composing in the intermediate grades. Teaching about form within the context of the reading and writing process is a major theme in this chapter.

## NARRATION, EXPOSITION, AND POETRY

## Reading and Writing Stories

The purpose of a narrative is to tell a story, either fictionalized or true. Long before attending school, children of diverse backgrounds experience stories. Storytelling is embedded in the social and cultural histories of humankind (Bruner, 1986). Parents often tell children their stories about growing up, while grandparents or other relatives may tell the history of the family settling in urban or rural areas. Other narrative listening experiences may involve fables and fairy tales, short stories and novels. Children also encounter stories through print and nonprint media: newspapers and magazines, computer and video games, radio, television, movies, and live plays. A child's sense of story is further reinforced through the mundane routines imbedded in daily life. For example, a shopping trip to the mall with friends is likely to inspire a relatively structured personal narrative. Personal narratives are a form of nonfiction frequently assigned in elementary school writing curricula (M. F. Heller, 1987). Robbie, a fifth-grader, wrote "The Story of My Bicycle" (which follows) after reading "The Dun Horse" (Grinnell, 1986), the story of a young Pawnee Indian's need for a horse, no matter how old or ugly.

### THE STORY OF MY BICYCLE

by Robbie, grade 5

*When I was eight years old and in the second grade, I used to have to walk six blocks to school every day. On days when it rained my mom had to take me to school. Other times when I had a bunch of books and things to carry, my mom had to take me again. Then one day my mom decided to go back to work. So my dad had to take me to school before he went to work at his office. Pretty soon my dad got sick of taking me to school. "You need a bike," my dad said. "Yeah!" I said. "Kids need bikes." So the very next weekend we went down to Wal Mart, and my dad and mom bought me a bike. From then on I never had to walk to school. Mom and Dad still take me to school only when it's bad weather because that's when you need a car. Pretty soon I'll need a car instead of a bike. How about it, Mom and Dad?*

Upon entering formal schooling, most children have internalized the basic structure of a story (Applebee, 1978; Bartlett, 1932; Stein & Glenn, 1979). Children know intuitively that stories have a beginning, a middle, and an end and that something happens in stories, which usually involve people or animals as characters. A child's intuitive knowledge of narrative structure supports story comprehension and composition. Over time, a child's concept of story develops as a result of listening activities, independent reading and writing, and direct instruction in story structure (Whaley, 1981).

***Developing Narrative Concepts.***    Within the research literature, the elements of a story are frequently referred to collectively as the story grammar (Mandler & Johnson, 1977). Story grammars are rules governing the parts that make up the underlying structure of a conventional narrative. Setting, beginning, reaction, attempt, outcome, and ending are six major story parts described by Mandler and Johnson. Variations in the labels of story parts appear throughout the literature (see Johnson & Mandler, 1980; Rumelhart, 1978; and Thorndyke, 1977) and will also vary across commercial language arts textbooks. What we call the parts of a story is not as important as how clear we are in our explanations and goals for teaching and reinforcing the structure of narratives through reading and writing.

Research into the influence of direct instruction in story structure on reading comprehension and written composition demonstrates a positive relationship. Gordon and Braun (1983) investigated the effects of "story schema training" on fifth-graders' reading and writing behaviors. The students in the experimental group were better able to use their newly learned framework for what a story is when encountering new selections and answering literal and inferential questions about the stories. They ultimately learned to rely on their knowledge of story during the writing process. Spiegel and Fitzgerald (1986) found that direct instruction in story structure significantly improved fourth-graders' knowledge of how stories are formed. In story production activities, the students in the "story structure group produced more complex and more fully formed stories. They had a greater awareness of time sequence and of cause and effect relationships between parts" (pp. 681–682).

In a study of fifth-graders' oral and written responses to multicultural children's literature, Heller and McLellan (1993) found that a child's concept of story can also be reinforced in the context of a reader response lesson. Following direct instruction in a simple story grammar, the children listened to the researchers read aloud multicultural fiction and nonfiction. The students then responded orally during whole-class discussions and then individually by writing a narrative. Open-ended response questions, such as "What did you think about the story?" were used to structure class discussions. Story grammar vocabulary was used in follow-up questioning, as in "Why was the scene with the invisible stick your favorite part of the *The Invisible Hunters* (Rohmer et al., 1987)?" Early in the study, the children began to use story grammar vocabulary, such as setting and character, spontaneously in their discussions. Story grammar vocabulary was also reinforced via the composing process. The children responded to the final response question, "Did the book give you any ideas for writing a story of your own?" by first filling out a story structure outline (Figure 4.1) and then composing a narrative. The results of the study revealed that reader response lessons do not necessarily preclude direct instruction in story structure. Open-ended responses appeared to encourage children to respond at higher levels of cognitive and metacognitive thinking about stories.

**MY STORY WRITING IDEAS**

After I listened to the book, I thought about writing my own story. These are my ideas:

**STORY TITLE—**

**SETTING**—When and where my story takes place

**PLOT**—What happens in my story

**CHARACTERS**—Who my characters are

**STORY PROBLEM(s) or CONFLICT(s)**—My characters' problem(s)

**RESOLUTION**—How my characters overcome their problem(s)

**THEME**—The special message of my story

**ILLUSTRATIONS**—On the back are some ideas for illustrating my story.

**FIGURE 4.1**   Story structure outline

SOURCE: M.F. Heller and H. McLellan, 1993. "Dancing with the Wind: Understanding Narrative Text Structure through Response to Multicultural Children's Literature, with an Assist from HyperCard," *Reading Psychology, 14* (4), 285–310. Reprinted with permission.

When teaching with any genre it is important to define relevant terms that will help children to respond to a text and to think about ideas for composing. Children need to know what stories are, how they are structured, and how they are best understood. In the intermediate grades, simple definitions and illustrations are best. For example, you could define a story something like this: A story is a series of related events that bring about change in a character or situation (S. Heller, 1987). The definition suggests that something must happen during the telling of events in order for it to qualify as a story. Change is an important factor in real stories. Further, the ideas in a good story connect with one another, brought together through the structures that underlie plot, characterization, and setting (Bruce, 1978).

As in kindergarten and the primary grades, listening to and talking about stories is fundamental to concept formation in the intermediate grades as well. What you read to the children should also be available to them later for independent rereading or as a resource for composing. Fourth-, fifth-, and sixth-graders ought to be read to daily either by the teacher or a peer. By listening to stories, children continue to develop their understanding and appreciation of narrative form. A reason to listen should always be established, with the children gradually assuming throughout the year independent responsibility for setting purposes. Because older children have a longer attention span, it is possible to read literature over a period of several days without sacrificing interest or comprehension. Setting aside a regular ten- to twenty-minute daily read-aloud time helps children to develop attentive listening skills. Allowing time for response through discussion or writing encourages critical thinking about an unfolding story.

Literal, inferential, and open-ended response questions help to structure class discussions after a read-aloud session. Teacher-directed queries that focus on the development of a story often lead to improved reading comprehension (Beck, 1984) and composition of narratives. To help frame a story for children, Sadow (1982) recommends using five generic questions that focus on setting, initiating event, reaction, action, and consequence—Rumelhart's (1975) basic story grammar. To avoid confusion, it is best to use the same terminology that is in the children's language arts text (i.e., plot instead of action). In addition, questions that stimulate metacognitive thinking are crucial to the process of understanding texts. Stauffer's (1981) recommended sequence of prediction/verification questions—"What do you think," "How do you know," and "Can you prove it"—are useful when teaching children to think out loud and talk about what they know and don't know about stories. Finally, open-ended response questions can be used to initiate discussions by encouraging students to express their thoughts and feelings about a story.

Surveys of intermediate-level students indicate that they are very interested in listening to and reading "here and now" stories, or narratives that closely related to the lives and experiences of children their own age (Higgins & Kellman, 1979). A balance of the here and now and the more distant stories afforded by myths, fairytales, folktales, historical fiction, and biographies is desirable. A well-rounded classroom and school library provide children with a wide variety of interesting materials appropriate for narrative reading and writing experiences. As children mature they are better able to handle abstractions, to work out problems through stories that are somewhat removed from their personal lives. A list of children's literature appropriate for intermediate-level grades is provided at the end of this chapter.

***Planning for Instruction.***     Intermediate-level children are older and more sophisticated in their world knowledge than kindergarten and primary grade students. Nevertheless, prereading/prewriting time is well spent when it is devoted to activating prior knowledge of concepts that underlie a central story problem. In a study of over 500 stories in more than ten basal-reader programs, Moldofsky (1983) "concluded that most fiction revolves around a central problem, and it is this problem that gives coherence to the story" (p. 741). Problems or conflicts central to a story are important to the author's overall intended message. An author may relate a conflict either explicitly or implicitly, through the narrator telling the story or through character development.

Determining the theme or controlling idea in fiction is an important comprehension and composition skill in the intermediate grades and beyond. Yet making such a determination often requires inferential thinking. Inferring a theme or main idea does not occur automatically to all children, especially if they have missed the important factual information in a narrative. However, getting at the central issues in a piece of fiction is easier if the children have been prepared in advance of reading and writing through appropriate concept formation activities that activate the children's prior knowledge of ideas contained in a narrative.

Deciding on what concepts are important is therefore a key element in lesson planning. It is possible to overload children with irrelevant background information at the expense of more process-oriented strategies needed to comprehend and to compose (Durkin, 1978–79). Irrelevant background information often manifests itself in the introduction of vocabulary words that are not necessarily essential for reading comprehension. For example, Mavis Jukes's (1984) award-winning story, *Like Jake and Me,* is the story of a young boy, Alex, and his need to be close to and accepted by his stepfather, Jake, a tough yet kind-hearted man. Concepts that are

Molly shares her writing with the principal,
Dr. Miller.

central to understanding this story of family relationships and conflict include individuality, acceptance, and fear. Story vocabulary words that are less relevant to the
main theme include cypress, grappled, and wolf spider. An appropriate prereading/prewriting discussion would focus the children's attention on concepts associated with the central story problem and overall theme. The following questions could
be used to stimulate whole-class discussion and encouragement of concept formation: "What does it mean to be an individual?" Who do you feel closest to in your
family and why?" and "What are you most afraid of?" Such questions prepare children to understand the events in the story and to identify the central story problem.
Identification of story conflict is essential to articulating the theme of *Like Jake and
Me,* which centers on the human need to be loved and accepted for who we are.

One way to teach narrative reading and writing is to teach the structure of a narrative by reading aloud fictional picture books and highlighting the connections

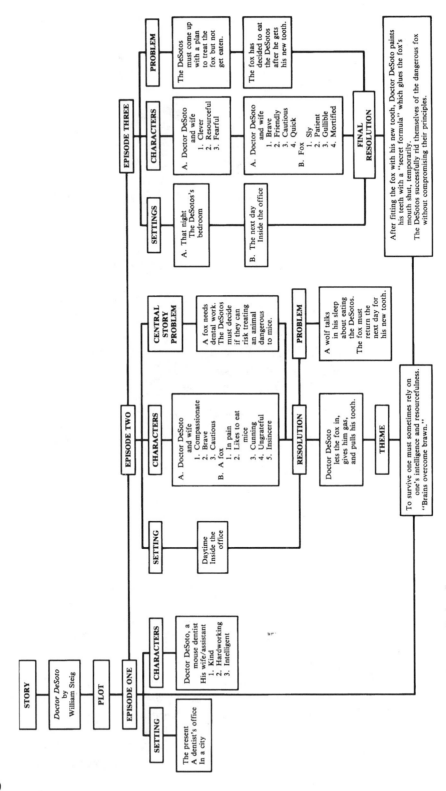

**FIGURE 4.2** "Doctor DeSoto" story map

between comprehending and composing throughout the lesson. The following model lesson integrates listening to, talking about, reading, and writing narratives. Through questioning and modeling, the teacher engages children's current knowledge about story structure and teaches new concepts as they emerge in the narrative. She also uses a story map (Figure 4.2) to aid in her instruction.

The teacher, Ms. Tyler, chooses a finely crafted story by William Steig, *Doctor DeSoto* (1983) on which to base her first lesson on narrative form. Although *Doctor DeSoto* is a story that appeals to audiences younger than fourth-graders, Ms. Tyler chooses this award-winning picture book for a number of practical reasons: (1) the structure of the story is clearly recognizable; (2) the author's writing style is filled with gentle humor and irony, which is appealing to any audience; (3) fourth-graders can identify with the realistic problems, the elements of fable, and the many messages presented in the story; (4) the story can be read aloud in one class period and the structure analyzed and discussed; (5) the story is simple enough to grasp and thus aids in the instruction of abstract terms, such as resolution or theme, associated with narrative structure.

This look inside a real fourth-grade classroom is intended to give you a feeling for the kinds of questions and models that teachers can use to teach narrative structure.

---

## INSIDE THE CLASSROOM
## What Is This Story About?

**A FOURTH-GRADE MODEL QUESTIONING SCENARIO**

### 1. Preparing to Listen
*(Discuss the concept of problems and their solutions; list ideas on chalkboard or overhead.)*

Today I am going to read a story to you entitled *Doctor DeSoto* by William Steig. As you can tell by the picture on the front of book, Doctor DeSoto is a mouse. He is also a dentist. What do you know about dentists? What is your most memorable experience going to the dentist's office? Most of us eventually go to the dentist because we have a problem with our teeth. Do dentists have problems with their patients? If you were a mouse dentist, what problems might you encounter trying to do your job? How would you solve the problems?

Doctor DeSoto has a special problem as a mouse dentist in this story. I want you to listen for his problem as I read the story aloud. While I'm reading, I'll stop after each *episode* in the *plot* and we'll discuss how we come to under-

*(continued)*

**Inside the Classroom (continued)**

stand Doctor DeSoto's problem and how he solves it in the story. As you all know, the plot refers to the sequence of events or episodes that make up the action in a story. As the plot unfolds, we will learn about Doctor DeSoto's problem and the solution. This knowledge will help us to understand what the story is all about, or the author's main reason for writing the story.

### *2. Listening and Talking*

*(Read the story aloud, stopping at appropriate points to engage the children in a discussion about the unfolding narrative. Ask questions that focus the children's attention on story structure.)*

*Synopsis: Episode 1, pp. 1–5. (Questioning focus: setting and character.)* Doctor DeSoto is a very kindly dentist. He and his assistant wife have set up shop in their home to attend to animals of all kinds, large and small. His one restriction, as indicated on a sign posted outside his office, is that he cannot treat animals that are naturally dangerous to mice, such as cats.

### Questioning Scenario

The *setting* of a story is the place and time at which the story is told. Knowing the setting of a story helps us as readers to visualize what is happening. Where and when does this story take place? How do you know? Is it hard for you to believe that a dentist could have an office in his very own house? Where are dentists' offices usually located?

The *characters* in a story can be people or animals or even inanimate objects. Characters carry out the *action* in a story. They are characterized, or described in certain ways, by the *narrator,* who tells the story and who may or may not be a character in the story. We learn about the characters in a story by what they say *(dialogue)* and what they do. How characters are described and how they behave help us to understand the overall meaning of the story. Who are the main characters in *Doctor DeSoto?* What is Doctor DeSoto like? How do you know? Does he behave like any dentists you know? If you were a mouse dentist, would you behave in a similar way?

Is the narrator in *Doctor DeSoto* a character in the story? How do you know? What do you think is going to happen in this story? How do you know? Can you prove it yet? [Retell portions of the unfolding story to answer questions that are not obvious to everyone.]

*Synopsis: Episode 2, pp. 6–17. (Central story problem is revealed.)* One day a fox who has a terrible toothache arrives at Doctor DeSoto's door. The fox begs to be treated. After discussing the dilemma of treating a dangerous fox, Doctor DeSoto and his wife reveal their compassion for suffering animals by letting him in and pulling his decayed tooth. The fox, though grateful that he is no longer in pain, reveals his true nature by dreaming about eating the

DeSotos, later thinking he might do just that the next day when he returns to pick up his brand-new gold tooth.

### Questioning Scenario

A *problem* has now developed in the story. A story problem "is a situation or situations around which an episode or the whole story is organized" [Cooper, 1976, p. 271]. *Conflict* is another term we sometimes use in connection with the story problem. What is Doctor DeSoto's problem? How do you know? What do you learn about his character in this episode? Will the way that he behaves help him to overcome the conflict? How do you think he will solve his problem? Does the fox have a problem? What do you think will happen next?

*Synopsis: Episode 3, pp. 18-28. (Resolution.)* Doctor DeSoto and his wife realize that they must prepare to defend themselves against the evil intentions of the fox. That night they formulate a plan to protect themselves. The next day the fox arrives and Doctor DeSoto sets his new tooth. During the procedure we learn through the wolf's inner thoughts that he indeed plans to eat the DeSotos. However, Doctor DeSoto and his wife have invented a "secret formula" that they paint on the fox's teeth, under the guise of a medication that will rid the fox of tooth decay forever. The secret formula in fact temporarily glues the fox's teeth together, thus enabling the DeSotos to rid themselves of the threat of death and at the same time be humanitarians. The fox leaves the dentist's office, dumbfounded at what has happened. The DeSotos breathe a sigh of relief and then take the rest of the day off.

Possible themes that can be inferred: (1) To survive, one must rely on one's intelligence and resourcefulness—or, brains overcome brawn. (2) Honesty, kindness, and hard work are often rewarded—good overcomes evil.

### Questioning Scenario

A *resolution* refers to the solution to a problem. How do Doctor DeSoto and his wife *resolve* their problem? Is the resolution of the central story problem in keeping with the character of Doctor DeSoto? In other words, do the DeSotos behave the same way throughout the story, even when they solve their problem? What evidence do you have? Does the fox now have a problem that needs to be resolved? What is it?

The underlying message in a story is called a *theme* or controlling idea. A theme is often a generalization about some aspect of life. Sometimes it is stated in a story; sometimes it is not and must be inferred. What do you think the theme of William Steig's *Doctor DeSoto* is? How do you know? Is there more than one theme? Can you go back through the story and trace the development of the theme? Summarizing behavior of the characters throughout the plot of a story helps to determine the underlying message or main idea.

*(continued)*

**Inside the Classroom (continued)**

### 3. Talking and Writing
*(Discuss possibilities for writing based on the story.)*

Through our discussion of *Doctor DeSoto,* we learned that narratives have certain parts or structures that an author uses to tell a story. Traditional stories have the following things in common: narrator, setting(s), character(s), plot, episodes (or events that depict the action), problems, resolution, and theme (or main idea). The most important part of a story may be the central story problem because this is what brings sense to what we are reading and writing. Does the story make you think of other problems and solutions that would make (or have made) good stories? Let's discuss some story ideas. Write the ones that interest you most on the front of your writing folders for future reference.

Example of central story problems from Ms. Tyler's fourth-graders:

1. After leaving Doctor DeSoto's office, the fox must figure out a way to get his mouth unglued so he can survive.
2. Doctor DeSoto and his wife are being sued by the fox for malpractice and are in danger of losing the business. They must figure out a way to win the court case. (Initial and final drafts are provided in Figure 4.3.)
3. A fox, who is also a doctor, has trouble treating his patients because he gets hungry on the job.
4. Doctor DeSoto has an enormous toothache on a weekend. The only dentist in town is at Leo the Lion's Dental Clinic for Large Animals.
5. Sharmain the shrimp is always being teased by the big fish in the ocean. One day Sharmain must do something dangerous in order to save Willy the whale.
6. Karla is a fourth-grader who wants to try out for the school band but is afraid she's not good enough.
7. Ten-year-old Peter is always getting into trouble because his little brother, Jimmy, blames everything on him. Peter wants to convince his parents that he's really a good kid.

### 4. Writing and Reading
*(The children now compose the first draft of their story and share their work with teacher and peers.)*

I would like for each of you now to begin working on the first draft of a story based on one of the story problems that we discussed or some other idea that you think would make a good story. If you need advice while you're writing, be sure to ask me or someone at your table. Use the story structure questions to help while you're writing your own story and when you're reading and reviewing someone else's story. After you've finished your first draft, your buddy will read and respond to it. I'll be around to read your stories, too. We'll be sharing our revised stories and talking about central story problems all year long as we read our basals and library books.

Foolish Fox

One day Doctor Desoto and his wife got a letter. The letter was a court order for them to stop working on peoples teeth because they didn't have a licence to work on {peoples teeth. Mrs. Desoto said, "Oh my what are we going to do? Doctor Desoto said," I now no know I have a licence...stop theif." The theif didn't stop luckly he landed on the secret formul (from Doctor Desotos last adventure). The Desotos called the police and found out who the robber was. It was the fox (from are last story)! He had sent the courtorder wich was fake and he almost got away with stealing his licecens to!

Doctor Desotos

Foolish Fox (Final Draft)

By Carl

(Grade 4)

One day Doctor DeSoto and his wife got a letter. The letter was a court order for them to stop working on people's teeth because they didn't have a license to work on people's teeth. They were going to be sued for malpractice by a fox.

Mrs. DeSoto said, ''Oh my, what are we going to do?''

Doctor DeSoto said, ''I know I have a license somewhere around here...''

As he walked into his office, Doctor DeSoto saw someone who dressed up like a sheep rummaging through the file cabinet. ''Stop thief!'' he said. But the thief didn't stop. He fell down the stairs and luckily landed in a tub of secret formula (from Doctor DeSoto's last adventure).

The DeSotos called the police and found out who the robber was. It was the fox (from our last story) dressed up in a sheep suit. He had sent the court order which was fake, and he almost got away with stealing Doctor DeSoto's license too!

**FIGURE 4.3** "Foolish Fox," by Carl, grade 4

*Reflections.*    Ms. Tyler's questioning provides her fourth-graders with a natural scaffold as they begin to think through the narrative structure in *Doctor DeSoto.* Questions about story content and structure lead to literal and inferential thinking and help children to develop a schema that can be applied to almost any narrative. An important point to remember, however, is that *experience* and *consistency* are necessary to internalize basic story concepts. Since it is our goal to enable children to comprehend and to compose stories with relative ease, it is helpful to use a similar sequence of questions each time you teach narratives of any kind, whether they be fables, fairy tales, sagas, conventional fiction, science fiction, or personal narratives.

Lessons similar to Ms. Tyler's introductory model may also be designed in conjunction with longer works written for the preadolescent. Judy Blume's (1972) *Tales of a Fourth Grade Nothing* and Marian Dane Bauer's (1986) award-winning book, *On My Honor,* are just two examples of the many well-written novels appropriate for intermediate grade children. Although longer works cannot be used as the basis of a single lesson, you could focus on one element of story structure at a time, such as character, during small- or large-group discussions.

As children begin to internalize the structure of a narrative, they will naturally become reflective during reading and writing. You may want to provide the following list of story structure questions to guide your students during the process of comprehending and composing stories written by themselves or others.

### Story Structure Questions
1. Who is the narrator of the story? Can I hear his or her voice? What is the point of view?
2. Does the story have a setting (time and place) that the reader can imagine?
3. Are the characters real and believable through what they do and say in the story?
4. What is the character's problem in the story? Will the reader understand the problem and how it is resolved?
5. Do the episodes or events in the story logically lead to a solution to the central story problem?
6. Can I make a general statement about the theme or main idea of the story?

This is my best advice for the author of the story: [student fills in]

## Comprehending and Composing Exposition

Expository writing explains or clarifies a subject. Exposition is found in virtually all stories, as authors explain an event or describe character and setting. Exposition dominates content area textbooks and is more prevalent in intermediate-level basal readers than in the primary grades. Children seem to know the basic differences between fictional narratives and nonfictional pieces of exposition, such as summaries, essays, or reports. In a comparative study of eight- eleven-, and fourteen-year-old children's awareness of text structures through reading and writing, Langer (1986) found that children described stories according to markers appropriate to the genre, such as "type of beginning, nature of the characters, presence of dialogue, nature of the plot" (p. 100). Conversely, they described reports as presenting the truth or factual information. When comparing their own story writing to report writing, the children in the study made a fundamental differentiation between fiction and nonfiction. The children believed the most important, distinguishing characteristic of their own stories was that they were "make believe," whereas their own reports were "truth telling."

Research into expository prose supports conventional knowledge that exposition is more difficult for children to read and to write, largely because of difficult vocabulary and concepts or the child's lack of experience with the structure of the text (Taylor & Berkowitz, 1980). Intermediate-level children themselves believe narratives to be easier to read than expository materials, and they know that exposition appears on tests designed to assess how much they know about a subject (Alvermann & Boothby, 1982). Such knowledge does not necessarily make it easier for children to comprehend and to compose exposition, however. A fourth-, fifth-, or sixth-grade child may in fact develop a fear of exposition, especially when the prose is accompanied by few illustrations (M. F. Heller, 1988c).

***Developing Expository Prose.***     Exposition, like narration, has a definite form or structure that authors use purposefully to convey a message. Readers expect text structures that bring cohesiveness to content and help them to remember what they are reading. There are several ways to develop expository prose. Methods of development include definition, description, process (collection, time order, or listing), classification, comparison, analysis, and persuasion. Each method of development carries its own unique rhetorical devices that an author uses to construct meaning and a reader uses to comprehend.

Text-driven models of writing instruction typically define a specific form, such as the descriptive paragraph, provide an illustrative example, and then assign student writing. However, intermediate grade children can still benefit from lessons that begin with very concrete activities that illustrate the abstract concepts of form and content. McGee and Richgels (1985) recommend using a hands-on, "tower-building" activity to demonstrate that expository paragraphs may be structured similarly but the content can differ significantly. An adapted version of the tower-building procedures follows.

## FOR YOU TO TRY
### Paragraphs Come in All Shapes and Sizes

**A CONCRETE ACTIVITY**

1. Materials needed: Collect a variety of containers of all shapes and sizes, such as milk cartons, plastic juice bottles, shoe boxes, paper towel rolls, and margarine tubs. Commercial toys such as wooden blocks or plastic blocks, Legos, Construx, Tinker Toys, or any plastic pull-apart toy are also excellent materials to use.
2. Build a demonstration tower that has different levels made from different materials.
3. Challenge the children to build their own tower, structured identically to yours but with different materials.
4. Compare the towers. Ask the children to infer what you have just demonstrated. Try to get them to draw the conclusion that two towers can have exactly the same structure but be built with completely different materials.
5. To continue developing the concept, discuss structures familiar to the children that are identical except for the materials: water towers, apartment buildings, houses, or even toys that come in plastic or metal versions.
6. Finally, have the children draw pictures of things familiar to them that have the same structure but are constructed of different materials. The pictures can then be used as the basis for descriptive or comparison paragraphs.

After the hands-on activities, introduce the lesson on exposition, drawing attention to the analogy between building towers and writing expository paragraphs. The form of the tower is to the structure of a paragraph as the materials of the tower are to the content or ideas in a paragraph.

Research-based strategies for teaching expository text structures begin at the paragraph level. Focusing on the single paragraph simplifies the task of explaining expository structures that might otherwise seem abstract and difficult. Theoretically, by learning about expository text structures through paragraph reading, analysis, and writing, multiparagraph texts in children's literature and the content areas will be easier to comprehend. An important instructional goal is to move to multiparagraph assignments as soon as possible, since children must deal with reading whole chapters in the content areas and with writing papers longer than a paragraph. Children soon learn that writing expository paragraphs and multiparagraph papers helps them to become better readers and writers of both nonfiction and fiction.

Since expository writing instruction starts at the paragraph level, a good definition of a paragraph is essential. Paragraph definitions are found in most language arts text, such as the following from *Your English* (1984): "A paragraph is a group of sentences about one idea. The topic sentence tells the main idea—what the paragraph is about. Detail sentences tell more about the main idea" (p. 70). Paragraphs vary in length, depending on the topic under discussion. Children's literature and content area textbooks are the major sources for model paragraphs, along with teacher-written examples. Listening to, reading, and writing paragraphs of differing lengths helps alleviate some of the anxiety related to the length of an assignment, since children often ask, "How long does my paragraph have to be?" One answer to this legitimate question is, "Your paragraph should be as long as needed to explain your ideas clearly."

***Methods of Development.***     As in kindergarten and the primary grades, it is important to read and write connected text every day. The following material describes typical methods of developing expository prose in the context of paragraph-level instruction. Although discussed separately here, authors often use several strategies in conjunction with one another to develop clear explanations of topics.

*Definition.*     Defining is an essential writing strategy that authors use to explain topics and ideas unfamiliar to readers. Children encounter definitions through daily reading experiences in all genres, in addition to dictionary and glossary activities. For instance, a pre-geometry math chapter may include the definition of a triangle, a science chapter on reproduction will probably define mitosis and miosis, a social studies chapter dealing with diversity will define culture, and a language arts textbook will define the parts of speech.

Fiction and biography can also contain definitions, especially when it is likely that readers are unfamiliar with important terms or subjects. Hoa, the protagonist in the picture book *Angel Child, Dragon Child* (Surat, 1989), explains the meaning of her Vietnamese nickname in this way: "Hoa is my true name, but I am Ut. Ut is my at-home name—a tender name for smallest daughter" (p. 8). Clear definitions enable children to build upon their growing understanding of concepts and issues that influence comprehension and composition.

*Description.*     Description occurs when an author portrays the characteristics and major attributes of a person, place, thing, or abstract idea. To describe we rely on our senses to help us notice detail, which we in turn use to create images that enable readers to visualize a character or scene. Descriptive paragraphs are in almost everything we read, from a short story to a novel to science books and library reference texts. Descriptive prose is, in fact, the most frequently occurring form of discourse found in elementary school textbooks (Meyer & Freedle, 1984), followed by process or collection. Chapter objectives sometimes articulate the form. "To describe our solar system," "to describe how a wet mound is set," "to describe how rainwater gets into our foods," "to describe two types of mammals" are just a few examples from intermediate-level science texts. Description is then required on short-answer or essay exams designed to assess chapter knowledge.

Description is an important form for developing a young writer's sense of audience. Effective descriptions enable the reader to visualize the person, place, thing, or event described. Details are what make the descriptive paragraph work for a reader. Comprehending detailed, factual information is also a prerequisite to inferring the main idea. The author's responsibility to the audience is to provide enough detail to enable the reader to reconstruct the intended meaning.

Professional models are useful in teaching the descriptive paragraph. When reading aloud a familiar piece of descriptive prose, have children listen for details and main ideas and then discuss the important concepts in the paragraph. For reinforcement you could then have the children reread the paragraph either in their text or on an overhead. They could also find other examples of description in self-selected fiction and nonfiction.

The following examples demonstrate the power of description in fiction and nonfiction:

*In the opening paragraph of* Julie of the Wolves, *Jean Craighead George (1972) describes the setting of her novel in this way:*

Miyax pushed back the hood of her sealskin parka and looked at the Arctic sun. It was a yellow disc in a lime-green sky, the colors of six o'clock in the evening and the time when the wolves awoke. Quietly she put down her cooking pot and crept to the top of a dome-shaped frost heave, one of the many earth buckles that rise and fall in the crackling cold of the Arctic winter. Lying on her stomach, she looked across a vast lawn of grass and moss and focused her attention on the wolves she had come upon two sleeps ago. They were wagging their tails as they awoke and saw each other. (p. 5)

*Marcia Keegan (1991) describes the kiva in her nonfiction picture book* Pueblo Boy: Growing Up in Two Worlds:

All pueblos, even the most ancient, had a special room known as the *kiva.* It was different from ordinary dwelling areas. It was usually larger, often circular, and placed in an important area of the pueblo. Much of the religious activity of the pueblo took place in the kiva. The dancers still go there to prepare for the dances. Public parts of the ceremonies are held in the plazas, but the private portions are held in the kiva. Timmy's village kiva is in the middle of the central plaza. (p. 28)

After reading an example of description, you can then provide a teacher-written model that demonstrates how one composes a paragraph. A paragraph outline illustrates the relationship among topic and detail sentences. Research suggests that paragraph outlines are effective in helping children to develop an understanding of the structure that underlies exposition (Flood, Lapp, & Farnan, 1986; McGee and Richgels, 1985).

The following is a model outline and descriptive paragraph written by Mrs. Stone, a fourth-grade teacher. After reading aloud Ernest Raboff's (1988) nonfiction *Renoir: Art for Children,* Mrs. Stone presented her models, which were inspired by Renoir's painting *Girl with a Watering Can.* She then engaged the children in a discussion of the process of writing a description of a painting. This was followed by the children's writing descriptive paragraphs on paintings selected from a variety of art books available in the classroom.

| | |
|---|---|
| Title: | The Pretty Girl |
| Detail Sentences: | 1. A little girl with blue eyes is holding a green watering can. |
| | 2. She has flowers in her other hand. |
| | 3. A red bow is in her blonde hair. |
| | 4. Her dress and shoes are both dark blue. |
| | 5. The blue matches her eyes. |
| | 6. Because she is smiling I think she is happy. |
| **Topic Sentence:** | 7. The little girl in the picture is very pretty. |

**The Paragraph:**

*The Pretty Girl*

*A little girl with blue eyes is holding a green watering can. She has flowers in her other hand. A red bow is in her blonde hair. Her dress and shoes are both dark blue. The blue matches her eyes. Because she is smiling I think she is happy. The little girl in the picture is very pretty.*

Topic sentences do not necessarily come first in a paragraph, as illustrated in the preceding example. Here the topic sentence comes last, as a final, summative comment that explicitly states the main idea of the paragraph. The topic is also reiterated in the title. By having children give a title to their written work, you will be helping them to focus on the overall reason for writing the paragraph—to convey a main idea based on description.

*Developing Descriptive Writing.*    Writing descriptively requires a sensitive awareness of audience. An author must provide adequate detail that allows the reader to reconstruct the intended meaning. Effective descriptions also enable readers to visualize the person, place, thing, or event. Comprehending detailed, factual information is is prerequisite to inferring main ideas.

Sensory experiences of all kinds are excellent activities in preparation for comprehending and composing descriptive discourse. We use our senses to become more aware of our world. Heightened awareness helps us to communicate thoughts and feelings through description. The following ideas for developing descriptive writing make use of the five senses:

Brian works on an expository piece based on encyclopedia reading and research.

LOOKING     The visual arts are particularly valuable in stimulating descriptive writing. Children's picture books are excellent resources to instill an appreciation of art and illustration. Tomie dePaola's *The Art Lesson* (1989) and *Bonjour, Mr. Satie* (1991) are beautiful picture books that will inspire the artist in every child. You could also visit an art or historical museum. While you're there, have the children orally describe some of the paintings and sculpture. The children could take notes to be used later in the first drafts of their descriptive paragraphs. If you don't have access to a museum, quality reproductions and posters are viable substitutes. In addition, Ernest Raboff's *Art for Children* series are quality paperbacks designed to introduce children to the lives and works of famous artists. A complete list of Raboff's books is at the end of this chapter.

HEARING     Nature walks are the classic environmental listening experience. While on a walk, the children take notes on the sounds they hear. Later they write a description of the listening experience. You can also tape-record the nature-walk sounds and replay them in the classroom prior to writing the first draft describing the sounds in the environment. An alternative to a nature walk is to use tape recordings of environmental sounds of the city, country, farm, household, or business office.

Classic or contemporary music is an excellent inspiration for descriptive writing. For example, Sergei Prokofief's *Peter and the Wolf* is a musical tale with instrumentation that creates an auditory representation of the story of a boy's adventure in a meadow. The music is so clearly descriptive that the listener can visualize Peter and his animal friends, the bird and the duck, outwit the cunning fox. David Godine Publishers' beautifully illustrated book, *Peter and the Wolf* (1990), is an adaptation of the classic tale. The book comes with an audiotape of the Philadelphia Orchestra playing "Peter and the Wolf," as Cyril Ritchard narrates the story.

SMELLING    A popular activity is to blindfold the children and have them guess what they are smelling. This activity works best in small groups, with a student leader in each group passing the "smelly objects" around: perfume, vinegar, coffee, potpourri, spices, after-shave lotion, shampoo, and so on. After the children have smelled the aroma, they describe the smell in detail to an audience that has never smelled it before.

TASTING    Tasting can be managed in the same way as smelling. The children could take turns bringing a mundane snack each day for a month. Foods appropriate for this activity include fruits, vegetables and dip, cheese and crackers, cookies, popcorn, and pizza. The food-eating experience would be the basis for a daily descriptive paragraph. At the end of the month, the children would write a paragraph describing the food they liked best.

TOUCHING    Grab bags or hidden object games stimulate the sense of touch. By keeping the object out of sight, the children must rely solely on their sense of touch to gather an impression that will enable them to describe it. Things to touch and feel include cotton balls, peeled grapes, cooked spaghetti, Velcro strips, velvet ribbon, silky material, rubber bands, small metal objects, and a wet washcloth.

*Skills in Context.*    The concept of detail in descriptive discourse can be taught in conjunction with traditional grammar lessons. Grammar describes the structure of our language, at word and sentence levels. Grammatical concepts that apply most directly to comprehending and composing description are adjective, adverb, and noun. An understanding of these parts of speech enables children to talk about and improve upon their writing during the composing process.

Traditional text-driven models of language arts instruction require children to define the parts of speech, recognize them in lists of worksheet sentences, and then apply the concepts during the writing process. A more efficient way to teach grammar is to begin instruction in the context of a whole paragraph. For example, after presenting a simple definition of an adjective, you could write a model paragraph that elaborates upon the definition. In this way you would be showing children how descriptive discourse makes definitions comprehensible.

### Can You Locate All of the Adjectives in the Following Definition Paragraph?

*An adjective describes a person, place, or thing. I can use adjectives to tell about special people and happy experiences in my life. For example, my great-aunt Angela was a beautiful woman who could shoot basketballs when she was ninety-three years old. When I was growing up one of my favorite places was my shady backyard. That's where my dad put up my basketball hoop. It was ten feet tall. But that wasn't too tall for Aunt Angela! She was a real wiry lady who could jump-shoot from eight feet.*

Following the brief lesson on adjectives, the children write their own definition or descriptive paragraphs. "This is an adjective" will be articulated more readily if a child has consciously thought about the words that describe, as opposed to underlining someone else's adjectives in a list of unconnected sentences. Additionally, by omitting the grammar worksheets, you will give children more opportunities to read and write connected text every day.

*Process.* A process is a clearly described set of instructions. Here the author tells the audience how to get where they are going, how to put something together or take something apart, how to make something, how to conduct an experiment, or how something works. The process form requires clear descriptions, sometimes definitions, and always rhetorical devices that signal the steps in a procedure. Transition words such as *first, next, now, before,* and *after* are essential in writing about a process. Detail is also a very important part of comprehending and composing a process, for without accurate knowledge and understanding of the facts in their proper sequence, the procedure may not be accomplished. Processes are prevalent in elementary school math, science, and social studies textbooks.

Time order, or collection, is a process form that requires the reader or writer to comprehend and compose such things as time lines, the sequence of events in a plot, or the ordered details of a nonfictional event. Time order is often encountered in children's literature and content area texts and is therefore worth teaching (McGee & Richgels, 1985; Vacca & Vacca, 1986). Composing autobiographical or historical time lines, outlining or summarizing the events leading up to a historical or scientific event, and listing the sequence of events in a story are typical activities that require a sense of time and how it relates to the orderly presentation of details. When teaching children about time order or collection, it is important to draw their attention to numbered steps and cue words, such as *first, second, then,* and *in the end,* that signal time-ordered texts and help them to understand and outline the steps in a time-related process.

## INSTRUCTIONAL GUIDELINES
### Teaching the Process Paragraph

The following guidelines for teaching the process paragraph suggest a step-by-step, enumerated procedure, as called for by the form.

1. Begin with a concrete experience, close to the children's daily lives, that calls to mind a process. The activity should require the children to manipulate objects, such as lacing and then tying a shoelace or making a peanut butter and jelly sandwich.
2. Demonstrate the process, talking through the procedure and using appropriate transition words that signal each step: "To make a delicious peanut butter and jelly sandwich, the *first* thing you need to do is get out the peanut butter, your favorite jelly, and two pieces of whole wheat bread. *Next,* place the two pieces of bread on a paper plate . . ." and so on.
3. *After* your demonstration, read a model process paragraph that you have written on chart paper or overhead. Draw attention to the structure of the paragraph, especially transition words that connect the ideas and the topic sentence.

### EXAMPLE PROCESS PARAGRAPH

*Tying your shoelaces can be very tricky work, especially if you are left-handed. The* first *thing you need to do is pull tightly on both laces with both hands to make sure your shoe fits snugly.* Second, *cross the left lace over the right lace, fold under and pull through, thus forming the base of your bow.* Now *you are ready to make the first bow loop. Using both hands, make a small loop with the left shoelace and hold the bottom of the loop between the thumb and forefinger of your left hand.* Next, *using your free hand, wrap the right shoelace around the bottom of the loop that you just made, forming a small circle at its base.* Now *slip the right lace through the small circle and pull it through with your left hand, thus forming the second loop of the bow.* Finally, *tighten the bow by gently tugging the two loops with both hands.*

4. Relate the concept of writing a process paragraph to reading and then summarizing processes, steps, or sequences of events that the children encounter in their daily reading. Stress the importance of learning how to explain the step-by-step procedures in a science experiment or the process that the pioneers went through in preparation for their travels westward.

*(continued)*

**Instructional Guidelines (continued)**

5. Have each child, working in pairs or small cooperative groups, complete a hands-on process, talking through the steps with their peers: making a paper airplane, cutting out snowflakes, making popcorn, making peanut butter and jelly sandwiches.

6. Upon completion of the activity, have the children (working in pairs or small cooperative groups) write a process paragraph. Encourage oral communication and collaboration as they write a paragraph that clearly describes to an audience of peers the process they just completed. Provide a list of transition words from the children's language arts text to aid in the development of their paragraph, for example, *first, second, third, fourth, fifth, sixth, last, now, before, next, after, then, during, when,* and *finally.*

    After writing their paragraph, the children would critique the draft, making sure that the steps in the process are logical and that the paragraph contains a topic sentence. Each group-written paragraph would then be read aloud to other class members to reinforce correct process form. The audience reacts to the oral reading, making suggestions for clarity and form.

7. The next step is independent writing of process paragraphs. Topic generation is critical here and may require teacher modeling, whole-class brainstorming, and one-to-one conferences. Example topics include the following: Tell your dad how to fly a kite, explain to your principal how to get from your house to school, write the directions for washing a dog, give these directions to the new owners of your dog's puppy, outline for your baby sister or brother the steps in putting together a Mr. Potato Head, explain to a Martian how to peel a banana, give your mother directions for driving you to your best friend's house. Writing topics should take the audience into consideration.

8. Upon completion of their first drafts, have the children share their work with a peer writing buddy and/or you. A process paragraph checklist is useful at this point.

**My Process Paragraph**

1. Did I include a topic sentence?
2. Are all of the steps in the process there?
3. Did I use transition words?
4. Did I include enough details so that my audience will understand what I'm trying to explain?

    My best advice for me or my friend:

9. *Finally,* have the children revise their first drafts and either place them in their writing portfolios or submit them for appropriate assessment.

*Classification.*    Classification is an organizational strategy whereby authors arrange groups of persons, places, things, or abstract ideas according to a common ground, or class. Definition, description, or illustration is then used to explain the topic in detail. Children encounter classification systems in all content areas. It is a strategy that gives coherence to texts and makes complex ideas more understandable by breaking them down into parts and subparts. Chapter titles and headings frequently signal groups under study, as illustrated in a sixth-grade mathematics chapter called "Ratio, Proportion, and Percent" (Ginsburg et al., 1991). Information books for children also address categories of subjects, as in Isaac Asimov's (1988) *Rockets, Probes, and Satellites* or Louise Quayle's (1988) *Dolphins and Porpoises.*

When teaching children to classify, visual aids in the form of concept maps and diagrams are important resources that help to show the relationships among the parts and subparts of whole groups. Discussing a topic close to children's interests helps to create enthusiasm for learning a new concept. Figure 4.4 is a diagram indicating groups of children's television programs, which a fourth-grade teacher used to introduce the concept of classification. In organizing her lesson, Ms. Ryan first asked the class to contribute to a list of programs that they enjoyed watching. She referred to the class list as the ultimate example or illustration of what fourth-graders choose to watch on TV. Next, the students classified the programs by type. This required them to determine a label that generally described the programs grouped together. Finally, they contributed details that illustrated the characteristics of the types of programs in each category. For example, a prime example of a cartoon was "Ren and Stimpy." Favorite cartoons were generally described as funny, silly, unreal, and gross. The final project was an individually written paper in which each student wrote about the three types of television programs they enjoyed watching.

*Comparison.*    Comparative writing explains a subject by indicating the similarities and the differences between two or more persons, places, things, or abstractions. Descriptive details are again important to the form, as well as words that signal likenesses and differences.

Comparison is an objective frequently included in intermediate-level curricula. For example, to compare sleet, snow, and hail is a typical objective in a fourth-grade science unit on weather. Although an instructional objective, little true comparison is found in elementary-level texts (Meyer & Freedle, 1984). What the science chapter is more likely to include are three separate sections describing different types of environmental phenomena followed by a comprehension question requiring the children to compare the concepts. To achieve the objective, the children must first understand the facts about sleet, snow, and hail from descriptive discourse in order to infer the relationships and then make accurate comparisons based on that knowledge—a formidable task, indeed.

Literary comparisons are found throughout children's literature. To understand some stories and most poetry, children must deal with similes (comparisons using the words *like* or *as*) and metaphors (comparisons that must be inferred from information provided in the text coupled with prior knowledge of the concepts being compared). Metaphorical language is difficult to comprehend and to compose with-

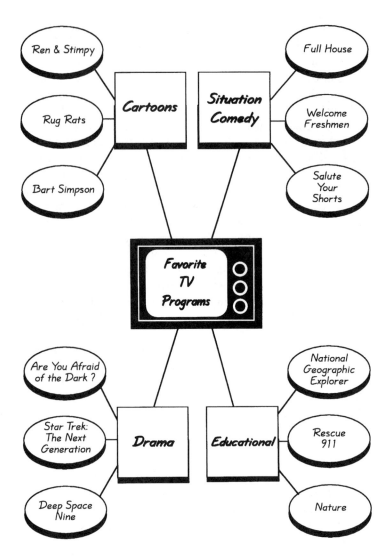

**FIGURE 4.4**   Classifying favorite TV programs

out an adequate understanding of comparison. The last section of this chapter deals with metaphor as it relates to reading and writing poetry.

To comprehend and compose comparative discourse, children must have acquired prior knowledge of and had some experience with the concepts of same and different. Experience with comparisons is not unusual for most children. By the intermediate grades virtually all children have made (or have been the subjects of) comparisons: Jill is taller than Jamie; Tim is a faster runner than John; My mom is the best cook in town. When first teaching the comparison paragraph, it is useful to point out comparisons that occur in our daily lives. In this way you will be helping children to place the concept in perspective and to draw on appropriate schema for comparisons when reading and writing.

*Skills in Context.*    Traditional grammar lessons on comparative adjectives and adverbs may be used in conjunction with writing whole paragraphs. Prior to reading and writing comparative discourse, it is important to teach key vocabulary words and phrases that signal comparison in a paragraph or larger work (i.e., *alike, same, similar, similar to, the same as, unlike, unalike, not the same as, dissimilar, different,* and *different from*). Semantic mapping (Johnson, 1986) is one way of presenting similarities and differences between two or more subjects. The following dialogue shows how one fifth-grade teacher taught comparison during a natural class discussion that followed a health unit. As an aid to instruction, he also used a semantic mapping strategy.

## INSIDE THE CLASSROOM
### Comparing Apples and Oranges

"Can you compare apples and oranges?" asked Mr. Baker as he ended a unit on vitamins in his sixth-grade health class. Holding an apple in one hand and an orange in the other, Mr. Baker continued: "How are they alike and how are they different? What we need first is a *basis* for comparison, or a basic idea that allows us to discuss similarities and differences."

The class thought for a few moments. Then Sheila raised her hand and said, "Fruit, Mr. Baker; apples and oranges are both fruit." "Very good," he said while writing the word on the chalkboard. Then one by one the students made further responses to the questions. As they talked, Mr. Baker wrote their answers on the chalkboard, placing each response under its appropriate category and drawing lines to indicate connections among ideas (Figure 4.5).

"This is a semantic map," said Mr. Baker, pointing to his drawing. "It's a diagram that helps us to organize our ideas. Today we are learning how to organize a comparison paragraph. Comparison paragraphs describe two or more persons, places, or things, such as apples and oranges. On my map I have circled words that represent the major concepts that will be in my paragraph (*apple, orange, fruit, similar, different*). The lines I'm drawing show the relationships among the ideas. The map is an aid when writing a comparison paragraph such as one that I've already written about apples and oranges. Listen to my paragraph called, "Apples and Oranges."

*(continued)*

**Inside the Classroom (continued)**

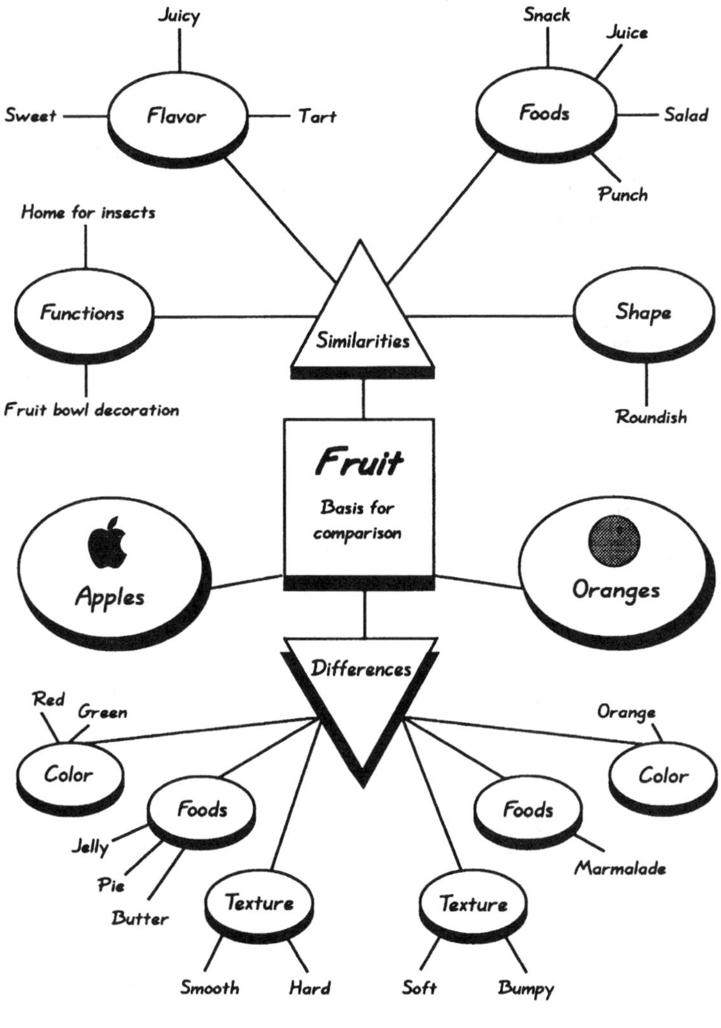

**FIGURE 4.5** Comparing apples and oranges

*Apples and oranges are alike and different. The most obvious similarity is that they are both fruits that grow on trees. Sometimes tart and sometimes sweet, we can eat these fruits raw, drink their juice, or cook them in a variety of foods such as pies, cakes, tarts, cookies, and candies. Because apples and oranges are relatively small and round and easily peeled, we often put them in our backpacks for a quick, nutritious snack. The differ-*

*ences between apples and oranges do not get in the way of our enjoying them! The smooth-textured apple skin may be bright red, green, or yellow, while an orange peel is bumpy and, of course, orange in color. While oranges prefer the more temperate climates of Florida and California, apples will thrive in cooler zones, as found in Washington State. And though it is said, "An apple a day keeps the doctor away," the vitamin C in oranges will also help our wintertime colds.*

"Are there any further comments about comparing apples and oranges?"

"I don't think you can really do it. Compare apples and oranges, I mean," said Kevin. "Why not?" said Mr. Baker. Kevin explained, "Because my mom's always telling me you can't compare apples and oranges. Like when I wanted to go on a ski trip over spring break with my best friend, Tom, and his older brother, Bill. My mom said, 'no.' And I said it'd be just like when I went camping last summer with Gramps in Rocky Mountain National Park. She said, 'No, it isn't. You can't compare apples and oranges.' "

The class groaned. Mr. Baker smiled and said, "Kevin, I think your mother was speaking metaphorically. What analogy was she making? How are apples like the ski trip with your best friend and oranges like the camping trip with your grandfather?" Kevin thought for a moment, then replied, "I guess she thought there was no *basis* for comparison. On the outside, apples and oranges don't seem very much alike. But they are both fruits, just like the two things I was comparing were both trips. She didn't see *any* similarities though. Only differences. I could have come up with lots of ways the two trips would have been alike."

"It sounds like a good topic for a comparison paragraph," said Mr. Baker. "How would you like to write a paragraph comparing the two trips?" In your paragraph try to convince your mother that the trips really could have been compared.

"In the meantime, can anyone else think of a similar situation you have experienced when your parents or someone else said you couldn't compare two things for the purpose of discouraging you from doing something? Would these experiences be good topics for comparison paragraphs? Let's list some ideas for comparison on the chalkboard. When we're through, choose a topic and write the first draft of your own comparison paragraph. If you have trouble coming up with a basis for comparing two or more things, I'll be around to help. You might want to make a semantic map before writing your paragraph to help organize your thoughts.

"If you can't think of words to explain your comparisons, review your language arts lessons 5 and 6 on comparing adjectives and adverbs. These lessons will give you some new ideas for vocabulary words to use when writing your comparisons. When each of you finishes with your initial draft, share your

*(continued)*

**Inside the Classroom (continued)**

paragraph with a friend or the students at your writing table. Look for these three important points: (1) a clear basis for comparison; (2) similarities *and* differences between two or more persons, places, or things; (3) key words that signal comparison. Underline the key words if you're not sure."

The following are examples of comparison topics that Mr. Baker's class suggested.

**Topics for Writing Comparison Paragraphs**

1. Taking piano lessons and going out for football
2. Mowing lawns and having a paper route
3. Junk food versus health food diet
4. Fish or fowl: Do guppies or parakeets make the best pets?
5. Summer is the best season of all compared to winter, fall, and spring.
6. The pros and cons of being a fifth-grader compared to being a fourth-grader.
7. Living on the West Coast compared to living on the East Coast

*Reflections.*    Mr. Baker's model lesson illustrates the power of using children's prior experiences as a stimulus for a comparison lesson. Such lessons make it easier to remind children of important concepts associated with comparison the next time a curricular objective requires them to compare two or more persons, places, things, or abstractions. Semantic maps, model paragraphs, and children's paragraphs should be available as reviews to help them write paragraphs in which they use their new knowledge of comparative form.

*Analysis.*    When analyzing a topic, the author or reader examines the relationships between the parts and the whole in order to communicate or comprehend the structure of the underlying ideas. Cause and effect, as well as problem and solution, are common forms of analysis that require dividing a subject into its component parts for the purpose of describing a causative relationship. Like comparison, causation is not often found in elementary textbooks (Meyer & Freedle, 1984), yet it is an important form for curricular objectives. Cause-and-effect questions are frequently used in comprehension checks at the end of science or social studies chapters: "Describe some causes and effects of air pollution in large metropolitan areas." "What would happen if the rain forests of the Ivory Coast were cut down?" "How does the environment affect housing in desert regions of the United States?" "What did America gain as a result of the Treaty of Paris in 1783?"

Cause-and-effect objectives require readers and writers to use analytical thinking that for some children may be initially too abstract to accomplish. Critical to understanding cause-and-effect relationships is the ability to draw correct and appropriate inferences and conclusions from facts presented in the text. The ability to differentiate between fact and opinion is crucial in understanding cause and effect. (See Chapter 6 for more about distinguishing facts from opinions.) Furthermore, understanding problems and their solutions is also fundamental to reading and writing causative discourse effectively.

Like all other forms of exposition discussed so far, cause and effect may be illustrated most effectively by first using children's personal experiences to stimulate analytical thinking. Concrete activities such as science demonstrations or experiments as well as field trips of all kinds are important means to use when teaching cause and effect.

Vicki Cobb and Kathy Darling's book, *Bet You Can't* (1980), is a wonderful resource when introducing intermediate-level children to cause and effect. The book, subtitled "Science Impossibilities to Fool You," is a collection of "tricks" that are grounded in basic scientific principles. For example, "Bet you can't pull apart two wet glasses" (p. 61) demonstrates the principles of cohesion and adhesion. The authors explain how to set up the trick (or experiment) and then explain why it is difficult or impossible to accomplish. After the children have taken the bet and tried to complete the directions, cause-and-effect questions logically follow: "What *causes* the glasses to stick together?" and *"Why* can't you pull them apart?" The answers are not obvious and require analysis, careful thought, and some knowledge of science: "You can't pull apart two wet plastic glasses *because* the water molecules between the glasses pull together and act like glue (cohesive effect) as they are attracted (adhere) to the plastic (or glass)." Cobb and Darling include a variety of safe tricks that use the laws of gravity, fluids and gases, energy, and mathematics to teach basic principles and at the same time make learning about cause and effect fun.

Remembering personal experiences also helps children to conceptualize cause and effect or problem/solution scenarios. A whole-class brainstorming activity produced the following list of writing topics, based on real events experienced by some sixth-graders in a small midwestern town.

### *Cause-and-Effect Topics, or What Really Happened*
1. The day my little brother did the laundry
2. When cold air meets hot: Living in tornado alley
3. Eliminating lunchroom noise (and food) pollution
4. My first stitches in the Memorial Hospital emergency room
5. Sisters can be best friends and worst enemies

The children's teacher encouraged his students to be as specific as possible when formulating writing topics. When children write with main ideas in mind, their composing progresses more smoothly. For example, Shelly's initial idea, number 5 above, was to describe how she got her very own room—the result of bickering with her sister. During a prewriting discussion with the teacher and the class, Shelly decided to focus on both the positive and the negative aspects of their relationship. The resulting title, "Sisters Can Be Best Friends and Worst Enemies," helped her to produce an interesting and substantive paragraph. Shelly's final draft paragraph, along with a graphic organizer that visually displays the organization of her ideas, follows. Graphic organizers are simple outlines that help students to see the relationships among the ideas in a paragraph. They are especially useful when teaching the structure of texts such as cause and effect or problem and solution (McGee & Richgels, 1985; Readence, Bean, & Baldwin, 1981).

### SISTERS CAN BE BEST FRIENDS AND WORST ENEMIES

by Shelley, Grade 6 (Final Draft)

*My older sister, Tracy, is my best friend, but she can also be my worst enemy. I think that we're best friends because she's willing to listen to my deepest, darkest secrets, and she never tells. On my birthdays she always gives me the present I've been wanting. And when I'm down she tries to cheer me up by offering to do my homework, free of charge! But sometimes she can be my worst enemy, like the time she threw a tantrum and moved all my clothes out of our room. She did it because she didn't want me reading her diary and borrowing her pink tennis skirt anymore. (The skirt used to be white before Dad washed it, but that's another story.) To get back at her I poured dusting powder in her underwear drawer. By the time Mom got home from work and saw the mess, Tracy and I had completely made up. But it was too late to save us. Mom and Dad both decided to give us separate bedrooms just to keep us out of trouble and to make sure that we stayed best friends. Now a brand-new wall separates our old bedroom, so we each have some privacy when we want it. But it's only a wall. Tracy and I are still best friends and worst enemies. And that's the way we like it.*

### MAIN IDEA

*My sister and I are both friends and enemies.*

### DETAILS

***Reasons or Causes/Why She's My Friend***

1. *Listens to me*
2. *Buys me nice things*
3. *Helps me with my homework*

***Reasons or Causes/Problems that Make Us Enemies***

1. *I read her diary. (Cause)*
2. *She gets mad. (Effect)*
3. *We get in a fight. (Effect)*

***Solution to Our Problems (Ultimate Effects)***

1. *We make up on our own.*
2. *Mom and Dad give us our own rooms.*
3. *We're still best friends.*

*Persuasion.*     Persuasive, or argumentative, discourse appeals to an audience's reason and emotion. The purpose of persuasion is to convince a reader or listener to accept a writer's or speaker's point of view on an issue. Children of all ages use argumentative language every day. For example, a fourth-grader may argue that he and his friends should be allowed just five more minutes to play soccer during the noon recess. A sixth-grader may try to persuade her teacher that the math assignment was unreasonably long for the short holiday break. And whole groups of kindergartners can be very persuasive on the topic of taking an afternoon nap.

The concept of persuasion is often associated with journalistic writing, such as editorials and advertisements. Reading newspapers and magazines and organizing and publishing classroom or schoolwide news are excellent activities that stimulate persuasive thinking. (See Chapter 8 for more on desktop publishing of school newspapers.) Persuasive language in advertising utilizes traditional propaganda techniques such as bandwagon ("Everyone's doing it!"), glittering generalities ("Buy it and you'll be popular forever!"), snob appeal ("Only the finest leather was used in our product"), just plain folks ("My neighbors all agree it's just like 'down home cookin' "), slogans (catchy phrases, jingles, and tunes), and endorsements (usually by well-known and popular persons or family, as in "Mom says its great!"). Writing and then acting out advertisements is a popular method that naturally evolves from teaching the specialized vocabulary and concepts that advertisers use. Because children themselves are consumers bombarded by media-driven propaganda, they respond enthusiastically to lessons on persuasion that involve topics close to their hearts, such as toys, food, entertainment, and clothing.

Tutolo (1981) discusses the importance of teaching children to be critical evaluators of company advertisements for *parity products,* which appear to dominate advertising aimed at children. A parity product is one in which almost all of the competing brands available are virtually identical, both physically and functionally. Toys, cereals, candies, soft drinks, and games of all kinds fall into this category. In his description of how advertising works, Tutolo suggests that advertisers transform nondifferences into significant differences and in so doing subordinate facts by pointing out the "special features" of their product compared to the competing brand. To accomplish their goal of selling the product, advertisers use ambiguous words to create the desired effect, with *weasel words* and *persuasive words* appearing again and again in both print and nonprint media. A weasel word evades or retreats "from a forthright statement or position." Examples are "help(s), refreshed, fortified, special, comforts, fights." Words typically used to persuade or catch children's attention to encourage a purchase include "free, new, now, quick, bargain, last chance."

Lessons on propaganda in advertising can be used successfully to enhance the process of teaching children to think critically, persuasively, and creatively.

## INSTRUCTIONAL GUIDELINES
### Teaching the Concept of Persuasion

The following are some practical suggestions for teaching the concept of persuasion through print and nonprint media advertising.

1. Prepare an audiotape or a videotape of about ten minutes of advertising aimed at children. (Ten minutes is likely to include twenty or more advertisements!) Saturday morning or late weekday afternoon programming provides an abundance of material from which to choose.
2. Before playing the tapes in class, define and discuss the concept of persuasion. For example, persuasion refers to a writer's or a speaker's attempt to convince an audience to agree with his or her ideas, opinions, and beliefs and ultimately to take some sort of action: "I believe that all upper elementary school children should (or should not) have an afternoon recess" is an opinion that could be presented along with an accompanying argument to the school administration.

    Next, ask the children to tell you everything they know about the word *persuade.* Elicit examples from the children's own experience with the concept, especially as it relates to the child as consumer. The following are some fourth-graders' real experiences with persuasion. Notice that the experiences are stated as titles or main ideas that can form the basis of a composition.

### Persuasion Topics
a. How I convinced my parents for more allowance money
b. Playground litter can be dangerous to your health.
c. Problems with too few computers in fourth-grade classrooms
d. Vote for me, Jessica Ray: Your #1 candidate for class president!
e. K-Mart stickers are the best in town.

3. After the concept of persuasion is fully discussed, introduce the idea of persuasive advertising by examining newspaper or magazine advertisements specifically for children. You may also want to list a few persuasive or weasel words in the ads on the chalkboard. Drawing children's attention to the rhetoric of propaganda helps to encourage critical thinking while reading and discussing the ads.
4. *Before* introducing the taped advertisements, instruct the children to listen for words and phrases that seem to appeal to their emotions and desire to purchase the product. Encourage the children to take notes *while* listening.

*After* the listening exercise, talk about the words that have caught the children's attention and categorize the ads according to the types of propaganda devices used. For example, the following advertisement uses testimonial (from Mom) and persuasive words such as *free* and *hurry* to try to convince children of the practicality and urgency of buying the product: "Hurry now while there's still time to buy a pink satin jogging outfit and still get your free Swatch watch. Mom will love the idea."

5. Next, generate more ideas that children might develop through oral and/or written language. For example, organize simple classroom debates in which small groups of children talk about issues that are important to them. Write letters to the editor of the school newspaper or write editorials on an important school-related issue; write mock or real letters to the manufacturer of a popular product explaining the impact of its current advertising strategies on intermediate grade children. The letter-writing process would include peer reviews, thus enabling the children to critique the argument being presented and make substantive suggestions.

6. *Extend* the concept of persuasion across the curriculum whenever possible to reinforce children's ability to think critically about their own opinions, beliefs, and ideas in relation to facts as well as other people's opinions. (See Chapter 6 for more discussion on distinguishing facts from opinions.) There are numerous opportunities in the sciences and social studies to talk about issues and to organize and present informed arguments.

Typical issues found in a fifth-grade social studies text (*Living in Our Country,* 1985) include concerns for the environment, United States involvement in space exploration, and government involvement in trade and industry.

*Summarizing.*     Twelve-year-old Jeffery defines summary writing in this way: "It's [writing summaries] when you have to put it in your own words but you can't really think of your own words so you use some of the author's words but not too many because that's copying." For Jeffery and almost all intermediate grade children, summarizing is difficult. But understanding summaries, what they are and how to produce them, is basic to comprehending and composing all forms of discourse. Indeed, the process of summary writing may be the ultimate example of making connections between reading and writing: Summaries require the writer first to read and fully comprehend the prose and then to reduce the text to its *gist,* or main ideas. It requires knowledge of the facts and the opinions plus the ability to infer main points and to judge what is important enough to include in the condensed version. Ordinarily, much rereading occurs in order to comprehend the text well enough to summarize. Oral summarizing should precede written summaries, to help organize one's thoughts. Finally, the writer must put it all together, using his or her own vocabulary. Putting it altogether in their *own words* is the hard part for most children, especially if they have not received direct instruction that includes teacher modeling as well as practice in summarizing orally. Instead, typical intermediate grade summary-writing exercises might include such assignments as "Summarize your library book," "Summarize the section on mammals in Chapter 3," or "Summarize the results of yesterday's mock election."

Summary writing appears to enhance children's ability to understand and remember important information from a text (Kintch & van Dijk, 1978). Vacca and Vacca (1986) compare good and poor summarizers in this way: Good summary writers are sensitive to the organization of ideas and events in expository or narrative writing. In other words, they are capable of analyzing *text structure*. They include only important information in their condensed or summarized version. They write in their own words but don't lose sight of the author's point of view or sequence of ideas or events. Furthermore, these students write their own topic sentences, which reflect important information that is not explicitly stated. The more skilled summary writers are usually among the older as well as better readers. Conversely, poor summarizers *retell* rather than condense information. They have difficulty distinguishing important from irrelevant information.

The recursive nature of the composing process is never so important as in summary writing. The process of writing, reading and rereading while writing, and finally rewriting is crucial to achieving a successful summary. Furthermore, children must have knowledge and understanding of the basic rules that control summary writing.

## INSTRUCTIONAL GUIDELINES
### Teaching Summary Writing

The following guidelines for helping intermediate grade children become good summary readers and writers incorporate an adapted version of the rules for summary writing first described by Kintch and van Dijk (1978). Included also are practical suggestions for teacher modeling of oral and written summaries.

1. Begin with oral summaries of events that the children have (or will have) experienced before gradually moving to oral summaries of stories and nonfiction that the children have read. Familiar fairy tales are especially helpful in teaching summary skills to older children.

   Oral summaries should precede written summaries because talk facilitates summary writing by helping students think about relevant and irrelevant information. To help children understand the abstract concept of summarizing, it is useful to define and model the process within a context that is meaningful to all students. Your initial model oral summary should be of something that has happened recently (or will occur soon), such as yesterday's school assembly, last night's favorite TV program, or tomorrow's field trip.

### TEACHER'S MODEL

*I want to summarize for you what will happen tomorrow when we go on our field trip. Listen carefully so you'll know what to do. In my summary I'm going to include some information that's not really necessary. I want you to listen for important and unimportant information because we're going to be studying summary writing in language arts today. Here goes:*

*"Tomorrow we will go on a field trip to the university dairy. The bus will leave at exactly 8:30 A.M. You will need to be ready to go at that time. You will be talking to your friends about how excited you are to be going on the field trip. All fourth-graders are to line up in Hall B. Mr. Campbell, the bus driver, is a very nice man. When you get on the bus, be sure to sit quietly and enjoy the ride. Your backpacks will be filled with books. Hall B is where the fourth-graders should have been. After we arrive at the dairy, Dr. Graham will give us a tour. Pay close attention to what he says because when we return to school at noon we will be summarizing what we did on our field trip."*

Display a written version of your oral summary on an overhead projector or chart paper and discuss the irrelevant or repetitious information, drawing lines through the sentences that are unimportant. What you have left is a summary paragraph that explains what the children must do in preparation for and while on the field trip.

2. Condense information by "collapsing lists" that might otherwise unnecessarily lengthen your summary. Categorization activities help children understand what you mean by placing lists of things or events under a common category, key word, or phrase that names the underlying concept (Vacca & Vacca, 1986). For example, after returning from the dairy farm trip, have the whole class participate in an oral discussion of what happened, listing all details on the chalkboard and simultaneously categorizing them.

### EXAMPLE LISTS

**(Facts)** *What we saw: holsteins, guernseys, goats, milkers, ice-cream machines, an old-fashioned butter churn, three secretaries, a yogurt maker, big chunks of cheese, feed, milk tanks, huge trucks, storage freezers, crates of boxes, the dairy manager, big rooms to milk the cows, dairy barns, the pipes*

*(continued)*

**Instructional Guidelines (continued)**

*where the milk goes through to get to the milk tanks, uniformed workers, a cook, hay, fly spray.*

*(Facts) What we learned: The dairy has over 100 cows and goats; sales from the dairy bar help to support university dairy research; whey is the watery liquid produced when you make cheese; to make yogurt, you have to culture the milk with two different kinds of bacteria.*

*(Opinions) What we thought: It was fun, the field trip was great, the milk barn was interesting, the dairy smelled good (sweet) and bad (sour), the ice cream tasted terrific, the yogurt maker was my favorite machine, the creamery was weird, dairy cattle are huge, the manager was nice to us.*

### Example Categories

*animals, employees, equipment, dairy products, educational information, sensory feelings, opinions*

3. Generate a topic sentence that reflects the gist of the summary. Writing a topic sentence is often easier *after* lists have been made. You can help the children develop a topic sentence inductively by focusing their attention on the relationship between the small bits of information on their lists and a logical main idea for the summary paragraph.

### Example Topic Sentence

*Our trip to the university dairy was both educational and enjoyable.*

4. Put it all together by having the whole class contribute to the paragraph summarizing the trip to the dairy. Write individual oral contributions on chart paper or overhead while encouraging (and modeling) rewriting and editing as the paragraph unfolds. Direct instruction *during* whole-group dictations is crucial to the process of eliciting a coherent and cohesive first draft (M. F. Heller, 1988b). It is important to model the use of transition words and phrases that bring cohesiveness to the summary. Be sure to point out that summaries do not have to include every single detail to convey a meaningful message.

   The following is a fourth-grade, teacher-directed and child-dictated (whole-class) summary paragraph.

### The University Dairy Farm

*Our trip to the university dairy was educational and enjoyable. After arriving on campus, Dr. Graham, the manager, first took us on a tour of the main dairy barn. While there we saw many different kinds of milk cows and goats, including holsteins, guernseys, and nannies. They are fed a special feed that helps them produce lots of milk. Next, we went inside the factory where the milk is pasteurized and the butter, cream, and yogurt are made. It smelled very sour inside that building, but the ice cream tasted terrific! We learned that you have to use two different kinds of bacteria to make yogurt. Unbelievable! Finally, we got to see the huge warehouse where the dairy products are stored. The money from the sales at the "Dairy Bar" help the university researchers learn more about producing quality products, like yummy frozen strawberry yogurt, our favorite.*

5. The next step is for the children individually to try summary writing. Oral summarizing should again precede the children's actual written summaries. Encourage the children to summarize their findings orally to you or to peers in a small group *before* writing their first drafts. Listeners could respond by telling the author what they found most interesting or what might have confused them. Talk facilitates and clarifies meaning as intermediate grade children struggle to put it all together in their own words.

 A good follow-up in the preceding example would be for them to research some aspect of the dairy industry that interests them and to summarize what they learn. Library books, encyclopedias, and classroom social studies or science texts would be good sources of information. Identifying and narrowing topics is a necessary whole-class activity before individual research begins. Example topics include the origin of yogurt as a popular food, the economics of dairy farming in the Midwest, the process of making cottage cheese, the "dairy belt," why dairy products are good for you (or the nutritive benefits of milk, cheese, and ice cream).

 There are many opportunities all day long to model the summarizing process. As children learn to listen to your literate, adult model, they will soon internalize this important form and become better summarizers themselves.

***Moving beyond the Paragraph.***     Intermediate grade children have a greater tolerance for listening to, reading, and writing longer works. Reading novels, biographies, or books of short fiction are by now expected. Writing multiparagraph papers and reports are standard curricular goals in grades 4, 5, and 6. Yet some children may resist required independent reading of chapter books. Further, the perennial question "But how long does it have to be?" is familiar to every teacher.

 During the intermediate grades, children may develop true fears of writing long reports, essays, or research papers, in spite of the good intentions of the teacher

Fifth-graders prepare to dramatize an original play about Native Americans.

who is trying to prepare them for the rigors of middle and high school. Some well-meaning teachers make the mistake of sending the children to the library the second or third week of school to do research and then to write a report on a subject they may or may not have been reading about. While this is a legitimate and important assignment, if given too early it can discourage any real reading and writing about a topic. For example, I once observed a group of four fifth-grade children go together to the library to do research for a report on "Puerto Rico." The exact assignment was "Write a two-paragraph report on Puerto Rico." No other direction was given. After locating a reference, the children decided to split an eight-paragraph section on Puerto Rico in the children's encyclopedia. Each child then copied two different paragraphs, verbatim, and turned them in as their respective "report." Obviously, the children had no concept of what a report is or how to go about writing a multiparagraph paper. Summarizing with descriptive discourse never entered their minds because "put it in your own words" had not yet been introduced or modeled.

Moving beyond the paragraph is essential to the development of literacy. Consider the following guidelines when teaching students to read and write longer works of fiction and nonfiction.

INSTRUCTIONAL GUIDELINES
**Making the Transition to Multiparagraph Papers
and Reports**

1. Model the process of reading and writing longer works of fiction and nonfiction. Your goal is to help children develop an appreciation of how authors develop stories, biography, and information books.
2. Encourage oral and written responses to literature through whole-class discussions, small-group readers' workshops, and journal writing. To encourage personal involvement in literature, ask open-ended questions such as "What did you think about the book?" or "How did you feel when . . ."
3. Design lessons that give students experience with a variety of text structures. Avoid overusing summary-writing assignments. Ask questions to stimulate interesting discussions and writing topics. For example, Describe the setting of the story as it unfolds.
   Compare a character in the story or nonfiction to someone you know.
   List the sequence of events in the narrative.
   Describe the causes and effects of the major issues described in the book.
   Write a paper to convince your classmates to read a particular book.
4. Set realistic goals for multiparagraph writing. For example,
   a. By the end of the first grading period, the fourth-graders will be able to write a two-paragraph descriptive report inspired by children's literature.
   b. During the first semester, the fifth-graders will write and revise a two-page biographical paper on a friend, relative, or historical figure.
   c. By the end of the year, the sixth-graders will have written three short stories publishable in the classroom's story collection.

## Reading and Writing Poetry

Like fiction and expository prose, poetry has form. Minot (1993) suggests four basic qualities of poetry that distinguish it from prose: "concern for line as opposed to the sentence, greater attention to the sound of language, development of rhythms, and a tendency to create density by compressing both meaning and emotions" (pp. 1–2). Poetry is personal expressive writing in the truest sense.

The poetic form can stimulate the imaginations of children of all ages. During the intermediate grades it is easy to lose sight of the primacy of poetry, or the idea that poetry is even more basic than prose, that it is an absolute prerequisite to reading and writing well (Sloan, 1984). Instead we may put aside the beauty and power of the form for narrative and expository prose that may be perceived as being more "important." As a result, we may read fewer poems or nursery or nonsense rhymes to our fourth-, fifth-, and sixth-graders for fear of treating the children like babies or boring them to tears (Tom, 1972). Yet children are natural poets whose overall reading and writing may be inspired through imaginative verse.

Teaching poetry well requires careful planning. It is not a simple matter of reading a model poem or two, then making an assignment. X. J. and Dorothy M. Kennedy's (1982) *Knock at a Star: A Child's Introduction to Poetry* is an excellent resource for teachers using a models approach. The classic and modern poetry in this collection is highly accessible and serves to amuse, delight, and engage children and adults. The poems are organized according to topics that can be used for lesson planning. For example, section one, "What Do Poems Do?" focuses our attention on the content and purpose of poems that "Make You Laugh," "Tell Stories," "Send Messages," "Share Feelings," and "Start You Wondering." In each section of the book, the reader is presented with model poems that illustrate a theme or special form, such as a formula poem. Overall, the poems in *Knock at a Star* are excellent choices for read-aloud sessions, silent independent reading, and models for poetry-writing assignments.

Because poetry has its roots in the oral tradition, it should be read aloud every day to help children understand and enjoy the rhythm and music of the form. Choosing good poetry to read aloud to children is an essential step in the planning process. Poetry appropriate for children may be rhymed or unrhymed, nonsense verse, lyrics, or ballads. Whatever the form, the subject should be of interest to the children. One study found that intermediate grade children preferred modern poetry over more traditional forms (Terry, 1974). First on their list of favorite poems was "Mummy Slept Late and Daddy Fixed Breakfast," by John Ciardi; second was "Fire, Fire," author unknown. Overall, the children in Terry's study liked humorous verse and poems about familiar experiences. Popular poetry collections among intermediate grade children include Shel Silverstein's *Where the Sidewalk Ends* (1974) and *A Light in the Attic* (1981), and Jack Prelutsky's *The New Kid On The Block* (1984) and *Tyrannasaurus Was a Beast* (1988). Both Silverstein and Prelutsky write humorous, sometimes nonsensical, rhymed verse that appeals to preadolescent children's sensibilities.

An important guideline when choosing poetry to read aloud is that the poem must be able to stand alone, without significant explication. If an explanation is needed, the poem may not be developmentally appropriate for the age level. Further, children may develop a lasting dislike for poetry because of a well-intentioned teacher's effort to explain the "true meaning" of every poem. Instead, poems ought to be read aloud and enjoyed for the absolute pleasure of listening to the sounds of the language; the images evoked; the rhythm, meter, and metaphors.

Children should never be forced to memorize poetry and perform in front of the whole class. When handled with diplomacy, poetry "readings," like prose "sharing," can be a successful part of the language arts curriculum. Always give the children the chance to practice reading poetry aloud prior to reciting before a group of any size. Encourage your students to read professional poetry as well as their own. *Illustrated Poems for Children* (1973) is an excellent collection of poetry written by major poets, including Robert Frost, Ogden Nash, and Emily Dickinson. Beautifully illustrated by Krystyna Stasiak, the book includes over 150 poems suitable for children of all ages. Other excellent anthologies of children's poetry are included at the end of this chapter.

***Writing from Experience.***     Topics for poetry writing should originate in the feelings and experiences of the children in your classrooms, for it is only then that a child can write from the heart. In his book *Wishes, Lies, and Dreams* (1970), Kenneth Koch describes his success in teaching poetry to elementary school children in a New York City public school. Koch's topics for poetry writing focused the children's attentions on matters of extreme interest and importance to them. He determined that "a poetry idea should be easy to understand, it should be immediately interesting, and it should bring something new into the children's poems" (p. 8). Children's desires, as expressed through wishes, lies, and dreams, became the focal point for numerous poetry lessons.

During his year-long experience teaching poetry to young children, Koch made some important observations about the developmental nature of poetry reading and writing:

> As poets, the primary graders tended to be buoyant and bouncy, the third graders wildly and crazily imaginative, the fourth graders warmly sensuous and lyrical, the fifth graders quietly sensuous and intellectual, and the sixth graders ironic (sometimes even slightly bitter), secretive and emotional. . . . The great and terrible onset of self-consciousness seems to begin around the fifth grade, and if children haven't written before that they may at first be a bit diffident about it. By the sixth grade they are more so, and by then some students have already decided that poetry is not for them, and they are tough to convince that they're wrong (though it can be done). (p. 43)

A key element in Koch's (1970) successful methods of teaching poetry writing was that he took the children seriously as poets. Children have a natural affinity for writing poetry, and there are many opportunities during the day to capitalize on their spontaneity and unaffected image making. Koch describes a variety of practical ways to instill a love of poetry reading and writing. He recommends freeing children from the idea that poetry *must* rhyme and have a preset rhythm and meter. His writing assignments include collaborative efforts as well as individual tasks. He suggests that poetry-writing activities can be structured to a point, and after that point the children are better left alone to be as creative and imaginative as they can be.

The models that Koch (1970) provided enabled every child to be a successful writer of poetry. His writing activities included Wish poems, in which each line begins "I Wish"; Used to/But Now poems, in which the children compare past and present; and Lie Poems, which were all "about how things might be but really aren't" (p. 19). The children also wrote other poems that were thematically based, including Dream Poems, Noise Poems, and Color Poems. In addition, Koch had the children write Comparison Poems as well as Metaphor Poems, the latter being more difficult for younger children because of the abstract nature of a direct comparison.

The following poems were written by intermediate grade children, whose teachers used some of Koch's ideas (1970) to stimulate poetry writing. The poetry-writing process began with each teacher reading aloud from the works of Shel Silverstein (1981) and Eve Merriman (1985) to model for the children how poets can write both rhymed and unrhymed poetry. Classes as a whole then brainstormed ideas for writing poetry based on experiences, desires, and feelings. In each instance, a class poem was first written.

### WE WISH

*I wish I had a million dollars.*
*I wish my hair was blonde.*
*I wish my baby brother was a baby sister.*
*I wish I could drive a car.*
*I wish we had five recesses and two lunch hours.*
*I wish Sherrie would move back to this school.*
*I wish Thanksgiving vacation was here.*
*I wish I had a bicycle for my birthday.*
*I wish I was taller than anybody in this class.*
*I wish I won the lottery.*
*I wish my mom and dad wouldn't get divorced.*
*I wish I could move to Arizona.*
*I wish people wouldn't throw trash on the playground.*
*I wish I had braces.*
*I wish I had a VCR.*

*An excerpt from Ms. Tyson's fifth-grade class wish poem*

The wish poem activity was followed by the children's individual compositions. As the poems were drafted, children read them aloud to partners or the teachers, who in turn responded to their form and content, telling the author what they liked best, what might have troubled them, and giving editorial advice that the poet was free to accept or reject. Here are some final drafts.

### I WISH I COULD RIDE UP HIGH

*I wish I could ride up high*
*In a huge spaceship with lots of*
*windows*
*And I could look out and see my*
*house and*
*Bicycle and all my friends down below*

Tammy, grade 4

### THE DREAM KEEPER

*Once I had a dream where a little old*
*lady*
*Popped out of my closet and*
*She said, "Here, Michael, I have a*
*pocket full of dreams."*
*"Pick whichever one you choose. But*
*only one."*
*I picked the best one: a bright red*
*porsche.*

Michael, grade 5

WHAT I AM (NOT REALLY)

*I'm a fish in a dish*
*Swishing.*
*I'm a frog on a log*
*Jogging.*
*I'm a clam with pearls*
*Twirling.*

Rene, grade 4

WHO I AM

*I used to be a baby*
*But now I'm 12*
*I used to be shorter*
*But now I'm taller*
*I used to be Jim's best friend*
*But now I'm Tod's best friend*
*I used to be afraid of playing soccer*
*But now I'm the goalie*
*I used to hate girls*
*But now I sort of like them sometimes*
*I used to rake the leaves for free*
*But now I get an allowance*

Allen, grade 6

***Humorous Verse.*** Children of all grade levels seem to enjoy funny poems. The limerick is often a first choice among intermediate grade children. Made famous by nineteenth-century poet Edward Lear, the limerick may be the most popular poetic form today (Kennedy & Kennedy, 1982). A limerick is a five-line, rhymed (a-a-b-b-a) poem that also has a distinct rhythm. The rhythm of the limerick is produced through length of line, the third and fourth lines (which rhyme) being shorter than lines one, two, and five (which also rhyme). The rhyme and meter of the limerick, coupled with a sometimes fantastic scenario, are what enable the poet to treat a subject in an amusing way.

*There was an old teacher from Spain*
*Who dreamed she was living in Main*
*She ate lots of lobster*
*And met a mean mobster*
*Who was sipping a glass of champaign.*

Eric, grade 5

Nonsense verse, including tongue twisters and riddles, are other humorous forms that children enjoy listening to, reading, and writing. An excellent source of classic nonsense rhymes is *A Great Big Ugly Man Came Up and Tied His Horse to Me* (1973). Clyde Watson's (1971) *Father Fox's Pennyrhymes* is another enjoyable book filled with home-spun humorous verse beautifully illustrated by the author's sister, Wendy Watson. *What's a Frank Frank?* (Maestro, 1984) and *Eight Ate: A Feast of Homonym Rhymes* (Terban, 1982) are books of homograph/homonym riddles that can be used in conjunction with a variety of grammar, vocabulary, and poetry lessons. The answers to the riddles contain alliteration and humorous plays on words, or puns.

Another very funny form is the hink-pink, or terse verse, which is a two-word poem that can be the answer to a riddle or stand alone to describe a person, place, or thing. The hink-pink can be extended to create other forms, including the hinky-pinkie, which contains 2-syllable words, and the hinkity-pinkitie which has two 3-syllable words (Geller, 1984). Here are some fourth-grade hinkie-pinkies:

| | |
|---|---|
| Name the fowl that won the lottery. | *Lucky Ducky* |
| What's a slothful flower? | *Lazy Daisy* |
| Who's your filthy friend? | *Muddy Buddy* |

The hink-pink form lends itself to illustrations, as does the "awesome alliteration." Alliteration is the repetition of initial sounds. A fifth-grade class studying the concept of alliteration in literature wrote their alliterative sentences, then illustrated them. These are some examples:

## AWESOME ALLITERATIONS

*Heaps of Hilarious Hamburgers*

*Lots of Lumpy Lambs*

*A Pair of Pink Ponies*

*A Ton of Terrible Teachers*

*A Heap of Hairy Hippos*

*Lots of Lumpy Low-Lifers*

*A Few Funny Fellows*

*Seven Slim Silly Swans Stuck to Slick Socks Square*

Using famous, well-loved poetry as a model is also a successful way to instill an appreciation of poetry reading and writing. Koch (1973) suggests several ways to incorporate classic poems into humorous poetry-writing activities. One example is the Apology poem, patterned after William Carlos Williams's free-verse poem "This Is Just to Say." Intermediate grade children are well acquainted with making apologies; thus making this particular poetry-writing activity very real and enjoyable.

| | |
|---|---|
| *This is just to say* | *This is just to say* |
| *I have burned* | *I ate the 12 chocolate* |
| *A hole in your* | *Cupcakes you were saving* |
| *Best pair of* | *For your bridge club.* |
| *Boxer shorts.* | *Forgive me, Mom.* |
| *I'm sorry, Dad. I* | *They were so sugary sweet.* |
| *Know how much you* | *I couldn't help it.* |
| *Loved the little* | *The bridge ladies don't* |
| *Golf clubs all over* | *Really need the extra* |
| *your underwear.* | *Calories like I do, a* |
| *Forgive me.* | *Growing boy.* |
| *I couldn't help it;* | |

Ron, grade 6

*I burned them because*
*The iron was so very*
*hot and steaming, and*
*The phone rang.*
*I had to talk to*
*Jill about Saturday*
*Night's slumber party.*

Julie, grade 4

*This is just to say*
*I read your boyfriend's*
*Love note that was out*
*In plain sight.*
*Forgive me.*
*It was so mushy and gushy;*
*I almost died laughing.*

Benjamin, grade 5

***Formula Poems.***    A prescribed form helps children to be successful writers. Highly structured formula poems include the unrhymed verse of the haiku, tanka, cinquain, and diamante. The haiku is a Japanese poetic form in which a single image is developed within a 17-syllable statement, arranged in three lines (5-7-5). The tanka is an extension of the haiku, with two 7-syllable lines appearing at the end of the poem (5-7-5-7-7).

*The wind is blowing*
*Very hard on my mother's*
*Best pot of flowers.*

Beth, grade 4

*The winter snowflakes*
*Fall softly on the playground*
*As my friends and I*
*Wish for warm summer breezes*
*Baseball, swimming, hiking, fun.*

Tom, grade 6

Cinquains also reflect a single image (or a story) but within a tightly structured five-line, 22-syllable 2–4–6–8–2) format. Line 1 contains the title, usually a noun; line 2 describes the title and often consists of adjectives and adverbs; line 3 expresses an action and therefore contains verb forms; line 4 relays a feeling or observation; and line 5 is a word or phrase that restates the subject in a different way. Cinquains are fun to use in conjunction with grammar lessons, thus enabling the children to use creatively their knowledge of nouns, adjectives, and adverbs. The following cinquain was written by a fifth-grader after his teacher read aloud the informational book *Journey into a Black Hole* (Branley, 1986).

*Black hole*
*Scary, dark, deep*
*Pulling, swirling, spinning*
*X-rays bombard me everywhere*
*Packed gas*

Jim, grade 5

The diamante (pronounced *dee ah MAHN tay*), invented by Iris Tiedt (1970), is another formula poem that encourages children to use their understanding of grammatical structures as well as opposites. Shaped like a diamond when it appears on the page, the diamante is a seven-line poem in the following formula:

Line 1: a one-noun subject

Line 2: two adjectives that describe the subject

Line 3: three participles (*-ing* verb forms) that tell about the subject

Line 4: four nouns—1 and 2 related to the subject and 3 and 4 related to the opposite (of the subject)

Line 5: three participles that tell about the opposite

Line 6: two adjectives that describe the opposite

Line 7: a one-noun opposite of the subject

> *KINDERGARTEN*
> *easy, happy*
> *coloring, clapping, playing*
> *ABC's, 1, 2, 3's, literature, math*
> *thinking, reading, writing*
> *hard, painful*
> *FIFTH GRADE*
>
> Roxanne, grade 5

***Free Verse.***    Most modern poetry is written in free verse. Free verse refers to unrhymed poetry written without meter. The poet creates rhythmical patterns through sentence structure, punctuation, and sometimes repetition of sound, words, and phrases (Minot, 1992). Langston Hughes "I, Too" and Eloise Greenfield's (1977) *Africa Dream* are two examples of free verse. As the label implies, free verse liberates the writer from the constraints of rhyme and rhythm patterns. Like rhymed poetry, free verse can tell a story or simply create an image.

The following examples of free verse were originally published in *Younger Kansas Writers** (1991; 1992; 1993), a yearly issue of *Kansas English.*

### PLAYING WITH RAYMOND

*I am all alone playing in my yard.*
*I play cars and trucks.*

*I see Raymond.*
*He sees me.*
*I am not alone.*
*I have Raymond to play with.*
*We play cars and trucks.*
*We play with the bikes,*
*but Raymond is going home.*

*I go home.*

Robert, grade 1

### AN INDIAN'S DREAM

*I had a dream*
*That I was a man;*
*That I was gray and old*
*And got my land*
*Got my land back!*
*Fair*
*And the white man knows*
*He better not dare!*
*Dare, to take it*
*Away*
*From me.*

Dorrell, grade 5

---

* Reprinted with permission from the Kansas Association of Teachers of English, *Younger Kansas Writers* (1991; 1992; 1993), Mary F. Heller, Editor.

## KANSAS

*Wild horses rove over*
*the flat-landed prairie.*

*The dust whirls up*
*as if it were a tornado.*
*But then it returns to the ground*
*    again*
*like it never happened.*
*The meadowlark sings its soft*
*and beautiful tune,*
*While the mares and their foals*
*fall to sleep.*

*The buffalo are grazing*
*and finally drift off to sleep.*

*The sunflower is almost like a fairy;*
*It closes up for bedtime too!*

*It will be a quiet night on*
*the Kansas prairie.*

                    Jorde, grade 4

## LIFTED

*She lifted me*
*    out*
*of my velvet-lined*
*    case.*
*She placed me*
*under her delicate*
*    chin.*
*With the newly rosined bow*
*She set me free.*

                    Leia, grade 6

## GETTING THE TREE

*The car slowed to a stop and*
*We all jerked open the doors.*

*We peered down the cheerful lane*
*With masses of breathtaking evergreens*
*Surrounding it.*

*We carefully examined various trees*
*Of all sizes and shapes.*

*Finally we spied the perfect tree*
*Swaying gently in the air current.*

*Dad sawed the trunk while we held*
*Our breath in anticipation.*
*At last, he dug in his deep worn pockets*
*For loose change, and then we drove*
*    off*
*With the sweet smell*
*Of pine filling the car.*

                    Shaina, grade 5

We should encourage children to experiment with a variety of structured and unstructured, rhymed and unrhymed, poetic forms in order to become knowledgeable about and appreciative of poetry. Experimentation with poetry reading and writing will flourish in an environment where children have access to the composing process. As during prose writing, children should be free to talk and write and rewrite their poems. They should not be held to the form or the content but rather gently guided to take risks without fear of the "red pen" making the ultimate comment on their effort. One of our most enjoyable tasks as teachers is to find the poet in every child and set the poet free.

## FOR YOU TO TRY
## Writing from the Heart

Make a list of images that are (or were) personally meaningful and very important to you, either as an adult or a child.

#### EXAMPLE LISTS

1. First's: *first day of school; first kiss; first time you drove alone;*
2. Important events: *graduation; wedding day; a special birthday.*
3. Humorous episodes: *getting caught in the rain; wearing unmatched shoes or socks; falling in a mud puddle.*
4. Favorite places: *Disneyland; World Trade Center; Museum of Natural History; Grand Canyon; Milford Lake; Hawaii.*
5. Most fun you've ever had: *Sailing on Tuttle Creek; overnight camping trip; riding on a roller coaster.*
6. Traumatic experiences: *saying good-bye; moving to another city; sibling rivalry; being left out; losing a best friend; surviving a natural disaster.*

*Transform your image into a poem. You may want to begin by just writing a paragraph about what literally happened. Then rewrite the image using poetic form, rhymed or unrhymed verse. Or you may simply want to write your thoughts using poetic form, instead of beginning with a summary paragraph. When you're ready, read your poem aloud to a friend. Talk about your poem. Revise if desired. Keep the final draft in your journal.*

#### *Example Teacher-Written Poem*

#### FIRST KISS

*Tonya kissed me on the cheek*
*For God, my brother, and everyone*
*On the playground to see me*
*Blush bright red and run*
*Inside the building right past*
*The monitor's watchful eyes,*
*Which had not seen the deed.*

*I heard the kids laughing at me as*
*I hid inside, ashamed of something,*
*But not really knowing*
*What shame there was in kissing.*
*Travis yelled, "Michael has a girlfriend."*
*And I cried big hiccup cries that only*
*My mother could stop when she came for*
*Me after school that day.*

## FOR YOUR JOURNAL

1. Observe the influence of text structure on children's reading and writing. Why do you think expository prose is more difficult to read and to write for some children?

2. Ask some children what they prefer to read and to write: fiction (stories, novels), nonfiction (expository prose, informational books), or poetry. Is there a difference in form between what children choose to read and write?

3. How do you (will you) help children to comprehend and compose a variety of structures?

4. Discuss the role of children's literature in the process of teaching text structures.

## SELECTED BOOKS FOR INTERMEDIATE GRADE CHILDREN

### Illustrated Fiction

Aiken, Joan (1988), *The Moon's Revenge,* Knopf.
Brittain, Bill (1987), *Dr. Dredd's Wagon of Wonders,* Harper & Row.
Byars, Betsy (1987), *A Blossom Promise,* Delacorte Press.
Carter, Dorothy (1987), *His Majesty, Queen Hatshepsut,* Lippincott.
Clement, Claude (1986), *The Painter and the Swan,* Dial Press.
Coerr, Eleanor (1977), *Sadako and the Thousand Paper Cranes,* Putnam.
Cooper, Ilene (1987), *Winning of Miss Lynn Ryan,* Morrow.
Cooper, Susan (1986), *The Selkie Girl,* Atheneum.
Delton, Judy (1987), *Angel's Mother's Wedding,* Greenwillow.
dePaola, Tomie (1989), *The Art Lesson,* Putnam.
dePaola, Tomie (1991), *Bonjour, Mr. Satie,* Putnam.

Eager, Edward (1985), *The Time Garden,* Harcourt Brace Jovanovich.
Eager, Edward (1985), *The Well-Wishers,* Harcourt Brace Jovanovich.
Eager, Edward (1986), *Magic by the Lake,* Harcourt Brace Jovanovich.
Eager, Edward (1986), *Seven-Day Magic,* Harcourt Brace Jovanovich.
Fleischman, Paul (1982), *The Animal Hedge,* Dutton.
Fleischman, Sid (1986), *The Whipping Boy,* Greenwillow.
Forbes, Esther (1969), *Johnny Tremain,* Dell.
Fox, Paula (1987), *A Likely Place,* Macmillan.
Fox, Paula (1987), *The Stone-Faced Boy,* Macmillan.
George, Jean (1988), *My Side of the Mountain,* Dutton.
Gormley, Beatrice (1987), *Paul's Volcano,* Houghton Mifflin.
Grahame, Kenneth (1980), *The Wind in the Willows,* Holt, Rinehart & Winston.
Greene, Bette (1974), *Philip Hall Likes Me, I Reckon Maybe,* Dial Press.
Hansen, Ron (1987), *The Shadowmaker,* Harper & Row.
Harmes, Patricia (1986), *Kevin Corbett Eats Flies,* Harcourt Brace Jovanovich.
Harvey, Brett (1986), *My Prairie Years,* Holiday.
Harvey, Brett (1987), *Immigrant Girl: Becky of Eldridge Street,* Holiday.
Haseley, Dennis (1983), *The Old Banjo,* Macmillan.
Hass, E. A. (1987), *Incognito Mosquito Makes History,* Random House.
Hearne, Betsy (1987), *Eli's Ghost,* McElderry.
Hooks, William H. (1987), *Moss Gown,* Clarion.
Howard, Ellen (1987), Edith Herself, Karl/Atheneum/Macmillan.
Howe, James (1987), *Nighty-Mightmare,* Atheneum.
Lewis, Naomi (1987), *Stories from the Arabian Nights,* Holt, Rinehart & Winston.
Lisle, Janet Taylor (1987), *The Dimpole Oak,* Orchard/Watts.
Lord, Athena V. (1987), *The Luck of Z.A.P. and Zoe,* Macmillan/Collier.
Macaulay, David (1990), *Black and White,* Houghton Mifflin.
Maccarone, Grace (1988), *The Haunting of Grade Three,* Scholastic Books.
MacClachlan, Patricia (1980), *Through Grandpa's Eyes,* Harper & Row.
McHugh, Elisabeth (1988), *Beethoven's Cat,* Atheneum.
Menotti, Gian Carlo (1986), *Amahl and the Night Visitors,* Morrow.
Minshull, Evelyn (1987), *The Cornhusk Doll,* Herald Press.
Molesworth, Mrs. (1877, 1977), *The Cuckoo Clock,* Dell.
Oz, Amoz (1981), *Soumchi,* Harper & Row.
Parks, Van Dyke, & Jones, Malcom (1986), *Jump! The Adventure of Brer Rabbit,* Harcourt
    Brace Jovanovich.
*Peter and the Wolf: Adapted from the Musical Tale by Sergei Prokofiev* (1990), Godine.
Quakenbush, Robert (1987), *Too Many Lollipops,* Golden Books.
Ray, Deborah (1987), *My Dog, Trip,* Holiday.
Rice, James (1987), *Texas Night Before Christmas,* Pelican.
Ryder, Joanna (1981), *The Snail's Spell,* Warner.
Selden, George (1987), *The Old Meadow,* Farrar, Straus & Giroux.
Service, Robert W. (1987), *The Cremation of Sam McGee,* Greenwillow.
Shura, Mary Francis (1987), *Don't Call Me Toad!* Dodd, Mead.
Snyder, Zilpha Keatley (1972), *The Witches of Worm,* Macmillan.
Snyder, Zilpha Keatley (1986), *The Changeling,* Dell.
Snyder, Zilpha Keatley (1986), *The Truth about Stone Hollow,* Dell.
Stevenson, Robert Louis (1916, 1987), *The Black Arrow: A Tale of the Roses,* Scribner.

Stoltz, Mary (1988), *Zekmet the Stone Carver: A Tale of Ancient Egypt,* Harcourt Brace Jovanovich.

Taylor, Mildred D. (1987), *The Gold Cadillac,* Dial.

Turner, Ann (1987), *Nettie's Trip South,* Macmillan.

Turner, Ann (1987), *Time of the Bison,* Macmillan.

Van Allsburg, Chris (1981), *Jumanji,* Houghton Mifflin.

Van Allsburg, Chris (1985), *The Polar Express,* Houghton Mifflin.

Van Allsburg, Chris (1986), *The Stranger,* Houghton Mifflin.

Waddell, Martin (1985, 1987), *Harriet and the Robot,* Joy Street/Little, Brown.

Wilson, Willie (1987), *Up Mountain One Time,* Jackson/Orchard/Watts.

## Fiction

Adler, C. S. (1987), *Split Sisters,* Macmillan.

Adler, C. S. (1988), *Always and Forever,* Clarion.

Aiken, Joan (1988), *The Last Slice of Rainbow,* Harper & Row.

Alexander, Lloyd (1987), *The El Dorado Adventure,* Dutton.

Alexander, Lloyd (1987), *The Illyrian Adventure,* Dell.

Auch, Mary Jane (1987), *Cry Uncle!* Holiday.

Babbitt, Natalie (1975), *Tuck Everlasting,* Farrar, Straus & Giroux.

Babbitt, Natalie (1986), *Boody Hall,* Farrar, Straus & Giroux.

Bauer, Marion Dane (1986), *On My Honor,* Clarion.

Bellairs, John (1974), *The House with a Clock on Its Wall,* Dell.

Brooks, Bruce (1984), *The Moves Make the Man,* HarperCollins.

Byars, Betsy (1973), *The Eighteenth Emergency,* Viking Press.

Byars, Betsy (1977), *The Pinballs,* Harper/Trophy.

Byars, Betsy (1981), *The Midnight Fox,* Penguin Books.

Cassedy, Sylvia (1987), *M.E. and Morton,* Crowell.

Christopher, Matt (1987), *Red-Hot Hightops,* Little, Brown.

Claro, Joe (1986), *Space Camp,* Scholastic Books.

Cleary, Beverly (1984), *Dear Mr. Henshaw,* Dell.

Cleaver, Vera (1987), *Moon Lake Angel,* Lothrop.

Clifford, Eth (1987), *Harvey's Marvelous Monkey Mystery,* Houghton Mifflin.

Collier, James L. (1974), *My Brother Sam Is Dead,* Macmillan.

Cooper, Susan (1970), *Dawn of Fear,* Harcourt Brace Jovanovich.

Corbin, William (1987), *A Dog Worth Stealing,* Orchard/Watts.

Dalgliesh, Alice (1954, 1987), *The Courage of Sarah Noble,* Scribner.

Disch, Thomas M. (1988), *The Brave Little Toaster Goes to Mars,* Doubleday.

Doyle, Brian (1986), *Angel Square,* Bradbury.

Emerson, Kathy Lynn (1987), *Julia's Mending,* Orchard/Watts.

Estes, Eleanor (1972), *Ginger Pyle,* Harcourt Brace Jovanovich.

Fox, Paula (1987), *Lily and the Lost Boy,* Jackson/Orchard/Watts.

Fox, Paula (1984), *One-Eyed Cat,* Bradbury.

Garden, Nancy (1987), *The Door Between,* Farrar, Straus & Giroux.

Grove, Vicki (1988), *Goodbye, My Wishing Well,* Putnam.

Hahn, Mary Downing (1987), *Tallahassee Higgins,* Clarion.

Hamilton, Virginia (1987), *The Mystery of Drear House,* Morrow.

Hammer, Charles (1987), *Wrong-Way Ragsdale,* Farrar, Straus & Giroux.
Holl, Kristi D. (1987), *The Haunting of Cabin 13,* Atheneum.
Honeycutt, Natalie (1986), *The All New Jonah Twist,* Bradbury.
Huberman, Crol, & Wetzel, JoAnne (1987), *Onstage/Backstage,* Carolrhoda.
Hughes, Dean (1987), *Nutty Can't Miss,* Atheneum.
Hughes, Monica (1987), *Sandwriter,* Holt, Rinehart & Winston.
Hunter, Mollie (1988), *The Mermaid Summer,* Harper & Row.
Jarow, Gail (1987), *If Phyllis Were Here,* Houghton Mifflin.
Jones, Diane Wynne (1988), *The Lives of Christopher Chant,* Greenwillow.
Jones, Rebecca C. (1987), *Germy Blew It,* Dutton.
Kelly, Jeffrey (1987), *The Basement Baseball Club,* Houghton Mifflin.
Kline, Suzy (1987), *Herbie Jones and the Class Gift,* Putnam.
Knudson, R. R. (1987), *Rinehart Shouts,* Farrar, Straus & Giroux.
Korman, Gordon (1986), *Our Man Weston,* Scholastic Books.
Krumgold, Joseph (1984), *And Now Miguel,* Harper & Row.
Lasker, Joe (1986), *Tournament of Knights,* Crowell.
Leroe, Ellen (1987), *The Peanut Butter Poltergeist,* Lodestar/Putnam.
Levitin, Sonia (1986), *Journey to America,* Macmillan.
Levoy, Myron (1988), *The Magic Hat of Mortimer Wintergreen,* Harper & Row.
Lewis, C. S. (1986), *The Lion, the Witch, and the Wardrobe,* Macmillan.
Lindbergh, Anne (1987), *The Shadow on the Dial,* Harper & Row.
Lowry, Louis (1985), *Anastasia Has the Answers,* Houghton Mifflin.
Lowry, Louis (1985), *Switcharound,* Houghton Mifflin.
Lowry, Louis (1986), *Anastasia on Her Own,* Dell.
Lowry, Louis (1986), *Autumn Street,* Dell.
Lowry, Louis (1987), *Rabble Starkey,* Houghton Mifflin.
Lyon, George Ella (1988), *Borrowed Children,* Orchard/Watts.
MacClachlan, Patricia (1985), *Sarah, Plain and Tall,* Harper & Row.
McGowen, Tom (1987), *The Magician's Apprentice,* Harper & Row.
Melling, O. R. (1986, 1987), *The Singing Tone,* Viking/Kestrel.
Namovicz, Gene Inyart (1987), *The Joke War,* Archway.
Naylor, Phyllis Reynolds (1987), *Beetles, Lightly Toasted,* Atheneum.
Nelson, Theresa (1986), *The 25 Cent Miracle,* Bradbury.
Nelson, Theresa (1987), *Devil Storm,* Jackson/Orchard/Watts.
Newman, Robert (1987), *The Case of the Watching Boy,* Karl/Atheneum.
Nixon, Joan Lowery (1987), *A Family Apart,* Bantam Books.
Nixon, Joan Lowery (1988), *Caught in the Act,* Bantam Books.
Park, Barbara (1987), *The Kid in the Red Jacket,* Knopf.
Paterson, Katherine (1988), *Park's Quest,* Dutton.
Rabe, Berniece (1987), *Margaret's Moves,* Dutton.
Rabinowitz, Ann (1987), *Knight on Horseback,* Macmillan.
Rinaldi, Ann (1986), *Time Enough for Drums,* Holiday.
Ruby, Lois (1987), *Pig-Out Inn,* Houghton Mifflin.
Ryan, Mary C. (1987), *Frankie's Run,* Little, Brown.
Sachar, Louis (1987), *There's a Boy in the Girl's Bathroom,* Knopf.
Sachs, Marilyn (1987), *Fran Ellen's House,* Dutton.
Seidler, Tor (1987), *The Tar Pit,* Michael D. Capun Books/Farrar, Straus & Giroux.
Slote, Alfred (1988), *Moving In,* Lippincott.

Snyder, Zilpha Keatley (1986), *The Egypt Game,* Dell.
Spinelli, Jerry (1990), *Maniac Magee,* Little, Brown.
Springer, Nancy (1987), *A Horse to Love,* Harper & Row.
Tate, Eleanora (1987), *The Secret of Gumbo Grove,* Watts.
Thomas, Jane Resh (1987), *Fox in a Trap,* Clarion.
Townsend, John Rowe (1986), *The Persuading Tick,* Lothrop.
Vivelo, Jackie (1987), *A Trick of Light: Stories to Read at Dusk,* Putnam.
Voight, Cynthia (1986), *Come a Stranger,* Atheneum.
Wallace, Bill (1987), *Red Dog,* Holiday.
Wiesner, David (1988), *Free Fall,* Lothrop.

## Poetry

Bauer, Caroline Feller (Ed.) (1986), *Rainy Day: Stories & Poems,* Lippincott.
Cassedy, Sylvia (1987), *Roomrimes,* Crowell.
Hopkins, Lee Bennett (1987), *Dinosaurs,* Harcourt Brace Jovanovich.
Janeczko, Paul B. (1987), *This Delicious Day: 65 Poems,* Orchard.
Lewis, Claudia (1987), *Long Ago in Oregon,* Harper & Row.
Livingston, Myra Cohn (1986), *Earth Songs,* Holiday.
Livingston, Myra Cohn (1986), *Sea Songs,* Macmillan.
Livingston, Myra Cohn (1987), *Cat Poems,* Holiday.

## Folk Tales and Fairy Tales

Baker, Olaf (1981), *Where the Buffalos Begin,* Lothrop.
Bierhorst, John (1987), *Back in the Beforetime,* McElderry/Macmillan.
Bierhorst, John (1987), *Doctor Coyote: A Native American Aesop's Fables,* Macmillan.
Farjeon, Eleanor (1984), *The Little Bookroom,* Godine.
Lewis, Naomi (1987), *Stories from the Arabian Nights,* Holt, Rinehart & Winston.
Martin, Eva (1986), *Tales of the Far North,* Dial Press.
Mayo, Gretchen Will (1987), *Star Tales: North American Indian Stories about the Stars,* Walker.
O'Shea, Pat (1987), *Finn Maccool and the Small Men of Deeds,* Holiday.
Ustinov, Mikolai (1987), *Fairy Tales,* Doubleday.

## Nonfiction

Aliki (1986), *A Medieval Feast,* Harper & Row.
Anderson, Joan (1987), *Joshua's Westward Journey,* Morrow.
Arnoksy, Jim (1987), *Sketching Outdoors in Spring,* Lothrop.
Arnoksy, Jim (1988), *Sketching Outdoors in Summer,* Lothrop.
Arnold, Caroline (1987), *Trapped in Tar: Fossils from the Ice Age,* Tichnor & Fields.
Ashabranner, Brent (1986), *Children of the Maya: A Guatamalan Indian Odyssey,* Dodd, Mead.

Branley, Franklyn (1987), *It's Raining Cats and Dogs,* Houghton Mifflin.

Brown, Tricia (1987), *Chinese New Year,* Holt, Rinehart & Winston.

Chiasson, John (1987), *African Journey,* Bradbury.

Cole, Joanna (1988), *Asking about Sex and Growing Up: A Question-and-Answer Book for Boys and Girls,* Morrow.

Faber, Doris & Faber, Harold (1987), *We the People: The Story of the United States Constitution since 1787,* Scribner.

Fischer-Nagel, Heiderose, & Fischer-Nagel, Andreas (1987), *Life of the Butterfly,* Carolrhoda.

Fisher, Leonard Everett (1986), *Ellis Island: Gateway to the New World,* Holiday.

Fisher, Leonard Everett (1987), *The Alamo,* Holiday.

Goble, Paul (1987), *Death of the Iron Horse,* Bradbury.

Hook, Jason (1987), *Sitting Bull and the Plains Indians,* Bookwright.

Lambert, David (1987), *The Age of Dinosaurs,* Random House.

Lauber, Patricia (1986), *Volcano: The Eruption and Healing of Mount St. Helens,* Bradbury.

Lauber, Patricia (1987), *Dinosaurs Walked Here,* Bradbury.

Lerner, Carol (1987), *A Forest Year,* Morrow.

Lye, Keith (1987), *Deserts (Our World),* Silver Burdett.

Patent, Dorothy Henshaw (1986), *Buffalo: The American Bison Today,* Clarion.

Patent, Dorothy Henshaw (1987), *All about Whales,* Holiday.

Perl, Lila (1987), *Mummies, Tombs, and Treasures: Secrets of Ancient Egypt,* Clarion.

Rahn, Joan (1986), *Animals That Changed History,* Atheneum.

Rinard, Judith E. (1987), *Wildlife: Making a Comeback,* National Geographic.

Rutland, Jonathan (1987), *Knights and Castles,* Random House.

Siegal, Beatrice (1987), *A New Look at the Pilgrims,* Walker.

Somme, Lauritz, & Kalas, Sybille (1988), *The Penguin Family Book,* Picture Book Studios.

Sussman, Susan, & James, Robert (1987), *Lies People Believe about Animals,* Albert Whitman.

Wakefield, Pat A. (1988), *A Moose for Jessica,* Dutton.

Weiss, Harvey (1988), *Shelters: From Tepee to Igloo,* Dutton.

Yue, Charlotte, & Yue, David (1986), *The Pueblo,* Houghton Mifflin.

## Biographies

Blumberg, Rhoda (1987), *The Incredible Journey of Lewis and Clark,* Lothrop.

Brown, Doelle (1987), *Belva Lockwood Wins Her Case,* Whitman.

Chadwick, Roxane (1987), *Amelia Earhart: Aviation Pioneer,* Lerner Publications.

Chadwick, Roxane (1987), *Anne Morrow Lindberg,* Lerner Publications.

Cleary, Beverly (1988), *A Girl from Yarn Hill: A Memoir,* Morrow.

Dahl, Ronald (1986), *Boy: Tales of Childhood,* Penguin Books.

D'Aulaire, Ingri, & Parin, Edgar (1987), *Abraham Lincoln,* Doubleday/Zepher.

D'Aulaire, Ingri, & Parin, Edgar (1987), *Benjamin Franklin,* Doubleday/Zepher.

Egan, Louise (1987), *Thomas Edison,* Barron.

Freeman, Russell (1987), *Lincoln: A Photobiography,* Clarion/Ticknor/Fields.

Fritz, Jean (1982), *Homesick: My Own Story,* Putnam.

Fritz, Jean (1883), *The Double Life of Pocahontas,* Putnam.

Fritz, Jean (1986), *Make Way for Sam Houston,* Putnam.

Harvey, Brett (1986), *My Prairie Year: Based on the Diary of Elenore Plaisted,* Holiday.

Hilton, Suzanne (1987), *The World of Young Herbert Hoover,* Walker.

Hiltz, Len (1987), *Quanah Parker,* Harcourt Brace Jovanovich.

Raboff, Ernest. *Art for Children Series,* Harper & Row. Titles: *Chagall* (1988), *Da Vinci* (1987), *Durer* (1988), *Gauguin* (1988), *Klee* (1988), *Matisse* (1988), *Michelangelo* (1988), *Picasso* (1987), *Raphael* (1988), *Rembrandt* (1987), *Remington* (1988), *Renoir* (1987), *Rousseau* (1988), *Toulouse-Lautrec* (1988), *Velasquez* (1988), *Van Gogh* (1988).

Stanley, Diane (1986), *Peter the Great,* Four Winds Press.

## Multicultural Books

Aamundsen, Nina R. (1990), *Two Short and One Long,* Houghton Mifflin.

Abells, Chana B. (1986), *The Children We Remember,* Greenwillow.

Adoff, Arnold (1990), *Sports Pages* (poetry), Harper & Row.

Amon, Aline (1981), *The Earth Is Sore: Native Americans on Nature* (poetry), Atheneum.

Ashabranner, Brent (1984), *To Live in Two Worlds: American Indian Youth Today,* Dodd, Mead.

Boyd, Candy D. (1993), *Chevrolet Saturdays,* Macmillan.

Carlson, Lori M., & Ventura, Cynthia (1990), *Where Angels Glide at Dawn: New Stories from Latin America,* Lippincott.

Conlon-McKenna, Marita (1990), *Under the Hawthorn Tree,* The O'Brien Press.

Cooper, Susan (1993), *The Boggart,* McElderry Books

Demi. (1991), *Chingis Khan,* Henry Holt and Company.

Goble, Paul (1992), *The Love Flute,* Macmillan.

Hamilton, Virginia (1988), *In the Beginning: Creation Stories from Around the World,* Harcourt Brace Jovanovich.

Hanamaka, Sheila (1990), *The Journey,* Orchard Books.

Hansen, Joyce (1980), *The Gift-Giver,* Houghton Mifflin.

Hayes, Joseph (1983), *Coyote:* Native American Folk Tales, Mariposa.

He, Liyi. (1987), *The Spring of Butterflies and Other Folktales of China's Minority Peoples,* Lothrop, Lee & Shepard.

Innocenti, Roberto (1991), *Rose Blanche,* Stewart, Tabori & Chang.

Jeffers, Susan, illustrator. (1991), *Brother Eagle, Sister Sky: A Message from Chief Seattle,* Dial.

Joseph, Lynn (1990), *Coconut Kind of Day: Island Poems,* Puffin Books.

Kalnay, Francis (1993), *Chucaro: Wild Pony of the Pampa,* Walker.

Keegan, Marcia (1991), *Pueblo Boy,* Dutton.

Louie, Al-Ling (1982), *Yeh-Shen: A Cinderella Story from China,* Philomel.

Matas, Carol (1993), *Daniel's Story,* Scholastic.

Patterson, Lillie (1989). *Martin Luther King, Jr and the Freedom Movement,* Makers of America.

Paulsen, Gary (1993), *Nightjohn,* Delacorte.

Pelz, Ruth (1990). *Black Heroes of the Wild West,* Open Hand Publishing.

Reynolds, Barbara (1988). *And Still We Rise: Interviews with Black Role Models,* USA Today Books.

Say, Allen *The Bicycle Man,* Houghton Mifflin.

Slote, Alfred (1993). *Finding Buck McHenry,* Harper Trophy.

Stanley, Fay (1991). *The Last Princess: The Story of Princess Ka'iulani of Hawaii'i,* Four Winds.

Soto, Gary (1990). *Baseball in April and Other Stories.* Harcourt Brace Jovanovich.

Taylor, Mildred D. (1987). *The Friendship,* Dial.

Yee, Paul (1989). *Tales from Gold Mountain: Stories of the Chinese in the New World,* New York: Macmillan.

# 5 THE MIDDLE SCHOOL READER AND WRITER

*Some people there are, who being grown, forget the horrible task of learning to read. It is perhaps the greatest single effort that the human undertakes, and he must do it as a child. . . . For a thousand thousand years humans have existed and they have only learned this trick—this magic—in the final ten thousand of the thousand thousand. . . . I remember that words—written or printed—were devils, and books, because they gave me pain, were my enemies. . . . Books were printed demons—the tongs and thumbscrews of outrageous persecution. Then one day, an aunt gave me a book and fatuously ignored my resentment. I stared at the black print with hatred, and then, gradually the pages opened and let me in. The magic happened.*

*John Steinbeck,* The Acts of King Arthur and His Noble Knights *(1976, pp. xi–xii)*

## CHAPTER CONCEPTS

Middle school students need time to read and write connected text.

Grammar is more effectively taught in the context of reading and writing whole texts.

Writing across the curriculum is a viable method that buys time for literacy.

The ability to articulate what one knows and does not know about any subject is crucial to language development and concept formation.

Sometime during the chaotic first week of my very first teaching job in a small junior high school in rural Oklahoma, I asked my twenty-eight second-hour students what writing and reading really meant to them now that they were in eighth grade. Not knowing exactly what responses I would get, but hoping for some clues to the personalities and attitudes of my students, I received a wide range of insightful answers. Fourteen-year-old Anthony's written response has followed me now for over two decades. I reread it occasionally when I want to be jolted back into the realities of classroom teaching:

> *To me writing in eighth grade means that you first have to read about history and stuff like that and then you have to summarize it and put it in your own words and then you have to spell all the words right and not forget to use commas. Then after you turn it in you can't just forget about it because the teacher makes you rewrite it if you didn't get it right the first time. And by then you've forgotten what you read anyway, so why bother? Writing's the pits; so's reading.*

Unlike the youthful John Steinbeck in the opening quote, not all adolescents believe reading and writing to be magical in middle school. Anyone who has been there will tell you that this can be a tough crowd. To a young adolescent, not much magic happens between grades 5 and 9. Everything is very real, very now, and often very frustrating. Growing into literate adulthood is simultaneously painful and joyous, while society views the middle school student as neither child nor adult.

Most students get through the middle school years relatively unscathed. However, an estimated 7 million youths (one in four adolescents), many from minority cultures, are feared "at risk of reaching adulthood unable to meet adequately the requirements of the work place, the commitments of relationships in families and with friends, and the responsibilities of participation in a democratic society" (Carnegie, 1989, p. 8). In short, the middle school years can be an exceptionally stressful time for many ten- to fifteen-year-olds, as they are "changing physically, maturing sexually, becoming increasingly able to engage in complex reasoning, and markedly expanding their knowledge of themselves and the world about them" (Feldman & Elliot, 1990, p. 4). It is a formidable task for middle-level educators to create an environment where all students can learn. Middle school teachers may at times wish they were magicians, capable of waving a magic wand and opening worlds through reading and writing. But much ground has already been covered in the elementary grades that has shaped ideas and attitudes toward schooling.

## MIDDLE LEVEL EDUCATION

Middle level education spans grades 5 through 9. These years are crucial to the development of literacy, school success, and an ultimate decrease in school dropouts (Epstein & MacIver, 1990). Since the 1980s, educators and parents have increased attention on the unique physical, psychological, cognitive, intellectual, and social development of adolescents. The importance of this pivotal life stage is clearly described by the Carnegie Council on Adolescent Development (1989), in its influential research report, *Turning Points.*

Young adolescents today make fateful choices, fateful for them and for our nation. The period of life from ages 10 to 15 represents for many young people their last best chance to choose a path toward productive and fulfilling lives. . . . This is a time of immense importance in the development of the young person." (pp. 20–21)

Where do we begin to help adolescents make connections among the language arts so that learning is a source of enchantment rather than persecution? One important observation about teaching is that to bring children with us to a more literate place, it is often helpful to take our cues from them. If you were to ask a group of adolescents what it is they like most about school, their first choice would very likely not be reading and writing. It would be friends. The social and emotional factors influencing adolescence "foster an urge in them to gain more control over how and with whom they spend their time" (Feldman & Elliott, 1990, p. 4). Goodlad (1984) in a survey of middle school students found that friends were mentioned most often

Carey and Sharon are eighth-grade friends who enjoy talking about books read in common.

as the single most important thing about school. Not surprisingly, similar data have turned up in other nationwide surveys of teens' attitudes (Caulkins, 1986). The importance of friendships made and broken during adolescence is a recurring theme in literature for the young (Young adult's choices, 1992).

George and Alexander (1993) suggest that "affective education—teaching about emotions, feelings, relationships—is critical in the middle school" (p. 13). Middle school students are often self-conscious and may develop feelings of incompetence, a low sense of self-esteem (Lipsitz, 1984). Taking advantage of the social nature of adolescents in the classroom environment is a special key to successful teaching at this level, just as it is during kindergarten and the elementary school years. Current views of successful middle school programs indicate that the child should be at the center of the curriculum, not the individual subject areas as traditionally seen in the secondary schools (Scales, 1992). Child-centered curricula utilize classroom organization and management strategies that take into consideration the unique needs of all children and support the emerging adolescents as they struggle to gain peer acceptance and self-identity. In her sensitive account of teaching in a middle school, Atwell (1987) uses the reading and writing workshop as the framework for encouraging the natural social behaviors of adolescence. She writes, "We give them [the middle school students] the workshop, that predictable environment that is itself an invitation to openness and change" (p. 262). Atwell uses the workshop as a basic classroom management strategy that allows for the integration of both theoretical and practical aspects of reading and writing processes. (See Chapter 8 for a full discussion of workshop formats appropriate for grades K–8.)

This chapter focuses on integrating the language arts in ways that are not traditional in middle school curricula. For practical reasons, many of the methods discussed in previous chapters can be adapted for middle school. For example, common sense coupled with knowledge of solid theory, research, and practice tells us that middle school children should be given many opportunities throughout the day to read and write connected text. Reading and writing will develop only if children engage in real reading and writing, and for many students school may be the only place this will occur. Young adolescents need to read and to be read interesting books written especially for them (Lesesne et al., 1993). Middle school students often search for the answers to persistent questions, such as "Who am I?" "Am I normal?" and "Who do you think I am?" (George & Alexander, 1993, p. 11). Adolescent literature is a valuable resource in helping children to understand themselves and their relationships with peers, family, and teachers. Daily read-aloud sessions reinforce listening comprehension skills and  instill an appreciation of prose and poetry. Reader response to literature is an effective way to motivate adolescent readers and writers. By asking the simple question, "What did you think about the story?" we reaffirm our respect for students' opinions and begin to establish an environment that bolsters self-esteem at every opportunity. Figure 5.1 illustrates the value of response activities, as a seventh-grader writes in his journal about the novel *Zeely* (Hamilton, 1969).

Middle school students, like elementary school children, appreciate hands-on,

*David*

Zeely was very quiet, She didn't speak much. She was very tall and wise. She was like that because her mother passed away. The story made me feel like I was really in the story. For instance when Geeder and Toeboy were on there way to their uncle Ross' form traveling on a train, I felt like I was with them. Virginia Hamilton wrote the book that way throughout, which was good. My favorite part was when Geeder and Toeboy slept outside of there uncle Ross' house, I thought that would have been fun. The story did not have a message for me, yet that doesn't hurt the quality of the book. It did not remind me of anything because I have not spent the summer at my uncles house before like Geeder and Toyboy did. Overall this story was one of the better ones I've read, because most other storys just speed things along, but this one didn't. Virginia Hamilton really knows what she's doing when she writes stories.

**FIGURE 5.1**   Journal response, David, age 12

direct experiences that are interesting and relevant and give them something to think, talk, read, and write about. As though we have come full circle, students in grades 5 through 9 need to engage in purposeful oral language, from reactions to conversations to discussions. Like kindergartners, young adolescents internalize concepts more readily when given new experiences and a chance to talk about their ideas.

## CREATING A LITERATE ENVIRONMENT

The daily classroom management realities in middle schools are significant, as teachers could have well over 100 students in five or six forty-five- to fifty-five-minute periods. In a traditional curriculum, middle school English and reading educators teach their students five days a week throughout the year. Some middle schools use inter-disciplinary teams of teachers, each responsible for a different subject. A middle school that houses grades 6 through 8 might utilize a collegial arrangement whereby two teachers divide the reading/language arts and science/math curricula and share responsibilities for social studies. Regardless of the curricular arrangements, large classes, limited instructional time, and frequent interruptions all contribute to the textbook-driven curriculum that is often implemented at the middle school level. Time for listening to prose and poetry as well as reading and writing connected text suffers at the expense of getting through the traditional reading and language arts programs.

Making more efficient use of time in middle level education requires making choices about course content. Be it kindergarten or ninth grade, it is neither possible nor desirable to cover all information contained in the textbooks. Making informed choices about what to teach in one's own classroom is difficult even for the experienced teacher. Well-intentioned teachers cover the same literature, grammar, and spelling material in the same order year after year for fear of missing a student or appearing not to be doing their job. Decisions about what, how, and when to teach important concepts require teachers making informed choices about the content of their textbooks. Together the teacher and the children, not the textbook, shape the curriculum. The middle school student is at the center of the classroom instruction.

Consider the following points when planning a fully integrated middle-level curriculum that fosters the development of literacy:

1. Provide guidance through a balance of direct instruction and child-centered activities that are supported by the reading and writing process.
2. Integrate listening to, talking about, reading, and writing a variety of prose and poetry.
3. Allow middle school students the freedom to talk about their learning. Foster oral language development through conversation, reaction, and discussion. Use reader response frequently to encourage free expression of ideas and feelings.
4. Teach grammar, mechanics, and spelling in the context of meaningful connected text.
5. Choose the best adolescent literature that you can find for read-aloud sessions as well as models for reading and writing. (A selected list of adolescent literature is located at the end of this chapter.)
6. Help middle school students develop a strong sense of self-esteem and discover who they are through daily reading, writing, and responding to connected text.

## THREE MODEL LESSONS

An integrated language arts curriculum is teacher-driven, not text-driven, as well as child-centered, not subject-centered. In the following sections of this chapter, I describe three model lessons that seek to achieve the six points outlined above. Each model lesson, "Inside the Classroom," is preceded by a "nonexample," or negative model. The three positive model lessons include explanations of how to plan the lesson, dialogue based on classroom observations where the lessons were put into practice (M. F. Heller, 1989a), and reflections. Reading and writing processes form the bases of each of three fully integrated lesson plans designed explicitly for middle school students. The models are "Grammar in Context" (1989c), "The Directed Reading and Writing Lesson" (1986a, 1986c), and "How Do You Know What You Know" (1986b).

## Grammar in Context

Rule of thumb: Never use grammar exercises as a classroom management tool.

### NONEXAMPLE: NOUNS? OH NO, NOT AGAIN!

*8:35 a.m.: Ms. Trabasko, a seventh-grade English teacher in her fifth year of teaching, says on the first day of the new semester, "Complete the exercises on pages 3–9 of your grammar text. Underline the nouns once and the verbs twice. [The class groans, "Not again. We did that last year!"] Quiet, class, or I'll assign the supplementary exercises. [A few more groans from the boys in the back row.]*

Sixth-graders are paired with kindergartners for a special art, reading, and writing project.

*Exchange papers when you're through and* quietly *check each other's work. When we're all through we'll review what nouns and verbs are."*

8:40–9:30 A.M.: *The students slowly open their books and begin the assignment while Ms. Trabasko sorts through a pile of spelling tests. The room is quiet, filled with gloom. No one admits finishing by the end of class.*

This is what might be termed a *nonexample* of what it means to teach language arts. It is a glimpse of reality, of the poorest of teaching methods, where assignments are used simultaneously for classroom management and punishment, the embodiment of everything that is and ever has been wrong with the teaching of English in middle and secondary schools. As I observed Ms. Trabasko's "lesson," I checked the calendar to make sure it was indeed January 1989. What this scene reminded me of was my own seventh-grade English teacher, Ms. McClure, who I believe used the very same words in 1963: "Underline the noun once and the verb twice." What troubled me most about my recent observation was that Ms. Trabasko, ten years younger than I, was probably relying on what she knew best, on what made her feel most comfortable in the English classroom. That is, she was probably teaching the way she was taught. Her choice was to use the grammar text "as is" because it was included in the prescribed curriculum for eighth grade. In this way she could control the class and at the same time be perceived by her peers and her superiors as doing the best job she could.

Extensive reviews of the research reveal that grammar study alone does not contribute significantly to the quality of student writing (Braddock, Lloyd-Jones, & Shoer, 1963; Hillocks, 1987). Yet curricular objectives in grades K–12 invariably include the study of grammar, largely because students are expected to understand grammatical concepts well enough to recognize and use them on standardized achievement tests. Thus grammar objectives remain in the elementary and middle-school English class. Hillocks suggests that grammar ought to be studied for its contribution to skill in proofreading and mechanics. He further suggests that the study of grammar might be undertaken by some professionals for "humanistic reasons" (p. 81). All things considered, the study of grammatical concepts is troublesome for teacher and student, especially if writing and reading connected text are priorities in the language arts curriculum.

Contrast Ms. Trabasko's nonexample with the following extended example in Mr. Weaver's traditional seventh-grade English class. "Grammar In Context" (1989c) is a method of teaching grammatical concepts within the context of reading and writing connected text. It is a method that buys instructional time for developing comprehension and composition by taking advantage of what we know about theory and research into the language arts.

INSIDE THE CLASSROOM
**Teaching Seventh-Graders about Nouns and Verbs—
Again, Again, and Again**

### 1. Prereading/Prewriting

*Activate the students' prior knowledge and understanding of the relevant concepts (in this case, nouns and verbs) by providing a very brief lesson on the topic. Nouns and verbs are reviewed briefly because seventh-graders have studied them since first grade. The short introduction, or "mini-lesson" (term coined by Caulkins, 1986), focuses the students' attention on the exact nature of the concepts to be discussed. It is then followed by oral reading or a good piece of literature. The purpose of the listening activity is for the students to articulate and apply their knowledge of basic grammatical concepts. The students write in their journals throughout the lesson. The journal entries are used to document progress.*

*Day 1, 8:35 A.M.*
Mr. Weaver, a veteran seventh-grade teacher, introduces the topic of nouns and verbs in this way: "I know that you all know what nouns and verbs are, though some of you may have forgotten the exact definitions. Let's see how many you can remember. Take about two minutes to write in your journals as many nouns and as many verbs that you can think of. Afterward, we'll see if we can come up with our own definitions. Ready, begin!" (Students furiously write lists of words.)

**WEAVER:** Eddie, read us your noun list.

**EDDIE:** Eddie, Mr. Weaver, desk, pencil, paper, journal, floor, table, chair, lights.

**WEAVER:** Good job. Do you agree that everything on Eddie's list is a noun? [The class agrees.] So what's a noun, Eddie?

**EDDIE:** Nouns name persons, places, and things.

**WEAVER:** Fantastic! Sounds like a definition I've heard all my life. Does anyone have an item on their noun list that they're not sure about? Read each other's list to make sure you're all straight about nouns. Now write the definition of a what a noun is in your journals.
   Now let's hear some verbs.

**CHARNELL:** Write, read, sit, stand, run, jump, play.

**WEAVER:** Excellent. What's a verb, Charnell?

*(continued)*

**Inside the Classroom (continued)**

CHARNELL: Verbs tell about action, about doing things.

WEAVER: Do they do anything else?

PATTY: Verbs also tell about who we are like; I *am*, or he *is*, or they *are*.

WEAVER: Yes, we sometimes call that "state of being." Now check your verb list to see if all the words are action or state of being words. Ask a friend if you're not sure. Then write the definition of a verb in your journal.

Mr. Weaver circulates to lend support and answer questions. In his brief sweep around the class, he notices three students, Ken, Jon, and Sandy, who do not have a firm grasp of nouns and verbs. He makes a note of this in his own journal for future reference.

WEAVER: Someone tell me why it's important to know what nouns and verbs are.

GEORGE: So we can get through this stupid course. [Class laughs.]

WEAVER: It's true, George, that you have to pass this course to go on to eighth grade. And you really do want to be an eighth-grader someday, don't you? [George shrugs.] Any other reasons to learn about grammar?

STAN: So we'll be able to write complete sentences. Sentences have to have subjects and predicates—that's what nouns and verbs are. And also so we'll be able to pick them out on those dumb standardized tests we have to take this year. [Class groans. Stan is the seventh-grade whiz kid.]

WEAVER: Thanks, Stan. You're right on both counts. Knowing about nouns and verbs is especially useful to us when we revise our writing. Grammar knowledge gives us the vocabulary we need to talk about our sentences and paragraphs. Understanding grammar helps us to understand the way we write. Being able to pick out nouns and verbs on a standardized test doesn't make us better writers, though. To become better writers we have to do a lot of writing *and* reading. It's a lot like swimming. You don't become a good swimmer unless you jump in the water and practice.

EILEEN: I'd rather swim than write, any day.

## 2. LISTENING/WRITING

*Choose a good piece of literature to read aloud. Help the students set a purpose for listening that is tied to the grammatical concepts under study. Have the students take notes in their journal* while *listening to help focus their attention on the purpose for listening.*

### 8:50 A.M.

>**WEAVER:** Now I want to know if you think you'd know a noun or a verb if you heard one or read one in a book. [Class nods yes. "Piece of cake," says Jim.] Today's read-aloud is a continuation of our unit on Edgar Allan Poe [1938]. As I read the beginning section of the story, "The Tell-Tale Heart," I want you to listen for Poe's use of nouns and verbs. While you're listening, write in your journals some of the nouns and verbs that you hear. Don't try to write them all down, just the ones that make an impression on you. Think about Poe's word choice and how it creates a special mood for the story. Try to predict what's going to happen.

Weaver reads the first page of the story, which is in the seventh-grade literature text, as the students listen intently and occasionally write words in their journals. After reading Weaver displays an overhead transparency.

>**WEAVER:** Here's my list of nouns and verbs. *Nouns: disease, vulture, blood, dissimulation, madmen, midnight; verbs: haunted, killed, fancy, thrust, undid, vexed, wronged.* Compare your list to mine. Was it as easy as you thought it would be to recognize nouns and verbs? What kind of effect does Poe create by carefully chosen words?

The class is not as confident as they were initially about their knowledge of nouns and verbs. They agree that the effect is "scary, spooky." But their lists are short, with adjectives and adverbs appearing in some of the journal entries—*evil, gradually, wisely.* Weaver and the students discuss the similarities and differences in their word lists, helping one another understand the differences between nouns and verbs and putting adjectives and adverbs "on hold" until Thursday's lesson. Poe's language is often archaic, and his word choice and syntax are difficult for some students to comprehend. Weaver rereads some of the more unusual words in context to clarify meaning and to try to get the students to infer the literal meanings of words like *dissimulation, fancy,* and *vexed.* Several students have trouble understanding that Poe's tale is a murder story being told by an insane narrator. They are nevertheless intrigued by Weaver's oral reading, which proved to be an excellent motivational technique for encouraging silent reading of the remainder of the story.

*(continued)*

**Inside the Classroom (continued)**

Even the teacher reads during sustained silent reading.

### 3. READING/WRITING

*Allow fifteen to twenty minutes for sustained silent reading of connected text. The purposes for reading will vary according to the selection. However, the grammatical concepts under study should remain at the forefront, as well as ideas for future writing activities. Encourage the students to think about grammar in the context of the story as they silently read during the remainder of the class period. Again, encourage the use of the journal to take notes about the purposes for reading and ultimately for writing connected text. Read and write with the students.*

*9:10–9:30 A.M.*

> **WEAVER:** Now I want you to finish reading Poe's "Tell-Tale Heart." As you
> are reading, notice his use of nouns and verbs. If there are some
> nouns and verbs that you don't understand, write them in your jour-
> nal, and we'll talk about them tomorrow. Think about the special
> nouns and verbs you might use when writing a story or a poem of
> your own. If while you're reading, you come up with an idea for a
> story or poem or piece of nonfiction, make a note of it in your jour-
> nal. For example, while I was reading to you this morning, I came up
> with an idea for a murder mystery that I'm going to try writing. I'm
> going to call it "The Case of the Missing English Teacher." [Class

groans.] Tomorrow we'll talk some more about nouns and verbs, Poe's "Tell-Tale Heart," and the stories or poems that you might like to write.

The students read until the end of the period. Mr. Weaver also reads and begins to make notes about his own mystery story. Those students who do not manage to finish reading are encouraged to bring their books home or to study hall.

### Reflections on Day 1

The first day of Mr. Weaver's lesson on nouns and verbs is a natural blend of direct instruction and student-centered activity. Within the fifty-five-minute time limit of a traditional seventh-grade English class, he is able to reintroduce the concepts of noun and verb in the meaningful context of connected text. Weaver has designed a lesson demonstrating that nouns and verbs influence comprehension and composition. Not incidentally, he has also given his students a powerful gift—the knowledge of how language works and the opportunity to use their own language to be expressive and communicative. He uses the journal to manage the lesson as well as to document student understanding and progress.

The second part of Mr. Weaver's grammar in context lesson follows up on the previous day's theme of the effective use of nouns and verbs in short fiction. The resulting dialogue reveals that most students were intrigued by Poe's story, though it is evident that not all the students comprehended the story with ease.

### 4. POSTREADING/PREWRITING/WRITING

*By way of review, orally summarize the grammatical concepts that are being studied, using definitions and examples. Again, place the concepts within the context of the prose or poetry that you have been reading. Ask for reactions to the literature in general, as well as to the author's use of grammatical constructs (nouns and verbs) in particular. Allow time to react, reflect, and think. Elicit suggestions for future writing topics inspired by the grammar/reading lesson. Model the process of taking preliminary notes on a writing project that was inspired by the reading selection. Allocate as much time as possible for writing, rewriting, and editing the final copy. This final step will vary according to the genre in which the students are working.*

### Day 2, 8:30 a.m.

WEAVER: Yesterday we talked about nouns and verbs, ideas that aren't new to any of you. We decided that nouns name persons, places, and things, like *Edgar Allan Poe, villains, officers, chamber, lantern,*

*(continued)*

**Inside the Classroom (continued)**

*bed.* Verbs tell us about action or being, like *tell, thrust, close, slept, cut, is, had been, was.* Then we decided to think about the nouns and verbs that Edgar Allan Poe used in his classic tale "The Tell-Tale Heart." Tell me what you thought about the story.

What followed was a lively discussion of the story, with wide-ranging reactions by the seventh-graders. Some thought the story was "too gross" and "too hard to read." One student suggested that Mr. Weaver should have read the whole thing aloud, "Because it sounds better, and I can understand more when *you* read it." The students were in general agreement that Poe's choice of nouns and verbs helped to create the "creepy" effect. "I loved the blood and guts part," said Randy. "It's a perfect Halloween story," suggested Rachel. Then Jason asked the ultimate question about Poe's work as an author.

JASON: How'd he come up with all those words? I could never think of that many different nouns and verbs in a million years.

WEAVER: Good question, Jason. Poe didn't just sit down and "think up nouns and verbs" to use in his story. He first had to have an idea for the story. Then he had to create a character to tell the story. This story is told in the first person. The *I* in the story is the madman who retells the terrible tale. I suspect that once Poe had the character in mind, the words that the madman used to tell the tale came more easily. Character is very important to a story. Some authors believe that characterization is *everything,* and without strong characters to sustain the action in a narrative, the story goes nowhere.

"Did you come up with some new ideas to write about as you read 'The Tell-Tale Heart'?" [Weaver writes the ideas on the chalkboard as volunteers read from their journal entries. He categorizes their ideas according to genre.]

| *IDEAS FOR FICTIONAL STORIES* | *POETRY IDEAS* | *PERSONAL NARRATIVES* |
|---|---|---|
| Murder in the School Lunchroom | Halloween | My First Halloween |
| The Mystery of the Squishy Sound | Haunted Sounds | Afraid of the Dark |
| Midnight Tales of Terror | Ghosts | Spooky Sounds in Gregory's House |
| The Mad Seventh-Grader of East Junior High | Creepy Creatures | Close Encounters with a UFO |

Some students who initially had no new ideas were inspired by their peers' responses and quickly wrote in their journals. Mr. Weaver suggested that the students write some of their ideas onto their writing folders for easier access during writing time. He then shared preliminary notes for his own mystery story.

> **WEAVER:** Want to hear what I've decided about my myster, "The Case of the Missing English Teacher"? [The class responds with enthusiasm. They enjoy hearing what their teacher is writing about.] The main character is going to be named Ms. Humphrey. She's going to be traveling on summer vacation in Europe, probably France, but she's not going to make it back for the beginning of the school year. When some seventh-graders hear about this, they try to come up with a plan to find her before the first day of class because the dreaded substitute, Mr. Speilman, is being contracted to take her place. And everyone hates Mr. Speilman because he forces you to underline the noun once and the verb twice in *everything* you write. [The students laugh because they remember a seventh-grade substitute English teacher who did just that!]

### 5. SUSTAINED BUT NOT NECESSARILY SILENT WRITING

*Allow fifteen to twenty minutes for sustained but not necessarily silent writing time. During this initial drafting period, the teacher should be readily available to help students who may still be experiencing writer's block. Encourage oral exchanges among students who can help one another clarify and develop their ideas. Remind the students again of the grammatical concepts that have been discussed throughout the lesson.*

### 9:10–9:30 A.M.

> **WEAVER:** Now I want you to start taking some notes on your next piece of writing. You can even start writing a first draft if you want. If you're stuck, talk to a friend or to me about your ideas. And if you need absolute quiet to get started, move to the partitioned writing area and put on a headset. While you're writing and rewriting, be sure to think about your choice of nouns and verbs and how those particular words will affect your audience of readers. You may want to use a thesaurus if you're having trouble coming up with just the right word. I'll be at the Editor's Desk in the writing area if you need me. Tomorrow we'll use the whole period for writing first drafts as well as reading some more Poe and maybe Hawthorne. If you get a chance, work on your piece outside of class.

These students cooperated to make a Conestoga wagon in conjunction with a reading and writing project on pioneer America.

***Final Reflections.*** Grammar in context is a way to introduce (or reintroduce) grammatical concepts in a way that is amenable to the middle school or junior high student, who from the onset may resist the subject of grammar altogether. The advantages of integrating grammar into the overall language arts curriculum are many. Time spent directly teaching the grammatical concept is directly proportional to the students' prior knowledge of the concept. For example, less time will be needed to discuss nouns and verbs, leaving more time available to introduce concepts new to seventh-graders, such as indefinite pronouns. Grammar in context lessons free the students and teacher from the boredom of lists of sentences in the grammar text that seem to bear no relation to comprehension and composition. Built into the lesson is the opportunity to recognize and define concepts that are so often a part of standardized tests. The teacher is a model and a mentor, guiding the students as they discover new ideas through reading and writing. Finally, the students are afforded the chance to read and write connected text for fifteen minutes or more a day, which gives them much needed practice that will carry over to other reading and writing situations.

## The Directed Reading and Writing Lesson

Pedagogical truth: Giving reading and writing assignments is *not* teaching; it is merely assigning.

### NONEXAMPLE: THE SCIENCE NONLESSON

*1:30 P.M.: Mr. Lyle, the eighth-grade science teacher, directs his fourth-hour students' attention to a map of the solar system displayed at the front of the room. "This week, class, we begin our study of the solar system. I want everyone to get out a piece of paper and a pencil and draw the solar system just as it appears on this map. Be sure to label the planets. Then I want you to read Chapter 7 in your science books and write the answers to the comprehension questions on another piece of paper. When you're through, I want you to get a library pass and go to the library to begin researching the planet of your choice. After you've done your research, I want you to write a paper about your favorite planet. Be sure to watch your spelling and your punctuation. Be neat. Papers are due on my desk by Friday. Any questions?" (No one has any questions. The students are very familiar with the way in which Mr. Lyle organizes his weekly lessons). "I'll be figuring nine-weeks' grades this whole week, so take care not to disturb me or others while you're reading and doing your research."*

*1:35 P.M.: The only sounds heard are the rustling of papers and whispers as students begin their week-long assignment.*

Mr. Lyle's science lesson is the ultimate example of a nonlesson in which the instructor makes an assignment but does little or no teaching. Ironically, his "lesson" contains several elements that are pedagogically sound practice. For example, there is a concrete activity—drawing a picture of the solar system—there is reading and writing of connected text—reading the chapter and answering the questions—and there is an extension of the main concept plus more reading and writing of connected text through research on the solar system. Finally, there is the illusion of a child-centered lesson, as the students participate in a great deal of independent decision making. But what is missing from the equation is the *teacher*, who guides the students in a systematic way through the learning process. Mr. Lyle's lesson contains the skeleton of a directed reading lesson, which has for years been recommended as a way to organize basal-reader and content area lessons. But a skeleton it will remain unless the combination of direct instruction and child-centered activity is systematically infused throughout his lesson.

The directed reading and writing lesson (DRWL) (M. F. Heller, 1986a) is one way to take advantage of the power of the composing process infused throughout prereading, reading, and postreading stages of the reading process. The organizational strategy that underlies the DRWL helps "buy time" to teach content area concepts that may be difficult for students to grasp on their own. At the same time it provides much flexibility through direct instruction, child-centered independent work, and reading and writing connected text.

The directed reading and writing lesson can be adapted for literature as well as other subject areas, including science. The following model lesson illustrates how Mr. Lyle's science lesson could have been organized to achieve a much greater effect on student learning.

# INSIDE THE CLASSROOM
## The Solar System*

**1. PREREADING**

A. Activate the students' prior knowledge of the major concept to be studied and provide a hands-on, concrete learning experience to help motivate listening, speaking, reading, and writing.

*Day 1, 8:05 A.M.*

**Ms. STEFFEN** [A first-year eighth-grade science teacher]: Good morning everyone. Today is the day we begin studying "The Earth and Space Science," and as I promised you last week I've brought my telescope to class for all of you to look through. You won't be able to see a lot today, though the moon is still visible this time of morning, and we can use a special projection filter and mirrors to see a reflection of the sun. The telescope is set up near the back windows with a clear view of the eastern sky. This viewing area is Station 1.

I also have a model of our solar system that I made during my student teaching semester. The model here on the work table, or Station 2, is constructed of Styrofoam balls, wire, and aluminum foil. Can you recognize the major planets and moons in our sun's system?

And displayed here over the chalkboard is a large map that shows the relationships of size and distance from the sun of all the planets. This is Station 3.

For the next fifteen minutes I want you to spend about five minutes at each station looking at these materials, which are intended to help you understand the small part of the universe in which we live. Talk among yourselves about what you see and think and feel. [The room is filled with excitement as the twenty-eight students wander from station to station, talking, observing, and reflecting. Ms. Steffen interacts with the students, observes their reactions, and makes notes in her journal about ideas that will need to be discussed later in the lesson.]

B. List on the chalkboard or overhead what the students already know about the concept (solar system). Model prediction strategies. Establish a teacher/student-generated purpose for reading and for writing.

---

*Adapted from M. F. Heller (1986a, pp. 173–182).

**8:25 A.M.**

**Ms. Steffen** [Everyone is now seated]: From what I overheard in your conversations, you already know a great deal about the universe in which we live. Tell me everything you know about our solar system. I'm going to write your ideas on the overhead, and while I'm writing I'll categorize the ideas so we will have an outline of the whole concept [Figure 5.2].

**Amy:** The solar system is made up of the sun and nine planets: Earth, Jupiter, Venus, Mars, Saturn, Pluto, Neptune, Mercury, and Uranus.

**Ted:** There's also our moon and all the other moons. I think Jupiter has lots of moons, but I don't know how many.

**Kenneth:** Yeah, and our moon looks real neat through the telescope. [Everyone in the class simultaneously agrees.]

**FIGURE 5.2** "The Solar System," eighth-grade concept map

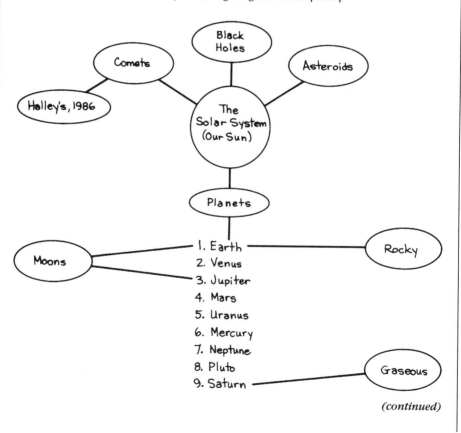

*(continued)*

**Inside the Classroom (continued)**

RONNY: What about black holes? Doesn't the solar system have black holes, too? I saw it in a movie once.

MINDY: There are comets and asteroids in the solar system, too. They're shown on that map. I saw Halley's comet in 1986 when it flew by. It wasn't all that great.

MS. STEFFEN: Those are excellent contributions. The title of our science Chapter 15 is "Astronomy" [Brockway, Gardner, & Howe, 1985, pp. 369–391], and we will be reading and writing about the Earth, moon, sun, and the solar system. So we'll probably learn quite a few facts about what makes up our planetary system. Besides what you've already mentioned, what else about the solar system do you think you will learn by reading the chapter?

TRACY: You mean like what the planets look like and how far away they are from earth?

MS. STEFFEN: Yes, exactly. You'll notice on page 376 that one goal or purpose for reading is "To identify the general features of the planets and other members of the solar system." What are some features of the planet Earth that you already know?

BILL: Dirt and grass and rocks and stuff like that.

MS. STEFFEN: Thank you, Bill. Dirt and grass are certainly features of our planet. And rocks too. That's why Earth is in the "rocky planet" category, which is also the title of the first section of the chapter. In that section I suspect we'll learn about other planets and objects that are rocky in makeup.

What about planets other than Earth? What do you think they look like? For example, does Saturn have any unique features?

SALLY: It has rings. But it probably doesn't have any grass or air. I don't think you can breathe on Saturn or any other planet except for Earth.

MS. STEFFEN: That's a fine observation, Sally. The second section of the chapter is titled "Gaseous Planets." I expect in that section we'll find out about those rings and whether or not there is air like ours on other planets.

Let's review the map of our concept I've been making here on the overhead during our discussion. [Ms. Steffen reviews the terms on her concept map.] We already know a good deal about what makes up our solar system. And I've introduced you to two new ideas, rocky planets and gaseous planets, which you'll be learning more about through reading the chapter.

If you were to write a paragraph using the facts on this concept map, what would the paragraph be like?

**SANDY:** It would describe what we already know about the solar system and also what we don't know very much about, like rocky planets and gaseous planets.

**Ms. Steffen:** Excellent! Writing about what we know and don't know not only helps us to comprehend the text but also helps us to begin thinking like scientists.

Our purpose for reading pages 369 to 381 is to learn more about the solar system, and our purpose for writing, then, is to describe the solar system.

### 2. PREREADING/WRITING (15–20 MINUTES)

Describe the assessment system that you will be using. Explain that the students' papers will be the first draft of a description of the solar system, which ultimately will include new terms and concepts learned by reading the assignment. First drafts are nongraded, but they are reviewed and responded to by peers during a prereading Writers' Workshop (described below) supervised by the teacher. Second drafts are written after reading the assignment and are reviewed and responded to by the teacher and/or peers during conferences before being returned to the student for final revisions. Only the final draft receives a letter grade. No exam is given on the chapter, although concepts and terms described in the student papers will be included on the unit exam.

### Prereading Writers' Workshop Format

1. Working in small groups of three or four, students exchange first drafts and critique one another's papers. The students are instructed to respond first to content by addressing questions such as

   What are the best parts of the paper?

   What parts confused you?

   How do you think the author can improve the paper?

2. Spelling, grammar, and punctuation *always* count and should be discussed in view of effective communication, but not at the expense of lowering the author's self-esteem. Form is a concern during the editing stage of the composing process.

3. Written recommendations by peers are given to the student author, who in turn uses them when revising the original draft after having read the assignment.

*(continued)*

## Inside the Classroom (continued)

**4.** The teacher is available at all times to lend support and encouragement throughout the workshop. If desired, the teacher may provide a model first draft, which the students could use for comparison during their discussions.

*8:40 A.M.*

> Ms. Steffen: Before reading the first four sections of Chapter 15, I want you to write the first draft of a paper describing the solar system as you presently understand it. You may write this first draft in your journal, since it won't be graded. This morning we will have a brief Writers' Workshop to go over your initial draft. Your second and/or final draft will be written *after* you've read the section on the solar system—after you've learned more facts about our universe. I'll be grading only your final draft, which will be worth 50 points: 10 = overall organization; 30 = content and factual information; 10 = spelling, grammar, and punctuation. [Ms. Steffen displays this system on an overhead. It is already familiar to the students.] You won't have a test on this chapter, but the information that you learn through reading and writing will be on the unit exam later this month.

Ms. Steffen circulates among small groups of three or four students, lending support whenever needed. A few students finish their first drafts quickly and begin reading, although there is not enough time for the majority to get started on Chapter 15.

## 3. Reading/Writing (Homework or Study Hall Assignment)

Encourage the students to think about their purposes for reading and writing while reading the chapter or chapter segment. Some internal composing may occur as students encounter new information about the concept. For example, they could think to themselves, "Asteroids are 'minor' planets. That's something new I've learned. I need to make a note to include it in my paper." Such metacognitive reflections can be later modeled by the teacher or students during the postreading phase of the lesson.

*9:00 A.M.*

> Ms. Steffen: For homework I want you to read pages 369–381 of the astronomy chapter. As you are reading, take some notes on the new facts that you learn about the solar system in general and the Earth, moon, and sun in particular. These notes will help you in revising your original draft and finalizing your solar system paper. Does anyone have questions before the bell rings?

**JAMES:** How *long* does the final draft have to be?

**MS. STEFFEN:** There's really no length requirement other than as long as it takes to describe the solar system fully, using both newly learned and already known information. I would guess that two to three paragraphs will be about right, though some of you may write more.

**KELLY:** Can we write our second drafts tonight?

**MS. STEFFEN:** Definitely, Kelly. Each of you should work on your papers whenever you get the chance. Tomorrow we'll discuss the chapter segment, work on second drafts, and continue responding to one another's writing.

### Reflections on Day 1

The first day of Ms. Steffen's directed reading and writing lesson is filled with a variety of teacher-directed and student-centered activities. Her decision to use three different "stations" to motivate interest in the solar system encourages a good deal of conversation and discussion. The eighth-graders' attention was focused immediately on the relevant concepts under study. Ms. Steffen's carefully planned use of concrete experiences produced a classroom environment that is conducive to oral language development. Oral language is fundamental in developing reading and writing skills and ought to be incorporated systematically throughout the curriculum in kindergarten through grade 12 (Loban, 1976). The students also engaged in writing connected text, the descriptive paragraph, that was directly related to comprehending the science chapter. This kind of prereading and writing activity is a powerful way to help students develop their cognitive abilities in reading and writing about scientific concepts.

### 4. POSTREADING/WRITING/REWRITING

After the students have read the assignment, model metacognitive skills to demonstrate what you (the teacher) were thinking as you read and reread the chapter. Skill in metacognitive thinking, or the ability to articulate what we know and don't know through reading, helps us to become better comprehenders and composers (Palinscar & Brown, 1984). Describe your thoughts as they relate to revising the initial draft of your own model paragraph. Display on the chalkboard or overhead all of the new concepts and terms that you expect the students to include in their second and final drafts, which in this example describe the solar system. In this way you will make sure that all relevant ideas are covered in preparation for the unit exam.

*(continued)*

**Inside the Classroom (continued)**

*Day 2, 8:05 A.M.*

MS. STEFFEN: What did you think about the chapter sections describing our Earth, moon, sun, and solar system? Did you learn anything new? I know I did. As I was reading I noticed several terms that were either in bold print or were italicized. When textbook authors highlight terms in this way, it's a clue that we need to pay attention to these ideas because they're important to our overall understanding. For example, when I was reading the section on comets, I had to slow down and reread certain italicized parts, especially when the author talked about the comet's nucleus, tail, and coma. [Ms. Steffen rereads the relevant paragraphs aloud.] Coma, I thought, is a strange name for what is evidently the glowing cloud that surrounds a comet's nucleus. I also thought to myself that I should definitely include this information in my paper on the solar system. So I made a note of these and other interesting terms below my first draft. But before I show you my list, I'd like to hear from you. What were you thinking while you read that will help you when revising your first drafts?

KAREN: I thought it [the reading assignment] was cool. Especially the part about Saturn's rings that are made of ice. I didn't know that before.

LARRY: And the part about meteors. Meteors are really falling stars. I saw a falling star last summer at my grandparents' farm.

MARY: I liked the chart that showed the size of each planet and its radius and how long it takes the planets to go around the sun. It's really neat.

MARK: I didn't understand anything I read in the chapter. Can we look through the telescope again, Ms. Steffen?

MS. STEFFEN: Yes, Mark. The telescope will be in the room for the next three weeks as we study the universe. During writing time I'll be over to help you with your first draft and your problems understanding the chapter. For now, listen carefully, and I think you'll learn a lot.

The class discussion of the first half of the chapter continued along these lines as the students made a variety of contributions. Ms. Steffen listened attentively and responded with genuine interest and enthusiasm. She then revealed her own model first draft and list of chapter terms that she had compiled while reading. She indicated to the students that these were concepts important enough to be included in revised drafts. After reading her example and reviewing the list of terms, she gave each student a handout made from the overhead transparency.

## OUR SOLAR SYSTEM BY MS. STEFFEN, EIGHTH-GRADE TEACHER

*Our solar system is made up of many interesting elements. The sun is at the center of the system, and nine planets orbit the sun. These planets are Earth, Venus, Jupiter, Mars, Uranus, Mercury, Neptune, Pluto, and Saturn. The planet Earth is a rocky planet that contains life as we know it. Saturn is a gaseous planet and probably does not support life forms like ours. Saturn has rings. Jupiter has many moons while Earth has only one. We can sometimes see comets or asteroids streaking across the sky at night. The last sighting of the famous Halley's comet was in 1986. Some scientists believe that black holes exist in our universe, but this has not yet been proven to be true.*

### New Concepts Learned While Reading "Astronomy"*

| | |
|---|---|
| astronomy | meteorite |
| rotation | coma |
| revolution | galaxy |
| constellations | nuclear fusion |
| satellite | sunspots |
| phases | solar eclipse |
| meteor | lunar eclipse |

### 5. WRITING/REWRITING/EDITING

Direct the students to revise their original drafts to include new information learned about the solar system as well as any recommendations made by peers during the prereading and Writers' Workshop (conducted the previous day). Point out that some rereading may be necessary to ensure full comprehension and accurate compositions. As the students finish their second drafts, these papers are responded to by the teacher and returned to the students during small-group or individual conferences (See Chapter 8 for more discussion on flexible grouping.)

### 8:40 A.M.

MS. STEFFEN: For the next twenty to twenty-five minutes I want you to get started on revising your initial drafts. Use the handout as a guide to make sure that you're covering all the important terms. Be sure to reread chapter parts if there's an idea you think you missed or don't understand. I'll be working on my revision, too, but I'm also available to help whenever you need it. You are also free to ask a friend for help provided you're not preventing that person from getting some good work done this morning.

*(continued)*

*Brockway, Gardner, & Howe (1985, pp. 369–381.)

**Inside the Classroom (continued)**

Tomorrow we'll reserve the whole class period for writing, rewriting, and editing. We'll also work in small groups so you can have an opportunity to respond to one another's work as we move along. By Thursday we should be ready to finish up our final drafts. If there's time on that day I'm going to read aloud the last two sections of the chapter. They are called "The Universe" and "Tools of Astronomy." The last part of the chapter will help you to think about possibilities for library research projects that we'll be doing as part of the whole unit on the Earth and space science. On Friday we will all go to the media center and learn where all of the science-related books, films, videotapes, and software are located.

*Reflections on Day 2*

The second day of Ms. Steffen's lesson reveals the importance of teacher modeling. She encourages listening and oral language through a focused discussion of the chapter content. And she demonstrates through metacognitive modeling and her own model paragraph how the reading and writing assignments are related, as well as how one goes about comprehending and composing. Her methodology combines declarative and procedural knowledge, both of which are necessary for students to develop adequate strategies to comprehend and to compose. Her willingness to participate in the students' learning process helps her to control the class. She uses a combination of direct instruction and child-centered activity that is effective largely because of the mutual respect between her and the students.

Not every reading assignment in a middle school or junior high course will lend itself to the incorporation of writing. The teacher will want to choose chapters or chapter segments exhibiting the following characteristics, which appear to influence reading comprehension in both theory and practice:

1. Choose a topic that is not altogether unfamiliar to the students to facilitate teacher modeling of the use of prior knowledge as an aid in comprehending and composing.

   Recent research clearly shows "that possession of relevant topic knowledge prior to reading strongly affects comprehension" (Anderson & Armbruster, 1984, p. 213). The first four sections of the chapter "Astronomy" (Brockway, Gardner, & Howe, 1985) cover topics familiar to most eighth-graders. Most will have heard of the solar system, stars, and planets but may not know such concepts as gaseous and rocky planets, comas, or meteoroids. Using familiar topics also aids in teacher modeling of metacognitive skills (Palinscar & Brown, 1984), recommended as a postreading activity in the directed reading and writing lesson.

2. Make certain the reading assignment reflects text structure that is clearly indicative of the structures found most often in a particular content area.

   A reader's recognition and knowledge of text structure appears to aid in understanding and retention of information (Meyer & Freedle, 1984). Structures typically found in most expository texts include description, collection, causation, problem and solution, and comparison (McGee & Richgels, 1985). Robinson (1983) provides a thorough explanation of the patterns of writing that occur in science, social studies, English, and math textbooks. Brockway, Gardner, and Howe (1985) use descriptive discourse, definitions, and illustrations in the chapter that explain the use of astronomy in the study of Earth and space.

3. Choose a reading assignment of manageable length, one that could be read in a single class period by most students.

   Controlling the length of the reading part of the DRWL is especially important in view of the writing assignment. Students will be expected to include in their compositions new information learned through reading. Too many new concepts could overload students' memory and therefore defeat the overall purpose of the writing assignment—to improve reading comprehension. The reading assignment in Ms. Steffen's lesson is the first eleven pages of an astronomy chapter in an eighth-grade general science text (Brockway, Gardner, & Howe, 1985). Her listening activity, reserved for later in the week, consists of the remaining six pages in the chapter.

***Final Reflections.***     The directed reading and writing lesson emphasizes direct explanation of reading and writing processes and activities (Roehler & Duffy, 1984). Throughout the lesson, the teacher is explaining, describing, defining, modeling, reminding, and most important, helping students to accomplish their purposes for reading and writing. The teacher is not just a classroom manager but rather serves as a model, who as Pearson (1985) argues, "assumes a more central active role in providing instruction" (p. 736). Such a role encourages active student participation in reading and writing processes because school takes on a new sensibility, one that is particularly pleasurable and meaningful to students. And once students realize how writing about what they read helps to improve their reading comprehension, they will more readily become independent readers and writers in the content areas. Reading and writing across the curriculum is an especially important goal for middle school and junior high students. The directed reading and writing lesson has the potential to fulfill this goal.

## How Do You Know What You Know?

Educational aphorism: You can lead a student to a textbook, but you can't make 'em think.

Seventh-graders are given valuable time in the library to read and respond to young-adult literature.

### NONEXAMPLE: THE UN-QUIZ

**MR. FLINT:** *Today's oral quiz is on Chapter 1 of* Huckleberry Finn [Twain, 1987a]. *Quinton, what is the setting for Mark Twain's novel?*

**QUINTON:** *It takes place on the Mississippi in a small town.*

**MR. FLINT:** *How do you know?*

**QUINTON:** *I don't know. I just know. You know what I mean?*

**MR. FLINT:** *No, I don't know what you mean. Can you explain how you came to know the setting of* Huckleberry Finn?

**QUINTON** (Now frustrated): *No! I mean I just can't say it. I can't think of the words. You know?*

**MR. FLINT:** *So you mean you just guessed the answer?*

**QUINTON:** *No. I didn't guess. I mean I really knew what the answer was* *before I ever read the dumb chapter. I just forgot how I knew it. You know? Or maybe I did read it someplace.*

**MR. FLINT:** *How could you know the answer before ever reading Chapter 1? I don't think you really know what this chapter is all about. If you can't tell me how you knew about the setting, then I think probably someone just whispered the answer in your ear. Right, Erica?*

**ERICA:** *I don't know.*

The somewhat amusing dialogue between Mr. Flint and his students is reminiscent of a 1920s vaudeville act in which the players' conversation is filled with exaggerations and puns, all for comic effect. In this eighth-grade classroom scene, however, the context is serious as the teacher as questioner attempts to probe the metacognitive awareness of the learner. *Metacognition* refers to "one's knowledge concerning one's own cognitive processes and products or anything related to them" (Flavelle, 1976, p. 232). Thinking and behaving metacognitively require us to articulate what it is we know or do not know about a subject. The task may seem simple enough. But as just illustrated, it is not so easy for students to explain what they know. Quinton's remark, "I can't think of the words," is a clear indication that he does not yet have sufficient vocabulary or conceptual knowledge to explain his understanding of setting in *Huckleberry Finn.*

Helping students to develop their metacognitive abilities is an important aspect of the reading and writing curriculum. Monitoring comprehension, for example, is one strategy necessary for active involvement in both reading (Wagoner, 1983) and writing processes (Birnbaum, 1986). A student who is not emotionally and intellectually involved in the text *while* reading or writing will probably not be an effective comprehender or composer. By asking students to tell us how they went about achieving their purposes for reading or writing, we learn if they have been actively involved in the reading, writing, and thinking process (M. F. Heller, 1986b).

Not all students have the language skills necessary to describe the cognitive processes they employ while reading and writing. Metacognitive modeling activities are useful when teaching students how to verbalize their understanding of an unfolding text. The following model lesson illustrates the think-aloud strategy we used in Chapter 3 entitled "What I Know." The setting for the lesson is an eighth-grade English class.

## INSIDE THE CLASSROOM
### What I Know*

**1. PREREADING/PREWRITING**

Explain to the students that you are going to show them how to become better readers of literature and also better writers by teaching them a "think-aloud" strategy. The strategy, called "What I Know," enables students to describe what they know and don't know (or find confusing) about a subject before, during, and after reading (or writing) a short story, poem, essay, or novel excerpt. (Grammar text chapters may also be used.) Being aware of what we know and don't know about any topic is useful in determining whether or not we can achieve our purpose for reading a lesson. This same knowledge helps us to monitor our composing efforts as we strive to construct a meaningful text while writing.

Distribute What I Know sheets that will include the following information:

**a.** The specific reading assignment that you and ultimately the students will use to model metacognitive strategies

**b.** The purpose for reading the lesson, stated in question form (This space is left blank until after a purpose for reading is established by the teacher and students.)

**c.** Three columns of information that reflect different types of cognition:

**Column A:** *What I Already Know (completed before reading). This column includes concepts that the student knew before reading the assignment and will thus aid in achieving the purpose for reading.*

**Column B:** *What I Now Know (completed while reading). This column includes new concepts encountered in the text that the student should think about to help answer the purpose question.*

**Column C:** *What I Don't Know (completed during and after reading). This column includes concepts that are still confusing to the student in the context of the reading assignment and therefore might interfere with the ability to answer the purpose question.*

**d.** The purpose for writing, with a preliminary topic and writing form identified (The teacher- and student-generated topics and forms for writing will be an outgrowth of the reading assignment and accompanying discussions. A purpose for writing may be established early in the lesson and revised later if necessary.)

---

*Adapted from M. F. Heller (1986b, 1986c).

Begin the reading/writing lesson by activating the students' prior knowledge of the literary subject by discussing a concept central to the main idea or theme of the reading lesson. Model for the students what you expect them to do in each column of their What I Know sheets. Together establish clear purposes for reading and writing.

### Day 1, 10:30 A.M.

DR. BRILEY (A master middle school English teacher with a PhD and twenty-five years of experience, Briley directs the students' attention to this sentence on the chalkboard: "This is for your own good."): Has anyone in here ever heard this before? *"This is for your own good."* [The students murmur among themselves.]

RODNEY: I have. I hear it every weekend when my folks lock me in my room so I can't sneak out at night with my friends and cruise the strip. But what do they know, right, Doc? [The class laughs. They know that Rodney is joking about being locked in his room.]

BRILEY: Knowing you *and* your folks, Rod, being locked in your room for the weekend might not be such a bad idea. [More laughter.] Any other examples?

KAREN: I used to hear it all the time when I was little. "Eat your peas. It's for your own good. Take your medicine. It's for your own good." Blah, blah, blah. Now it's "Do your homework. It's for your own good." I'll be glad when I'm eighteen so I can make my own decisions.

BRILEY: But don't you think you'll always have to make decisions about what's good for you and for those you're responsible for? I'm forty-seven years old, and I still have to think about what's good for me. Like exercise. My doctor tells me that I need to exercise thirty minutes every day, "For your own good," he says. I look at my physical and take him seriously. I hate to exercise, but I want to be around at least another forty-seven years.

LOUIE: Gee, Dr. Briley. I knew you were fat, but I didn't know you were *that old.* [Class laughs. Briley smiles and takes the comment with good humor. He has already established the kind of rapport with his students that allows for joking during a serious lesson.]

BRILEY: Thanks for your observations, Louie. Glad you're paying attention this morning. The sentence "This is for your own good" is from Chapter 12 of Mark Twain's [1987b] novel *The Adventures of Tom Sawyer,* which we're going to be reading and then writing about. Tell me what you already know about Mark Twain and Tom Sawyer.

*(continued)*

**Inside the Classroom (continued)**

EVELYN: Twain wrote *Huckleberry Finn*. We read it last year. And Tom Sawyer was in that book. He was Huck's friend. They got into trouble a lot.

BRILEY: Very good, Evelyn. And we're going to be reading all of *The Adventures of Tom Sawyer* this semester. Chapter 12 stands nicely alone, like a short story. I'm hoping it will get all of you interested in reading the entire novel. I have here on the overhead what's called a "What I Know" sheet. It has three columns. Column A is labeled "What I Already Know." I'm going to write Evelyn's comment in this column because it represents what many of you already know about the author and the character in our reading assignment. What do you think the chapter is going to be about, given the fact that "This is for your own good" is a sentence taken from the chapter and that it is sometimes called "The Cat and the Pain-Killer"?

BOB: It's probably about a cat that gets sick and eats some painkiller. Or maybe Tom Sawyer gives the cat some drugs. Hey, maybe Tom Sawyer's really a drug dealer. [Class laughs.] Or a cat killer! [More laughter.]

BRILEY: I doubt it, Bob. Mark Twain's stories are a bit tamer than that, don't you think? Can anyone give me a good reason or purpose for reading the short story, based on what you think it's about?

CARLA: I think Tom Sawyer is going to give a cat some medicine for its own good. Tom Sawyer's always getting into trouble. The cat's probably going to die or something like that.

BRILEY: Sounds like a reasonable guess. Can anyone put Carla's suggestions into question form so we can have a *purpose* question in mind while we're reading? [The class is used to formulating purposes for reading and writing.]

CYNTHIA: Why does Tom Sawyer give the cat some painkiller?

BRILEY: Good. Notice I'm writing the purpose question on the What I Know sheet right here where it says, "Purpose for Reading." While you are reading the short story, I want you to think about the purpose question and try to answer it.

   As you are reading you'll be learning new things about Tom Sawyer that will allow you to answer the question. Those new ideas should be written here in Column B, called "What I Now Know," or what you learn while you're reading that helps you to comprehend the story and achieve your purpose for reading. For example, while I was reading the story I learned that the cat's name is Peter. I think that's important enough to put in Column B.

Column C, "What I Don't Know," is for those vocabulary words, events, or whole ideas that are confusing to you while you're reading or even after you've finished the story. These are ideas that you might have questions about during our discussions. In other words, information that you write in Column C might get in the way of understanding the story. For example, a sentence in the story that confused me was "Tom tried to whistle her down the wind." I wrote it in Column C because it confused me, and I wanted to find out what it meant.

It's just as important to know what you understand as well as what you don't understand while reading or while writing. I'm distributing a blank What I Know sheet to each of you now, and I'd like you to try using it with the reading assignment. When we're all through reading, I'll show you my sheet and tell you about what I was thinking while I read "The Cat and the Pain-Killer." Questions?

**JACK:** You mean we're supposed to write all that stuff down just so we can answer the purpose question?

**BRILEY:** Yes. Writing these ideas down helps you to be really actively involved in the story. It will keep you alert. There's one more reason to write what you know and don't know, and that has to do with a purpose for writing. While you're reading the short story, I want you to think about one more thing—that is, what would be a good topic for you to write on after reading about "The Cat and the Painkiller"? For example, since we know this story has something to do with things in our lives that we have to do for our own good, what might be a simple writing topic?

**LESLIE:** How about the time I had to go to the dentist for my own good?

**ROCKY:** Yeah, and the time I had to chop wood at my grandad's for my own good.

**BRILEY:** That's the kind of thinking I like to hear. If you already have some purposes for writing in mind, write your topic ideas on your sheet where it's labeled "Purposes for Writing" so you don't forget.

You have the rest of the class period to read the novel excerpt. [Briley distributes copies of the reading assignment.] If you have questions about filling out the sheet while you're reading, I'm available to help. I'm going to be writing a paper called "Exercise Is for My Own Good," which I'll be sharing with you later in the week. Tomorrow we'll talk about the story and about what you know and don't know.

*(continued)*

## Inside the Classroom (continued)

### 2. Sustained Silent Reading/Prewriting

Instruct the students to read silently. Encourage them to use their What I Know sheet and to take some notes that will help them achieve their purpose for reading.

#### 10:55 A.M.

The class reads for the remaining twenty-five to thirty minutes of class. Dr. Briley answers individual student's questions about filling out the What I Know sheet.

### Reflections on Day 1

A key element in Dr. Briley's success as a teacher is his obvious rapport with the students. He is able to make jokes at his own expense, he listens carefully to the students' responses, and they in turn listen to him. The teacher as mentor is a concept to be highly regarded in the middle level and junior high classroom, where impressionable adolescents need role models. Before one can be a model teacher, however, one must have the students' respect and attention. What I Know is an activity that requires a good deal of teacher planning. Modeling what we think about before, during, and after reading is not as simple as it may seem on the surface. Dr. Briley had thoroughly prepared for this lesson, providing excellent visual aids in the form of a clear overhead transparency and handouts. When middle school and junior high students sense that their teachers know what they are doing and simultaneously care about learning, they will be more willing to listen, read, and write.

### 3. Postreading/Prewriting

A. When everyone has completed the reading assignment, write on the chalkboard or place on an overhead a copy of your own completed What I Know sheet. Next, describe for the students what you were thinking—what metacognitive strategies were used—while reading and constructing the answer to the purpose question. For example, you may choose to illustrate compensatory monitoring strategies, such as slowing down, rereading, or ignoring confusing parts and reading on (Collins & Smith, 1980). While you are talking, the students should be comparing their What I Know responses to yours.

### Day 2, 10:30 A.M.

>    **Briley:** I'd like everyone to take a look at my What I Know sheet here on the overhead.
>
>    You'll notice that I really didn't have to write a whole lot to come

**What I Know**

Reading: Chapter 12, *The Adventures of Tom Sawyer,* pp. 96—102.
Purpose for Reading: Why did Tom Sawyer give Aunt Polly's cat some painkiller?

| What I Know | What I Now Know | What I Don't Know |
|---|---|---|
| Tom Sawyer is very mischievous.<br>He likes Becky Thatcher but doesn't want anyone to know.<br>He is Huck's best friend. | Tom Sawyer misses Becky Thatcher very much. Aunt Polly gives him medicine to try to cure his indifference.<br>She tells him it's for his own good.<br>Tom thinks the painkiller is quack medicine. Tom poured the painkiller down a crack in the floor; later, he gave it to the cat that just happened to walk by. When the cat behaved strangely, Tom decided to use this as an example of what it felt like to drink the terrible medicine. Aunt Polly felt bad and decided to stop making Tom take the painkiller. | Tom tried to "whistle her down the wind." |

**Purposes for Writing:** To describe why exercise is good for me. My writing topic will be "Exercise Is for My Own Good."

up with an answer to the purpose question. For example, look in Column B, where I wrote, "Tom Sawyer misses Becky Thatcher very much; Aunt Polly gives him medicine to try to cure his indifference."

While I was reading the first few paragraphs of "The Cat and the Pain-Killer," I learned that Tom Sawyer was heartsick because Becky Thatcher had stopped coming to school. This made him so moody that Aunt Polly thought he was ill and started giving him home remedies to cure him. I thought this might have something to do with his eventually giving the cat some painkiller, so I wrote that information in Column B.

Would anyone care to share some of the new things you learned that helped you answer the purpose question?

*(continued)*

**Inside the Classroom (continued)**

A good discussion followed, with several students volunteering information from their sheets. Typical responses in Column B, What I Now Know,
included such details as these: Aunt Polly believed in quack medicine. Tom had
to take painkiller medicine, which tasted terrible. Tom pretended to like the
painkiller when he was actually pouring it down a crack in the floor. When
Aunt Polly figured out that Tom gave the cat a dose of painkiller, she felt sad.
She thought that she had been inhumane to Tom, even though she meant well.

> BRILEY: Would anyone care to suggest an answer to our purpose for read-
> ing question? Why did Tom give Aunt Polly's cat, Peter, the
> painkiller?
>
> SYLVIA: I think he did it to show Aunt Polly what it really felt like for a boy
> to have to take that awful medicine.
>
> BRILEY: How do you know? What makes you think so?
>
> SYLVIA: Because when Aunt Polly asked Tom why he did it, he said he did
> it out of pity for the cat. Tom said that the cat didn't have an aunt
> who could try out medicines on him.
>
> BRILEY: Where in the story did you learn this information?
>
> SYLVIA: Tom said it right here on page 100: "Heaps. Because if he'd a had
> one [an aunt] she'd a burnt him out herself! She'd a roasted his bow-
> els out of him 'thout any more feeling than if he was a human." That's
> what got Aunt Polly to thinking about what she'd done. That's why
> she decided not to make Tom drink the medicine anymore.
>
> BRILEY: A very fine answer, Sylvia. Does anyone have a different answer
> to the purpose question?
>
> [Several students volunteer variations of Sylvia's answer. Typical
> responses are "Tom gave the cat some painkiller so his aunt would
> stop giving him medicine"; "Tom pretended the cat was him and
> gave it the painkiller to show Aunt Polly what it felt like."]
>
> BRILEY: Take a look at my purpose question response. I wrote that Tom
> Sawyer probably gave the painkiller to the cat for two reasons. As I
> was reading I thought that Tom Sawyer behaved as he usually does.
> He was really a mischievous boy who probably gave Peter the
> painkiller only because the cat happened to walk by as Tom was
> pouring the medicine down the crack. This information is on pages
> 98-99. I reread this part slowly to make sure I fully understood what
> was going on. After the cat acted so strangely and Aunt Polly was
> astonished by the cat's behavior, Tom realized that he could use the

incident to his benefit by comparing himself to the cat. That's what made Aunt Polly feel guilty and stop forcing the painkiller medicine on Tom. I thought to myself, Tom's a quick thinker, too.

B. Following the explanation of your comprehension monitoring strategies, encourage the students to explain how they came to understand the story. Use this whole-class discussion as a time to reinforce think-aloud strategies that help us to be better comprehenders and composers, that is, to fulfill our purposes for reading and writing.

An alternative to whole-class discussion is to have the students form small, heterogeneous discussion groups of three or four good and poor readers. The purpose of this type of follow-up activity is to give the students immediate practice modeling their own metacognitive strategies with the same reading material. Direct the students to take turns describing what they did to achieve their purpose for reading. During this phase of the lesson, it important to move among groups, lending support and encouragement. The students should compare their concepts and answers to those of the teacher and their peers, discuss similarities and differences, and ultimately decide which strategies seem to offer the best answer to the purpose question.

BRILEY: Would anyone like to share with the class information that you put in on any part of your What I Know sheet? Listen to one another's contributions and compare what your classmates say to what you wrote.

Several students volunteer information from their What I Know sheets.

BRILEY: I mentioned yesterday my problem with "whistle her down the wind," which you can see I've written in Column C, What I Don't Know. Can anyone tell me what Tom meant?

SALLY: He meant that he tried to forget about Becky Thatcher, to put her out of his mind, by whistling and thinking about someone else.

BRILEY: How do you know? What makes you think that's what Tom meant by "whistle her down the wind"?

SALLY: Because of what he says and does just before and just after. He didn't really want anyone to know that he liked her. He was too proud to admit it. But then he was miserable because she was sick and couldn't come to school. He couldn't put her out of his mind. It's a lot like my older brother Ken, who's in college. He likes this girl named Laura but she doesn't even know he exists so he tries to put her out of his mind by doing other stuff.

*(continued)*

**Inside the Classroom (continued)**

**BRILEY:** So Tom Sawyer was lovesick?

**SALLY:** Right.

**BRILEY:** Is that why Aunt Polly gave him the painkiller?

**ROSEANNE:** Yes. I put that part in Column B. I also wrote that Aunt Polly was stupid. Everybody knows that medicine doesn't cure puppy love.

**CARL:** You mean cat love, Roseanne. [Class groans.]

**BRILEY:** Do you think Aunt Polly is a bad person?

**ROSEANNE:** No. She's probably really nice, but weird. She reminds me of my Aunt Eleanora. My Aunt Eleanora sleeps with a bunch of garlic around her neck to ward off evil spirits whenever her zodiac chart tells her to. Strange. [Class laughs.]

**BRILEY:** Does anyone have a purpose for writing that they would care to share?

**KEVIN:** I'm going to write about the time my dog, Tisha, ate some rat poison that was behind our piano.

**BRILEY:** How did you come up with your topic, Kevin?

**KEVIN:** When I read the part about the cat acting so nutty it reminded me of how Tisha acted when she ate the poison. We had to take her to the vet.

**BRILEY:** I look forward to your narrative.


#### 4. SUSTAINED BUT NOT NECESSARILY SILENT WRITING

The transition between the reading and writing assignment begins when students fulfill their purpose for writing by completing the first draft of their paper. Purposes for writing should be primarily student-generated, as in the previous example, although teacher-directed writing assignments could include such topics as a descriptive paragraph on "Knowing What I Know." In this paragraph, the students describe how their own understanding of what they know and don't know will help them to be better readers of literature and ultimately better writers. Paragraphs are then shared with classmates.

The students' What I Know sheets are kept in a folder to be used as references in future comprehension monitoring activities. The teacher will also find the information on the sheets and in student writing useful when observing comprehension and composition progress over time. The What I Know assignment remains a written record of the students' thinking process before, during, and after reading.

**11:00 A.M.**

> **DR. BRILEY:** For the next twenty-five to thirty minutes I'd like you to get started on your first drafts [printed below]. You'll want to keep your What I Know sheets handy to refer back to, especially if there's information from the story that you want to include in your paper. I'll be around to answer questions. Anyone who's still struggling with a topic to write about should meet with me here at the Editor's Desk. [Three students move forward to a table located at the front of the room.] You may quietly ask one another's help. Tomorrow we'll devote the whole class period to writing, and then on Thursday we'll have a Writers' Workshop and go over first, second, or final drafts, depending on how far each of you has progressed by then.

## TISHA AND THE RAT POISON

by Kevin, Grade 8

> *One day my dog Tisha ate some rat poison that was behind our piano. We didn't notice that she had done it until she started acting weird. She started running around the room rubbing her nose in the carpet. Then she whined like she wanted to go outside. I took her outside and she went to her water dish and drank all the water up. Then she laid down and sort of had a spasm like a fit. Just then my dad discovered the torn apart rat poison container, and he figured out that Tisha probably ate it. We rushed her to the vet. The vet gave her some medicine that coated her stomach and made her throw up. After that she stayed at the hospital all night. The next day we got to bring her home.*

### Peer Response (Amy)

1. What did you like best about the writing?

   *I liked Kevin's story because it seemed true to life. He told everything that happened, except for maybe the last part after they brought Tisha home.*

2. Did anything confuse or bother you about the writing?

   *How did you get Tisha in the car? How did the vet get the dog to eat the medicine? If the rat poison was behind the piano, how did Tisha get to it to eat it?*

3. What advice do you have for the author?

   *I'd like to know the answers to my questions. When you rewrite the story, tell a little bit more about what happened after you brought Tisha home. Did she stay away from behind the piano?*

***Final Reflections.***    For students to become independent monitors of their own reading comprehension, the teacher's metacognitive modeling ought to be an ongoing event in any classroom. Such demonstrations should take place again and again—perhaps as often as once a week. Middle school teachers will want to vary the assignment to accommodate a variety of text structures and purposes for reading and writing both fiction and nonfiction. Ultimately, teacher modeling should give way to student modeling within small groups and finally to independent modeling and improved reading, writing, and thinking among all students.

## FOR YOUR JOURNAL

1. Interview an adolescent or group of adolescents. Ask them about their memories of learning to read and write in the elementary grades (K–4). What insights do the students give you about schooling?
2. Analyze the curriculum language arts at one middle school grade level (5–9). Answer this question: "What skills are expendable?" In other words, can you eliminate reteaching certain ideas that seem to have been covered again and again during the previous years (e.g., "Underline the noun once and the verb twice")?
3. Choose a traditional grammar lesson from a middle school language arts textbook. Write a lesson plan that teaches the grammatical concepts within the context of composing and comprehending connected text.
4. Prepare a What I Know sheet on a favorite piece of adolescent literature, complete with a model writing assignment. Teach the literature lesson to a group of middle school students. Make some observations about the students' metacognitive abilities before, during, and after your lesson.

## SELECTED BOOKS FOR ADOLESCENTS

### Illustrated Fiction

Arnosky, Jim (1988), *Gray Boy,* Lothrop.
Branscum, Robbie (1987, *Johnny May Grow Up,* Harper & Row.
Byars, Betsy (1987), *The Not-Just-Anybody Family,* Delacorte Press.
Fleischman, Paul (1982), *Graven Images,* Harper & Row.
Fox, Paula (1973), *The Slave Dancer,* Bradbury.
Fox, Paula (1984), *The One-Eyed Cat,* Bradbury.
George, Jean Craighead (1972), *Julie of the Wolves,* Harper & Row.
Hamilton, Virginia (1986), *The Planet of Junior Brown,* Macmillan.
Houston, James (1977), *Frozen Fire: A Tale of Courage,* Macmillan.
Jaques, Brian (1987), *Redwall,* Philomel.
Jukes, Mavis (1985), *Blackberries in the Dark,* Knopf.

Paterson, Katherine (1977), *Bridge to Terabithia,* Crowell.
Pinkwater, Daniel (1986), *The Muffin Friend,* Lothrop.
Noyes, Alfred (1983), *The Highwayman,* Lothrop.
Van Allsburg, Chris (1984), *The Mysteries of Harris Burdick,* Houghton Mifflin.
Wisler, G. Clifton (1986), *The Antrain Messenger,* Lodestar.
Yolen, Jane (1987), *A Sending of Dragons,* Delacorte Press.

## Fiction

Adlers, C. S. (1987), *Carly's Buck,* Clarion.
Aiken, Joan (1985), *Midnight Is a Place,* Dell.
Aiken, Joan (1986), *The Shadow Guests,* Dell.
Alcock, Vivien (1986), *The Cuckoo Sister,* Delacorte Press.
Alcock, Vivien (1987), *The Mysterious Mr. Ross,* Delacorte Press.
Alexander, Lloyd (1978), *The Book of Three,* Dell.
Alexander, Lloyd (1987), *The Eldorado Adventure,* Dutton.
Anderson, Margaret J. (1980), *Journey of the Shadow Bairns,* Knopf.
Bacon, Katharine Jay (1987), *Shadow and Light,* McElderry.
Baehr, Patricia (1987), *Falling Scales,* Morrow.
Bawden, Nina (1973), *Carrie's War,* Harper & Row.
Bedard, Michael (1987), *A Darker Magic,* Atheneum.
Blackwood, Gary L. (1987), *Wild Timothy,* Atheneum.
Blume, Judy (1987), *Just as Long as We're Together,* Orchard/Dell.
Brett, Simon (1987), *The Three Detectives and the Knight in Armor,* Scribner.
Brooks, Bruce (1986), *Midnight Hour Encores,* Harper & Row.
Brooks, Bruce (1986), *The Moves Make the Man,* Harper & Row.
Byars, Betsy (1981), *The Summer of the Swans,* Penguin Books.
Cameron, Elanore (1973), *The Court of Stone Children,* Dutton.
Cavanna, Betty (1987), *Banner Year,* Morrow.
Chetwin, Grace (1987), *The Riddle and the Rune,* Macmillan/Bradbury.
Christopher, John (1967), *The White Mountains,* Macmillan.
Cleaver, Bill, & Cleaver, Vera (1969), *Where the Lilies Bloom,* Harper & Row.
Climo, Shirley (1987), *A Month of Seven Days,* Crowell.
Cole, Brock (1987), *The Goats,* Farrar, Straus & Giroux.
Collier, James L. (1974), *My Brother Sam Is Dead,* Macmillan.
Cooper, Susan (1986), *The Dark Is Rising,* Macmillan.
Corbin, William (1987), *A Dog Worth Stealing,* Orchard/Watts.
Creswell, Helen (1987), *Moondial,* Macmillan.
Danzinger, Paula (1987), *Remember Me to Harold Square,* Delacorte Press.
DeFord, Deborah H., & Stout, Harr S. (1987), *An Enemy among Them,* Houghton Mifflin.
de Trevino, Elizabeth Borton (1965), *I, Juan De Pareja,* Farrar, Straus & Giroux.
DeJong, Meindert (1987), *The House of Sixty Fathers,* Harper & Row.
Desei, Anita (1988), *The Village by the Sea: An Indian Family Story,* Chivers Press.
Dunlop, Eileen (1987), *The House on the Hill,* Holiday.
Edwards, Pat (1987), *Nelda,* Houghton Mifflin.
Fitzhugh, Louise (1986), *Nobody's Family Is Going to Change,* Farrar, Straus & Giroux.
Fleischman, Paul (1983), *Path of the Pale Horse,* Harper & Row.
George, Jean Craighead (1987), *Water Sky,* Harper & Row.

Gorman, Crol (1987), *Chelsey and the Green-haired Kid*, Houghton Mifflin.

Greene, Bette (1986), *Summer of My German Soldier*, Bantam Books.

Guest, Elissa Haden (1986), *Over the Moon*, Morrow.

Hall, Lynn (1987), *Ride a Dark Horse*, Morrow.

Hamilton, Virginia (1983), *The Magical Adventures of Pretty Pearl*, Harper & Row.

Haynes, Betsy (1986), *The Great Mom Swap*, Bantam Books.

Hill, Douglas (1987), *Planet of the Warlord*, Dell.

Hinton, S. E. (1980), *Tex*, Dell.

Holl, Kristi D. (1987), *Patchwork Summer*, Atheneum.

Hoppe, Joanne (1987), *Pretty Penny Farm*, Morrow.

Howker, Janni (1987), *Badger on the Barge*, Penguin Books.

Hughes, Monica (1981), *The Keeper of the Isis Light*, Atheneum.

Hughes, Dean (1987), *The Zephr*, Atheneum.

Hunt, Irene (1988), *Up the Road Slowly*, Scholastic Books.

Hunter, Mollie (1975), *A Stranger Came Ashore*, Harper & Row.

Irwin, Hadley (1987), *Kim/Kimi*, McElderry.

Jacobs, Paul Samuel (1988), *Born into Light*, Scholastic Books.

Jones, Diana Wynne (1988), *Dobsbody*, Greenwillow.

Jones, Diana Wynne (1981), *The Homeward Bounders*, Greenwillow.

Jones, Diana Wynne (1988), *The Eight Days of Luke*, Greenwillow.

Johnston, Norma (1986), *The Watcher in the Mist*, Bantam Books.

Kherdian, David (1987), *Bridger: The Story of a Mountain Man*, Greenwillow.

Killien, Christi (1987), *All of the Above*, Houghton Mifflin.

Kipling, Rudyard (1987), *Kim*, Penguin Books.

Langton, Jane (1973), *The Diamond in the Window*, Harper & Row.

Levoy, Myron (1987), *Alan and Naomi*, Harper & Row.

Lunn, Janet (1983), *The Root Cellar*, Scribner.

Mark, Jan (1985), *Handles*, Atheneum.

Mark, Jan (1987), *Thunder and Lightnings*, Harper & Row.

Mayhar, Ardath (1987), *Makra Choria*, Atheneum.

Mayne, William (1986), *Drift*, Delacorte Press.

Mazer, Norma Fox (1987), *A, My Name is Ami*, Scholastic Books.

Murphy, Shirlye Rousseau (1987), *The Ivory Lyre*, Harper & Row.

Murray, Marguerite (1987), *Odin's Eye*, Atheneum.

Murrow, Liza Ketchum (1987), *West against the Wind*, Holiday.

Naylor, Phyllis Reynolds (1986), *The Keeper*, Atheneum.

O'Dell, Scott (1960), *Island of the Blue Dolphins*, Houghton Mifflin.

O'Dell, Scott (1987), *The Serpent Never Sleeps: A Novel of Jamestown and Pocahontas*, Houghton Mifflin.

Park, Ruth (1980), *Play Beatie Bow*, Atheneum.

Paterson, Katherine (1978), *The Great Gilly Hopkins*, Crowell.

Paulsen, Gary (1984), *Tracker*, Bradbury.

Paulsen, Gary (1985), *Dogsong*, Bradbury.

Paulsen, Gary (1986), *Sentries*, Bradbury.

Paulsen, Gary (1987), *Hatchet*, Macmillan/Bradbury.

Peck, Richard (1983), *The Ghost Belonged to Me*, Dell.

Ransom, Candice (1987), *Fourteen and Holding*, Scholastic Books.

Richter, Hans Peter (1987), *I Was There*, Penguin Books.

Rodgers, Mary (1972), *Freaky Friday*, Harper & Row.

Rostkowski, Margaret I. (1986), *After the Dancing Days,* Harper & Row.
Rylant, Cynthia (1986), *A Fine White Dust,* Bradbury.
Sachs, Marilyn (1979), *A Summer's Lease,* Dutton.
Savage, Deborah (1986), *A Rumor of Otters,* Houghton Mifflin.
Sebestyen, Ouida (1983), *Words by Heart,* Bantam Books.
Shura, Mary Frances (1986), *The Josie Gambit,* Dodd, Mead.
Sleator, William (1986), *The Boy Who Reversed Himself,* Dutton.
Smith, Doris Buchanan (1986), *Return to Bitter Creek,* Viking Press.
Smucker, Barbara (1979), *Runaway to Freedom,* Harper & Row.
Snyder, Carol (1986), *The Leftover Kid,* Putnam.
Snyder, Carol (1987), *Leave Me Alone, Ma,* Bantam Books.
Snyder, Zilpha Keatley (1981), *A Fabulous Creature,* Atheneum.
Speare, Elizabeth George (1983), *Sign of the Beaver,* Houghton Mifflin.
Steiner, Barbara (1986), *Is There a Cure for Sophomore Year?* New American Library.
Taylor, Mildred D. (1976), *Roll of Thunder, Hear My Cry,* Dial Press.
Taylor, Mildred D. (1983), *Let the Circle Be Unbroken,* Bantam Books.
Voigt, Cynthia (1981), *Homecoming,* Atheneum.
Voigt, Cynthia (1986), *Izzy, Willy-Nilly,* Atheneum.
Walsh, Jill Paton (1970), *Fireweed,* Farrar, Straus & Giroux.
Walsh, Jill Paton (1974), *The Emperor's Winding Sheet,* Farrar, Straus & Giroux.
Walsh, Jill Paton (1980), *A Chance Child,* Avon Books.
Wells, Rosemary (1987), *Through the Hidden Door,* Dial Press.
White, T. H. (1978), *The Sword in the Stone,* Dell.
Wiseman, David (1981), *Jeremy Visick,* Houghton Mifflin.
Wolff, Virginia E. (1991), *The Mozart Season,* Holt.
Wolff, Virginia E. (1989), *Probably Still Nick Swansen,* Holt.

## Nonfiction

Arnosky, Jim (1984), *Drawing Life in Motion,* Lothrop.
Bell, Ruth (1988), *Changing Bodies, Changing Lives,* Vintage.
Benedict, Helen (1987), *Safe, Strong, and Streetwise: The Teenager's Guide to Preventing Sexual Assault,* Little, Brown.
Boorstin, Daniel (1987), *The Landmark History of the American People,* Random House.
Cheney, Theodore A. Rees (1987), *Living in Polar Regions,* Watts.
Currimbhoy, Nayana (1987), *Living in Deserts,* Watts.
Freedman, Russell (1987), *Indian Chiefs,* Holiday.
Gehrts, Barbara (1975), *Don't Say a Word,* McElderry.
Goor, Ron, & Goor, Nancy (1986), *Pompeii: Exploring a Roman Ghost Town,* Cromwell.
Hintz, Martin (1987), *Living in the Tropics,* Watts.
Jespersen, James, & Fitz-Randolph, Jane (1987), *From Quarks to Quasars: A Tour of the Universe,* Atheneum.
Madaras, Lynda, & Saavedra, Dane (1988), *The What's Happening to My Body? Book for Boys: A Growing Up Guide for Parents and Sons,* Newmarket Press.
Madaras, Lynda, & Saavedra, Dane (1988), *The What's Happening to My Body? Book for Girls: A Growing Up Guide for Parents and Daughters,* Newmarket Press.
Markl, Julia (1987), *Living on Islands,* Watts.
Meltzer, Milton (1986), *Poverty in America,* Morrow.

## Biography

Haskins, James (1988), *Corazon Aquino: Leader of the Philippines*, Enslow.
Hautzig, Esther (1987), *The Endless Steppe: A Girl in Exile*, Harper & Row.
Miller, Robyn (1986), *Robyn's Books: A True Diary*, Scholastic Books.
Randolph, Blythe (1987), *Amelia Earhart*, Watts.
Randolph, Sallie G. (1987), *Gerald R. Ford, President*, Walker.
Van Steenwyk, Elizabeth (1987), *Dwight D. Eisenhower, President*, Walker.
Watkins, Yoko Kawashima (1986), *So Far from the Bamboo Grove*, Lothrop.

## Poetry

Glenn, Mel (1986), *Class Dismissed II: More High School Poems*, Clarion.
Hearney, Seamus, & Hughes, Ted (1985), *Rattle Bag: An Anthology of Poetry*, Faber & Faber.
Janeczko, P. (1987), *Going Over to Your Place: Poems for Each Other*, Bradbury.
Livingston, Myra C. (1982), *Why Am I Grown So Cold: Poems of the Unknowable*, McElderry.
MacKay, David (1970), *A Flock of Words: An Anthology of Poetry for Children and Others*, Harcourt Brace Jovanovich.
Poe, Edgar Allan (1987), *Annabel Lee*, Tundra.

## Folk Tale

Price, Susan (1987), *The Ghost Drum*, Farrar, Straus & Giroux.

## Multicultural Books

Ada, Alma F. (1993), *My Name Is Maria Isabel*, Macmillan.
Adoff, Arnold (1982), *All the Colors of the Race*, Lothrop, Lee & Shepard.
Berry, James A. (1988), *A Thief in the Village & Other Stories*, Orchard Books.
Broker, Ignatia (1983), *Night Flying Woman: An Ojibway Narrative*, Minnesota Historical Society Press.
Childress, Alice (1989), *Those Other People*, Putnam.
Crew, Linda (1989), *Children of the River*, Delacorte.
Drucker, Malka, & Halperin, Michael (1993), *Jacob's Rescue*, Bantam.
Gordon, Sheila (1987), *Waiting for the Rain: A Novel of South Africa*, Bantam.
Hamilton, Virginia (1990), *Cousins*, Philomel.
Hamilton, Virginia (1989), *A White Romance*, Harcourt Brace Jovanovich.
Ho, Minfong (1990), *Rice without Rain*, Lothrop Lee & Shepard.
Hobbs, Will (1989), *Bearstone*, Atheneum.
Jenkins, Lyll Becerra de (1988), *The Honorable Prison*, Penguin.
Lyons, Mary E. (1990), *Sorrow's Kitchen: The Life and Folklore of Zora Neale Hurston*, Scribner.
McCullogh, Frances, ed. (1984), *Love Is Like the Lion's Tooth: An Anthology of Love Poems*, Harper & Row.
Maguire, Gregory (1989), *I Feel Like the Morning Star*, Harper & Row.
Marino, Jan (1990), *The Day That Elvis Came to Town*, Little, Brown.
Meltzer, Milton (1988), *Rescue: The Story of How Gentiles Saved Jews in the Holocaust*, HarperCollins.

Myers, Walter D. (1988), *Fallen Angels,* Scholastic.

Myers, Walter D (1991), *Now Is Your Time! The African-American Struggle for Freedom,* HarperCollins.

Newth, Mette (1989), *The Abduction,* Farrar, Straus & Giroux.

Nye, Naomi S. (ed.) (1992), *This Same Sky: A Collection of Poems from around the World,* Four Winds Press.

Orlev, Uri (1991), *The Man from the Other Side,* Houghton Mifflin.

Paulsen, Gary (1985), *Dogsong,* Bradbury.

Patterson, Katherine (1983), *Rebels of the Heavenly Kingdom,* Avon.

Peck, Robert N. (1972), *The Day No Pigs Would Die,* Knopf.

Say, Allen (1991), *El Chino,* Houghton Mifflin.

Schami, Rafik (1990), *A Hand Full of Stars,* Dutton.

Speerstra, Karen (1980), *The Earthshapers,* Naturegraph.

Staples, Suzanne F. (1989), *Shabanu: Daughter of the Wind,* Knopf.

Taylor, Mildred D. (1981), *Let the Circle Be Unbroken,* Bantam.

Thomas, Joyce C., (Ed.) (1990), *A Gathering of Flowers: Stories about Being Young in America,* Harper & Row.

Watkins, Yoko K. (1986), *So Far from the Bamboo Grove,* Lothrop, Lee & Shepard.

Wolff, Virginia E. (1991), *The Mozart Season,* Holt.

# 6 CONCEPT FORMATION
## Developing Reading and Writing Vocabularies

*A word is like a picture in your mind.*

*Kathleen, age 7*

*The meaning of a word represents such a close amalgam of thought and language that it is hard to tell whether it is a phenomenon of speech or a phenomenon of thought. A word without meaning is an empty sound; meaning, therefore, is a criterion of "word," its indispensable component.*

*L. S. Vygotsky,* Thought and Language *(1962, 1979, p. 120)*

## CHAPTER CONCEPTS

Real and vicarious experiences contribute to reading and writing vocabularies.

Children internalize new vocabulary words through direct instruction and incidental encounters with words in reading.

Vocabulary instruction that is conceptually based enables readers and writers to understand words in a variety of contexts.

Dictionaries, thesauri, brainstorming, semantic maps, semantic feature analysis, word sorts, and newspapers are useful in developing child-centered vocabulary instruction.

The concept of word is fundamental to the development of literacy. Sometime during the kindergarten and first-grade years, most children come to realize intuitively that printed words are labels for concepts, or abstract ideas about the world in which we live. Finding just the right words to express what we mean is crucial to oral and written composition. Knowing all the right words to understand what we read is critical to comprehension. Everyone has experienced difficulty with individual words during the process of reading and writing. To be stopped at the word level of any text frustrates even the best readers and writers. "I can't think of the word!" or "What *does* this word mean?" are expressions that reflect experiences common to us all. Knowledge of words, lots of words, makes us confident as we become literate.

Vocabulary instruction is an essential part of schooling, for it is during those formative years that we acquire the vocabulary associated with being an educated adult (Carroll, 1971). How children acquire reading and writing vocabularies is the subject of extensive educational research, but there are still many uncertainties about what contributes to effective classroom practices (McKeown & Curtis, 1987). Undeniably, the better comprehenders and composers have larger, more sophisticated vocabularies from which to draw when constructing meaning from text. Although vocabulary is often directly taught through the language arts curriculum, most researchers feel that memorization of word definitions alone does not add significantly to a child's knowledge of words (Stahl & Fairbanks, 1986).

It is estimated that children learn about 3,000 words per year. This knowledge cannot be accounted for solely through direct instruction. Rather, children appear to learn words quickly and incidentally through repeated exposure during reading (Nagy & Herman, 1987). Other experiences with language also facilitate vocabulary growth. Conversation and discussion along with composition and creative writing will naturally extend the concepts underlying the new words that ultimately become a permanent part of reading and writing vocabularies. Writing especially helps to internalize difficult concepts that may otherwise go unlearned through minimum exposure to key terms during reading (Pearce, 1984).

The close relationship among words, concepts, and experience is important to consider when planning for instruction. The ability to define a single word does not guarantee that a student understands the underlying concepts. Many concepts require thousands of words to describe the network of ideas that are involved. For this reason, direct instruction in vocabulary definitions alone has limited value (Herman & Dole, 1988). Better comprehenders ordinarily have better conceptual knowledge about the world because they usually have read and written more, experienced more, and learned more as the result of a variety of environmental factors in the home and the schools. Prior world knowledge in general appears to form the best possible base for comprehension and composition. Enlarging children's views of the world is a formidable task that all teachers must undertake. Daily reading and writing of connected text offers an excellent environment to facilitate concept formation, the fundamental cognitive process that enables us to organize our knowledge of the world.

## CONCEPT FORMATION

A concept is the structure of an idea. Concept formation refers to the process of acquiring and developing an understanding of any idea. It is a complex process that also involves the intellectual ability to integrate and organize new and old informa-

Emily and Joe are second-graders who thoroughly understand the concept of prehistoric times by talking, reading, and writing about dinosaurs.

tion into common relationships (Harris & Hodges, 1981). In other words, as we conceptualize our life's experiences, we simultaneously categorize the ideas to bring order and sense to the world. This organization of category networks, or schemata, is what makes orderly retrieval of information possible from short- and long-term memory. Concepts themselves are an ever-changing, "active part of the intellectual process, constantly engaged in serving communication, understanding, and problem-solving" (Vygotsky, 1979, p. 53). We are bombarded with thousands of ideas daily. To cope with the dynamics of day-to-day learning, we must assimilate and accommodate new information into already existing schemata. The ability to conceptualize, or think abstractly about any idea, is basic to learning.

Concept formation occurs as we interact both verbally and nonverbally with the environment. The emergence of a concept can be directly observed in the classroom by listening to children interacting either formally or informally with teachers or peers. Consider the following example of a group of four kindergarten children's understanding of the concepts normally associated with school, specifically classroom, teacher, and students (M. F. Heller, 1988d).

### CLOSE ENCOUNTERS IN A COLLEGE CLASSROOM

*A few weeks ago I invited David, Kirk, Jessica, and Cynthia, four kindergarten children, to visit my undergraduate language arts seminar. My purpose was to give my college students an opportunity to interact with and observe "real live" children. The class began with my students interviewing this panel of four youngsters about what it was like being a kindergartner. "What do you like best about kindergarten?" was the first query. "Recess" was the typical first response.*

*Then it was the children's turn. "What questions do you have for me or for my students?" I asked.*

*Cynthia asked, "These are your students? [I had only ten]. Where's the rest of them?"*

*Jessica asked, "Where do you put your coats and backpacks?"*

*David asked, "Where's your [the instructor's] desk?"*

*Kirk asked, "What's for snack?"*

*The children then went on to make observations about their new surroundings:*

**KIRK:** *Those are funny lights, like in our bathroom at home. Florexent.*

**CYNTHIA:** *These are really* long *and* high *tables.*

**JESSICA:** *Where's the reading* rug?

**DAVID:** *Your students sure are* old!

*We answered those and other questions as best we could and responded to their observations with smiles. Then we made valentines, the children dictated a valentine story, I did a magic trick and read them* Sylvester and the Magic Pebble *[Steig, 1969] and finally as a special treat the four children and I went to McDonalds after class was over. After that I collapsed in utter exhaustion.*

***Reflections.***    The kindergartners' questions are telling. Unlike their own classroom, for them the college classroom was an alien place with too few students, no coatracks and cubbies, no teacher's desk, and definitely no sign of snacks forthcoming. To understand the situation, they questioned the setting and fit the explanations into their already-existing knowledge about what school and classrooms are like. Their inevitable conclusion was best summed up by Kirk's casual, yet ironic, statement: "Your classroom is kinda empty. But that's OK. It's just college." The children's concept of schooling was broadened by the real experience of visiting a college classroom and interviewing college students. Most important, they came away from the experience equipped with new information that would enable them to describe, to compare, and to evaluate. Their newly acquired vocabulary that they associated with college classrooms—empty, long tables; fluorescent lights—was born of the experience itself. Language indeed has its roots in concrete behaviors (Piaget, 1973).

This scenario is a reminder of the important role of real experiences in concept formation and language development. It is essential to seize every opportunity to elaborate and extend concepts that children develop incidentally, either through reading and writing or through participation in a more direct experience. Here are just a few activities that would naturally follow a field trip to a college classroom:

Talk and then write about the differences and similarities between college classrooms and elementary, middle, or junior high school classrooms.

Draw a picture to show the similarities and differences between the two classroom settings.

Dictate or write a descriptive paragraph about the field trip.

Write about how you felt being in a college classroom (personal expressive writing).

Write a fictional story based on the field trip.

Read some children's literature that has a classroom setting, such as *Miss Nelson Is Missing* (Allard, 1985).

Read one another's writing that was inspired by the experience.

Field trips are only one example of the opportunities that lend themselves to concept formation. In his now classic Cone of Experience model, Edgar Dale (1969) outlines eleven levels of abstraction, ranging from nonverbal, concrete activity, which he terms "direct, purposeful experience," to the most abstract experience that is received from the spoken word, "verbal symbols." Combining real or vicarious experiences such as field trips, exhibits, television, audiotapes, and visual aids with listening and discussion, plus reading and writing, provide optimum opportunities for concept development across all subject areas. The model lessons described throughout this text attempt to provide the basic structure that encourages concept formation every time something is taught.

## VOCABULARY INSTRUCTION

Like all good teaching, guidance during the development of reading and writing vocabularies involves a balance of direct instruction and child-centered activity. In other words, "the experiences with words that lead to large-scale growth come through both explicit instruction and incidental encounters with words in reading" (Nagy, 1988, p. 32). Providing many opportunities to read and write connected text is only the beginning. A major goal of vocabulary instruction is to help children develop a love of words and at the same time become independent word learners (Carr, 1985). Developing independence in learning new words takes time. Effective vocabulary instruction involves using a variety of approaches that encompass concept-formation activities, teacher modeling, wide reading, and copious writing.

### Instructional Decisions

What vocabulary words should be directly taught in the context of connected text? It is important to realize the significance of learning fewer words well as opposed to many obscure words less well. Vacca, Vacca, and Grove (1987) recommend focusing instruction on four categories of words that are likely to result in long-term payoffs for readers and writers. The categories are *key words, useful words, interesting words,* and *vocabulary-building words.* The following instructional guidelines contain practical suggestions for locating words in each category and organizing conceptually based vocabulary-building activities.

## INSTRUCTIONAL GUIDELINES
### Selecting Vocabulary Words for Instruction

The following guidelines for selecting vocabulary words offer definitions and examples of each category.*

#### KEY WORDS

Key words represent the major concepts in basal readers, language arts, and other content area readings. They are ordinarily introduced at the beginning of a lesson and sometimes appear in bold print throughout the text. A thorough understanding of key words is essential for complete understanding of the text. The concepts underlying key words may be reinforced through oral discussions and writing.

 *Example source: Living in Our Country,* fifth-grade social studies text

*(continued)*

---

*Adapted from Vacca, Vacca, & Grove, 1987, pp. 183–184.

### Instructional Guidelines (continued)

(Armeto, Garcia, & Erickson, 1985), "From Many Colonies to One Nation," pp. 223–243)

*Key words: representatives, boycott, patriots, militia, privateer*

*Developing the concepts:* (Discussion/composition) "Choose *one* of the key words from the social studies chapter about the colonies. Discuss with a friend everything you know about that word and all the other words and concepts that it brings to your mind in relation to the colonization of America. Individually write a poem or a paragraph that explains what the word means to you. Share your work with your partner and the class."

#### USEFUL WORDS

Useful words are utilitarian in nature. They are the high-frequency words that children encounter or require again and again during reading and writing. Useful words are also relevant to the child's particular age and grade level, and their usefulness may change over time.

*Example source:* First-grader's personal writing dictionary containing alphabetized sight words from the basal reader and other words needed by the child during the writing process (New words are handwritten into the dictionary by the child or teacher at the moment of most usefulness.)

*Useful words: about, beautiful, couldn't, dear*

*Developing the concept:* (Talk/write). Encourage children to add useful words to their personal dictionaries to facilitate writing fluency. By incorporating sight words into their daily writing, the children will internalize not only word meanings but also spelling patterns.

#### INTERESTING WORDS

Interesting words pique the child's interest and imagination, stimulating an enthusiasm for learning about word origins and usage. Children will often mention words that they are curious about and want to learn more about. New experiences, either real or vicarious, will provide opportunities to notice words of special interest to the children.

*Example source:* Fourth-grade field trip to a simulated tropical rain forest

*Interesting words: tropical, biotron, ecosystem, niche*

*Developing the concept:* (Write/read/discuss). "Using as many as you can of the new vocabulary words and concepts that you learned during our field trip, describe an imaginary trip through a real tropical rain forest in Africa. Do some library research on rain forests in North America. How is a terrarium like a tropical rain forest? Is a terrarium also a biotron? Is it an ecosystem? What plants and animals have a special niche in the tropical rain forests of North America?"

### VOCABULARY-BUILDING WORDS

Vocabulary-building words offer the best possible structural analysis to determine word meanings. Structural analysis involves careful study of the base or root word and its surrounding prefixes and/or suffixes. Creating new words from known base words is a quick way to extend concepts already familiar to the children.

*Example source: Houghton Mifflin Spelling, Book 3* (Henderson, et al., 1982)

*Vocabulary-building Words*

| | |
|---|---|
| *remake* | *unlike* |
| *redo* | *undo* |
| *return* | *unload* |
| *rewrap* | *unkind* |

*Developing the concept:* "The prefix *re* means again, and *un* means not. Each day this week during sustained silent reading, notice all of the words that begin with the prefix *re* or *un*. Write them in your journal. As you write your drafts this week, underline all of the words that you use that begin with *re* or *un*. On Friday we'll compile our list of *re* and *un* words and see how many we've discovered through reading and writing." The study of word origins often begins with structural analysis of words that are good vocabulary builders. Etymology is a discipline that many intermediate and junior high students enjoy, especially when you begin with vocabulary study that focuses on words that are personally meaningful (i.e., the children's names).

*Example source:* The children's names, first, middle, and family; *Oxford English Dictionary* (1971, 1975).

*Vocabulary-building Words*

*Amber*—Middle English; a golden, somewhat translucent fossil resin that is polished and used in costume jewelry

*Lance*—Old French; a weapon of war made of a long shaft and a sharp steel head, often carried by knights

*Smith*—Greek; a wood carving knife

*Developing the concept:* "Look up your name in the *Oxford English Dictionary* and discover its origin. Describe how your name can be used in other contexts as an object, an action, an event, or some other concept that is not a name. Interview your grandparents or another elderly person about their family names. Make a list of the family names that interest you. Create a family word-origin tree.

***Selecting an Instructional Method.***    The three general categories of vocabulary instruction are definitional, contextual, and conceptual. No single approach is adequate to maximize the children's opportunities to develop their vocabularies to the extent needed for excellent comprehension and composition. Because conceptual approaches have by far the most lasting effect on vocabulary acquisition and retention (Thelen, 1986), each strategy described here encourages concept formation. Teacher modeling, as well as reading and writing connected text, also contributes to more comprehensive vocabulary instruction. The overall goal is to help children acquire a multitude of words that they know very well and that they can independently draw on during reading and writing.

## The Definitional Approach

Definitional approaches to vocabulary instruction focus on the literal meanings of words, as well as words with similar or dissimilar meanings. Typical definitional methods involve dictionary, glossary, and thesaurus usage. All educated people at some time or another use dictionaries and thesauri to help construct meaning during reading and writing. The importance of these resources is highlighted by the frequent inclusion of dictionary-related activities in the reading and language arts curriculum. Dictionary and thesaurus usage is an important skill to develop, but not at the expense of interest and enthusiasm for words and language learning. Looking up words in the dictionary, passively writing the definitions, writing the word in a sentence, and then memorizing the definition for an end-of-the-week test does not significantly improve children's reading comprehension, nor does it guarantee that they will use the words in their writing.

Classroom instruction in definitions should be accomplished within the broad context of day-to-day learning. Beginning with picture dictionaries in kindergarten and first grade, and progressing to more elaborate editions of child and adult volumes, students should be taught how to use a dictionary to look up words needed for comprehension and composition. Richard Scarry's (1966) *Storybook Dictionary* is an excellent picture dictionary for young children. In this creative nontraditional reference book, Scarry puts words directly in the context of a brief story. The reader must infer word meaning through context and picture. For example, the entry for the word "above" reads as follows, "A mosquito is flying above Flossie's head. It is over her head. Look out, Flossie!" (p. 7). Flossie, a mouse, is seated on a chair. A mosquito is pictured flying around her head. Other excellent examples of dictionaries and thesauri for children and adolescents are listed at the end of this chapter.

Dictionaries should be readily available during the reading and writing process, to clarify important terms that are crucial to topics under study and to aid during rewriting and editing. Whenever appropriate, model the process of looking words up in the dictionary, reading the literal definition, and extending the concept through brief discussions of literal and implied meanings in the context of a lesson. Through repeated exposure to positive models of dictionary and thesaurus usage, students are more likely to value these important resources for comprehending and composing.

***Teachable Moments.***    In the following vignette, Charley's questioning during his search for just the right word provides what teachers enthusiastically call the "teachable moment." Teachable moments are those numerous occasions sprinkled throughout the day when we quickly seize the opportunity to make language learning meaningful and permanent. It is important to recognize those moments when a child demonstrates genuine interest and enthusiasm about words in particular and language in general. Ms. Smith, a model teacher, takes her cue from Charley when he asks, "Got any ideas?"

> CHARLEY: *But Ms. Smith, how can I look the word up in the dictionary if I don't really know what word it is I want? I mean all I really want is a word that sort of means "rad" but not really, more like* cool dude *only that's two words. I want a* long *word that sounds better than* rad *but is just as good. Anyway,* rad's *not in the dictionary. Know what I mean? Something like* neat *but better. Got any ideas?*
>
> MS. SMITH: *I know what you mean, Charley. You want a word that isn't slang but that expresses more exactly what you want to say. What I usually do when I'm stumped for a word, and I can't find it in the dictionary, is to look up a similar word, like* cool, *and see if I can get some ideas. If that doesn't help, then I'll go to the thesaurus since the thesaurus contains lots of synonyms and antonyms for words we use in our writing. Since you already know the definition of your word, I'd try the thesaurus first to come up with an alternative to* rad *or* cool. *Let's look up* cool *together and see what we find.*

The happy ending to this scenario is predictable. Charley and Ms. Smith discover numerous synonyms for the word *cool* in the thesaurus—*easygoing, unemotional, self-controlled, composed,* and so on. Charley chooses the word *easygoing* to describe his main character and happily continues writing.

The time that it took to describe the process of using a dictionary and a thesaurus to locate the word is well spent because it occurred in the context of constructing meaning. Ms. Smith demonstrated that she, too, is a writer and a reader who is willing to share her experiences with a student for pedagogical reasons. This kind of instructional sharing builds a trusting relationship between teacher and student, making the teacher a model for literacy rather than a commander of dictionary-related assignments.

***Definitions in Context.***    It is important to provide many opportunities for students to be creative in their approaches to dictionary and thesaurus usage. The definition paragraph is one way to combine knowledge and understanding of the concept of definition with creative writing. Definition paragraphs can range from the commonplace—definition of a banana—to the more esoteric definition of a "bodacious Eighth-Grader." (A bodacious eighth-grader is rad to the max, of course!) Students can have fun writing mystery definitions of unnamed objects or definitions for out-of-towners or alien audiences.

Making definitional approaches work is contingent on choosing a limited number of appropriate words to define, then extending the underlying concepts to ensure thorough knowledge and understanding of single words. It is always important to make the task of defining words enjoyable. Children will enjoy learning new words only if it gives them a sense of accomplishment by making conceptualization easier during reading and writing. Writing mystery definitions and playing simple word games are two ways to encourage curiosity about word meanings.

### WHAT IS IT? MYSTERY DEFINITIONS

by Evan (Sixth Grade)

*This fruit is round and can be red, yellow, or green in color. It is smooth on the outside but crunchy when you bite in. Some of the different kinds that you see at the grocery store are Jonathon, Washington, and Delicious. They all grow on trees. This fruit is used to make juice, pies, and cake. At Halloween time you can dip one in carmel or cinnamon syrup, then eat it on a stick. Usually your mom puts one in your lunch every day for a nutritious snack during SQUIRT time. My father always says, "An _____ a day keeps the doctor away." WHAT IS IT???*

Practice in writing a concise definition is a worthwhile endeavor because it helps students to appreciate the economy of language used in dictionaries. Individual definitions can be collected into a class collection. Class "slang" or regional dialect dictionaries are popular volumes that are frequently published and make their way into the school library. Dialect dictionaries are useful during genealogy units and studies of regional and state history. Here is a sample entry from a sixth-grade regional dialect dictionary written by children in a small western Kansas town.

*Rat /rat/* adv: *To accomplish immediately (as in* Do it rat now).

***Word Games.***    Just for fun, occasionally use dictionary- and thesaurus-related games to create enthusiasm about words. "Stick the Teacher" (Maleska, 1981) is a fun-filled activity in which the students take turns picking out words in the dictionary for the teacher to define. When the teacher misses, the class gets a point. Later in the day, the teacher has an opportunity to win back points by using the word in an appropriate context. During the game the dictionary definitions are read aloud, and the overall activity focuses on improving listening comprehension while learning new concepts. The game can be extended to small groups and renamed "Stump the Student." One word of caution: Competitive games should always be used sparingly in the classroom and never without the ground rules firmly stated ahead of time. Otherwise competition can encourage undesirable playground behaviors inside the classroom.

Concepts may be extended through library research, reading, and writing.

## The Contextual Approach

The context of the spoken or written word influences meaning. Independence in reading requires the use of context to comprehend an author's intended meaning. Writers manipulate words in written context in order to create a clear and meaningful message. Efficient use of context while comprehending and composing any genre requires knowledge of how word meanings can vary from one context to another and how information contained in the surrounding text influences word meaning. During the comprehending and composing process our prior word knowledge also effects our growing conceptual understanding of words. Overall, effective use of context clues during reading and writing is a prerequisite to developing facility with language.

Determining the meaning of a word through context is not a simple matter. Consider the following exercise in which a short list of words is first presented in isolation, then in the context of a single sentence. Can you comprehend the sentence without the dictionary definition of the key word?

## FOR YOU TO TRY
## Vocabulary Words in Context

### AN INFORMAL INVENTORY

1. *precipitancy*     Precipitancy creates prodigality.
2. *vitreous*     Tenants of vitreous abodes ought to hurl no lithoidal fragments.
3. *pulchritude*     Pulchritude does not extend below the surface of the derma.

How did you do? The exercise demonstrates the importance of prior world knowledge in constructing meaning from context. It further highlights Nagy's (1988) point that use of context alone to derive meaning from text is an inefficient method of comprehending.

Just in case you don't know, here are the literal meanings of each word:

1. acting hastily
2. of or like glass
3. beauty

Now do you understand each sentence? To help in your comprehension, try to rewrite each sentence by using synonyms or a simpler vocabulary. Here's the rewrite:

1. Haste makes waste.
2. People in glass houses should never throw stones.
3. Beauty is only skin deep.

Obviously, prior knowledge of aphorisms and how they are constructed is very helpful when constructing meaning from the text, especially if you do not already know the definitions of the key words in isolation. Now can you do the reverse? Rewrite this sentence in your most sophisticated vocabulary: "Rolling stones gather no moss." (One possibility: "A rotating lithoidal fragment never accrues lichen.") Too hard? Always remember the difficulty of the task the next time you ask elementary or middle school children to "figure out the meaning of the word by the surrounding words in a sentence."

***Context Clues.***     Clues to the meaning of specific vocabulary words in sentences may be either explicitly or implicitly stated in the context. Explicit context clues may be actual definitions or synonyms of the word in question, whereas implicit clues to meaning are more subtle hints, which the reader must infer from information contained in sentences surrounding the target word. Context clues should help children derive the meaning, or at least enough of the meaning to keep on reading without losing comprehension of the whole text. Here are some examples:

### EXPLICIT MEANING CLUES

*Mom painted the guest bedroom chartreuse, a brilliant yellow green.*

*Tim was a gregarious fellow. In fact he was the friendliest, most sociable guy in the class.*

As illustrated in the exercise above, it's not always easy to figure out the meaning of a word in context. To be efficient users of contextual knowledge, readers and writers must ultimately be familiar with both denotative (literal) and connotative (implied) word meanings. For example, most primary grade children are very familiar with color words such as blue, green, and yellow. They can recognize the word, define it as a color, and even give examples of those hues in the environment. However, it will be several years before the same children will know that blue, green, and yellow in certain contexts can mean something other than color, as in "He's feeling blue today," "She is green with envy," and "The cowardly lion was yellow with fear." In the example sentences, blue connotes a feeling of sadness or melancholy; green and yellow imply an undesirable character trait. Thorough knowledge of word meanings, denotations, and connotations, help in choosing just the right words to express what we mean during the composing process. Correctly using words denotatively and connotatively requires conceptual knowledge that is acquired through a combination of direct experiences, wide reading, and abundant writing.

### IMPLICIT MEANING CLUES

*The shade of the flower petals ranged from rose to fuchsia.*

*Tim's gregarious nature made him the life of every party. He loved being around friends and family.*

The use of context to determine word meaning is often directly taught through single-sentence examples presented by the teacher or included in the child's text. Typical preteaching activities involve key concepts presented in isolation and then used in a sentence from which the meaning of the word may be inferred.

*Key word:* mysterious

*Context: The dark old house with broken window panes looked mysterious.*

Having children put vocabulary words into their own sentences is another common way of reinforcing the use of context plus prior knowledge of the word to convey meaning. However, the same pitfalls associated with the definitional approach can befall contextual approaches, especially if single-word or single-sentence exercises dominate instruction. It cannot be overemphasized that conceptual knowledge forms the basis of truly knowing word meanings in any given context. Most texts are *not* rich in clues to meaning, thus making teacher- or child-created examples somewhat artificial. For example, consider the word *sauntered,* a fifth-grade spelling word, in each of two contexts:

1. The boy sauntered into the classroom knowing full well that he was late.
2. The girl sauntered near the ice-cream palace.

To a child who has never encountered the word before, *saunter* in sentence 1 could mean anything from "walked" to "ran." Sentence 2 contains even fewer clues, as exemplified by one fifth-grade child's guesses: "fell down" and "lived." Although the subtleties in meaning of the word *saunter* are more easily inferred in sentence 1—"knowing full well he was late" being the best clue—the sentence itself does not help the reader extract a meaning that is closely synonymous with the word. Synonyms such as *strolled, meandered,* or *loitered* will not be easily called to mind unless children have prior knowledge of and experience with the concept of "walking in a leisurely or idle manner."

***Teacher Modeling.*** Teaching children to use context to derive word meanings while comprehending or composing requires both direct instruction and a good deal of teacher modeling. It is important for teachers to demonstrate the process of determining word meanings within the context of connected text. Children's literature is a valuable resource for teaching word meanings in context. For instance, Karen Lynn Williams's (1990) *Galimoto* is the story of Kondi, an African child, who has collected old wires to make a "galimoto," which we know only from reading the copyright page means "car" in Chichewa, the national language of Malawi, Africa. The author never explicitly defines galimoto in the story. She instead leaves it up to the reader to infer the meaning of the word. The events in the story take Kondi on a journey through his village to acquire more wire for what is portrayed through action and dialogue as a coveted object. The last few illustrations show Kondi and his friends enjoying his creation—a push-toy car. This picture book provides an excellent text to model inferential thinking required to determine word meaning in the context of a story.

Demonstrating what one is thinking while constructing meaning requires metacognitive behavior that can be rehearsed and then modeled by the teacher, as in this example that uses an excerpt from a fourth-grade teacher's description of her grandmother. The words *gracious* and *graciousness* are on the children's weekly spelling list, therefore making the example timely from a pedagogical point of view.

### TEACHER'S WRITTEN EXAMPLE—GRANDMA HALE

*Grandma was a* gracious *person. Whenever friends were over for dinner, she would make them all feel like family, waiting on their every want and need. Grandma would smile at even the most suspicious-looking stranger who might come to the door, though she was cautious, too, never letting her* graciousness *get in the way of protecting those she loved.*

### TEACHER'S METACOGNITIVE MODEL

Gracious. *Now what does that word mean? I know that it describes Grandma as a person, i.e.,* "gracious *person." Because it describes a person,* gracious *must be an adjective. But what is its meaning? It must also have something to do with the way Grandma behaves or acts. I know this because of the next few sentences, when I learn how she treats friends who come to dinner. Because she is so kind to everyone,* gracious *must mean something like "kind."* Courteous *is another word that comes to my mind. She is* courteous *to strangers, smiling at them but not necessarily letting them in the door. As I keep reading, I'll probably come to more examples of Grandma's kindnesses.*

When demonstrating this process, it is important to be as clear and concise as possible. Brevity is desired above elaborate explanations that go on for too long and tax the children's listening capacity. In the example, the teacher uses a synonym, *courteous,* to help explain the meaning of the word. This also shows children the importance of making connections between already-known vocabulary words and new words encountered as we read. Crucial to metacognitive modeling is a follow-up activity that engages the children in a similar think-aloud strategy to practice the skill that was just demonstrated. Working in small groups, the children could describe to one another how they figured out the meaning of an unknown word through context or how they determined a new word needed in their writing. Practice during group discussions helps to reinforce the critical thinking skills introduced by the teacher during her demonstration.

***Cloze Procedures.***    Fill-in-the-blank activities, or cloze procedures, exemplify the contextual approach to vocabulary instruction because they necessitate using the context of a sentence and surrounding text to determine the exact or an appropriate vocabulary word. More specifically, cloze procedures require children to read sentences or paragraphs and supply a missing word, which has been systematically (every fifth word, every useful word, every interesting word, etc.) or randomly deleted. Based on the Gestalt theory of closure, cloze exercises take advantage of our natural urge to complete or make whole any structure in the environment, including a reading passage (W. L. Taylor, 1953). An additional benefit of cloze passages is that we are able to ascertain a child's use of syntax and semantics in determining the word that best fits (Johnson & Pearson, 1978, 1984). For example, in the simple sentence "Jill _____ away from the barking dog," we would expect a primary grade child to fill in the blank with an appropriate verb, such as *walked* or *ran.* Inappropriate words, such as *come, talk, or boy* would indicate the inability to infer the correct word from context. Cloze passages are frequently used to determine the extent of reading disability among remedial readers (Jongsma, 1971).

Inference training is another viable use for cloze passages. Carr, Dewitz, and Patberg (1989) describe a modified cloze exercise that is useful in presenting a model of inferential thinking. Their Inferential Training Technique, which has been shown to be successful in fifth- and sixth-grade classes (Dewitz, Carr, & Patberg, 1987), utilizes expository passages from any content area. The teacher deletes "selected words," which could be key concepts or any vocabulary deemed important enough to teach directly. Initially the students fill in the blanks and then discuss as a class the inferential thinking that took place while trying to determine the correct word.

During inference training particular emphasis is placed on forward and backward inferencing, using the text itself plus prior knowledge. The teacher takes the opportunity to model the process of making inferences and filling in the correct word. Next, the students and teacher reread the passage aloud to answer inference-level questions about the passage itself. According to the researchers, the thinking required to infer selected vocabulary words and concepts during the cloze procedure acts as a "bridge" in preparing the students to continue thinking inferentially while answering the comprehension questions accurately. Important to the entire exercise is teacher-directed class discussion of clues to meaning, found both within and outside of the text. Later, the students use a self-monitoring checklist as they become independent readers.

## INSTRUCTIONAL GUIDELINES
### Constructing Cloze Passages

Cloze passages are one of the more flexible methods of teaching children about vocabulary words in context. When designing a cloze activity, teachers can choose from a wide array of syntactic and semantic problems relative to comprehending and composing. Here are just a few ideas for making cloze procedures that are conceptually based.

#### Steps in Constructing Cloze Passages for Vocabulary Instruction

1. Use a wide variety of subject areas and contexts when designing cloze activities. Math, science, and social studies textbooks as well as good children's literature are rich sources of vocabulary and concepts that are worth developing. The cloze exercise is a unique kind of exposure to key words and concepts that often need to be encountered in a variety of situations for full understanding.
2. Begin at the *paragraph* level (as opposed to the sentence level) to provide an explicit model of reading and writing connected text. The length of the cloze activity will vary from grade to grade, ranging from short paragraphs in the primary grades to more elaborate multiparagraph stories or nonfiction in the middle grades. Take care not to make the exercise too long because lengthy passages could discourage children who are already having difficulty constructing meaning from whole texts.

3. In general, keep the first sentence of the passage intact, as recommended by traditional approaches to cloze construction, particularly when reinforcing reading comprehension. However, there may be times when you can legitimately omit a key word from the beginning sentence, especially when very specific vocabulary words and concepts are under study.
4. When choosing vocabulary words to delete, utilize the four general categories mentioned previously: key words, useful words, interesting words, and vocabulary-building words. Include a list of the words deleted plus a few distractors to aid the children in their search for just the right vocabulary. Model for the children the thinking that takes place while determining the correct word.

## LOGICAL THINKING[†]

*There are four _____.*
*The _____ of the first two*
*_____ is _____ than 2.*
*The _____ of the last two _____ is 9.*
*The last _____ is _____.*
*The _____ between the last two _____ is 1.*

*Vocabulary (\* means a distractor):*

*digits   figures\*   greater   lesser\*   sum   even\*   odd   difference*

## WHAT IS A DESERT?[‡]

*What comes to mind when you hear the word desert? . . . The three things found in most deserts are _____ air, _____ , and _____ earth. The air is _____ over a desert. There are very few _____ . The sun shines almost all day. It is hot during the day but it _____ off at night. _____ does not often fall in the desert. When _____ does fall, it comes down hard. The _____ flows in many _____. It forms small _____ that run into larger _____. Every time it _____, the water cuts a deeper _____. After thousands of years the beds of the larger _____ become wide and deep with _____ sides. They become _____. In some deserts there are large deep _____.*

*Vocabulary*

*factories\*   sunshine   lakes\*   bare   streams   canyon(s)   rain clouds   dry\*   water   streambed   shallow\*   steep   cools*

*(continued)*

---

†From Orfan and Vogeli (1987, p. 115).
‡From Kaltsounis (1986, p. 90).

## Instructional Guidelines (continued)

### OXYGEN—AN IMPORTANT ELEMENT*

*Think for a moment how important the element oxygen is. It is one of the most important _____ _____ in the world. It combines with so many different _____ to build _____. We need some of these _____ as much as we need oxygen itself. We must have _____, for instance. Without oxygen, _____ could not take place. _____ takes place when oxygen combines with the _____ in _____. Without oxygen, _____ would not light. The _____, or _____ or _____ we use for heat could not _____. The _____ in the engine of a car would not _____ and provide the _____ to make the car go.*

*Vocabulary*

*burn(ing) water food\* carbon dioxide\* building blocks compounds fuels substances elements\* matches electricity\* wood gasoline oil coal gas energy*

5. Be as creative as you can be when designing a cloze activity to maintain the children's interest and enthusiasm about learning new words. Fill-in-the-blank exercises can become pure drudgery if the children do not see short- and long-term benefits to reading and writing. One way to make the cloze activity interesting is to combine vocabulary study with word play in general, metaphorical language in particular. Riddles, nonsense rhymes, and guessing games that feature language play can be highly motivational. Guilio Maestro's (1984) *What's a Frank Frank?* is an illustrated collection of homograph riddles that could be used with cloze activities. Homographs are words that are not only spelled alike but also pronounced alike. The differences in meaning occur as a result of the words' positions in the sentence, for example, *class* the noun and *class* the adjective. Can you fill in the blanks and answer Maestro's first riddle? "What's a frank frank? A _____ who gives his _____ opinion" (p. 4). (Answer: *hot dog; honest*). Other interesting books that feature language play are those written by Marvin Terban (1982, 1983, 1984) and published by Clarion Books. They include *Eight Ate: A Feast of Homonym Riddles, In a Pickle and Other Funny Idioms,* and *I Think I Thought and Other Tricky Verbs.*

6. Use the children's own writing to help them understand the importance of word choice. For example, using a computer or word processor, type a

*From Cooper, Blackwood, Boeschen, Giddings, & Carin (1985, p. 146).

child's first draft of a poem, expository paragraph, or short fiction and delete several adjectives. The child substitutes with synonyms or antonyms and then compares the original version to the new version. Word processing in this instance makes deletions and retrieval of the original text easier. The child could make the substitutions directly into the computer and even create several versions of the original for comparison. This particular activity combines dictionary and thesaurus usage with the cloze procedure, thus building on children's growing knowledge of how to construct meaningful texts by using a wide range of interesting and descriptive vocabulary words.

***Creative Dramatics.***      Drama effectively encourages interest and enthusiasm about words in contexts created by the children themselves. Pantomime, puppet shows, skits, and plays can focus on one or more interesting vocabulary words and concepts. The experience of acting out a word or concept through children's theater helps elementary and middle school children acquire word meanings more efficiently (Duffelmeyer, 1980). The dramatizations can be written by small or large groups and acted by the teacher or children. The most important component is the

This cooperative learning group has designed a semantic map around the concept of "volunteering" on volunteer appreciation day.

actual production of the work, which gives children real and meaningful experiences with words and concepts in contexts of the children's own creation.

Word categories that lend themselves to creative dramatics include

*Feelings:* happy, sad, angry, pleased, ecstatic, frightened
*Sensory words:* sweet, sour, soft, hard, bright, dull, loud, fragrant
*Action words:* stumbled, sauntered, walk, run, jump, sit
*Value-laden words:* honesty, integrity, courageous, forthright, sincere

When using creative dramatics to internalize new concepts, limit the number of new words to be incorporated into the dramatization. For example, a single feeling word, such as *ecstatic,* and its various synonyms and antonyms is sufficient material around which to develop a dramatization.

Effective use of context clues in combination with prior knowledge is an important intellectual process. As children encounter key concepts in a variety of contexts, their knowledge and understanding of new words will deepen. Over time new vocabulary words and concepts will become a permanent part of the children's reading and writing vocabularies. This is the ultimate goal of vocabulary instruction.

## The Conceptual Approach

Conceptual approaches to vocabulary instruction strengthen students' knowledge of the underlying concepts that form the basis of a vocabulary word. Ideally, all vocabulary instruction should be conceptual in nature because conceptual knowledge is what enables readers and writers to understand a word in virtually all contexts. To know fully the underpinnings of a word requires an understanding of the concept first at a personal level (Carr & Wixson, 1986). Experience, either real or vicarious, provides the personal knowledge necessary to build our repertoire of conceptual knowledge. Concept-building experiences should be as real and as direct as possible, giving children every opportunity to manipulate personally a wide range of things in the environment. As mentioned previously, field trips, artwork, games, experiments, and demonstrations are just a few examples of real experiences that help to build conceptual awareness.

Ironically, the idea of a direct, or hands-on, experience is sometimes difficult to grasp. Picture drawing is probably the lowest level of a hands-on experience since it requires the child to use paper and pencil to create his or her own vision of a person, place, thing, or event. An adult's understanding of the concept of concrete experience often requires direct experience with the varying degrees of concreteness that are possible within the confines of a classroom. The example activity For You to Try: A Hands-On Experience is designed to give individuals experience with a concept from its most abstract level to more explicit, concrete awareness. This particular example requires a minimum of two people, a ball, paper and pencil, and a story that contains some references to any kind of ball, such as Stephen Kellogg's (1978) *The Mystery of the Magic Green Ball.*

## FOR YOU TO TRY
## A Hands-On Experience

### THE BALL

*Close your eyes. Think of the word* ball. *Try not to visualize.*
*Now visualize the word itself.* B-a-l-l. *Now visualize the object.*
*Open your eyes. Watch me and listen as I say the word* ball.
*Say the word* ball.
*Look at the word as I write it on the chart paper:* b-a-l-l.
*Write the word on your paper. Read the word aloud.*
*This is a book about a magic green ball.* (See Kellogg, 1978.)
*Listen as I read the book. Discuss the book.*
*Draw a picture of a ball. Share it with a friend.*
*Write a narrative about your picture of a ball.*
*Look at this ball. What kind is it? Describe it orally.*
*Catch the ball. Touch it, feel its shape. Describe it in writing.*
*Bounce the ball. Pitch the ball. Play a game with just the ball.*
*Write a poem, fiction piece, or nonfiction piece about your experiences*
*with balls.*
*Share your work with a friend.*

This exercise is only one example of many vocabulary words and concepts that can involve manipulation of an object in conjunction with reading and writing connected text. Once one begins thinking about ways of presenting concepts through an experience-based curriculum, the process of incorporating concrete activities becomes a natural part of reading and writing instruction.

***Brainstorming.***     Brainstorming, or whole-class discussions about any topic, may be the most often used prereading and prewriting activity across all subject areas. "Tell me everything you already know about _____" is a typical question eliciting children's knowledge and understanding of important concepts. During whole-class discussions of a word, free associations play a role in individual children's memories of real and vicarious experiences with the concept.

Basing vocabulary instruction on experience is an important part of conceptual approaches since our concept of the world in general is grounded in experience. A concrete, hands-on experience of some kind should be a part of the brainstorming session whenever possible, thereby adding to the stimulus for remembering and discussing the target concept. During whole-class discussions, the teacher also facilitates memory of the concept by asking leading questions that encourage children to think about their past experiences with the word in particular and the underlying concepts in general. Following is a concept-formation activity set in a fourth-grade classroom.

## INSIDE THE CLASSROOM
### Tornado in a Bottle

**Ms. Cook:** Look what I have here, a mayonnaise jar half filled with water. I've put a few drops of dishwashing liquid in the jar along with three or four very tiny pebbles. Now when I shake the jar quickly in a circular manner, look what happens. What does this remind you of? [Ms. Cook has created an artificial "tornado" in a bottle.]

**Gregory:** It's a tornado! A baby tornado.

**Ms. Cook:** It does look like a little tornado or water spout, doesn't it? I'm going to pass the jar around the room and let all of you have a chance to make the tornado in the jar and to see it up close. While we're doing that I want you to tell me everything you know about the word *tornado*. [While the children talk, Ms. Cook plots a semantic map of their responses, Figure 6.1, on the chalkboard.]

**Ann:** They're real bad storms with a lot of wind and rain. Sometimes hail too.

**Tim:** And they can suck up trees and even whole houses.

**Ms. Cook:** So a tornado is a very destructive storm. Have any of you ever seen or been in a tornado?

**Kimberly:** I have. It's scary. I saw one out on my aunt's farm. It was black and huge and sounded like a freight train. It looked like it was coming right at me.

**Ms. Cook:** I've been in just one tornado in my life. Just after a heavy rainstorm and hail the sky darkened and everything was very calm. No wind at all. Then suddenly a tornado hit the town. It destroyed several buildings.

**Bill:** I've just been in regular storms. But I've seen pictures of them. Some of 'em are white. They're shaped like funnels. They look kinda pretty, but they're not really.

**Ms. Cook:** What else do you know about tornadoes? Where are tornadoes most likely to occur?

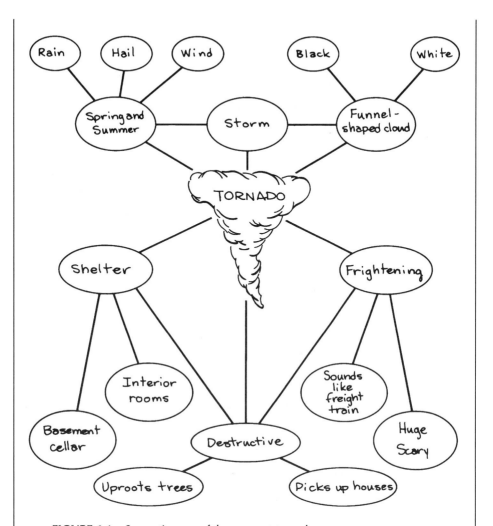

**FIGURE 6.1**    Semantic map of the concept tornado

**CONNIE:** In Kansas!

**MS. COOK:** Why do you say that, Connie?

**CONNIE:** Because I saw *The Wizard of Oz* about ten times. My dad says that movie was made in Kansas. It's the tornado capital of the world.

**RAY:** My grandpa says he lives in "tornado alley." That's in Oklahoma where they have lots of tornadoes too.

**MS. COOK:** Are there other names we often use that mean the same thing as tornado? What are some other severe tornadolike storms?

*(continued)*

**Inside the Classroom (continued)**

**KARLA:** Do you mean like *cyclone?* That's what my big brother who lives in Texas calls them.

**BARB:** What about *whirlwinds* and *dust devils.* Aren't they just baby tornadoes?

**MS. COOK:** Good answers. A *cyclone* is really another name for tornado. It's a very powerful and destructive windstorm with swirling winds. And you're right, Barb. Whirlwinds and dust devils are very similar in shape to tornadoes. We often see them from a distance in the desert or on prairies, especially in very dry weather. They're not so destructive but can be annoying if they pass in front of your car while you're driving along the highway. What time of year are tornadoes likely to occur?

**BOBBY:** Usually in the spring and summer, like last year when the sirens blew during school, and we all had to move into the hallway and get down on the floor and cover our heads.

**MS. COOK:** I remember. Tornado drills are very important. They can save lives. The weather stations are very good at warning the public to be on the alert for these massive storms. But tornadoes are sometimes unpredictable. We have to be prepared to take shelter whenever one is near. What kinds of cover make the best shelter?

**LAURA:** Basements and cellars. Anything underground.

**PAM:** My mom always makes us go in the inside linen closet.

**MS. COOK:** How are tornadoes formed? [There is no response.] We're going to find out how tornadoes are actually formed and also more facts about these storms.. Listen while I read this very special book by Franklin Branley (1990) called *Tornado Alert.* Afterwards we'll talk about the new information we've learned about tornadoes. This will get us ready to read and write as we study tornadoes, hurricanes, monsoons, and other tropical weather during our science unit on natural disasters.

***Reflections.***    Research indicates that the prereading and prewriting portions of a lesson may have the greatest potential for fostering comprehension (Durkin, 1984) and, because the process is similar, composition. Time spent activating children's prior knowledge of important concepts is well worth the effort. Teacher-directed discussions, as in the preceding example, are often a prelude to child-centered lessons that may involve independent reading, researching the concept further, composition, creative writing, and creative dramatics. Figure 6.2 is an example of a first draft about a "baby tornado" written by a fourth-grader in Ms. Cook's class.

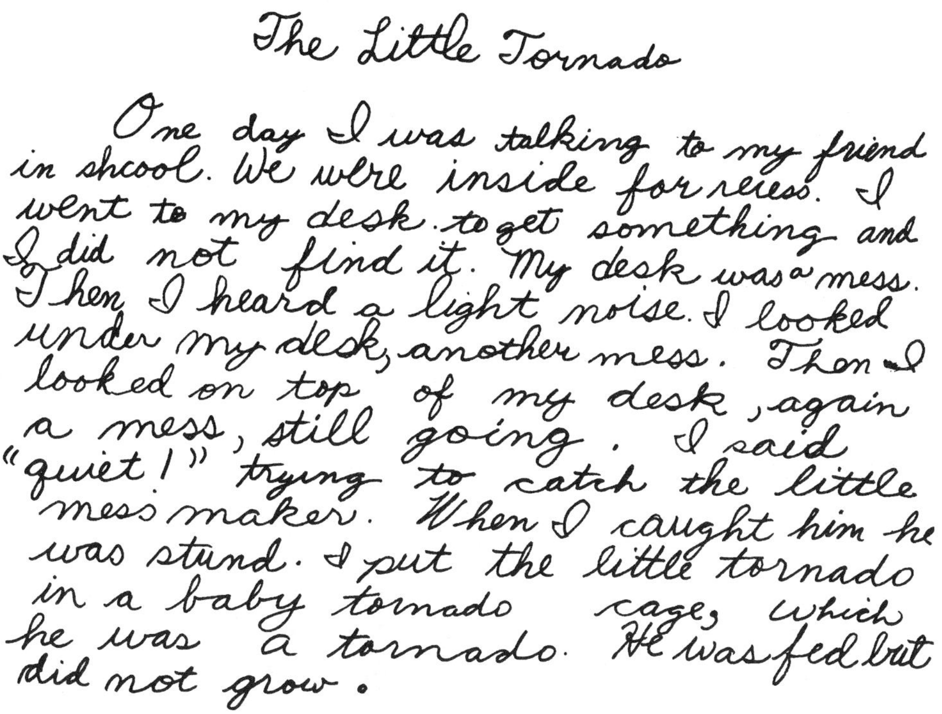

# The Little Tornado

One day I was talking to my friend in shcool. We were inside for recess. I went to my desk to get something and I did not find it. My desk was a mess. Then I heard a light noise. I looked under my desk, another mess. Then I looked on top of my desk, again a mess, still going. I said "quiet!" trying to catch the little mess maker. When I caught him he was stund. I put the little tornado in a baby tornado cage, which he was a tornado. He was fed but did not grow.

**FIGURE 6.2**    "The Little Tornado," by Catherine, grade 4

***Semantic Maps.***    Semantic maps, sometimes referred to as *concept maps* or *webbing,* are visual representations of the relationships among ideas underlying a concept. The semantic map is perhaps the simplest and most often used visual aid for helping children to categorize and classify important information relative to the vocabulary under study. Graphic representations of the children's ideas can be drawn spontaneously, as they emerge, or prepared ahead of time and used as a stimulus for discussion. A variety of configurations are possible, including circles, boxes, grids, matrices, and simple squares with connecting lines to designate relationships among ideas. Chalkboard, overheads, and chart paper are the best media for presenting a semantic map. Semantic maps can be as simple or as elaborate as the teacher and grade level dictate. The most important point to remember is to make the relationships among the ideas clear to the student. Concept circles (or blocks) are particularly useful in the primary grades for demonstrating examples and nonexamples of simple ideas (Figure 6.3).

***Semantic Feature Analysis.***    Semantic feature analysis (SFA) (Johnson & Pearson, 1984) is a schema-based strategy that encourages analyzing, comparing, and contrasting new and old information about vocabulary words belonging to the same class, such as people, animals, and buildings. "Semantic features" refers to the "phrases describing components of meaning shared by some of the words or that dis-

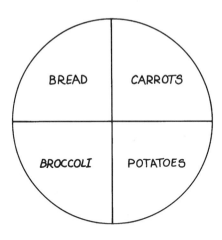

*There are four foods in the circle. One of them does not belong. Describe the relationship among the three foods that do belong and explain why the one food is miscategorized.*

**FIGURE 6.3** Concept circle: Food groups

tinguish a word from other meanings" (Nagy, 1988, p. 14). More specifically, the strategy involves analyzing the parts of a concept in relation to the whole and comparing the features of each part by using a matrix. The vertical columns of the matrix represent the basic features of the vocabulary words that are listed horizontally. Used during prereading or prewriting, SFA activates children's prior knowledge of difficult concepts that will influence comprehension and composition (Anders & Bos, 1986).

Figure 6.4 describes the concept of *transportation* as it evolved during a class discussion. Pluses, minuses, zeros, and question marks in each cell signify the relative value of each feature in relation to the vocabulary word. For example, *cars* get pluses in the cells corresponding with characteristics most often associated with automobiles (for people, ground transportation, etc.), and minuses are placed in the cells intersecting with features more commonly associated with airplanes and space travel (wings, jets, cargo bay). Zeros indicate ambiguity about whether or not the feature applies or is applicable only in certain circumstances (i.e., *bicycle* and long-distance travel). Question marks indicate that further research is necessary to make an appropriate response, as in *airplane* and keys. These matrices are valuable adjuncts to class discussions and follow-up research activities. The graphic is a clear repre-

| Mode of travel | For people | For animals | For products | For children | Short distance travel | Long distance travel | Gasoline | Rocket fuel | Wings | Keys | Seat belts | Other: |
|---|---|---|---|---|---|---|---|---|---|---|---|---|
| Car | + | O | O | + | + | + | + | − | − | + | + | |
| Bus | + | O | O | + | + | + | + | − | − | + | − | |
| Airplane | + | O | O | O | O | + | − | ? | + | ? | + | |
| Train | + | O | O | O | + | + | ? | − | − | ? | − | |
| Bicycle | + | − | ? | + | + | O | − | − | − | − | − | |
| Mini-van | + | O | O | + | + | + | + | − | − | + | + | |
| Space shuttle | + | ? | + | − | − | + | − | + | + | ? | + | |
| Other: | | | | | | | | | | | | |

Legend:  + Always  — Never  O Sometimes  ? Needs research

**FIGURE 6.4**  Transportation matrix: Semantic feature analysis

sentation of categories in the concept under study, and there is room to expand the matrix as ideas evolve during class discussion. The next step in the activity is to put the concept into a context involving reading and writing connected text, as could be required through descriptive writing or further research.

***Word Sorts.***    Word sorting is a simple categorization strategy that fosters a deeper understanding of and memory for concepts. Based on the principles of inductive reasoning and discovery learning, word-sorting activities focus on classifying words according to their common properties, "one of the most basic and powerful operations of human thinking that is responsible for much of a child's natural learning ability, particularly the acquisition of linguistic concepts" (Gillet & Temple, 1989, p. 205). In word-sorting activities, as the name implies, children sort through familiar and/or unfamiliar words written on index cards, study and compare them to determine the features they have in common, and sort them accordingly. Vocabulary-building words may be the best kind for word-sorting activities, especially when you are introducing the strategy. However, other useful words, interesting words, or key concepts can also make successful sorts.

## INSTRUCTIONAL GUIDELINES
### Developing Word-Sorting Activities

The following are some guidelines for creating vocabulary activities that utilize both open and closed sorts.

**MATERIALS**

1. Three-by-5-inch lined note cards
2. Pencil, pen, or fine-tip markers
3. Recipe card boxes, small shoe boxes, small pocket folders, alphabet tabs
4. Rubber bands
5. Picture file

**COLLECTING THE WORDS**

The majority of the words for sorting games should be easily recognized at sight by the children. Allow the children to help develop their own word cards. This saves time and energy and is simultaneously educational.

**EXAMPLE SOURCES**

1. Word banks—words that children have collected as a result of language experiences
2. Personal dictionaries (put words on cards)
3. Sight-word vocabulary from basal-reader lessons

4. Words that have been derived from children's literature in read-aloud activities and follow-up writing
5. Content area key vocabulary words

## USING WORD SORTS

### Closed Sorts

In a closed-sort activity, the feature that all words contain is stated in advance. This activity teaches convergent thinking.

### TEACHER-DIRECTED EXAMPLES

1. Search for the words that have similar meanings (synonyms): *ecstatic, lament, happy, sad, bright, cheerful, optimistic, anguish, joyous, sorrow, grieve.*
2. Which words in the stack are derived from a similar base or root word? *forgive, unforgiven, forgetful, forgetfulness, forgotten, forget, forgot.*
3. Sort through these color words and match them with the vocabulary word that could represent the connotative meaning of the color word: *yellow, blue, green, red, envious, angry, sad, cowardly.*
4. Match all of the words in your word bank with a picture in the picture file. Classify the words as person, place, thing, or idea (no picture required).
5. Find all of the homonyms. Sort them according to homophone and homograph: *read, read, red, knight, night, to, too, two, their, there, they're*
6. Locate all of the key words associated with the concept of energy: *conservation, watt, battery, sun, wind, wire, plug, waterfall, conduct, heat, light.*
7. Read these words and identify the word(s) that cannot be associated with the concept of freedom: *autonomy, emancipation, independence, confinement, liberty, sovereignty, slavery*

### GAMES

Tracking the Unknown is a closed-sort game in which the teacher or a peer presents groups of several semantically similar, easily recognized words, such as *pretty, lovely, gorgeous,* and then shows a word or words similar in meaning but not likely to be known, such as *comely.* The purpose of the game is to determine if the child can generalize from the known words to the unknown words and recognize the new words' meanings by applying the generalization. *Comely* must mean "good-looking"!

### Open Sorts

In an open-sort activity, no criteria are stated in advance. Instead the children examine the words in their stack of cards, categorize them according to their own ability to discover similarities, and classify them through discovery learn-

*(continued)*

---

### Instructional Guidelines (continued)

ing. The children are guided toward discovering ways to sort the words by teacher assistance as well as peer involvement through small-group efforts. Once the cards are sorted, the children are encouraged to come up with the category, classification, or generalization that underlies the logic of their sort. Open sorts encourage divergent thinking because the children can choose among many alternatives when sorting and classifying their words.

#### CHILD-DIRECTED EXAMPLES

1. puppy, grass, molecule, flower, tiger (living things)
2. Sesame Street, Mr. Rogers, Electric Company (children's programs)
3. books, newspapers, street signs, captions (things to read)
4. jump, walk, run, skip, crawl (action words)
5. mail, tail, sail, nail, jail (rhyming words)
6. circle, square, rectangle, triangle (shapes)

#### GAMES

Read My Mind is an open-sort game in which children work individually to sort their words according to a generalization that they determine. A partner with whom they are working then tries to guess the generalization or tries to add words from his or her word cards that fit their partner's word sort.

---

***Skills in Context.***    Word-sorting activities can be extended to more contextually based situations. For example, in closed-sort activities the children could go on to write definition, comparison, or classification paragraphs to demonstrate full understanding of the concepts that underlie their lists of words. In open-sort activities, the children could examine their own or professionally written fiction, nonfiction, or poetry for words that could be easily categorized. Word sorting is deceptively simple in design, yet it is a powerful activity that will generate an interest in word learning and simultaneously encourage broad conceptual thinking.

## USING THE NEWS

Newspapers and magazines are a rich source of vocabulary words and interesting concepts that form the basis of quality vocabulary instruction. The comic strip page is an especially good place to start. Almost all children read and enjoy "the funnies." Goldstein (1986) found cartoons and comic strips to contain more difficult vocabulary words than most people imagine. And if you can't figure out what the words mean, the cartoon isn't humorous! Cartoonists are also fond of using figurative language, including similes, metaphors, and puns. Puns are plays on words that have a

The newspaper is a rich source of vocabulary words for instruction.

humorous effect, as in "That's very punny." Children can search the funny papers for figurative language or interesting words that can be used in word sorts, cloze activities, or comics rewritten with synonyms (or antonyms) to make the original strip more accessible to younger audiences. Class cartoons are also popular, with comic strip characters based on classmates and "balloon bubble" dialogue that relates to real classroom discussions and events. Class cartoons are often successful when written in groups, with a designated illustrator and lots of interaction about choosing just the right humorous vocabulary words and contexts.

The newspaper is a classic resource for teaching the concepts of *fact* and *opinion,* two very important terms to be reckoned with throughout our lifetime. The editorial page and advice columns are the most logical places to find opinions, whereas front-page news articles, public notices, and classified ads contain the most facts. But which vocabulary words denote facts and which denote opinion? The difference can be subtle. Differentiating fact from opinion during the reading process sometimes requires a sophisticated knowledge of word meaning, connotations, and special contextual usage, coupled with a worldly knowledge that only prior experience can offer. When composing expository or argumentative discourse, presenting clear facts and convincing opinions is essential. Teaching children to be critical readers and writers requires them to have a full conceptual understanding of what makes up the facts and the opinions.

Cartoons often provide interesting concepts for vocabulary instruction.

## Getting the Facts

Regardless of the age of the child you are working with, it is important to begin with a good definition of fact and opinion, followed by an experience that will make the definition real and meaningful. *The Macmillan Dictionary for Children* (1987) gives us a place to start. The dictionary definition of *fact* is "Something that is known to be true or real; something that has really happened" (p. 231). Although we know that facts are known to be true or real, there is another dimension to factual information that the definition alone does not address. Facts can be tested or verified, and they can be either accurate or inaccurate. These elements of the concept are what enable us to make the idea real and meaningful.

A simple way to demonstrate the concept of a fact is to involve the children in role-playing a situation from which factual information, as well as opinions, can be explicitly and implicitly derived. Ms. Carpenter utilizes paired role playing in her third-grade class as she attempts to bring the concepts of fact and fantasy close to home.

### JEREMY'S BEDTIME

> **Ms. CARPENTER:** *Angela, I want you to pretend for a moment that you are a mom or a dad. Explain to your child, Jeremy here, why he has to go to bed at 8:30 P.M. Include as many facts as you can imagine. The rest of the class is going to listen for all the facts and write them in their journals. I'm going to tape-record your skit so that we can listen later and verify the facts and any opinions that we heard.*
>
> **CAST:** *Mom—Angela P., Jeremy—Jeremy L.*
>
> **MOM:** *It's 8:30, Jeremy. Time for bed. You have to get up early in the morning and go to swimming lessons.*
>
> **JEREMY:** *Awe, do I have to? It's still light outside. And I want to ride my bike. You let me ride my bike last night after 8:30.*
>
> **MOM:** *Yesterday was Saturday. And you rode your bike until 8:00. Remember, the whole family watched a movie after you came in. You got to stay up late because it was Saturday. This morning you were exhausted.*
>
> **JEREMY:** *But I won't be tired. You're not being fair.*
>
> **MOM:** *I am being fair. Tomorrow's going to be a great day! Goodnight, Jeremy. Sleep tight.*

The brief skit provides a scene that is close to every child's experience—arguing with a parent about bedtime. It is a real context in which to talk about facts. What are the facts?

1. Jeremy's bedtime is 8:30 P.M. (explicitly stated and verifiable fact).
2. Jeremy got to ride his bike after 8:30 P.M. last night (explicitly stated, verifiable, yet inaccurate according to authority—Jeremy's mother; Jeremy has created a fiction about bike riding last evening).
3. Mom let Jeremy watch a movie Saturday night and stay up late (explicit and verifiable—the whole family watched the movie).
5. Jeremy went to bed (implied, verifiable fact—"Goodnight, Jeremy").

## Recognizing Opinions

"Jeremy's Bedtime" may also be used to help children recognize opinions. After listing the facts brought out in the dialogue between Jeremy and his mother, ask the children if they know what an opinion is. Begin again with a good dictionary definition such as Macmillan's (1987): An opinion is "a belief that is based on what a person thinks rather than on what is proved or known to be true" (p. 437). The concept of opinion is even more abstract to a child than factual ideas. The truth or falsity of an opinion cannot in the end be verified. The vocabulary words that surround and form the opinion give us clues to the verifiability of the statement. For instance, the opinions in "Jeremy's Bedtime" are as follows:

1. "This morning you were exhausted."
2. "I won't be tired."
3. "You're not being fair."
4. "I am being fair."
5. "Tomorrow's going to be a great day!"

Both Jeremy's and his mother's opinions contain adjectives that deal with quality—*exhausted, tired, fair, great*—as opposed to quantity. Qualitative information is almost always in the realm of opinions, whereas quantitative data are factual in nature. It would be difficult to prove just how tired Jeremy really was. Although we probably believe that Jeremy's mother is really being fair, there's no way of knowing for sure without more information. And who's to know just how "great" tomorrow is really going to be? Degrees of tiredness, fairness, and greatness are difficult to quantify. Providing children with contrasting statements is sometimes useful in showing the relationship between quality and quantity, opinion and fact. For example, contrast these statements. Which is fact? Which is opinion?

1. Karen is prettier than Darlene.
2. Darlene is a faster swimmer than Karen.

Obviously, statement number 2 would be much easier to test empirically than number 1. Degrees of prettiness are subject to opinion.

Other special vocabulary that signals opinions are words that express qualification, exaggeration, or an appeal to the emotions. Phrases that qualify the author's statement include *I think, I truly believe, it is our opinion, in my honest opinion, in her mind, it is his belief,* and *in their view.* Qualifying adverbs also cue us to opinions since the writer will use them whenever he or she is expressing an uncertainty, as in *probably, usually, likely,* and *possibly.* To stimulate a discussion of qualifiers, use examples close to the students' awareness. For example, "In the school board's view, the fall semester break is probably unnecessary" is a statement that will stimulate a lively discussion filled with opinions from the class, as well as some pertinent facts relative to the issue of semester breaks. Comparing and contrasting the opinions and facts in a class discussion will also elicit more qualifying statements, which can be added to the list for future reference.

Exaggeration, often in the form of an overgeneralization, very often denotes an opinion, as in "The sixth-graders are the greatest kids in the school!" However, placed in the context of a school newspaper article that specifically addresses the sixth-graders' contributions to a recent fund-raising drive, the statement becomes more factual in nature. An important point to make when teaching fact and opinion is that the more specific one can be, the more likely the information will be interpreted as fact.

Finally, emotion-laden words, or words with connotations that appeal to our emotions, are also signs of opinions. *Courageous, heart-rending, hideous, daring, forthright, noble, mean,* and *ugly* are just a few examples. News articles should be as objective as possible and not contain vocabulary that reveals the author's bias. Recognizing the difference between objectivity and subjectivity is closely aligned to the task of differentiating between fact and opinion. Reading and writing a news or informational article and an accompanying letter to the editor on the same topic is one way to teach elementary and junior high children appropriate uses for subjective and objective language, as in the following exercise.

## FOR YOU TO TRY
## Children's News Writing

Children's news writing is often filled with lots of opinion that may color the facts. Read the following pieces taken from an actual elementary school newspaper.

### FOURTH-GRADERS WIN ALL DURING FIELD DAY

*Ms. Thompson's fourth-grade class won all the events in last Friday's field day competition. The 12 girls and 16 boys were fantastic in every race. Billy N. was especially sensational in the 50-yard dash, and Sally R. was the prettiest and the fastest hopper in the gunnysack race. The boys' and girls' sportsmanship was also astonishing. They got really excited when they won the big trophy. Nobody said anything mean to anybody. The whole school was extremely proud of them.*

*Dear Editor,*
*I am writing about last week's dumb article about Ms. Thompson's fourth-grade class being such goody-goodies during field day. No way were those kids as nice as the article said they were. Billy N. himself stuck his tongue out at me after he won the race. You'd have to be blind not to see it. I guess you are blind because Sally R. isn't all that pretty. Besides, I think the whole thing was rigged. Our fourth-grade class in Ms. Bernard's room was better than they were. Everybody said we were. Didn't you notice all the "boos" from the crowds when we didn't win. I'd say we really won at least six of those ten events. It's just not fair.*

*A mad fourth-grader from room 206*
*(continued)*

---

**For You to Try (continued)**

Now design a Writers' Workshop that focuses on the concepts of objectivity and subjectivity. To create the teacher-written models for your workshop, complete the following steps:

1. List the words and phrases that reflect the opinion of the author.
2. Rewrite the article to make it more objective.
3. Rewrite the letter to the editor to make it less subjective.

---

Concepts form the basis of all vocabulary words, indeed of all that we know. Carefully chosen words learned well help to build a vocabulary that enables children to conceptualize about things experienced during reading and writing. An essential goal of vocabulary instruction is to give students every opportunity to conceptualize about new vocabulary words. In the end, it is only through a wide variety of real experiences with concepts that we are able to make individual words a permanent part of our reading and writing vocabularies.


## THEMATIC UNITS

### VIGNETTE

*"How was school today?" asked Mitchell's mother, as the second-grader entered the kitchen.*

*"Terrible! I'm sick, sick, sick to death of apples," Mitchell shouted.*

*"Why are you so sick of apples? You like apples," she replied, somewhat puzzled.*

*"Because all we ever do is talk about apples. It all started when Miss Philips read us* Johnny Appleseed. *Then we went on that field trip to Britt's farm and picked apples. And then Joey's mommy helped us make no-bake apple cookies. And then we had to color apples. And then we had to draw apples and cut them out and paste them on the apple bulletin board. We even have to see what happens if you put an apple in a jar and leave it there for three weeks. If you ask me, that's gross. And today we had to count apples in math and do apple story problems. And you know what, next week we have to go to the library and look up all the books we can find with the word apple in the title. Second grade's dumb. I wish we could just read about dinosaurs and stuff like that. What's for dinner?"*

*"Your favorite: apple dumplings!" his mom said, as Mitchell bolted for the door.*

Thematic units are gaining prominence in elementary and middle school curricula, with recent interest in whole language and integrated language arts. A thematic unit is a lesson-planning method that integrates listening, speaking, reading, and writing in the context of a theme, which spans several subject areas. The length of a unit varies according to topic, objectives, and grade level. Units can last a week, a month, a grading period, or a whole year. Like any successful teaching strategy, units of study must be carefully designed in order to meet intended outcomes and at the same time sustain children's interest and attention. Functional thematic units have as their basis a conceptually based theme that ties ideas together in meaningful and interesting ways. Thematic units introduce children to concepts in a wide range of contexts, thus encouraging a deeper understanding of new information.

To be effective, themes need to be broadly defined and grounded in the major concepts to be studied. Whereas some teachers organize integrated lessons according to motifs or topics, such as apples or dinosaurs, conceptually based themes are universal in nature. For example, Figure 6.5 is a Rain Forest unit that has as its basis

**FIGURE 6.5**   Thematic unit: The rain forest

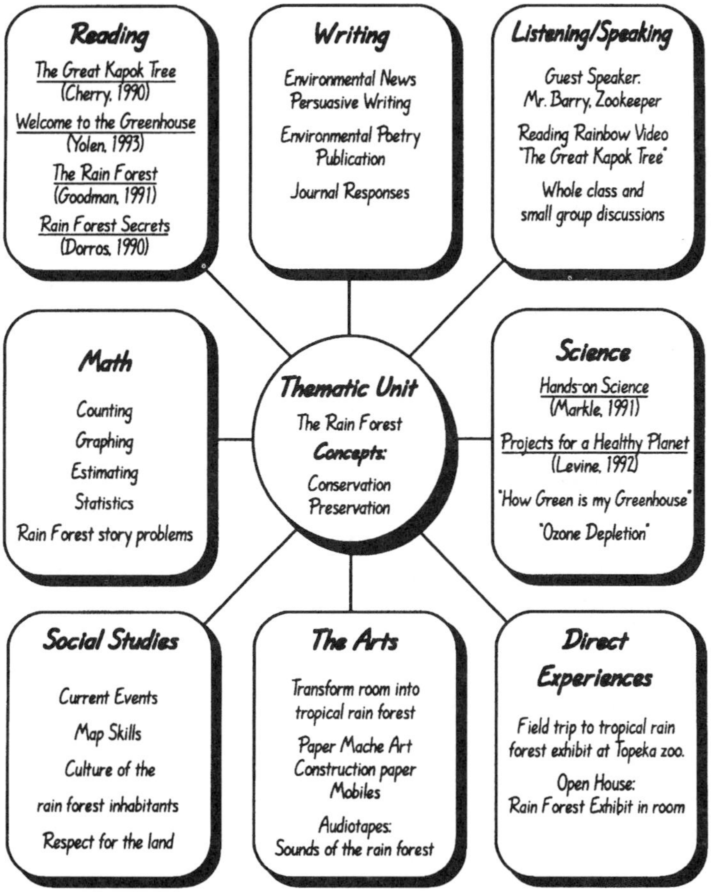

the concepts of conservation and preservation. This two-week unit is designed for use in a multiage classroom housing grades 1–3. In this community of learners, the social nature of learning is prominent as the children work together in achieving unit objectives. Conversation and discussion are primary vehicles for exploring new ideas. Whole-class activities include taking a field trip to a rain forest exhibit, listening to children's literature and a guest speaker, creating a classroom rain forest for open house, and publishing a class environmental newsletter and poetry collection. Small-group cooperative learning focuses on math and science concepts, such as estimating and preserving, through experimentation and manipulation. Individualized learning occurs throughout the unit via independent reading and writing. The children's new knowledge is assessed informally through observation and analysis. Final drafts of writing projects are placed in the children's portfolios.

Thematic units are often thought of as all-encompassing, and this can frustrate planning. While it is possible to develop a unit of study that includes all subject areas, it is not always practical. To artificially impose a theme on a subject area can adversely affect children's motivation to learn. As illustrated in the vignette above, Mitchell's complaints about school were due in part to his teacher's overuse of the topic "apples." Consider the following guidelines when planning functional thematic units for your classroom:

## INSTRUCTIONAL GUIDELINES
### Creating Thematic Units

#### CHOOSING A THEME

The inspiration for a thematic unit can come from a variety of sources. The more broadly defined the theme, the easier it is to connect subject areas. There are several categories of themes to consider.

#### *Universal Themes*

Very broad, generally stated themes are universal in nature, touching everyone's life experiences in some way. Universal themes are frequently suggested by content area readings, children's literature, and current events. School districts and curriculum planning committees sometimes recommend very broad themes for each grade level. Some examples are:

communication

patterns

change

diversity

### Literary Themes

A literary theme is a generalization about life and the human condition. Such themes are typically defined as the overriding main idea of a short story or novel. Literary themes are interpretations of prose and poetry, rather than literal statements about what happens in a story, nonfiction, or poem. They can usually be expressed in a sentence, as in the following examples:

> Everyone needs to be wanted and loved.
>
> Growing up involves joy and pain.
>
> We learn from life's experiences.
>
> Good often overcomes evil.
>
> Friendship brings obligation.
>
> We must develop respect for differences among each other.

Two sub-categories of literary thematic units are author studies and genre studies.

### Author Studies

An author study focuses on the works of a single author. Reading many or all works written by a single author enables students to understand better the concepts of writer, writing style, and audience. The idea of recurring literary themes can also be introduced when a single author is studied.

### Genre Studies

Genre studies refers to a unit plan centering on one form of literature at a time: fiction, nonfiction, biography, autobiography, poetry, or drama. The literary form, or text structure, is what gives the unit cohesion. Studying one genre in-depth gives students a better sense of how authors go about developing narratives, expository prose, and poetry.

### Topical Themes

Topical themes are more specific in nature. They are frequently inspired by the subject areas. Topical themes usually lend themselves to shorter units of study that may connect children's literature with a few subject areas. Some example topics are:

> Friends and Family
>
> The Environment
>
> Communities
>
> War and Peace
>
> The Southwest

*(continued)*

**Instructional Guidelines (continued)**

A subcategory of topical themes is the content area unit of study.

### Content Area Units

Textbooks in the contents areas of math, science, and social studies, frequently organize information thematically. For instance, *People in Time and Place: Comparing Communities* (Joyce & Erickson, 1991) is a third-grade social studies textbook with four distinct thematic units: Communities and Maps; Communities and Natural Resources; Government and Citizenship; and Communities Yesterday and Today. Within each unit are several chapters that address the broad theme more specifically. Also included in each unit are thematically relevant children's literature selections and journal writing activities.

Content area units need not be limited to textbook use alone. One can build upon any topic in any content area, integrating wide reading in math, science, or the social studies with listening, speaking, reading, and writing and in the contexts of children's literature, the arts, and direct experiences.

### *Motifs*

Motifs are superficial themes that can tie together several subject areas, but not necessarily in a substantive manner. Motifs are best thought of as tools to motivate children's interest and attention. They can be used in conjunction with broader-based themes. Example motifs are:

Colors
Animals
Food

### PLANNING A UNIT

Carefully planned units of study stand the test of time and can be used year after year with minor adjustments. The following is an organizational procedure intended as an aid to unit planning.

1. Survey curricular objectives for your grade level and make a list of major concepts that span two or more major subject areas.
2. Decide upon a thematic approach: universal theme, literary theme, topical theme, or motif. Choose an approach or combination of approaches that will effectively deal with important objectives and concepts.

3. Decide which subject areas lend themselves naturally to the theme. Not every subject lends itself to inclusion in a thematic unit. When a content area does not fit into a theme, omit the subject rather than force the ideas.
4. List materials and activities that will help you to develop concepts across two or more subject areas.
5. Determine the length of the unit, based upon the curricular objectives and amount of material you wish to cover. Keep in mind the students' probable attention span.
6. Gather materials, arrange for special activities, and implement the unit.

Thematic units can be very rewarding experiences for teacher and students. Appendix D contains samples of functional thematic units written for a variety of grade levels, K–8.

These second- and third-graders display artwork that accompanied a thematic unit on "The Rain Forest."

## FOR YOUR JOURNAL

1. Observe the development of a new concept that has been introduced in a primary, intermediate, or middle school classroom. Comment on how much or how little the students already seem to know about the ideas being discussed. Draw some conclusions about future direct instruction and child-centered activities that elaborate and extend the concept.

2. Spend a day discovering the *interesting words* that elementary or middle school children are naturally curious about. Can you categorize them? How would you incorporate these concepts into the daily curriculum to encourage curiosity about words?

3. Make a list of "feeling" or sensory words (e.g., *gooey, creepy, hot,* and *cool*) and read them aloud to a group of elementary or middle school students. Ask for reactions. Are there a variety of connotations within and across grade levels?

4. Pick a word from your favorite children's book and design a concept map around that word. See how far you can extend the concept. Describe how you would help children use the concept within the context of reading and writing connected text.

5. Describe a concept-formation activity that is experience-based. Carefully explain how you would provide a real or vicarious experience with a concept that not only stimulates memory of past experiences but also extends the children's personal experience.

6. Design a print media-based vocabulary activity that incorporates a real experience with reading and writing connected text.

7. Design a functional thematic unit.

## DICTIONARIES AND THESAURI

### Kindergarten and Primary Grades

*American Heritage First Dictionary* (1986), Houghton Mifflin.
*Good Morning, Words!* (1990), Scott, Foresman.
*Macmillan First Dictionary* (1990), Macmillan.
*My First Dictionary* (1990), Scott, Foresman.
Root, B. (1993), *My First Dictionary,* Dorling Kindersley.
*The American Heritage Picture Dictionary* (1986), Houghton Mifflin.
*The Kingfisher First Thesaurus* (1993), Kingfisher Books.
*The Doubleday Children's Dictionary* (1989), Doubleday.

*The Doubleday Children's Picture Dictionary* (1987), Doubleday.
*The Macmillan Picture Wordbook* (1990), Macmillan.
*Webster's New World Children's Dictionary* (1991), Prentice-Hall.
*Words for New Readers.* (1990), Scott, Foresman.

## Intermediate Grades and Middle School

*Macmillan Dictionary for Children,* newly revised (1989), Macmillan.
*Macmillan Dictionary for Students* (1984), Macmillan.
*Roget's 21st Century Thesaurus* (1991), Dell.
*The American Heritage Student's Dictionary* (1986), Houghton Mifflin.
*The Merriam-Webster Thesaurus* (1989), Merriam-Webster.
*Thorndike-Barnhart Student Dictionary* (1992), HarperCollins.
*Webster's Elementary Dictionary* (1986), Merriam-Webster.
*Webster's Intermediate Dictionary* (1986), Merriam-Webster.
*Webster's New World Children's Dictionary* (1991), Simon & Schuster.
*Webster's New World Dictionary for Young Adults* (1992), Prentice-Hall.

## SELECTED BIBLIOGRAPHY OF PERIODICALS FOR CHILDREN AND ADOLESCENTS

## Kindergarten and Primary Grades

*Boomerang* (an audio magazine—storytelling, music). 123 Townsend Street, Suite 636, San Francisco, CA 94107

*Chicadee.* The Young Naturalist Foundation, 56 The Esplanade, Suite 306, Toronto, Ontario, Canada M5E147

*Cricket* (archeology, fantasy, history). P.O. Box 51144, Boulder, CO 80321-1144

*Hidden Pictures Magazine* (mazes, puzzles). 2300 W. Fifth Ave, P. O. Box 269, Boulder, CO.

*Highlights for Children.* 803 Church Street, Honesdale, PA 18431.

*Hopscotch: The Magazine for Girls.* PO Box 1292, Saratoga Springs, NY 12866

*Kid City* (formerly *Electric Company*). Lincoln Plaza, New York, NY 10023

*Kids Discover* (historical and scientific facts). 170 Fifth Avenue, New York, NY 10010

*Ladybug* (songs, rhymes, fiction). P. O. Box 58343, Boulder, CO 80321-8343

*Penny Power* (consumerism). Consumers Union of the U.S., 256 Washington Street, Mt. Vernon, NY 10553

*P3: The Earth-Based Magazine for Kids.* PO Box 52, Montgomery, VT 05470

*Ranger Rick.* 8925 Leesburg Pike, Vienna, VA 22184-0001

*Scholastic News.* Scholastic, 2931 E. McCarty Street, PO Box 3710, Jefferson City, MO 65102-9957

*Seedling Series: Short Story International.* 6 Sheffield Road, Great Neck, NY 11021

*Sesame Street Magazine.* Lincoln Plaza, New York, NY 10023-80322

*The Mini Page* (tabloid). Diane Galante, UNiversal Press Syndicate, PO Box 41950, Kansas City, MO 64141

*Your Big Backyard* (nature and animals) 8925 Leesburg Pike, Vienna, VA 22184-0001

U*S* Kids (health and fitness). 245 Long Hill Road, Middletown, CT 06457

*World Newsmap of the Week/Headline Focus.* Field Publications, 4343 Equity Drive, PO Box 16630, Columbus, OH 43216

*Zoobooks.* Wildlife Education, Ltd., 3590 Kettner Blvd., San Diego, CA 92101

## Intermediate Grades and Middle School

*Boy's Life* (nature, sports, hobbies). 1325 W. Walnut Hill Lane, PO Box 152079, Irving, TX 75015-2079

*Calliope: World History for Young People,* 30 Grove Street, Peterborough, NH 03458

*Cobblestone: The History Magazine for Young People.* 30 Grove Street, Peterborough, NH 03458

*Dolphin Log.* The Cousteau Society, 8440 Santa Monica Blvd., Los Angeles, CA 90069

*Faces: The Magazine About People* (anthropology and natural history). 30 Grove Street, Peterborough, NH 03458

*Know Your World Extra* (news, science, narratives). Field Publications, 4343 Equity Drive, PO Box 16630, Columbus, OH 43216

*National Geographic World.* National Geographic Society, 17th and M Streets, NW, Washington, DC 20036

*Native Monthly Reader.* Scholastic Newspaper for Young Adults. RedSun Institute, PO Box 122, Crestone, CO 81131

*Odyssey* (astronomy, space travel, and technology). Kalmbach Publishing Company, 2107 Crossroads Circle, PO Box 1612, Waukesha, WI 53187-1612

*Owl: The Discovery Magazine for Children.* The Young Naturalist Foundation, 56 The Esplanade, Suite 306, Toronto, Ontario, Canada M5E147

*¿Que Tal?* (articles about Hispanic-Americans). Scholastic Classroom Magazines, 2931 McCarty Street, PO Box 3710, Jefferson City, MO 65102-3710

*Sassy* (contemporary teen magazine for girls). 230 Park Avenue, New York, NY 10169

*Scholastic Voice.* Scholastic, 2931 E. McCarty Street, PO Box 3710, Jefferson City, MO 65102-9957

*Skipping Stones: A Multi-Ethnic Children's Forum.* SKIPPING STONES, 80574 Hazelton Road, Cottage Grove, OR 97424

*Sports Illustrated for Kids.* Time & LIfe Building, Rockefeller Center, New York, NY 10020-1393

*Student Series: Short Story International* (contemporary short stories). 6 Sheffield Road, Great Neck, NY 11021

*Teen Power.* Amy Swanson, TEEN POWER, Box 632, Glen Ellyn, IL 60138

*US Express* (ESL). Scholastic, 2931 E. McCarty Street, PO Box 3710, Jefferson City, MO 65102-9957

*Young American: America's Newspaper for Kids* (news, sports, entertainment, cartoons). YOUNG AMERICAN, PO Box 12409, Portland, OR 97212

*Zillions: Consumer Reports for Kids.* 101 Truman Avenue, Yonkers, NY 10703

# 7

# ASSESSING THE LANGUAGE ARTS

*The unexamined life is not worth living.*

*Socrates*

## CHAPTER CONCEPTS

The purpose of assessment is to give children a positive sense of their progress toward literacy.

Assessment portfolios are child-centered management techniques for evaluating oral language, listening, reading, and writing progress over time.

Both process and product are important in assessing the language arts.

Effective assessment systems involve children, peers, teachers, and parents throughout the process of observing, responding, analyzing, and grading.

Reader response to literature is an important vehicle for assessing comprehension and composition.

Assessment is a fact of life. We live in a society where standards of excellence exist in every social setting. In our homes and our workplaces as well as in the classroom, we are constantly comparing or being compared. The schools are centers for assessment. Children's reading and writing are scrutinized in many different ways throughout the academic year. The methods of measuring academic performance range from simple observation to reaction to grading to standardized tests. How our students fare on any formal or informal instrument is viewed as a direct reflection of our teaching, hence the pressure to assess in the most objective manner possible.

The ultimate purpose of assessment in the language arts is to facilitate learning to read and to write (Morrow & Smith, 1990). Viewed as a whole, assessment is an ongoing and dynamic process that utilizes a "variety of information collected simultaneously" (Farr & Carey, 1986, p. 2) and involves the child and teacher, parents, and peers. Throughout the process of assessing reading and writing, we are concerned with many aspects of a child's learning behaviors as they develop over time, including cognitive, affective, and in the case of handwriting, psychomotor development. A primary objective of educational assessment is to  inform individuals about their progress toward a predetermined goal. For children in elementary and middle school, the process should also provide a sense of accomplishment, of getting better at reading and writing across all subject areas. If children do not believe that they are steadily progressing toward literacy, their motivation to keep reading and writing is impaired. They may simply stop reading and writing altogether, as seen in some remedial students who become depressed at the thought of failure, which to them seems to result no matter how hard they try. As Anthony, an eighth-grader quoted in Chapter 5, said, "Why bother? Reading's the pits; so's writing."

Standardized testing remains prominent in our schools, yet the merits of this familiar practice have been recently called to question. Following a three-year study of testing in the schools nationwide, the National Commission on Testing and Public Policy (1990) identified several limitations of large-scale testing. The commission warned that standardized tests are imperfect and often give misleading views of a child's true scholastic ability. All too often test scores are used unfairly to label individuals or groups, especially minorities. Further, students are tested too much. Teachers feel the pressure of state and local mandates and often spend valuable instructional time teaching to the test. Finally, test developers need to be held accountable for the reliability and validity of their products, as more and more educators observe that test scores do not reflect an accurate account of student performance.

As a result of the growing dissatisfaction with conventional evaluation, alternative strategies, such as portfolio assessment, are beginning to emerge. A common characteristic of alternative assessment is that it encourages teachers "to move beyond the 'one right answer' mentality and to challenge students to explore the possibilities inherent in open-ended, complex problems, and to draw their own inferences" (Herman, Aschbacher, & Winters, 1992, p. 6). O'Neal (1991) predicts that by the year 2000, "language arts classrooms will engage in constant data collection on all students. The ebb and flow of instruction and assessment will occur in most classrooms as a matter of routine, assisted by technology" (p. 72).

This chapter deals with alternative ways of assessing children's literacy development in the context of an integrated curriculum. Central to the assessment systems discussed here is the importance of assessing the reading and writing process as well as any products associated with becoming literate. I begin with a description of portfolio assessment as a viable alternative for teachers. I then describe the three basic forms of assessment—observation and reaction, analysis, and grading—that contribute to the organization of a portfolio assessment system in the language arts classroom. Finally, I explain the process of assessing language arts via reader response to literature.

## PORTFOLIO ASSESSMENT

Portfolio assessment is an alternative technique for observing and evaluating a student's oral language, reading, and writing development over time. Simply defined, portfolios are "collections of student work that exhibit the student's efforts, progress, and achievements in one or more areas" (Paulson, Paulson, & Meyer, 1991). Portfolios support a child-centered classroom, where students actively engaged in establishing criteria for learning, reflecting upon their accomplishments, thinking about the processes they use when reading and writing, and choosing reading and writing products to share with peers and parents. When utilizing a portfolio system, teachers are also empowered, as they no longer rely exclusively upon standardized tests and grades to demonstrate student competence. Instead, the teacher, in collaboration with children and parents, assemble portfolios that truly reflect children's reading and writing as it develops along a continuum throughout the school year.

Little experimental research exists to demonstrate the statistical reliability and validity of portfolio assessment. Nevertheless, educators recognize the merits of a system that takes into account the daily reading and writing behaviors of all children. DeFina (1992) suggests that portfolio assessment provides a more accurate view of the abilities of culturally different students—often the majority in our schools—who do not perform well on standardized tests normed in a different culture. He also contends that nonmainstream students may be classified disabled or disadvantaged when in fact they are not *culturally deprived* but are *other-culture enriched*. In short, portfolios have the potential for allowing "differently abled students to state and affirm what they have learned, to make judgments about their learning—processes no less important to nonmainstream students than to mainstream students" (p. 56).

How do we organize an assessment program that utilizes the portfolio? Valencia (1990) suggests that assessment portfolios be organized around broad curricular goals. For example, simple checklists of learner outcomes, described later in this chapter, bring the contents of a portfolio into focus. We are able to look through a student's portfolio and make the connection between completed language arts assignments and curricular goals. Overall, the portfolio should give students a sense of self-satisfaction and accomplishment in making progress over time.

While the content of a portfolio will vary across classrooms, the following items are essential for a grading period with an accompanying parent conference.

## The Language Arts Portfolio

### Written Work
Examples of initial and final drafts of written work.
Best work submitted by student for a grade

### *Checklists and Benchmarks*

Simple records of oral language, reading, and writing development: process and product

Description of relative placement on continuum between emerging and fully literate reading and writing behavior

### *Grading Criteria (if applicable)*

### *Audio Tapes or Video Tapes*

Examples of students reading, discussing, reflecting upon literature for children and adolescents, and their own writing

Examples of students interacting with one another

### *Student Reflections*

Self-assessment of oral language, listening, reading, and writing

Peer assessment of written work

Journal responses

Sally assesses her own work, while David and Best continue writing at the Editor's Desk.

***Teacher Reflections***
Anecdotal journal entries
Reading and Writing Conference notes

***Parent Reflections***
Parents' assessment of their child's progress in and attitudes toward reading, writing, thinking, and responding

Portfolios in progress may be sent home at any time during the grading period for parents to peruse. A brief note from the teacher requesting a written response accompanies materials sent home.

Teachers must somehow manage a delicate balance between what and when to scrutinize and to avoid too much assessment too soon or too little assessment too late. Some commonsense guidelines are useful when developing a portfolio system for use in grades K–8.

- Remember that everything a child reads or writes does not have to be assessed.
- Link assessment with short- and long-term curricular goals.
- Use a variety of measures, including observation/reaction, analysis, and grades.
- Utilize both qualitative and quantitative information.
- Assess both process and product.
- Assess both form and content of written discourse.
- Assess both content and context for learning.
- Allow the children to have some say in what is to be assessed.
- Take further advantage of the social aspects of the classroom by using self-assessments as well as peer responses.
- Design a system that motivates reading, writing, and responding to connected text.
- Keep the paperwork simple, usable, and flexible.
- Make records accessible to children.
- Involve parents in the assessment of their child's progress, especially as it relates to home involvement in the literacy process.

## FORMS OF ASSESSMENT

### Observing and Reacting

Observation is the simplest form of assessment and perhaps the most valuable. It is a practical way of focusing our attention on children in the classroom. Through observation we can record our reactions to children's oral language, reading, and writing behaviors that might otherwise go undocumented through more formal assessment procedures, such as standardized tests. Teachers are indeed "kid watchers," as Yetta Goodman (1978) has suggested. They watch children all day long but may not realize that their observations are useful in assessing progress toward literacy. This phenomenon is true in part because we often take our observations of children for granted.

Observing changes in process and product is important as we listen to children orally describe how they came up with a writing topic, ask for help with spelling, or respond to another child's work in progress. Reacting to children during the process of becoming literate is equally important. Children want to know what our reactions are to their work. The most formal setting for reacting to a child's work is an individual conference, sometimes held with a parent present. Our reactions range from simple responses such as "I like the way you're developing the character in your story" to more complex suggestions for further reading or revising of a writing project.

Structuring observations is helpful in gaining a new perspective on students' classroom behaviors. For example, the stance used to assess children should vary from day to day and task to task. A teacher may simply watch her students from a distance as they engage in talking, reading and writing, or she may observe more closely specifically defined oral language, reading, and writing in small-group settings or one-to-one conferences (D. H. Graves, 1983). By observing children first hand, we get to know them a little better, day by day. This knowledge helps us to be better teachers of language by enabling us to interact meaningfully with children concerning their abilities, interests, and ambitions.

***Knowing Our Students.*** The inextricable nature of children's cognitive and affective development requires attention to both domains during assessment. Educators have long believed that how students feel about themselves and about schooling is important knowledge in understanding growth toward literacy. Positive self-esteem is critical to learning. One middle school teacher I know uses a bulletin board technique called "Today I Feel" to help in the daily observations of her sixth-graders. Each morning as the children enter the classroom, they choose a student-drawn symbol that expresses how they happen to be feeling that day and then "hang" their feelings on the bulletin board just below their names (Figure 7.1). The symbols are drawn on three-by-five-inch cards and include both verbal and nonverbal messages, such as happy faces, sad faces, neutral faces, abstract drawings, or slang expressions, such as *rad, groady, excellent, cool, dorky,* and *not*(!). A Christmas ornament hook or opened paper clip attached to the card is easily attached to a cup hook located below the child's name. The teacher can determine at a glance how her students are feeling and thus be more sensitive to their individual day-to-day needs.

Interest inventories are among the more traditional ways of getting to know students. Knowledge so gained helps teachers to become more astute observers, to understand language behaviors more clearly. Administered at the beginning of the year, the interest inventory can aid in short- and long-range planning. Student inter-

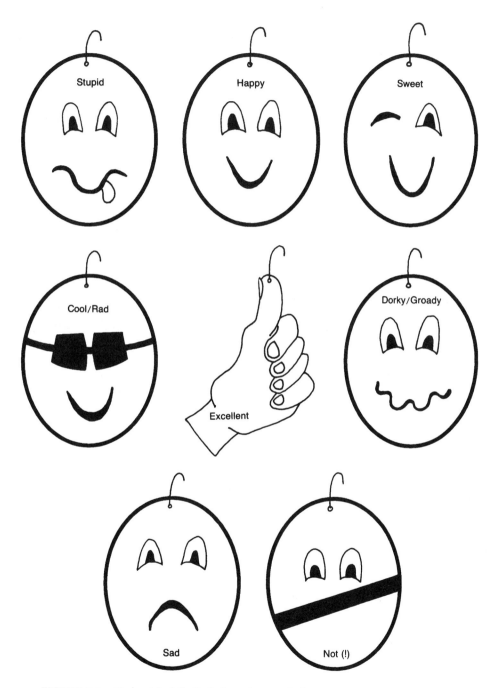

**FIGURE 7.1**   Today I feel (bulletin board examples)

est groups are a popular classroom management strategy, made possible by surveying the entire class about what they like to read and write. (See Chapter 8 for further discussion of interest grouping.) As student interests change during the academic year, parts of an inventory can be readministered to observe the evolution of interests and in some cases to broaden students' horizons. Surveys of student interests take many forms, ranging from interview techniques (Wixson, Bosky, Yochum, & Alvermann, 1984) to paper-and-pencil interest and attitude inventories (Figure 7.2). Incomplete-sentence (Boning & Boning, 1957) or cloze surveys, interest checklists, and Snoopy and Happy Face inventories are just a few popular examples.

***Keeping Records.***    Methods of recording what one sees and hears are as variable and individual as the observed behavior. The record-keeping system should be simple enough to be usable yet substantive enough to yield information that informs the child and parents about progress being made. Because assessment by observation is usually an informal approach, data collection can take many forms. For example, teachers may design a checklist that identifies cognitive behaviors that they wish to observe in their students, or they may simply make notations in an observation journal. Observing children's reading and writing behaviors is not as simple as it at first seems. It requires knowledge of what to look for as well as a sensitivity to issues surrounding the development of literacy in grades K–8. Although it can be used virtually on a daily basis, observation as assessment can become unwieldy and therefore not useful if it is more complicated than it has to be.

***Checklists.***    Observation checklists are one example of managing informal classroom data collection. To be useful both during and after the assessment process, checklists must be manageable. Three important points to remember when designing a useful checklist for observing reading and writing behaviors are these:

1. Keep the checklist as short and as simple as possible.
2. Align short- and long-term curricular goals and objectives to the checklist.
3. Include quantitative as well as qualitative information. The qualitative aspect of a checklist becomes crucial over time as the teacher begins to analyze the students' progress in a nine-week, semester, or year-long period. Numbers may become useless information without commentary to support the quality of the students' performance on a task.

Checklists are useful as aids to whole class as well as individual observations. Figure 7.3 is an example of a checklist for a language arts class that is appropriate for kindergarten and primary grades. Checklists that include information about all children in one class should be readable at a glance and provide a broad overview of how the children fared on either a specific reading or writing task or a group of similar activities.

Figure 7.4 is an observation checklist that may be stapled to each child's writing folder. The checklist gives the child an opportunity to observe himself or herself throughout the reading and writing process and to reflect on his or her work.

**Incomplete-Sentence Survey**

1. Today I feel _____
2. I think that reading means _____
3. I think that writing means _____
4. I like to read because _____
_____
5. Sometimes I don't like to read because _____
_____
6. I like to write because _____
_____
7. Sometimes I don't like to write because _____
_____
8. My favorite things to read about are _____
_____
9. My favorite things to write about are _____
_____
10. When I'm at home, I read _____
and I write _____

**Draw a picture of how you feel when you read. Draw a picture of how you feel when you write.**

**FIGURE 7.2** Incomplete-Sentence Survey (adapted from Boning and Boning, 1957, pp. 196–200.)

**Basic Lesson Plan Scenario:** Listen to story, discuss, decide on writing topic, compose first and final drafts.

**Objective:** After listening to (or reading) *Alexander and the Terrible, Horrible, No Good, Very Bad Day* (Viorst, 1972), the students will contribute to a discussion of the story. The students will write and illustrate a personal narrative about the worst or best day they or someone they know ever had (or imagined). The narrative will be revised for publication in a class collection.

| Name | Oral Contributions + ✓ o | | Written Narrative (1st/2nd) | |
|---|---|---|---|---|
| Emily | + | Very talkative | 1st<br>2nd<br>Ill. | ✓ "My Birthday"<br>✓ "<br>✓ Child & birthday cake |
| Sarah | + | Lots to say – just lost a tooth | 1st<br>2nd<br>Ill. | ✓ "The Lost Tooth"<br>✓ "<br>✓ Wanted to glue "lost" tooth on paper. |
| Mark | + | "Christmas & New Year" – Best Days | 1st<br>2nd<br>Ill. | ✓ "Trains"<br>none<br>✓ Trains & RR tracks. |
| Kevin | ✓ | "Summertime" best days | 1st<br>2nd<br>Ill. | ✓ "Camping Out"<br>✓ "Yellowstone Park"<br>✓ Change title in revision |
| John | o | Sad today. Doesn't know why. | 1st<br>2nd<br>Ill. | ✓ "My Dog" – About a dog John once had.<br>Resisted revision<br>✓ Excellent drawing. |
| Brad | o | Inattentive today | 1st<br>2nd<br>Ill. | ✓ "The Special Day"<br>none<br>✓ Picture of a circus tent. |
| Cynthia | ✓ | Good response | 1st<br>2nd<br>Ill. | ✓ "Saturday"<br>✓<br>✓ Picture of child "sleeping in". |
| Robert | + | Great ideas! | 1st | ✓ "The Shopping Trip" |

**FIGURE 7.3**   Whole-class observation checklist (K–3)

**Date:** **Title:** **What I Think About My Reading & Writing:**

L
R 12-1-89
W̲

My Trip TO space.

Beucase it is my novel.

L 11-17-89
R̲
W

The Astronauts

Because I ingoy it.

L̲ 11-10-89
R
W The big orange spot.

Because it is funny.

L
R
W

_____

L
R
W

_____

**Legend: L = Listened to     R = Read     W = Wrote**

**FIGURE 7.4** Individual writing folder checklist (K–3)

Simplicity is again the watchword, as a kindergartner or primary grade child will not be inclined to keep up with a complicated recording system. After a child has completed a checklist, he or she places it in a portfolio.

***Journals.***    Anecdotal journals are another example of observation record keeping. Making notations during or just after a lesson while it is still fresh in one's mind is a convenient way to record important cognitive and affective behaviors. Flexibility is a key element in this kind of assessment. The teacher decides on one or more lessons per day to observe, and the only material needed is the paper on which to make notations. Again, the observations are linked to curricular objectives.

A teacher's journal can be anything from a spiral or loose-leaf notebook to a computer disk. Anecdotal records are of most use when they are readable and accessible. If you are using a computer to record your observations, be sure to make a backup disk. Some teachers have the luxury of one or more computers permanently housed within the classroom. Through data base and spreadsheet programs, the children themselves can learn how to store and retrieve evaluative information about themselves. Separate computer files can also be set up for children's individual responses to literature or reactions to peers' writing. In the final chapter of this book I will talk more about computers and how they can enhance the development of literacy.

Although observation journals are more formative than summative, teachers may wish to compile a list of frequent observations about the class in general or individual students in particular, to be used later in a conference. The following is a journal observation made by a fifth-grade teacher. Mr. Gerard made his entry both during and after a language arts textbook lesson on cause and effect taught to a whole class.

### MARCH 3, 1989

*The class is having trouble with cause and effect. Only Jay, Dennis, and Teresa contributed. Things got better when we talked about personal examples of cause and effect. Marcia and Marlene are acting out again—name calling, making faces. Move them even further apart. Arrange another conference with them and maybe their parents. Tom's attitude is improving every day; he's at least trying to participate today. Have the librarian find some books with cause/effect concepts that the fifth-graders can read. Write a better cause/effect example paragraph for them for tomorrow. Try small-group discussions. Talk together about the concept and maybe add some kind of easy hands-on activity before we get started writing.*

Mr. Gerard's observations are focused on many aspects of classroom behavior, from the students' understanding of the concept under study to attitudes and social behaviors. Anecdotal accounts need not be lengthy to be useful. In just a few sentences Mr. Gerard recorded what occurred in the class and began planning for a more effective lesson. He also has a written record of the development of the concept's cause and effect and the social interactions that may be affecting learning. His journal entries will eventually show how the students' conceptual and social skills change over time.

In general, journals are also useful for children's self-assessments of their own progress in reading and writing. Elementary or middle school students observing themselves and then articulating those observations is an important activity that enables children to grow both intellectually and emotionally.

Children's journals can take many forms. In the primary grades, stapled sheets of line-free paper, as well as lined, primary newsprint, are a popular way to introduce children to the concept of the journal. To add to the life of the journal, make a cover of laminated construction paper that has been decorated by each child. In the intermediate grades and middle school, spiral notebooks make the best kind of journals because of the secure nature of the binding. Next best is the loose-leaf pocket folder, in which the children can add sheets of paper as their journal grows. Journals should be stored in file boxes kept in an accessible, central location.

A child's journal entries also add an important perspective to the portfolio, as parents get a glimpse of how their child's feelings and attitudes develop and change over time. At the beginning of fourth grade, ten-year-old Jeremy's entries, for example, reflect a dislike for reading and writing in general.

### SEPTEMBER 9 *(Focus: How do you feel about reading and writing?)*

*I don't understand why we always have to go to the library and pick out a book. I don't like to read. I hardly ever write except maybe a thank you note to my grandma because my mom made me do it.*

### NOVEMBER 15 *(Focus: How do you feel about the reading and writing you've been doing? What are you reading and writing?)*

*Today we got to go to the media center and work on computers. I like to write stories on the computer. It's lots funner than paper and pencil. I think my writing is good. I'm working on a car story. I like Ms. Jarmel the librarian. She showed me where to find all the books about car racing.* Wheels [Fitzpatrick, 1988] *is my favorite book. I've read it six times.*

### APRIL 20 *(Focus: Describe what you've been reading and writing.)*

*My story about driving in the grand prix is 20 pages long! That's the most I've ever written in my whole life. I'm working on publishing it so all the other kids can read it. I like my illustrations except for the classic car part which is hard to draw. Ms. Steffen's going to help me with it tomorrow. She's the art teacher. I read* Wheels *again. Also* Hot Rod [Nicholas, 1978]. *Super cool!*

As the months passed, encouragement by the classroom teacher and library media specialist stimulated Jeremy's interest in and enthusiasm for reading and writing about topics that interested him. His literacy skills blossomed as the year progressed. The journal entries serve as a permanent record of Jeremy's fourth-grade reading and writing development as seen through his eyes.

The interactive nature of dialogue journals (Staton, 1988) makes them very useful tools for getting to know students through private written conversations. These dialogues can be used informally to observe changes in children's attitudes about reading and writing as well as their development in reading, writing, and thinking, as seen in the following excerpts from a seventh-grader's journal:

> **LESLIE:** *Today is the worst day of my life. I made a 20 on the spelling pretest. I hate spelling. Why do we have to learn how to spell anyway?*
>
> **MS. CARLYLE:** *Cheer up, Leslie. You know that I don't record the pretest score. And you* always *do better by Friday after you've studied. Your spelling is getting better and better. Just look through your written work since the beginning of the year. Fantastic progress!*
>
> **LESLIE:** *Thanks. I forgot the 20 doesn't really count. I feel better sort of. I still don't like to study spelling words. You're right. I do spell lots better now. I think it's probably because I remember words from reading and then when I write them I can spell them the right way. Were you a good speller in 7th grade?*
>
> **MS. CARLYLE:** *I was a terrible speller in middle school. I think it was because my teachers put a lot of emphasis on memorizing lists of words that we never got a chance to use in writing. Your experiences are going to be better than mine were.*

***Peer Response.***    Reader response means reacting to writing like a reader, not like an expert (Temple & Gillet, 1984). "What did you think about the story?" is a frequently asked question that elicits a free response containing evaluative information, not only for the student writer but also about the peer reactor. For example, a peer's response will reveal the level of thought—literal, inferential, or evaluative—that was engaged in while reacting to a classmate's work or any piece of literature (Studier, 1981). Peer responses are an important element of assessment because they take advantage of the social aspects of the classroom by encouraging verbal interactions about one another's work. Requests for simple responses are best, with short lists of questions to help peers formulate their reactions. Questions that structure a response should be worded to encourage positive comments and constructive criticism, to avoid antagonistic remarks that could potentially destroy another child's confidence in his or her reading and writing abilities. As mentioned in Chapter 3, three typical questions in response to a peer's writing are:

What did you like best?

What confused you?

What advice do you have for the author?

Peer responses may be written or oral, depending on the classroom management strategies that you are using. Responding to writing as a reader helps students

Small-group Writers' Workshop gives children time to read and respond to one another's work.

gain a sense of the relationship between author and audience. Written responses encourage openness and sincerity through private advice to a classmate. Mutual respect for one another's work and opinions is a major purpose of reader response. Student authors are free to accept or reject the advice of their peers. The ultimate goal of peer responses is to help classmates feel good about themselves as readers and writers, as well as to help improve reading and writing proficiency. During the process of reacting to a peer's work, the respondents, themselves readers and writers, develop valuable critical thinking skills. Written responses can be collected and analyzed over time to see the development of students as readers, writers, and reactors.

***Teacher Response.*** Conferences are special times set aside for teachers to respond to children's work in progress. The reading conference and the writing conference are two ongoing activities that help teachers get to know children better and at the same time provide a forum for positive reactions to each child's developing comprehension and composition. Both the reading and the writing conference help to promote positive contacts between teacher and student. The conference need not be long to have a positive effect on the child. It can be as short as a thirty-second dialogue in the hallway or as long as a regularly scheduled fifteen-minute session at the teacher's desk. Daily interactions with individual children is what matters, not the length or location of the conference. Frequent and positive encounters with a teacher help children to feel good about themselves and about their academic progress. All children need this kind of special attention at school.

*The Reading Conference.*     The primary purpose of a reading conference is for child and teacher to engage in a conversation about books. The most frequent statement during a reading conference is "Tell me about what you've been reading lately." The teacher listens attentively, sometimes comparing the child's choice to his or her own favorite books or suggesting another book of a similar or different nature. Such an interaction can take as little time as one minute, anytime, anywhere, from hallway to library to playground. Yet this kind of brief interaction yields a great deal of information about the child's interests in and attitudes about independent reading. For instance, if a child's response is "I haven't been reading anything good," the teacher probes a bit further to determine the reason for the child's negative feelings and then gives suggestions for finding something of interest to read: "I know that you really like dinosaurs. Have you read *Tyrannosaurus Was a Beast* (Prelutsky, 1988) yet? I have a copy right here that you can look over." One-on-one dialogues about books communicate to students that teachers also read and really care about what the individual child is reading and thinking. It is useful to keep a checklist of these brief encounters, just to make sure that every child is contacted sometime during the week.

Reading conferences can also be more formal, regularly scheduled parts of the weekly lesson plan. If the classroom management system is designed for totally individualized reading, reading conferences are important avenues for assessing a child's progress in reading and to engage in direct instruction whenever needed. This would be a time for teacher modeling of comprehension monitoring strategies, oral reading and rereading, concept formation, and developing ideas for further reading and writing. Harris and Smith (1980) recommend that formal reading conferences be about fifteen minutes long and occur at least once a week, with adjustments in time according to the individual needs of the child.

*The Writing Conference.*     The writing conference is an occasion for the teacher to respond to an individual child's work in progress. Ordinarily a writing conference involves only the teacher and child. Whole-class or small-group writing conferences can also be held to model appropriate responses to peers' works in progress. Like the reading conference, the quality of a writing conference is enhanced by the amount of knowledge the teacher has about the child and his or her writing. Over time, children gain confidence in themselves as writers and arrive at the conference with a set of questions for the teacher.

Writing conferences usually take place during the period that has been designated as sustained (but not necessarily silent) writing time. Brief two- to three-minute individual conferences often occur at the beginning of the period as the teacher moves about the room to make sure everyone is clear about the assignment. At this time the teacher may also give short, positive comments about the children's writing or answer simple questions about some aspect of composing: "I like the way you've begun your story." "Spell the word the way you think it should be spelled." "I see that you're writing about the book you've been reading. Terrific!" "So you're having a lot of trouble deciding what to write about? Why don't you sign up for a conference and we'll talk about it right now."

Formal writing conferences are structured yet predictable activities designed to fit the individual needs of the child writer (D. H. Graves, 1983). The predictable nature of writing conferences is what gives children the confidence and security to sign up for them so that they can talk with the teacher openly and honestly about their writing. The setting and the questions that the teacher uses are what create the secure and positive atmosphere. During the conference, the child and teacher sit alongside each other at a table with some clear work space. The teacher does not need to read the child's work ahead of time but rather learns the skill of reading and responding to drafts in progress during the conference itself. The teacher learns to identify problems, to focus on one or two trouble areas, and to help the child develop a plan to solve the writing dilemmas (Murray, 1985). The children come to the conference, usually at their own initiative, bringing a piece they are working on, which could in fact be a blank page. In the beginning the teacher structures the conference through open-ended, nonthreatening questions and responses. As the teacher and child become more involved with a draft, questions and requests are used to focus attention on matters of form, style, and content (Figure 7.5).

Questions that stimulate talk about ideas are very important to the writing conference. Children who think that they have nothing to write about will often surprise themselves at conference time with a verbal rendition of a narrative or nonfiction that they can't seem to start writing, as illustrated by Ms. James and her third-grade pupil Tony.

**Ms. James:** What is your story about, Tony?

**Tony:** I don't have nothin' to write.

**Ms. James:** You're having some trouble getting started today? That happens to me a lot, especially when I have to come up with an idea all by myself. What have you thought about writing?

**Tony:** Nothin'.

**Ms. James:** Did you look over your topic list on your writing folder? Maybe that'll help.

**Tony:** No. It don't help neither. I don't like any of those ideas. They're boring.

**Ms. James:** Are you still working on your skateboarding? I saw you yesterday after school on the concrete playground. Looked pretty good to me.

**Tony:** I am good.

**Ms. James:** How do you do it? I mean stay on that skateboard and make all of those fancy maneuvers? I could never get a skateboard to move a foot without falling on my face.

**Tony:** Sure you could. It just takes practice.

**Ms. James:** Who taught you how to ride a skateboard?

### Beginning the Conference

Tell me what you're writing about today.
How do you feel about what you're working on?
Do I get to hear more about . . . ?
What can I help you with?
Which draft am I seeing now?
I'm so happy to see you smiling about your paper; tell me about it.

### Focusing Attention

Where do you want to begin this story?
Who will be the main character(s)?
Have you thought about a problem or conflict between your characters?
What did you have in mind as a central metaphor for your poem?
Tell me what will happen next in the story.
Show me which sentence sums up your main point in the paragraph.
What does this paragraph have to do with all the others?
Can you tell me why you used so many commas in your paragraph?

### Rereading/Rewriting Drafts

This draft seems more developed. What did you add?
I see that you've changed the title. Tell me why.
Do you still like this piece?
Do you need to read more about . . . , since you're having so much trouble getting started?
How has this draft changed since I last saw it?
Show me the new vocabulary words you've tried since the last draft.
What do you have left to do before moving to the editor's desk?

### Editing the Final Copy

Underline all of the words you think you don't know how to spell.
What do you want to work on first, commas or capitals?
Which sounds better to you? "My dogs done got lost for good," which is the way you wrote
the sentence, or "My dog is lost for good," which is another way of saying the same
thing.

**FIGURE 7.5**    Writing conference questions

TONY: Nobody. I been ridin' the skateboard since I was three years old. Since my big
brother Ronny brought one home. Then when I was five I got my own. Now
I'm eight, and I'm good. I practice every day. I ride it to school and home after
school. That's how I got so good.

Ms. JAMES: Do you think you could teach me how to handle a skateboard?

TONY: Yeah. But you can't wear high heel shoes. You have to wear tennis shoes or
sneakers. Some kids go barefoot, Not me. I wear my sneaks.

Ms. JAMES: You've already told me quite a lot about what it takes to be a good skateboard rider. Do you think you could write about it?

TONY: Sure. Then maybe I can get you on the board at recess?

Ms. JAMES: It's a deal. But I'll have to change into my sneaks.

The five-minute exchange between Ms. James and Tony was all that was needed to stimulate thinking about a writing topic of interest. Ironically, skateboarding was listed on Tony's writing folder. Although it was already an important subject to him, Tony needed the verbal exchange of ideas with his teacher before he could get started on his own. Further, Ms. James showed genuine interest in Tony and volunteered to get involved in a real experience that would extend his concept of skateboarding. It was, of course, Ms. James's goal to encourage Tony to write about teaching her to ride a skateboard, which according to Ms. James, he ultimately did.

Ordinarily children sign up for a writing conference when they are ready to share a first draft. Some teachers manage a writing conference with each child every week or two, while others may confer with children more frequently in small groups of two or three. The following are suggested guidelines for conducting an individual writing conference that promotes positive communications between teacher and student.

## INSTRUCTIONAL GUIDELINES
### Conducting a Writing Conference

**RESPONDING TO THE WORK—TEACHER/CHILD INTERACTIONS**

1. *Responding.* The teacher responds in a positive and friendly manner to the content of the work. Tell the child what you like about his/her work so far.
2. *Telling.* The teacher asks the child to tell about what he/she is working on and where he or she is in the composing process.
3. *Reading.* The child then reads his/her work aloud. The child's purpose for reading is to think about what he/she is trying to communicate, to compare his/her retelling to his/her written work.
4. *Talking.* Together, the teacher and child talk about the similarities and differences between the oral telling of the story/nonfiction/poem and the written version.
5. *Responding.* The teacher again tells what he or she liked about the child's piece of writing. Next, the teacher indicates confusing or unclear writing and asks the child to clarify meaning.

**ANALYZING THE WORK**

6. *Focusing.* While discussing the text, the teacher focuses the child's attention on the content and structure of the text by using appropriate terminology. If the child is working on fiction, use a simple story grammar that includes setting, character, plot, episodes, central story problem, resolution, theme. For nonfiction, focus on the elements of structure being used, such as description, comparison, process, persuasion, and so forth. Poetic structure is also important to consider at this point and may

*(continued)*

**Instructional Guidelines (continued)**

include aspects of poetry such as rhythm, meter, rhymed or unrhymed verse, and metaphor.

**7.** *Rereading.* During the analysis, the teacher and/or the child rereads the whole or parts of the work in order to clarify the author's intentions.

**8.** *Responding to Content.* The teacher offers advice to the child-author with regard to content. The author is free to accept or reject the advice.

**9.** *Responding to Form.* In addition, the teacher makes positive comments about the text form, or the surface features of written language that we associate with grammar, spelling, and punctuation. The teacher reminds the child that form is very important to communication. And while we attend to matters of form during the editing stage of the composing process, we nevertheless must be aware of our spelling, grammar, and punctuation while we are writing. If there are several problem areas, focus the child's attention on one aspect of form at a time—i.e., "In your next draft, make sure that you've capitalized the beginning of every sentence."

**10.** *Rewriting and Editing.* While the purpose of a writing conference is primarily to talk about the work in progress, some rewriting and editing will occur naturally during the process. It is important for teachers to recognize the teachable moments during the conference, to point out that the student may have left out a character's name or forgotten to put an apostrophe here or a comma there. Have the child make corrections directly on the paper, or keep a running list of items to attend to during independent rewriting and editing of work, which may later be submitted for a grade.

ENDING THE CONFERENCE

When children leave a writing conference, they should feel good about their work in progress and know what must be done to make their writing even better. Clear expectations are necessary in order for children to fulfill curricular objectives. Language arts objectives will vary across grade levels. Although all children may be writing every day in your classrooms, not everything written necessarily needs to be revised, edited, and submitted for a grade. The writing conference is a powerful social event that can nurture the writing process and give children a sense of self-satisfaction in the knowledge that their writing is getting better day by day.

An anecdotal record of what occurs during a reading or a writing conference is useful to keep. The record design should be simple and manageable (Figure 7.6). Some teachers keep a conference notebook with dated entries that include brief notes taken during and just after the meeting with a child. This kind of information is very valuable when planning short and long-term intervention strategies and when summarizing and sharing information (Figure 7.7) during parent-teacher conferences.

Name: _Jennifer C._

| Date | RC | WC | Comments |
|------|----|----|----------|
| 8-29 | ✓ | | Jennifer's favorite author is Judy Blume. She's read all of Blume's books twice! |
| 8-31 | | ✓ | "I hate to write." Jenny's not had very many positive experiences writing. Need to work on her self-concept as an author. |
| 9-04 | | ✓ | First draft--"My Brother Kenny." Nice detail about little brother. Jenny has trouble with transitions from event to event in the narrative. She's aware of this--doesn't know how to fix it. Suggested outlining/numbering events first-- 1, 2, 3, etc. |
| 9-06 | ✓ | ✓ | Current book: The Little Princess (Burnett). Glad she took my suggestion to try a new author. Second draft of brother narrative much more cohesive. She tried outlining and it seemed to help. Still doesn't like writing. Says she'd rather read. |

*(continued)*

**FIGURE 7.6**   Reading and writing conference notes

## Instructional Guidelines (continued)

Nine-week's goal: The student will develop an understanding of exposition through paragraph writing.

First Quarter: September 5 – November 10: *(I) Initial Draft   (F) Final Draft*

| Titles | Comments |
| --- | --- |

1. Space (I)

   *Concept of space is rather narrow in scope. Encourage more reading in science text and trade books.*

2. How to Wash a Dog (I)
   How to Feed a Cat (I)

   *Good sequencing. No need to revise significantly.*

3. Pioneer Days (I/F)

   *Excellent use of information in social studies text.*

4. Fish Make Good Pets (I/F)
   Zoo Eagles (I)

   *Description improves with second draft. Read more about eagles.*

5. Why I Hate Math (I)
   Why I Hate Science (I)

   *Similar paragraphs-- These two subjects difficult for Kevin.*

6. PE Is My Favorite Subject (I)

   *Nice use of detail. Clearly explains what goes on in P.E. class.*

7. Computers Are Great! (I)
   Nintendo Is Great! (I/F)

   *An obvious motivation for Kevin. These were both composed at the computer.*

8. My Family (I/F)
   My Best Friend (I/F)

   *Worked hard on these. Made good use of peer interaction.*

9. A Definition of Thanksgiving (I)

   *Lovely definition. Included new knowledge about Plymouth, Pilgrims, etc.*

**FIGURE 7.7**   Summary of compositions, by Kevin, grade 4

The computer printout facilitates the composing process as children read, analyze, and respond to work in progress.

Writers, whether children or professionals, never really become fully independent in the sense that they need a reader to respond to their work. Writers learn from the reader's response whether or not their intended message was received. Although our goal as teachers is to enable children to be independent readers and writers, this does not mean that at some point they will never need us again. Rather, the teacher should always be the ever-present mentor who helps the child become a better writer as the result of sensitive responses and constructive recommendations. The writing conference is the forum for such teaching endeavors.

*A Final Note.* Reading and writing conferences are opportunities for teachers to learn about the real person inside the student. Knowing children as individuals significantly improves the assessment process. The conference setting has a reciprocal bonus in that children will ultimately arrive with their own questions. When this happens the student has become a thinking individual who has learned how to learn through reading and writing.

## Analyzing

Analysis requires breaking down a process or product into components in order to examine the relationships among parts and wholes. The purpose of analyzing skill in the language arts is to provide students a detailed and objective account of their progress, especially over time. Like reaction and observation, analytical assessment employs checklists and anecdotal journals to examine and record information gained from careful scrutiny of a student's listening, speaking, reading, and writing behaviors. When used throughout the comprehending and composing processes, analytical checklists provide students with explicit information about what is expected. Checklists and anecdotal records are placed in the student's portfolio for use during conferences.

***Process.***    Analytical assessment of a process should be simple and concise. Figure 7.8 is a checklist that reflects a student's literate behaviors, as observed by the teacher, during the processes of composing and comprehending. The teacher shares her analysis with students and parents during individual conferences each grading period. Together they reflect upon what the student does best and what areas might need extra attention. Students may also analyze their own skill development by using similar self-checklists, reflecting upon the processes they undertake while reading, writing, and thinking. The process of being self-reflective helps students understand the complexities of learning to comprehend and to compose.

***Product.***    Analyses of products associated with the language arts may also be accomplished through checklists. Informal teacher made or commercially prepared checklists of language arts skills typically describe progress in oral language development, reading word recognition and comprehension, and written composition form and content. Such informal assessment instruments often include simple questions that direct children's attention to the surface features of written language or the levels of thinking employed during comprehending and composing (Figure 7.9). Analyses of oral and written language are useful during the postreading and editing stages of the comprehending and composing process because they heighten students' metacognitive and metalinguistic awareness. Research suggests that student writing improves significantly if analytical checklists are consistently used during the rewriting and editing phases of the composing process (Hillocks, 1987). A key factor in the successful design of an analytical checklist is to keep it simple so that students are not overwhelmed.

Formal analysis of student writing is also possible. Statewide mandates to assess student writing are becoming more prominent in American education. The movement is an attempt to hold educators accountable for teaching writing in the elementary and middle schools. Several states in the northwest and in Kansas use an analytic assessment instrument patterned after Spandel and Stiggin's (1990) "Six Trait Analytic Model." Originally developed in 1984 by a group of Oregon teachers, the model provides a criterion-referenced, analytical scoring guide focusing on the following characteristics of written language: ideas and content; organization; voice; word choice; sentence fluency; and conventions. Each trait receives a score of one to five, with five being the highest. Scoring criteria are given for levels 5, 3, and 1. Levels 2 and 4 are assigned when the rater perceives the writing to fall somewhere in between the stated criteria. To administer the writing assessment instrument, students normally write on a predetermined topic. Trained teachers at the district or

**Before Reading and Writing**

How does the student prepare to comprehend and to compose?

_____ by listening attentively and orally contributing to class discussions?

_____ by making predictions about the reading text?

_____ by reading *before* writing?

_____ by writing *before* reading?

_____ by formulating topics to write about?

_____ by describing verbally the purposes for reading and writing?

_____ by identifying the intended audience?

**During Reading and Writing**

What does the student do *while* reading and writing in order to construct meaning?

_____ asks the teacher or peers for help with new or difficult concepts.

_____ refers to other text sources, such as dictionaries, grammar books, or library references. (Reads more to write better.)

_____ seeks out other adults (other teachers, parents, relatives, friends) for help with new or difficult concepts.

_____ takes notes while reading (things to ask about).

_____ makes notes while writing (reminders of things yet to do).

**After Reading and Writing**

What does the student do to demonstrate that he or she has constructed meaning from print (reading) or with print (writing)?

_____ orally contributes to class discussions.

_____ demonstrates reading comprehension by writing about what was read.

_____ uses new knowledge in current and future writing activities.

_____ readily shares writing with teachers, parents, and peers.

_____ verbally responds to the writing of professional and student authors.

_____ articulates what he or she knows and does not know about topics read or written about.

**How does the student feel about his or her reading and writing processes?**

1. _____ The student enthusiastically engages in reading connected text every day.
2. _____ The student enthusiastically engages in writing connected text every day.
3. _____ The student has developed a variety of reading interests as seen by the personal reading checklist of books read and to be read.
4. _____ The student has developed a variety of writing interests as seen by the personal topic checklist of papers written and to be written.

Optional legend: A = Always,   S = Sometimes,   N = Never.

**FIGURE 7.8**   Analysis of comprehending and composing processes

**Now that I'm finished reading:**

_____do I remember what happened in the story?

_____do I know how to reread to find out what I can't remember?

_____do I share what I've read with a friend?

_____can I think of something new to write about?

_____do I feel good about reading?

_____do I want to keep reading?

**Now that I'm finished writing:**

_____did I reread my work to be sure it says what I want it to say?

_____did I share my work with a friend?

_____do I need to read something else to help me with my writing?

_____did I remember to capitalize and put end marks on my sentences?

_____do I feel good about writing?

_____do I want to keep writing?

**FIGURE 7.9**   Self-analysis of comprehension and composition (primary level)

state departments of education typically score the papers. Trait ratings are then sent to teachers who in turn may use them for diagnostic purposes.

Overall, analytical assessment of product and process should be closely aligned with instructional objectives. For example, Figure 7.10 illustrates how a fifth-grade teacher and her students analyze the oral language, reading, and writing that accompanied study of a novel. Here the analytical checklists are directly associated with the goals of the lesson plan and assess both product and process.

Analyses of process and product enable us to develop a clear understanding of children's progress toward literacy. During individual conferences, printed checklists and anecdotal records improve communications between teacher and student. Sensitive responses based upon careful analysis of language development, in turn, positively influence children's thinking while they are engaged in reading and writing connected text. The development of thought and language is a primary goal of language arts instruction.

## Grading

For better or for worse, grades are currently a permanent part of our educational system. Children and their parents want to know if they've "made the grade" and how they "measure up" against other students in the same class. It is their right to have such information. Grades are ingrained in the classroom atmosphere and sometimes take on a life of their own that governs a child's inner motivation. If points and letter grades are allowed to dominate the curriculum, the quality of life in the classroom diminishes, as even young children can become stressed by the scores they

**Objectives:**

1. The students will develop their oral language and listening skills throughout the process of reading and responding to the novel, *The Secret Garden* (Burnett, 1984).

2. The students will demonstrate their reading comprehension of *The Secret Garden* through a series of journal entries written in response to each chapter.

3. The students will develop their narrative writing skills by composing a story inspired by the novel.

**Oral Language/Listening** (Criteria: (S) Satisfactory; (N) Needs Improvement)

———————— Working in small groups, the student actively responded to *The Secret Garden*.

———————— The student formulated a topic for writing inspired by the novel.

———————— The student responded to one or more peer's story in progress.

**Reading** (Criteria: (S) Satisfactory; (R) Rewrite)

———————— The student's journal responses reflected good comprehension of the novel, *The Secret Garden*.

**Writing** (Criteria: (S) Satisfactory; (R) Rewrite)

**Story Content**

———————— The setting was clearly described

———————— The characters were believable

———————— The central story problem was evident

———————— The plot supported the development of character through action and/or dialogue

———————— The problem was resolved—something happened in the story to bring about change in character or situation

———————— A theme could be identified in the story

**Story Form**

———————— There were no significant grammar, spelling, and punctuation errors

**FIGURE 7.10**    Assessing a novel study

achieve on an assignment. Yet when "incidental writing," such as letters, cards, or classroom rules, are unnoticed or unassessed, children may learn that such writing "doesn't count," that only writing produced on tests is valued because a grade is assigned (Florio & Clark, 1984).

Grades are indeed an important aspect of schooling, but their importance should not be overemphasized at the expense of children's attitudes toward reading and writing. To help children understand grading, it is important to explain your assessment system early in the school year and to adjust the process whenever a task calls for flexibility. For example, holistic grading, or applying a single numerical score or letter grade, is rarely informative. However, explaining the criteria, or how the score or letter grade is to be determined, is valuable information from which a child can learn. Criteria for grading composition as well as comprehension may be arrived at in many ways, including suggestions by the children themselves.

## INSTRUCTIONAL GUIDELINES
### Grading Language Arts Assignments

**SOME SUGGESTIONS**

**1.** Decide on the minimum number of reading and writing assignments to be assessed during a specific grading period, such as nine weeks or a semester. Allow the students to help select their best work to be graded.

**EXAMPLES**

*During the first nine weeks, the first-grade students will write a minimum of eight to ten personal narratives or fiction. Editing will be introduced gradually so that by the end of the first semester the children will have edited at least one of their stories. The students will submit their best papers for grading.*

*E = Excellent       = + 10 (at least one edited)*
*S = Satisfactory    = 8–10 (at least one edited)*
*U = Unsatisfactory = –8 (did not attempt editing)*

*During the first eighteen-week semester, the seventh-grade students will write, revise, and edit a minimum of eight paragraph-level assignments, including fiction and nonfiction. The form and content of the assignments will be assessed separately and points assigned accordingly. The students will submit the best four of the eight papers for grading.*

*A = 93–100%      B = 85–92%      C = 75–84%      D = 65–74%*

**2.** Establish clear criteria for grading both the content and process of any assignment that has as its fundamental goal the improvement of reading and writing.

**EXAMPLES**

*After listening to* Doctor DeSoto *(Steig, 1982), the second-graders will write and illustrate a personal narrative about a trip to their dentists' offices. The paragraph will be shared with a friend, revised, and edited. The final draft will be published in a class collection entitled "Our Trips to the Dentist."*

### Final Draft Grade
E  = Excellent

S  = Satisfactory

NI = Needs Improvement

### Criteria for Grading:
#### Initial draft(s):
*Sentences related to trip to dentist's office.  + −*

*Illustrated their story.  + −*

*Shared with a friend.  + −*

#### Revised (final) draft (ready for publication):
*Wrote a personal narrative that told story about a trip to the dentist's office.  + −*

*Took into consideration reader response to content of first draft.  + −*

*Included illustration.  + −*

*Sentences were complete.  + −*

*Spelling errors corrected.  + −*

*Capitalization and punctuation corrected.  + −*

*Shared with a friend.  + −*

*After reading* There's a Party at Mona's Tonight *(Allard, 1985), the fourth-graders will demonstrate their understanding of character by writing a character sketch of Potter Pig. The final draft of the character sketch will include details from the story that reflect the main character's personality, his problem-solving abilities, and any changes in character that take place during the narrative.*

### Initial Draft
*Shared in a small group + −*

### Final Draft (Graded)
#### Content:
*Fully characterizes Potter Pig.          30*
1. *Contains explicit/implicit details from the story.*
2. *The reader clearly understands who Potter Pig is, how he behaves, and what motivates him.*

*(continued)*

**Instructional Guidelines (continued)**

*Form:*

| | |
|---|---|
| *Complete sentences* | *5* |
| *Spelling* | *5* |
| *Punctuation* | *5* |
| *Handwriting* | *5* |
| *Total* | *50* |

*A = 45-50   B = 40-44   C = 35-39   Below 35 = rewrite*

**3.** Emphasize that *everything* a child reads or writes "counts" in making progress toward literacy. Even though a piece of written work does not receive a score or letter grade, it is nevertheless important. Children need to understand that your response to and informal analysis of their comprehension or composition all contribute to the development of reading and writing. This knowledge bolsters children's confidence in the assessment system by relaying the message that *all* classroom reading and writing is valued.

Examples of reading and writing assignments that might not receive a letter grade or points include journal writing, letters, diaries, sustained silent reading, number of books checked out of the library and read independently, initial drafts of any written work, and group efforts.

## ASSESSMENT STRATEGIES

### Responding to Literature

Assessing reading comprehension through oral and written composition is an important option to consider when planning a comprehensive assessment system. Traditionally, reading comprehension has been assessed through comprehension questions. The answers to the comprehension questions, which are often dominated by literal-level queries, are then graded "right" or "wrong," and points are assigned accordingly. Virtually all basal-reader series as well as literature texts and content area books include comprehension checks. Essay exams are another traditional way of assessing reading through writing, although they are used more often in the secondary schools than in elementary and middle schools. Used exclusively to assess reading comprehension, end-of-chapter questioning and essay exams could contribute to poor attitudes toward reading and writing.

An alternative to chapter-end comprehension questions and essay exams is composition and creative writing. To understand how this kind of integrated assessment works, consider the following model lesson, beginning first with a nonexample.

### A NONEXAMPLE: ALEXANDRIA AND THE TERRIBLY HORRIBLE, NO GOOD, VERY BAD GRADE

**MS. GARFIELD** (a sixth-grade teacher in her tenth year of service): *Alexandria, I see that you didn't get a single question right at the end of Chapter 7. This seems to be a developing pattern that's gone on for over nine weeks, and I'm starting to get concerned. Why do you think you're having so much trouble understanding what happens not only in reading but also in all the other subjects?*

**ALEXANDRIA** (a twelve-year-old sixth-grader with a history of language difficulties but who does not qualify for special help outside of the regular classroom): *I don't know. I guess I'm going to get bad grades again.*

**MS. GARFIELD:** *Yes, I suppose you are. Probably F's. And whose fault do you think it is, Alexandria? I just don't think you try hard enough. Look at this paper. You didn't even attempt questions 9 through 20. And I gave you the whole class period to answer the questions.*

**ALEXANDRIA** (head bowed): *It's just too hard.*

**MS. GARFIELD:** *I want you to take all of your books home over the Thanksgiving holiday and answer every comprehension question at the end of every chapter that we've already covered. After you're through I want your parents to check your work. Maybe they can help me get you ready for middle school next year. Heaven knows I've tried.*

**ALEXANDRIA:** *Yes, Ms. Garfield. Can I please go now?*

**MS. GARFIELD:** *Very well. Don't forget your books.*

## INSIDE THE CLASSROOM
### Integrating Writing into a Second-Grade Literature Lesson

1. Survey all of the literature you wish to use during a grading period. Decide on as many stories that you feel lend themselves to composing to assess comprehension. Make a list of the central story problems, themes, characters, concepts, and vocabulary words that you believe are necessary for the students to know to demonstrate complete comprehension of the text.

*(continued)*

**Inside the Classroom (continued)**

| | |
|---|---|
| Story: | "Frederick's Alligator" (E. A. Peterson, 1985) |
| Story problems: | No one believes Frederick's stories about wild animals that he keeps in his room. Frederick brings a live baby alligator to school. It gets loose and eats the class' tadpoles and worms before it is found. |
| Central themes/main ideas: | Wild animals belong in natural settings, not home or school. Alligators (wild animals in general) don't make good pets. |
| Concepts: | Make-believe friends/pets Cause and effect Fantasy/reality |
| Characters: | Frederick, Frederick's mother, Frederick's teacher, baby alligator, Frederick's friends. |
| Essential vocabulary: | Alligator, lion, egg, baby, river, carried, hid, "yonk," pet, tadpoles, bug, worms. |

2. Introduce the lesson with a direct, hands-on experience related to the central story problem or theme. Prepare the children to read (silently) by activating their prior knowledge of the major story concepts and by making some predictions about the story. Relate the major story concepts to previously encountered stories or nonfiction with similar themes. Integrate the essential vocabulary words into the discussion and display them on the chalkboard or overhead. (Italicized in following example.)

*8:45 A.M.*

MS. MYERS (a second-year, second-grade teacher): Good morning, second-graders! Today we're beginning a very special unit on animals that lay eggs. And we have our *baby* chick incubator full of eggs that Mr. Lyle brought yesterday. Do you remember how carefully he *carried* the eggs from their containers and placed them gently in the incubator? I want everyone to gather around the incubator now and carefully turn one *egg* over just like Mr. Lyle demonstrated yesterday. Do you remember why we turn the eggs over every day for twenty-one days?

SALLY: So they can get warm and all hatch on time.

MS. MYERS: Yes. It takes twenty-one days for a baby chicken embryo to develop before it is ready to peck its way out of a shell. The warmth of the temperature inside the incubator is kept constant. When you turn the eggs over every day you are helping to warm each side of the egg. [Children gently turn eggs over and return to their seats.] Thank you for being so gentle with the eggs. Does anyone know of other animals that are hatched from eggs?

**ROB:** Goldfish! My goldfish laid eggs and baby goldfish popped out once.

**KAREN:** Robins lay eggs. They're blue! My brother brought a cracked one home once.

**MS. MYERS:** Robins and goldfish lay eggs. Good! Rob has a goldfish for a *pet*. Would robins make good pets? Could you keep a robin in your house?

**SALLY:** If you put it in a cage.

**TONY:** But it wouldn't be happy. Like the robin in that story we read about Little Bear. It'd be sad.

**MS. MYERS:** You're right, Sally. We could keep a robin in a cage. But robins are wild animals, and like bears they wouldn't make good pets. Thanks for remembering the story about Little Bear, Tony. Can any of you think of other animals that would be sad if you tried to keep them for pets? [The class names a variety of undomesticated animals, including *lions,* tigers, bears, and baby chicks. Ms. Myers suggests *tadpoles, bugs,* and *worms.* She lists the children's responses on the chalkboard.] Would an *alligator* make a good pet?

**WHOLE CLASS:** No!

**MS. MYERS:** Remember the story I read to you yesterday by Mercer Mayer, *There's an Alligator Under My Bed* [1987]. Was that a real alligator or a make-believe alligator?

**WHOLE CLASS:** Make-believe!

**MS. MYERS:** Right! Where do real alligators live?

**TED:** They live in the sewers, don't they?

**TOM:** Nope. They live at the zoo and in swamps.

**MS. MYERS:** Well, Ted, alligators really have been found in sewers in large cities. Back in the 1960s it was legal to buy alligators at a pet store and take them home. Some people got tired of their alligator pets and flushed them down the toilet. That's how they got into the sewer system and continued to grow! Can you imagine that? Alligators usually live in swamps. Sometimes they're found in *rivers* or lakes. In America alligators live in the swamps of Louisiana and Florida [points to states on globe]. Do you think that alligators are hatched from eggs?

**WHOLE CLASS:** No!

*(continued)*

**Inside the Classroom (continued)**

Ms. Myers (smiling): "Guess what! Alligators do hatch from eggs. The mommy alligators *hide* their eggs under warm mud and leaves, where the baby alligator incubates and gets ready to hatch. And today we're going to read a story called "Frederick's Alligator." It's about a little boy named Frederick who has an alligator for a pet. What kind of sound do you think a baby alligator makes? [Class responds with a variety of animal noises ranging from growls to grrr.] In this story, Frederick's alligator makes this sound: *"Yonk, yonk."* That's a funny sound, isn't it! [Children laugh.] While you're reading the story silently, I want you to pay attention to the real animals and the make-believe animals that are in the story. You'll also notice a problem that Frederick has with his alligator. When we're all through reading, we'll talk about Frederick's alligator and how he and his mother, teacher, and friends solved the problem. When you finish reading, I would like you to write in your journal what you think Frederick's problem was in the story. I also want you to write what you liked best about the story. Does anyone have questions?"

*9:10 A.M.*

3. Allow about twenty minutes for sustained silent reading. Remind children who finish early to write in their journals. Children who are not reading at grade level may listen to a tape recording of the story, while others who may have minor difficulties are encouraged to ask questions while reading. All children should respond in writing.

*9:20 A.M.*

4. Discuss the central story problems and themes. Relate the details of the story to the children's lives. Write important concepts and vocabulary on the chalkboard. Engage the children in a whole-class discussion that encourages inferential and evaluative thinking. Suggest several possible writing assignments that measure the children's overall understanding of the story. Give the children a choice of topics and make clear that only the second or final drafts will receive a satisfactory or unsatisfactory mark in the grade book.

Ms. Myers: What was Frederick's problem in the story? [She writes children's responses on the chalkboard under the heading "story problems."] Would anyone like to read from their journal?

Stacy (reading from her journal): Nobody would believe him about the baby alligator.

Ms. Myers: Why wouldn't anyone believe Frederick?

**CAROLINE:** Because he said he had bears in his room but he really didn't and then when he really did find an alligator egg at the river and he told his mother she didn't believe him and neither did his teacher but they finally did when he brought it [the alligator] to school.

**MS. MYERS:** Very excellent answer, Caroline. Were there any other problems in the story? For instance, where did Frederick keep the alligator egg?

**TRUDY:** He kept it in his shoe box under his bed. The shoe box had grass in it.

**MS. MYERS:** How are Frederick's shoe box packed with mud and leaves and our baby chick incubator alike?

**JOHN:** It's warm inside so the baby can hatch. Frederick's alligator hatched inside the shoe box. But it didn't take twenty-one days. It didn't take hardly any time at all.

**MS. MYERS:** Great answer, John. So the baby alligator hatched inside the shoe box because it was warm, just like our incubator. We didn't learn in the story how long it took for the baby alligator to hatch, but we could do some research later to find out how many days it really takes. What was the problem after Frederick brought the alligator to school?

**MARIANNE:** The alligator got away and ate the worms and tadpoles. Yucky! [Class laughs.]

**MS. MYERS:** What do you think would happen if a baby alligator got loose in our room? Would that be a problem?

**WHOLE CLASS:** It would eat the baby chickens!

**TERRY:** It might eat our lunches or our bookbags!

**STACY:** Or it might hide inside the coat room and jump out and scare us like this: "Boo!"

**MS. MYERS:** Yes, good. Those are all real problems that we might have with a baby alligator in our room. How did Frederick solve his problem?

**LYLE:** He took it [the alligator] to the river where its home is at and it lived happily ever after.

**MS. MYERS:** What did you think about that? Would you have taken the alligator back to the river?

**PENNY:** Yes, because it'd be happier there. It's not a good pet to keep.

**MS. MYERS:** Do you think that Frederick's teacher and friends and mother would believe him now when he told stories about make-believe animals? How do you know?

*(continued)*

**Inside the Classroom (continued)**

CARL: They'd believe him because his mother looks under his bed now. It said so on the last page. My mom believes me every time I tell her there's something under my bed because there was once this huge cockroach under my bed. She made my dad get it out because she's scared of bugs.

Ms. Myers: Very good, Carl. What do you think is the most important thing [lesson] that we learned by reading this story?

JENNY: Look under your bed every night for wild animals. [Class laughs.]

PAUL: Don't ever bring home a pet alligator or he'll eat your sheets!

MS. MYERS: Did you like this story?

WHOLE CLASS: Yes!

MS. MYERS: I'm so glad! I think that you probably all agree that alligators don't make the best pets. Now I would like you to name some animals that would make good pets. These kinds of animals are called domestic, which means we can easily take care of them in our homes. I'll list them on the chalkboard next to the wild animals that you named earlier. [Class names dog, cat, rabbit, parakeet, gerbil, goldfish, white mice, and hamster.]
Let's look at our list of wild animals and domestic animals. Could any one of these animals on either list be an imaginary pet? For example, could you pretend that you had a pet lion? Could you pretend that you had a pet cat? I have a little boy named David who's a second-grader just like you. When he was four years old he had an imaginary pet he called "jack rabbit." Jack rabbit lived in David's backpack. Do any of you have imaginary pets or brothers or sisters who have imaginary pets?

CHARLENE: My baby brother thinks his blankie is his pet blankie. He talks to it all the time.

PAUL: I had an imaginary pet rhinoceros one time. I used him to hang up my coat.

CHARLENE: What happened to him?

PAUL: One day he just decided to go back to Africa to see his friends.

MS. MYERS: We can use our imaginations to make any animal (or thing) we want into our pet, just like Charlene's baby brother and Paul and Frederick did. Today's author's club activity is going to be a follow-up to our basal-reader story, "Frederick's Alligator." If you were going to write a story about an imaginary pet or a real pet, what would it be about? Remember, when we write fictional stories, like "Frederick's Alligator," we include the place or setting where the story happens, characters, a problem, a solution to the problem, and a story ending. [The story grammar parts are written on the chalkboard.]

You might want to start with a story title or with the name of your character and a problem that the character has. I'm going to write a story called "My Pet Canary." Its going to be about a real pet canary that gets loose one day and flies away to the Canary Islands, where it has an adventure with lots of other birds. As you begin thinking about what you want to write about, remember the story of "Frederick's Alligator" and how wild animals can often cause problems if we try to keep them as pets. If you're stuck on where to begin, ask your pen buddy or me. I'll be around to help everyone as you begin writing. Would anyone care to share their ideas for a story? [Several children volunteer ideas for writing, and Ms. Myers writes their suggestions on the chalkboard: My Dog, My Kitty, Cloe the Gerbil, and My Brother's Pet Hamster.]

*9:45–10:15 A.M.*

5. Allow at least thirty minutes for writing first drafts. Prepare the children for what is to come the next day, revising and editing, since this is to be a graded paper. To whatever extent possible, write with the children, but be available to help when needed.

> **Ms. Myers:** Now I want all of you to begin writing the first drafts of your papers. We have about thirty minutes left before recess, so I'm sure you'll get a good start. Tomorrow we'll have small-group conferences, and we'll use the Editor's Desk to help with our revisions and editing. Don't forget to use your writing checklist to help you say clearly what you want to say. All of your papers should be kept in your writing folder. Remember that each of your drafts gets a sticker, but only the final copy of your story will get an S, S+, or E in the grade book. So let me know when you're ready for me to grade your last revision. [The children begin writing, as does Ms. Myers, who interupts her own work during the next thirty minutes to answer questions and lend assistance.]

***Reflections.*** Ms. Myers's lesson buys time for literacy by eliminating worksheets from a traditional basal-reader lesson and substituting reading and writing connected text. By writing about topics relative to what has been read, children begin to develop the ability to think like a writer, to read and reread their own writing and the writing of others to construct and reconstruct meaningful texts.

Students' oral or written responses to children's literature are also an important assessment technique. Research into fourth-, fifth-, and sixth-grade reader responses to literature indicates that children respond in predictable ways, and what they say about the books they read gives us insights into their cognitive and affective development (C. R. Cooper, 1976; Purvis, Rogers, & Soter, 1990). Studier (1981) found that fifth-graders consistently responded to content rather than form or style and were primarily concerned with the literal aspects of literature rather than generating inferences. She also discovered that children are fully capable of responding as critical readers of literature. In other words, they will articulate what it is that they like or do not like about a selection. Kiefer (1988) describes a longitudinal study in which she observed children's responses to picture books in kindergarten through grade 4. She concluded ". . . that as children communicate with and about picture books they seem to develop growing awareness of aesthetic factors and of the artist's role in choosing these factors to express meaning." Atwell (1984) used a letter-writing technique, similar to dialogue journals, to elicit responses to literature from her middle grade students and then to engage in a written conversation with the children about their responses. Written reflections about books gave her students the chance to talk with another reader about what makes good writing and about the process of learning to understand and love literature. During the year Atwell was able to observe positive changes in the students' attitudes and thinking about reading and writing prose and poetry.

When organizing reader response to literature activities, keep in mind that simple instructions are best. For example, "Tell me and your friends what you liked and didn't like about the book. And tell us why," is a typical instruction that encourages freedom of expression as well as critical analysis of the text. It is also important to vary the activities from time to time by including nonverbal responses, such as picture drawing, crafts, or pantomime, in which the children demonstrate how a book made them feel. Creative dramatics, including child-written plays and skits, are also excellent variations that encourage analysis and synthesis of ideas learned through reading.

You may want the children to keep their observations about literature in a response journal. In this way you will have a written record of their progress throughout the year. Above all you will want to give children *time* to respond to the literature they are reading. A scheduled thirty-minute period per week for response activities is not unreasonable for middle grade students. Because primary grade children often read numerous books per week (sometimes per day!), the opportunities to write or draw about what they've been reading should be frequent—perhaps as many as two or three times a week. By affording many opportunities to respond to literature, you will be helping your students to become reflective readers, writers, and thinkers. This is an important goal in the development of literate individuals.

## Journal Writing

Journals are valuable tools for assessing children's comprehension and composition. What children write in their journals is a matter of short- and long-term curricular goals. You may wish to reserve journals for personal expressive writing, a type of nonfiction in which the children freely express their opinions and feelings about a subject. "Today I Feel" is an example of an assignment that encourages children to express how they are feeling about themselves on a particular day. It is a good way to encourage writing when children might otherwise refuse to compose because they can't think of anything to write about. Other teacher-directed journal-writing activities can focus on more academic concerns, such as "Write in your journals your observations about today's science experiment when we watched the baby chickens hatch from their eggs." or "What did you learn in math today? Tell me about it in your journal."

Though journal topics can be teacher-directed, child-generated topics are used more often. It is best to set aside a specific, uninterrupted time during the day for the children to write in their journals. Anywhere from five to fifteen minutes per day is a good span of time for primary grade children. The class need not be silent during journal writing because collaborative talk will facilitate the composing process. Instead, quiet interaction supports the social atmosphere that nurtures composition (Dyson, 1987). Ordinarily, journals are nongraded efforts, although you could use a credit/no credit method, especially if the children are motivated by your assessment system. Some children may be more likely to write in their journals every day if they understand that what they are writing not only helps their overall writing and reading but also "counts" in terms of the grade they receive in language arts each nine weeks. Journals are an excellent record of the children's writing progress over time and may be used as formative assessments of composition skill.

Journal writing may or may not be shared with peers or the teacher. Dialogue journals (Staton, 1980) are a way to interact with children privately through informal message writing. They are an especially good way to highlight the interactive nature of reading and writing. Furthermore, they give teachers and children an opportunity to develop a special reader-writer relationship. Your response to the children's journal entries can take the form of statements, questions to clarify meaning, or answers to question that the children have asked. You would write your response alongside the children's work in their journals, modeling written language that is appropriate for primary grade children. If you cannot read the kindergartners' or first-graders' invented spellings, you would simply ask them to read their entry to you before you respond.

### SECOND-GRADE DIALOGUE JOURNAL ENTRY

*I likt it wen Joey brot his dog to scol for sho and tel. It mad me hapy to see the pupy. I like pupees. I wat a pupy for my bertday. Do you hav a dog?*
*Jamie,*
*I like dogs, too, especially when they are puppies. I don't have a dog now, but I did have one when I was in second grade. His name was Boots. He was a black terrier with white paws. What kind of dog do you want for your birthday? What do you think you will name him?*

The children could also communicate with one another, sharing private thoughts and feelings, solidifying their community of readers and writers in which they reside during the school day. At home, written dialogues between parents, grandparents, and siblings provide valuable practice with written language. When children communicate in writing at home as well as at school, they begin to realize that written language is an important form of communication in daily life.

### HOME DIALOGUE JOURNAL ENTRY

> *Cindy,*
> *Tell me about your first day of first grade. [Cindy's mother read this sentence to Cindy as she looked on.]*
>
> > *Mommy*

> *Mommy*
> *Fis grd wuz fn we plad gamz I rad mi nam I lic mi techr [Translation: First grade was fun. We played games. I read my name. I like my teacher.]*
>
> > *Love Cindy*

## ASSESSMENT RECORDS

The portfolio system that you develop to manage and maintain assessment data is partly mandated by the schools but mostly developed by individual teachers. School districts will often prescribe and provide the exact kind of grade book to be kept by teachers, along with recommendations for other record-keeping systems, including folders of children's work. Computer printouts of grades as well as standardized test results normally go into a child's permanent cumulative folder, which is kept in the principal's office except during parent conferences or special staff meetings. Records that are kept in the assessment portfolio are more informal and include examples of children's work, checklists, and interest inventories.

Managing enormous amounts of data is an important issue, as children read and write connected text on a daily basis. Data collection can be more manageable during the year if you follow a few commonsense guidelines. Noncommercial, teacher- and childmade reading and writing folders should be of sturdy manila with the children's names clearly printed on the tab. Use different-colored folders to signify different language arts assessment objectives. For example, green could signify final drafts, and white folders could contain works in progress. You may also have the children decorate their folders to help identify their purpose. The more expensive folders with pockets on each side may be more practical in that loose papers are less likely to get lost, an inevitable fate of many works in progress. Each grading period make some decisions with the child about what should be placed in the assessment portfolio and what can be sent home. Be sure to copy any piece of work sent home that you still want to have on file.

The children should keep their folders in the same place at all times to minimize wasted time hunting for their work. Heavy cardboard file boxes located on a table at the back of the room are a practical alternative to steel file cabinets, which may not be accessible to all children, especially in the primary grades.

Sheila looks for her writing portfolio, which is accessible at all times.

Checklists should be securely stapled to the appropriate folder so that the children can fill in the information when the opportunity arises. When a checklist is completed, remove it from the child's folder and place in the child's portfolio, which contains all summative information gathered during the year about the child's progress in reading and writing. Make sure that each piece of data has a clearly marked date so that progress can be more easily documented.

Commercially prepared writing portfolios are available with side pockets for writing samples and preprinted writing checklists. The *Heath English* series (1986), for example, has three levels of folders, which include prewriting, writing, and revising/editing checklists, or guidelines, which are printed directly on the pocket-style folder. The level-1 folder, which is intended for primary grade children, includes a revising and editing checklist with such questions as "Did you write clearly about your idea? and "Does each sentence begin with a capital letter?" Such systems encourage the young child to become self-critical about work in progress. A disadvantage of the commercially prepared folder is that the cost may be passed on to the student.

## Closing Thoughts

Portfolio assessment contributes positively to a literacy-rich school environment. In such classrooms, all children feel good about themselves and their growth in the language arts. A carefully organized portfolio system is beneficial to all. For students, teachers, and parents soon realize that becoming literate is an ongoing process, where risk taking in reading, writing, and thinking is abundantly rewarded.

## FOR YOUR JOURNAL

1. Be a "kid watcher" for at least one hour in an elementary or middle school classroom. Observe the listening, speaking, reading, and writing behaviors in the classroom. Record what reflects the development toward literacy.

2. Design an assessment portfolio that you would feel comfortable showing to a child's parent. Name the grade level. Describe the contents you would include. Be sure to use both short- and long-term assessment instruments and examples of the child's work, if possible.

# 8 THE LITERACY-RICH CLASSROOM ENVIRONMENT

*It feels good to read and write in Mrs. Wallace's classroom.*

*David, age 7*

*Look, Mom. I've covered up all the ducks with my papers from school!
These worksheets sure do make great wall paper, much better than the
ducks. You don't mind, do you Mom? I am getting older you know.*

*Lisa, age 8 (from a mother's personal journal)*

## CHAPTER CONCEPTS

The classroom environment of instruction is crucial to literacy.

Instructional grouping is most effective when varied and flexible.

The workshop format facilitates growth in reading and writing.

Reading and writing conferences help teachers know children well.

Word processing naturally supports the integration of reading and
writing.

Time should be reserved each day for reading and writing connected
text.

The relationship between classroom environment and learning is significant.
Scholarly research into classroom management concludes that the most successful
teachers are those "who approach classroom management as a process of establishing and maintaining effective learning environments" rather than emphasizing their
roles as authority figures or disciplinarians (Brophy, 1988, p. 1). Many factors contribute to a positive classroom atmosphere, including time management, instruction-

al methods, teacher-student and student-peer relationships, and parental involvement.

There is no single recipe for pulling together the elements that lead to successful teaching and learning in positive settings. Because teaching is as much an art as it is a science, creating a classroom environment that optimizes learning is complex. To be artistic in our approach to classroom management and instruction requires a fundamental knowledge of both content and process across all subject areas. Knowledge of content gives us freedom to concentrate on the process of teaching. Creative and consistent use of the reading and writing process in lesson planning helps to build a foundation for successful teaching experiences. Ultimately our successes as teachers enable us to deal confidently and affirmatively with children. Effective classroom management has its roots in teachers' confidence in themselves as individuals and as professionals.

To reiterate a theme that is central to this text, the wise combination of direct instruction and child-centered activity is the goal for which classroom teachers should strive. This final chapter is designed to help teachers achieve that goal. The first section addresses a variety of instructional management strategies, including flexible grouping and computer-assisted learning, that support the integration of reading and writing instruction. The second section details the practical scheduling techniques that support quality instruction.

## INSTRUCTIONAL MANAGEMENT

### Whole Group, Small Group, No Group

Classroom teachers are very familiar with the dilemma of how to manage instruction for the fifteen to forty students in their classrooms. Research supports the concept of flexible grouping as the most desirable strategy (Hallinan, 1984). Flexibility in grouping students means that the group setting varies, sometimes daily, and depends on the objectives of the lesson and the individual needs of the students. One key to making group instruction workable is the teacher's willingness to remain open to change in his or her own classroom. Changes in attitudes, abilities, interests, and peer relationships, as well as the curriculum itself, will dictate change in any group arrangement. The language arts are very social processes that will flourish in a wide variety of settings, from one-to-one tutorials to whole-class instruction. It is important for teachers to recognize when the social interaction of a particular group breaks down for any reason, for it may then be time to disband, reorganize, and begin anew.

No matter how positive the group setting may seem in the beginning, constant monitoring and assessment is necessary to ensure its continued success. Using grouping effectively requires teachers to be acute observers of the children in their classrooms, to listen to the children interact within groups and, most important, to listen to the children's own observations about the groups in which they participate. Very often the children themselves will be direct in their opinions. As one sixth-grader I know aptly observed, "I've been in the 'mammals group' now for six months. I'm sick, sick, sick of mammals. I wanna be in the bird group." Without careful observation, potentially harmful situations could occur without the teacher's awareness. For example, during a conference with eight-year-old Tanya's mother, the second-grade teacher learned that Tanya had been complaining about her book buddy. It seemed that John had been teasing Tanya for the last six weeks about how slowly she reads. Tanya was too shy to say anything to the teacher. Her mother reported, "Tanya thinks she's doing something wrong," and she went on to appropriately request, "Would you please give her a different partner?"

Sometimes no group at all is the best strategy. It is important to remember that comprehending and composing are essentially solitary activities. Although reading and writing flourish within an atmosphere of frequent interactions among teacher, students, and peers, the individual child must ultimately construct meaning. Individualizing instruction occurs as a natural part of classroom management when teachers encourage children to read and write about what interests them and to contribute to the assessment system that measures the individual child's progress toward literacy. No-group situations mean that the children are on their own, working at a pace that has been agreed on by child and teacher. In the best of all possible classroom environments, children successfully read and write independently and, at the same time, learn from and contribute to small-group and whole-group activities.

What follows are descriptions of various instructional settings that support an integrated language arts curriculum in which reading and writing connected text is a valued and daily activity.

***Whole Groups.***    Whole-group, or whole-class, instruction dominates classroom organization and activities in the United States and in Great Britain, with the possible exception of reading instruction (Galton & Simon, 1980; Stodolsky, 1984). However, whole-class reading instruction is having a renaissance because of recent interest in more holistic teaching in general. A major contributor to this movement is teachers' and researchers' concerns about the adverse impact of small-group instruction on individual children, particularly when they have been grouped by ability, the most common instructional grouping practice (Good & Marshall, 1984; Hiebert, 1983). No matter what the label, children placed in the "blue birds" know that in fact they are the "low" reading group and consequently often experience negative self-esteem and reduced social status (Jongsma, 1985).

Whole-class instruction involves a heterogeneous group, in which everyone is given a chance to participate, children are not as likely to feel the pressure of participating at a competitive level. Whole-group instruction also eliminates competition between ability groups, which could account for the lower self-image of children who perceive their situation in the smaller group as irreversible. Moreover, whole-class instruction gives children an opportunity to practice appropriate social behaviors dictated by large-group situations. Working together as a whole group helps the class develop solidarity, to develop a feeling of belonging to "room 555," of being important individuals in the eyes of their peers. In summary, effective handling of whole-group situations makes teaching more efficient and ultimately enhances contact with small groups and individual students.

Whole-group instruction often includes brainstormed ideas that the teacher then writes on the chalkboard.

## INSTRUCTIONAL GUIDELINES
### Teaching Whole Groups

The instructional decisions for choosing whole-group instruction over some other arrangement can be based on a few guiding principles.

Choose whole-group instruction when:

1. *You are reading aloud to the children.* Position yourself so that all children can hear you. Gather young children around you so they can see the pictures more easily.
2. *You are engaging the children in a direct experience.* Concept-formation activities that are real and concrete require a great deal of careful planning, and there is rarely time to repeat the activity. Since this portion of any lesson is crucial to internalizing important concepts, the whole class should always be involved. Examples of direct experiences include field trips, videotapes, slide shows, puppet shows, creative dramatics and

role playing, guest speakers, art or music, experiments and demonstrations, and library research.

3. *You are explaining a new concept and you want everyone to hear what everyone else has to say about it.* Whole-class brainstorming sessions are valuable listening and thinking activities that give children the opportunity to be models for their peers. Children who ordinarily have trouble coming up with responses or ideas for further reading and writing are stimulated by the talk that surrounds them.

4. *You are modeling a process, procedure, or product that is crucial to the language arts lesson.* Modeling is a valuable yet underused strategy for teaching comprehension and composition. There are numerous opportunities throughout the day to be an adult model of the language behaviors that you want the children to develop. Children need to see their teachers engaged in reading, attentive listening, thoughtful discussion, and writing connected text. Other modeling situations involve metacognitive and metalinguistic thinking, topic generation and topic selection, composing a first draft, rewriting, editing, dictionary and thesaurus usage, and selecting a book just for fun.

5. *You are formulating rules for classroom behavior and academic expectations.* Classroom rules should be a combination of ideas contributed by the whole class and by the teacher. Rules should be positive statements clearly printed on posterboard, or some other sturdy paper, and displayed in a prominent place. Discussing classroom rules early in the year helps to set the tone. It is therefore desirable that rules are stated in the most positive manner possible, as in the following examples from a multiage class, grades 4, 5, and 6. Children may need help stating their ideas affirmatively. "Don't interrupt when somebody else is talking" could be better phrased: "Listen carefully to what others have to say." The following classroom rules were developed by a fourth-grade class during a whole-class discussion at the beginning of the year. Rules were suggested, discussed, and voted on to formulate the final list.

    *Our classroom is great because we . . .*
1. *Respect one another as individuals.*
2. *Listen carefully to what others have to say.*
3. *Contribute often to our discussions.*
4. *Read and write every day to learn.*
5. *Express our opinions openly and honestly.*
6. *Help each other as we become readers, writers, and thinkers.*

Separate, more specific rules for group behavior may be formulated from time to time, especially for field trips or small-group interactions that are new to the children, such as a Writers' Workshop or some other cooperative learning situation.

***Small Groups.***     Traditional American classrooms place a great deal of emphasis on students doing their own work, even when working alongside others in a small group (Stodolsky, 1984). Yet letting children work cooperatively in pairs or in small groups toward a common goal is an effective teaching method. In his comprehensive review of the literature, Slavin (1987a) concluded that students across all grade levels appear to benefit academically and socially from working cooperatively on learning tasks. He defines cooperative learning as an instructional method "in which all students of all performance levels work together in small groups toward a group goal" (p. 8). Although heterogeneous small-group activities are not new to teachers, they are nevertheless uncommon in most elementary and middle school classrooms.

How small is a small group? Ideally small groups range in size from three to six children, depending on the objectives of the lesson. More children interfere with the amount of individual contributions that any one child can make. As in whole-group situations, small groups are social settings in which rules and procedures govern the group's functioning and help to make it run smoothly. Small-group instruction works best when the objectives are clearly stated and the children know exactly what is expected of them. Students may be organized into wide variety of groups, including interest groups, research groups, script writers, drama casts and crew, and classroom helpers, just to name a few. Both reading and writing processes give teachers many opportunities to group children in small clusters. For example, the Editor's Desk, described in Chapter 3, is a way to involve small groups of children in the task of editing their work with the help of a peer leader, the "guest editor."

The small-group workshop is relatively new to the elementary and middle school classroom. Readers' and Writers' Workshops are important small-group settings in which children can learn to appreciate the work of professionals and peers alike. Additionally, the workshop is a social situation that demands cooperation by all members of the group, who are there to learn with and from each other.

*Readers' Workshop.*     Sometimes referred to as literature discussion or response groups, Readers' Workshop is a small-group activity. The Readers' Workshop management system requires each child to silently read the *same* piece of prose or poetry before coming together for the workshop. An alternative procedure occurs when one child reads aloud as the rest of the group listens attentively. The latter arrangement is sometimes difficult to manage in crowded classrooms but is nevertheless worth trying occasionally if conditions permit. The purpose of the workshop varies according to the selection and the specific objectives that the teacher wishes to fulfill.

Workshop guidelines are normally written on chalkboard or chart paper for the children to refer to during their discussion. When several groups are having workshops at once, the teacher floats among groups, contributing when appropriate and taking note of the group's progress in general and individual contributions in particular. The workshop promotes cooperation through small-group interactions. Children and teacher collaborate to establish workshop rules, as in the following examples.

### OUR READERS' WORKSHOP (K–3)

1. *I will read the book before workshop.*
2. *I will tell what I liked and didn't like.*
3. *I will listen carefully to everyone else.*
4. *I will think about what the story (or poem) says to me.*
5. *I will help my friends talk about the book.*
6. *I will write about what I've read.*

### RULES FOR READERS' WORKSHOP (6–8)

> *To help our workshop run smoothly, I will:*

1. *Come to workshop having read the book.*
2. *Tell the group what I thought about the book.*
3. *Try my best to analyze and discuss the text according to the guidelines.*
4. *Listen carefully to what others have to say.*
5. *Help others to understand the book.*
6. *Connect reading to writing by responding to the book in my journal or by writing my own prose or poetry that the book inspired.*

The selection for the Readers' Workshop may be from children's literature or content area reading. The primary goals are to read, respond, analyze, and discuss a piece of fiction, nonfiction, or poetry. The level of response and analysis is directly related to the age of the child. However, most children are fully capable of critical thinking. For instance, primary grade children could analyze and discuss sibling relationships as they are portrayed in Judith Viorst's (1978) *Alexander Who Used to Be*

Readers' Workshop for middle school students

*Rich Last Sunday* or Bernard Waber's (1972) *Ira Sleeps Over.* Intermediate grade children would enjoy responding to the drama, adventure, magic, and mystery in Arielle North Olson's (1987) *The Lighthouse Keeper's Daughter* or Frances Hodgson Burnett's (1963) *A Little Princess.* Middle school students love describing the author's use of humor in Daniel Pinkwater's (1984) *Blue Moose.*

## INSTRUCTIONAL GUIDELINES
## Conducting a Readers' Workshop

The following organizational scheme describes how a Readers' Workshop can be managed.

### READERS' WORKSHOP: ORGANIZING PRINCIPLES

### When to Have a Workshop

Readers' Workshops should be regular and frequent events in order to maximize the effects of small-group cooperation and interaction. Depending on the length of the books being read and discussed, a workshop could take place either weekly or biweekly.

### What to Read

Readings for the workshop should come from the best possible children's literature that can be obtained in multiple copies. Six copies each of five different single titles is the minimum requirement for getting a workshop organized in a class of thirty children. The cost of multiple copies may be prohibitive for some school systems. Teachers and administrators could elicit the help of the Parent Teachers Organization to raise funds for such an investment. Often the school library will have more than one copy of a single title; several school libraries in a district could work cooperatively to pool resources through an interlibrary loan system, thus making enough copies available in one school for a limited time. Anthologies of children's literature and literature-based basal readers or language arts books are also an alternative since such series are often adopted by the entire district and therefore each child has his or her own copy. In the beginning the teacher usually decides on groups of books that will be used for Readers' Workshops. However, as the year progresses the children are given the opportunity to suggest books that they have read and enjoyed and want to reread and share. This kind of information is elicited frequently in order to have time to obtain enough copies of the children's choices.

### How to Form Groups

Group assignments can be either random or interest-related. Assign students to one group of no more than six children. In a class of thirty, this would mean five different heterogeneous groups. Small workshop groups should be dynamic, ever-changing entities that meet the interests and needs of individual students. The teacher is a floating member of each group. During workshops she moves about, taking note of which personalities seem to work best together and which interests seem to wane over time. She also provides model comments and observations that help keep the discussion going if it appears to be in trouble. Usually an anecdotal record is kept for the purpose of organizing groups for subsequent workshops.

### Where to Hold Workshops

Most teachers are used to average-size classrooms filled with the usual desks, tables, bookshelves, and cubbies. Six groups of five children each simultaneously discussing what they have read is obviously a *noisy* scenario. Although classroom talk is mandatory in such situations, too much talk at once could defeat the workshop's purposes. Some teachers solve the problem by arranging ahead of time with the school librarian or media specialist to allow one or more groups to hold the workshop in the library. The hallway is also a possibility, provided the children do not disturb students in adjacent classrooms. The disadvantage of removing students from the main classroom is that additional supervisory help is needed by either the librarian or aide. If a workshop is held some place other than the classroom, the teacher may want the children to videotape or audiotape their discussion. In this way he or she can later view or listen to the group's interactions and make notes accordingly.

### Why Conduct Readers' Workshops?

Readers' Workshop is a forum for introducing excellent models of professionally written fiction, poetry, and nonfiction. For most students the concept of a workshop is new and different from the usual read-the-book-present-a-boring-book-report scenario. Instead, the workshop provides a fresh approach to reading and responding to literature. When presented in the context of "new and different," workshops can carry very positive connotations of reading for enjoyment, writing about what is read, and learning from peers in a small-group setting.

Readers' Workshops may be designed to meet a wide variety of curricular objectives. Here are just a few examples from a third-grade teacher's language arts curriculum.

> *Through Readers' Workshop the children will learn:*
> 1. *To enjoy discussing books read in common.*
> 2. *To respond orally and in writing to quality children's literature.*
> 3. *To analyze the structure of stories, poetry, or nonfiction.*
> 4. *To recognize the theme or main ideas in stories, poems, or nonfiction.*
> 5. *To describe how they came to understand the book.*
> 6. *To write their own fiction, nonfiction, and poetry inspired by what they have read.*

*Writers' Workshop.*     Writers' Workshop is a small-group setting in which children read and critically respond to one another's work in progress, under the guidance and supervision of the classroom teacher. The overriding purpose of the workshop is for children to help one another become *better* writers of prose or poetry. Writers' Workshops enable children to think of themselves as authors, to develop a sense of audience, and to come away from the workshop with the knowledge that what they are writing is of consequence. The primary difference between Writers' and Readers' Workshops, of course, is the child-written text under discussion. The children themselves decide when they are ready to put their work before the group. Ordinarily the workshop takes place when a first or second draft is available. Criteria may be established ahead of time so that the students understand that a certain number of drafts are expected during a grading period.

Since children write at varying paces, Writers' Workshops require flexible if not modular scheduling. Flexible workshop schedules are possible when large time blocks are allotted during the day for language arts (A.M.) and other content areas (P.M.). The teacher could also place some time restrictions on when drafts are due and workshops are held, especially if modular scheduling is out of the question. For instance, workshops could always be scheduled on Thursday, with final drafts due on Friday or the following Monday. For optimum interaction with the least amount of tension, the group should probably have about three or four members. Keeping the group small is also a practical consideration, given the children's different writing paces. There may simply be no more than two other children, in addition to the author, available for the workshop when the draft is ready.

Because children may not be used to critiquing constructively one another's work, and therefore do not really understand what is expected, teachers should conduct one or two model workshops with the whole class. You may wish to provide a teacher-written model to critique or, with the permission of the child, an actual work in progress from the class.

## INSTRUCTIONAL GUIDELINES
### Conducting a Writers' Workshop

The organization and management of a Writers' Workshop is governed by rules established collaboratively by teacher and student, as in the following illustration from a fourth-grade class.

*When*              *Writers' Workshop happens when I decide that my draft should be read by my classmates. I know that I must put up four drafts every nine weeks. Workshop is usually held during reading and language arts time, unless other arrangements are made.*

| | |
|---|---|
| *Where* | *Writers' Workshop takes place in a small circle of friends inside the classroom, out in the hallway, or in the library, depending on the available space.* |
| *Who* | *No more than three of my classmates volunteer to join the workshop. My teacher is also a part of the workshop, especially if we need help.* |
| *What* | *I give my story, poem, or paragraph(s) to my workshop members, and they read my work before we talk about it.* |
| *How* | *During the workshop, my friends tell me what they liked best, what confused them, and what advice they have for me as an author. Workshop members are considerate of my work. They respond to what I wrote (content) and how I wrote it (form). Sometimes we reread parts of what I have written. I listen carefully. I take notes so I don't forget what my readers have suggested. I take their suggestions into consideration when I rewrite my paper.* |
| *Why* | *Writers' Workshop helps me to become the best writer that I can be. I learn from my classmates and they learn from me.* |

Children will develop self-satisfaction from composition and creative writing only when they know that their writing is getting better. Good writing is hard work, no matter what age the author is. Elementary and middle school Writers' Workshops help the author move steadily along through positive reinforcement and constructive criticism from peers and teacher.

***Collaborative Writing.***    Collaborative writing, a popular small-group activity, can be either very successful or utterly disastrous because of the individual nature of the composing process. Group-written or group-dicated stories are often recommended for less able readers. However, when children have not successfully read very many stories, the structure of the narrative in a group effort may be completely distorted. Consider the following group dictation by four sixth-graders in the "low" reading group. Their only instructions were to tell the story of a fly that had become trapped inside a Venus flytrap and to use as many of the science vocabulary review words as they could. The following is the product of their efforts (M. F. Heller, 1988b, p. 131).

**MARK:** A fly flew into a Venus flytrap.

**JIM:** The fly died.

**TOM:** The fly flew back outside.

**KELLY:** It was just hiding inside one of the lobes.

**MARK:** The fly met another fly inside.

**JIM:** The fly flew back out the back door.

**TOM:** The fly went back inside the flytrap again.

**KELLY:** The flytrap tried to digest the fly.

**MARK:** The other fly tried to escape.

**JIM:** The fly is stupid.

**TOM:** The two flies got married.

**KELLY:** They had fifty children which were all insects.

**MARK:** They named one of the kids Venus Flytrap.

**JIM:** The fly was grossed out.

**TOM:** He works for WKRP in Cincinnati.

**KELLY:** The fly don't like carnivorous plants.

As evidenced by each contribution, the children do not individually have a clear concept of what a story is. As a result, their collaborative effort consists of a list of sentences that lack the cohesion necessary to support a narrative structure.

The traditional language experience approach does not give students total access to the composing process, particularly rewriting and editing. The flytrap story was the children's first and only draft. No direct instruction occurred during the dictation. One way to help small groups of children dictate a more unified story is to encourage use of the recursive nature of the composing process as the children are engaged in telling their story. Children and teacher should actively monitor the work in progress, read and reread what is being composed, and make modifications while dictating (or writing) to model the composing process more closely as it naturally occurs on an individual basis. For instance, when Jim suggests that the fly dies, the teacher could have asked, "If the fly dies now, what happens to the story?"

Compositions that are the result of collaboration among small-group members can be successful, as can be documented through research (Slavin, 1987b). Collaborative ventures work best when very specific instructional objectives are made clear to the students. Working together to produce a skit, play, short story, or poem requires a good deal of negotiating that depends on group contingencies. The whole group will be rewarded, but the reward is contingent on each individual's completion of assigned specific tasks. Rules are very important to collaborative efforts, especially when a quality process is expected during the group's interactions and a quality product is expected at the end.

Teachers should realize that if a group is assigned a single writing project, it will be the product of the entire group only if the children can work together cooperatively. Otherwise, one child will emerge as the major composer while the others merely look on. For example, one fifth-grade teacher I know instructed six students to write a play together for a kindergarten audience. She made it clear to them that *everyone* was to contribute to the play. But no further instructions were given. That evening the group gathered at one of the children's homes. According to the mother's report, there was an unresolvable argument over what the play was to be about.

So the children, being resourceful, bright fifth-graders, divided up the work as follows: Sarah wrote the play, Kate found the music, Britt and Tom made the puppets, and Tammy made the scenery. The teacher's goal of everyone *writing* the play was not achieved, although the group worked well together once roles were defined. They all had a part in producing a very successful play, *Miami Mice,* for an enthralled kindergarten class. Clearly, small-group efforts will succeed if the ground rules are laid and everyone in the group knows what is expected of them.

Following is an excerpt from a group-written story that is an example of the ultimate in successful lessons. Unlike the sixth-grade Venus flytrap dictation, "What Would You See in China?" was written and illustrated by four sixth-grade children who had been heterogeneously grouped for the activity. The children, members of a central Kansas elementary school, wrote the story at the conclusion of a social studies unit on China, during which they read from their texts and completed a good deal of library research on the history and culture of mainland China. Their teacher, Ms. Grimes, wanted the children to work together on some kind of group writing project having to do with China. To stimulate the small-group writing projects, she thought of using a unique pattern book called *What Would We See?* (Johnson, 1963). The book, which is now out of print, was written by a Kansas elementary school teacher and illustrated by her students. It is a highly predictable story filled with alliteration and images of animals that may or may not be seen in the Kansas countryside (i.e., a lamb and an alligator).

Ms. Grimes decided to use the pattern book about Kansas as a model for her students. The main objectives of the lesson were that the children, randomly assigned to groups of three or four, write and illustrate a book about China patterned after Johnson's book. (See the accompanying excerpts.) The children's creation had to contain *accurate* facts about China plus alliteration and a predictable pattern of sentences throughout. The entire process of negotiating content, writing, rewriting, editing, illustrating, and publishing took about two weeks. The results were six different China books carefully handwritten and illustrated by Ms. Grimes's class. Each group collectively received a final grade on its finished product, which then was placed in the school library. The children were extremely proud of their accomplishments. Ms. Grimes believed that the true success of the project was seen by the children's renewed enthusiasm for writing, not just in groups but individually as well.

## SMALL-GROUP COLLABORATIVE WRITING

### *Professional Model (an excerpt)*
*What Would We See? Norma Johnson (1963)*

What would we see if we were riding along—

Riding along in the middle of Kansas?

Would it be an elephant?

An elegant elephant clumping along in the middle of Kansas?

No, but we could see a pony—

A prissy-proud pony. A pony with mane blowing about in the breeze.

Yes, we would see a pony—a pretty, proud pony

Prancing about as proud as you please. (pp. 3–5)

### Sixth-Grader's Collaborative Story (an excerpt)

What Would We See in China? by John, Kathy, and Jana

*What would we see if we were riding along, riding along in the middle of China?*

*Would it be a purple Porsche driving along in China?*

*No, but we could see a beautiful brown bike bouncing along on Beijing boulevard.*

***The Mini-Lesson.***    Mini-lessons (Caulkins, 1986), or mini-lectures, are brief yet concise explanations of concepts. These short lessons are organized for one of two reasons. First, a teacher may determine through direct observations of individual children that a specific concept needs to be reviewed or retaught. For example, in a second-grade class of twenty-five children, five students may still be having difficulty with something as general as topic selection or as specific as the use of plurals. The teacher designs a brief lesson on the problem area, specifies the group, teaches the lesson, and then disbands the group as soon as the concept has been fully internal-

Rules for proofreading are clearly displayed during a small-group mini-lecture.

Jessica and Mary are book buddies sharing their favorite picture book.

ized. This approach is prescriptive in nature since the teacher isolates problem areas, focuses only on the children who need help, and then addresses the problem in an efficient small-group setting.

Mini-lessons are also appropriate for whole-class instruction, especially at the beginning of the academic year, when a review of basic concepts and processes is all that is needed to refresh the children's memory. Whole-class mini-lessons or mini-lectures are also useful when presenting new concepts, especially when the lesson is presented in the context of a direct experience before reading and writing. The overall advantage of lessons presented in brief is that they help to buy more time for reading and writing connected text.

***Diads.***     Diads, or pairs of students working together, are yet another way to organize children for specific instructional purposes. As in small-group settings, relationships should be monitored and pairs rotated whenever two children do not appear to be enhancing one another's learning. Following are some typical reasons for having children work in pairs.

*Book Buddies*.     Children in the same class read their favorite books aloud to each other or children are paired with a different grade-level child, for example, a sixth-grader with a kindergartner.

*Pen Pals.*    Children are randomly assigned a pen pal from their own class, a child from another class at the same grade level, an older child in the same building, a child in a different school, or a college student. Pen pal activities serve many instructional objectives. When an older child or an adult is the pal, the younger child sees appropriate models of letter writing, which help to improve their reading and writing abilities (M. F. Heller, 1988a).

*Writing Mates.*    Writing mates, or partners, help one another during the composing process. Children are encouraged to ask their partners to help them with aspects of content and form as their writing emerges. "How do you spell . . ." and "What do you think about . . ." are typical questions.

*Peer Tutors.*    "I never really learned grammar until I had to teach it." This statement by a first-year middle school English teacher reflects a common truth about teaching, that we really learn a concept well through the act of teaching others. This is the philosophy on which peer tutoring is based. It takes careful planning, teacher modeling, and supervision to guarantee that peer tutor and tutee relationships work (Cazden, 1981). Tutors should never feel that they are being denied the opportunity to read and write connected text at the expense of time spent schooling a peer in a particular area. Peer-tutoring programs work best when the tutors are highly motivated to teach their friends (or younger students) and are rewarded intrinsically for their efforts. At the same time, the tutees should feel good about working with a peer.

*Computer Tutors.*    The need to educate children about computers is an important instructional goal, yet teachers are often overwhelmed by large classes and few microcomputers. It is very desirable to have children working in pairs at a computer, teaching one another computer basics with simple programs, keyboarding, word processing, spread sheets, and data base. Schoolwide tutor programs are usually voluntary, after-school activities during which interested children of all ages learn the basics of computer usage and then return to their classrooms to help the teacher with one-to-one peer tutorials.

*No Group.*    Sometimes children are best left alone to learn independently. Developing independence is an important life skill that can be effectively reinforced at school. Reading and writing centers are popular instructional settings that when creatively designed, can also be powerful aids to classroom organization and management.

*Reading and Writing Centers.*    Centers are special areas located somewhere in the classroom where children can work independently (or in very small groups) for a very specific purpose. Although the center is typically associated with kindergarten and primary grades, reading and writing centers are possible in any grade, K–8, and are an appealing alternative to independent seat work. Directions for using the center are first explained to the whole class, and then children are assigned times when the center is available. For older children, the directions for using the center are reinforced in writing. Tape-recorded instructions are often used with younger children or less able students.

The reasons to participate in a reading and writing center are as varied as the curriculum itself. Traditional approaches utilize centers for drill and practice, especially on worksheets for reading and writing skills. However, a much more holistic approach would be to design centers that reinforce conceptual development. Such centers take advantage of all of the language arts areas—listening, speaking, reading, and writing—and are often thematic in content. The focus of center learning then becomes the assimilation and accommodation of ideas, new and old, through independent study of concepts related to a wide variety of topics across all subject areas. Conceptually based themes range from the very simple and concrete (shapes, colors, textures) to more abstract ideas concerning friendship, freedom, or scientific explorations (Figure 8.1). Ideally reading and writing centers contain many audiovisual aids, including tape recorders, headphone sets, videocassette recorders and a monitor, typewriters, a computer and printer, art materials of all kinds, pictures, posters, and books.

## The Multiage Classroom

Imagine a classroom of twenty-two children in grades 1, 2, and 3, working together as a community of learners. The children are not labeled first-, second-, and third-graders. They're just students in Mrs. Reynolds' multiage class. Mrs. Reynolds is their teacher for three years. In her classroom, the children learn from one another in a supportive and nurturing atmosphere that underlies the family grouping model. The environment is child-centered and highly individualized, as students' literacy develops at individual rates. Older children serve as models and mentors for their younger peers. Mrs. Reynolds is the facilitator who employs all combinations of whole-, small-, and no-group instructional settings. She designs developmentally appropriate lesson plans that are often arranged in thematic units. In addition, she uses many of the traditional teaching methods employed in a more traditional classroom setting.

Mrs. Reynolds's room looks a lot like any other literacy-rich environment. Tables are arranged in clusters where children can face one another and communicate ideas. There are small, private spaces for children to work alone or in pairs. There's a listening/music center in the back of the room, complete with headphones and tape recorders. Shelves lining the walls contain volumes of picture books, novels, poetry, and desktop publications. Print is everywhere, from chalkboard to chart paper to bulletin board and computer monitor. The noise level gets high, as children work in small groups. But when asked to come together as a class, the room is suddenly hushed as everyone moves to the center carpeted area and sits quietly as Mrs. Reynolds reads them a story or engages in direct instruction of a skill or process.

Multiage grouping has its roots in the American one-room schoolhouse where children often stayed with the same teacher over a period of several years. New

**"Close Encounters of an Uncertain Kind"**

**Objective**

As we enter the twenty-first century, the students will gain an appreciation for scientific inquiry and space travel through reading, writing, and thinking about concepts relative to humankind and our place in the universe.

**Student Options:**

1. Read one or more of the books about space that are provided in the learning center.
2. Write an original space story or poem inspired by what you have read.
3. Create your own UFO or alien, using the materials provided. Write a story or play in which your creation(s) are characters.
4. Make a list of "questions for further research" that you'd like to answer. Write your questions on your writing folder.

**Materials**

*Suggested Art Supplies:*

Paper plates, glue, yarn, aluminum foil, cellophane tape, crayons, magic markers, bottle caps, cardboard containers (all sizes), pipe cleaners, scissors, Popsicle sticks or tongue depressors, toothpicks, paper cups, fabric swatches, contact paper, construction paper, string, paper towel or toilet tissue tubes, plastic tableware.

*Children's Literature:*

*Making UFOs,* Dave Ross (1980), Watts.
*Guys from Space,* Daniel Pinkwater (1989), Macmillan.
*The Glow in the Dark Night Sky Book,* Clint Hatchett (1988), Random House.
*Journey Into a Black Hole,* Franklyn Branley (1986), Harper & Row.
*The Planets in our Solar System,* Franklyn Branley (1981), Harper & Row.
*The Eagle Has Landed,* Bill Martin, Jr. (1970), Holt, Rinehart & Winston.
*Goodnight Moon,* Margaret Wise Brown (1942), Harper & Row.
*The Golden Book of Stars and Planets,* Judith Herbst (1988), Western.
*The Astronauts,* Dinah L. Moche (1978), Random House.
*Glow in the Dark Constellations,* C. E. Thompson (1989), Brooke House.

*Media and Props*

Record or tape of "Also Sprach Zarathustra," Richard Strauss (theme from *2001: A Space Odyssey*)
Tape recorder
Transistor radio
Dog dish or colander
Flashlight
Computer
VCR
*Earth Versus the Flying Saucers* (videotape)
*War of the Worlds* (audiotape)

**FIGURE 8.1** Thematic language arts center (1–4)

Children in grades K–3 work together in a multiage classroom.

Zealand, which has the highest literacy rate in the world, commonly uses multiage grouping throughout its educational system (Connell, 1987). While much of the scenario from Mrs. Reynolds' classroom is seen in a traditional first-, second-, or third-grade classroom, there are nevertheless fundamental differences between multiage and unit grouping. The major suppositions underlying multiage grouping are philosophically in line with whole-language and integrated language arts methods. The following assumptions about teaching and learning distinguish the multiage classroom from age-segregated grouping, typically found in American schools (Kasten & Clarke, 1993).

The multiage grouping model:

1. Supports interactive models of teaching and learning
2. Considers student diversity to be a given
3. Views learning as a dynamic, ongoing process
4. Values learning how to learn as much as what to learn
5. Sees the teacher as the primary facilitator of learning, who provides a variety of developmentally appropriate learning experiences that meet the needs of all children (pp. 11–13).

While not all educators and parents feel comfortable with the idea of the multiage classroom, progressive educators are nevertheless giving it a try. In time, research may give us an indication of the positive effects of family grouping models over more traditional classroom management systems.

## COMPUTERS IN THE SCHOOLS

Computers are here to stay. As children progress through kindergarten, elementary, and middle school grades and into the twenty-first century, personal computers will have become a permanent fixture in the classroom. Since it was first introduced in the late 1970s, the personal computer has enjoyed a dramatic increase in use. School administrators mandate computer curriculum objectives, and school boards approve funds for investing in thousands of dollars worth of hardware and educational software. The computer is thus thrust into classrooms with the promise of helping teachers to improve the reading, writing, and thinking skills of their students. Regardless of intensive in-service training and preservice preparation in computer usage, classroom teachers may still be reluctant to use available technology when planning for instruction. More often than not, computer usage is limited to pro-

First-graders collaborate while learning to use a computer.

grammed drill and practice that is dictated and monitored by the software, not the teacher. Balajthy (1989) reports that in 1985, "drill and practice activities accounted for 73 percent of computer time, and tutorial instruction an additional 24 percent" (pp. 84–85). Very little time appears to be devoted to word processing or computer programming.

## Computer-Assisted Instruction

Computer-assisted instruction (CAI) is frequently based on a skills viewpoint, with software packages that divide language learning into specific skills areas, such as letter and word identification, vocabulary and dictionary definitions, and comprehension with emphasis on right or wrong answers (Reinking, 1988–89). Used only in this way, the computer is simply an expensive substitute for worksheets. Although it may be argued that some CAI provides immediate feedback to the student, thus freeing the teacher to attend to other classroom needs, it is important to remember that the computer is only as good as the information contained in the software.

Computer software programs were never intended to replace reading and writ-

David, a sixth-grader, composes at the computer.

ing instruction or the instructor. In a study of social interactions during microcomputer instruction, Allen (1988) found that a significant amount of teacher intervention necessarily occurred within the fourth-, fifth-, and sixth-grade classes observed. Both child- and teacher-centered questions were important to the learning process. Allen also found that the majority of the children enjoyed working in small, collaborative groups to solve computer program problems and that little antagonism or off-task behavior occurred. The computer can certainly be used to maintain children's attention, and this particular aspect of computer instruction should be exploited whenever possible.

Computers have tremendous potential for teaching the language arts, especially if teachers are knowledgeable about word-processing programs as well as graphics tools designed for elementary and middle school students. With the recent interest in teaching writing as a process, designers of computer software have responded with whole categories of programs that exploit the process viewpoint through interactive stories or story makers. Unlike word-processing programs that present the child with a blank screen on which to write, interactive programs such as *Story Maker* (Bolt, Beranek & Newman) encourage children to write a story by selecting one of several story lines provided by the program. Using the *Story Maker* program, children construct a variety of plots suggested by the "story tree," or they can add their own original story segments. The program "tells" the children if they have actually met the predetermined goal of creating a story or if they need to work on the plot line further. For children who are experiencing difficulty with logical plot development, either in their reading or writing, *Story Maker* could help them to develop a clearer understanding of the logic of story lines. Nevertheless, the program itself limits the children's thinking along preprogrammed ideas. Even though a wide variety of plots can be constructed by using story makers and interactive story programs, they should be used sparingly.

Other process-oriented computer software are prewriting programs in the form of outliners, data bases, and activity disks; postwriting programs, which include spelling checkers, grammar checks, and editing helpers; and total writing programs such as the *Writing Workshop* (Miliken). Some programs help children organize their thinking before writing through prewriting questions that encourage creative and critical thinking. Because a question-and-answer session with a computer requires a child to be a competent independent reader, most of the available software, such as *Writing a Narrative* (MECC), is designed for intermediate grades or secondary-level students. Proofreading programs, such as *Bank Street Speller* (Broderbund) also require a certain amount of independence in reading. Spell checks will only frustrate children if they are unable to recognize the correct spelling of the word from a list of alternative spellings. Nevertheless, the proofreading component of a comprehensive word-processing program is a useful adjunct to the editing stage of the composing process.

An important question for teachers to ask when reviewing software that claims to improve the process of reading and writing is this: "Does the program encourage critical thinking, concept formation, and extended practice in reading and writing connected text?" That is a lot to ask of a piece of software designed for young children. As software writers become better at their craft, we will begin to see better and better materials to help us in our fundamental instructional goals. In the meantime, there appears to be no real substitute for a good word-processing program that puts the child in charge. A selected list of computer software and publishers appears at the end of this chapter.

## Word Processing

Word-processing programs, compared to computer-assisted instructional programs, allow the students and the teacher to create their own reading and writing agendas. Graphics tools enable children to experiment with drawing pictures and designs by using simple programming languages such as LOGO (Pappert, 1980). Word-processing programs and graphics tools more explicitly model real-world computer applications than do games or CAI (Brown, 1986). However, before children can be expected to sit before a blank computer screen and compose and illustrate their own work, the teacher must be a model to the students, frequently using the computer during language experience activities and for other real experiences such as letter and memo writing, as well as in teacher-written models of fiction, nonfiction, and poetry. Being a model, computer-literate teacher is important because it communicates to students the value of using computers to their fullest without fear or hesitation.

The act of electronically typing words into a computer, which then displays the writing on a screen, supports and amplifies the recursive nature of the composing process. As writers compose on the screen before them, the word-processing program allows them the flexibility to shape their work through deletions, additions, substitutions, and rearrangements of individual words or whole sentences and paragraphs. Reading and writing connections are fully realized as the writers, who are the first readers of their own work, simultaneously write, read, rewrite, reread, and then write some more. Anywhere in that process they may choose to print a draft for their readers to respond to.

The ease with which writers can rewrite and ultimately edit a piece is one of the major advantages of composing at the computer. Children who become practiced at word processing soon revise and edit more than they ever did with pencil and paper (Daiute, 1986). Yet there are pitfalls: Computers can be either a tool or a trauma, depending on how the teacher handles word-processing instruction (Rosegrant, 1986). Clements (1987) suggests that when used as effective tools, computers encourage exploration and experimentation with language and at the same time facilitate communication. The traumatic effects of the computer are felt when a child or teacher misuses its capabilities by overemphasizing correctness of form and content or becoming overly critical about first drafts right off the printer. Regardless of the promise of computer technology, word-processing lessons can suffer from the same poor teaching methods as the more traditional paper-and-pencil, textbook writing and reading curriculum.

Angela, a third-grader, learns to manipulate a mouse as her teacher observes.

It is never too early to introduce children to computers and word processing. Not surprisingly, children in grades K–8 already know a lot about computers. Although children's knowledge and experience will vary widely within and across grade levels, almost all will have had some experience with digital machines, from dishwashers to microwaves to video games. As users of everyday equipment in the home, children are already acquainted with the minimum skill level necessary to follow a set of directions and use a computer for word processing (L. K. Brown, 1986). It then becomes the job of the teacher, with the help of a good word-processing program and graphics tools, to guide the children in their use of the computer's vast potential for learning.

## INSTRUCTIONAL GUIDELINES
### Teaching Word Processing

The following are some tips and example lessons for introducing and using word processing in the elementary and middle school language arts curriculum.

1. Be a model computer user. There is nothing worse than a beautiful piece of new computer equipment sitting sedately at the back of the room year-round, untouched by the classroom teacher's hands. Teachers should take every opportunity to use computer equipment for lesson planning, home and school communications, and printed or illustrated bulletin board materials.

For language experience activities (LEA), the computer is ideal (Heller, 1993). Either one-to-one or in small groups, the children dictate their stories as the teacher types them directly into the computer. The children are seated so that they can easily see and read their words as they appear on the screen. During the oral composing process, the teacher can talk about how the word processing program may be used to make deletions and insertions, move the text around for greater clarity, and help with editing the first draft through spell checks and grammar features.

Language experience lessons also give teachers the opportunity to reinforce key terms that may already have been introduced in a large-group setting. Additionally, when the children are finished with their initial draft, the teacher can immediately print a copy for each child in the group. These hard copies may then be used for rereading as well as rewriting. The immediacy of having their own personal copy of their story is a tremendous advantage. When children have the hard copy in hand, it is then that the relationship among oral language, writing, and reading becomes real.

A way to involve the whole class in computer-assisted language experience activities is to have the children first individually hand-write their experience stories. As each child finishes the first draft, he or she reads it to the teacher, who in turn types it into the computer, using conventional spelling. The teacher then prints a copy of the conventionally spelled version and hands it to the child to reread. Both the child's story and the computer printout (Figure 8.2) are then placed in a folder for later use in reading and writing activities. In a class of thirty students, with the help of a teacher aide who reads to the children after they completed the write, read, reread process, one first-grade teacher reported easy completion of the lesson in about an hour (M. F. Heller, 1989b).

When young children themselves begin composing at the computer, a

*(continued)*

**Instructional Guidelines (continued)**

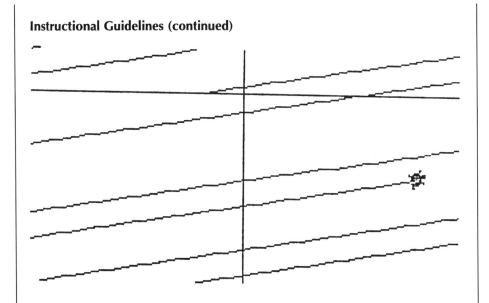

David.

I LIKe computersit is
fun.IVLrnd UBaNtcomPuters.
I nohaw to mac the turti
Muv

```
David

I like computers.  It is fun.  I've
learned about computers. I know how to
make the turtle move.
```

**FIGURE 8.2**  Computer-assisted language experience story—1

similar LEA procedure can be used. As the children complete their computer LEAs, the teacher types directly below their story the conventionally spelled version (Figure 8.3) and then has the child reread (M. F. Heller, 1989b). It is important when using this particular procedure that the children do not think that what they have written is "wrong," but rather that the conventionally spelled version will help them to become better readers, writers, and ultimately spellers. When presented in this light, children usually have no difficulty accepting the teacher's version alongside their own. Because young children's invented spelling sometimes contains minimal cues for rereading and comprehending, the conventionally spelled version becomes much easier for the children to read and reread as the school year progresses. For most children, being able to read what they wrote earlier in the school year creates a sense of pride and self-satisfaction.

2. Introduce key terms gradually. Sometimes teachers are not sure which computer-related terms should be introduced first. The vocabulary of the computer often changes, according to the equipment and the program. Therefore it is important to be consistent in the use of terminology for the computer and software available in the school.

As in any encounter with a new subject area, the concepts underlying the vocabulary are of utmost importance. In the beginning it is best to go slowly and introduce only a few word-processing terms at a time and then provide practice with meaningful reading and writing lessons, as described throughout this textbook. Logic and common sense about what is developmentally appropriate should be followed. For example, young children in the primary grades will initially struggle with an unfamiliar keyboard just to find the letters of the alphabet. Young children should first become familiar with the location of all the letters and second be introduced to the *space bar.* Tab and shift key instruction would logically follow.

If graphics are a part of the word-processing program, such as Logo-Writer (Logo Computer Systems, Inc.), the commands for creating a picture or design should also be introduced gradually, first separate from word processing but soon thereafter in conjunction with an actual writing activity. Figure 8.4 is an example of a mid-year first-grader's "shape story," composed at the computer with the Logo-Writer program.

Direct instruction in correct keyboarding techniques can begin as early as the kindergarten or first-grade year. Research indicates that children who develop their keyboarding skills early learn to compose more quickly at the computer than those left to "hunt and peck" (Schmohe, 1990). Formal keyboarding techniques should always be practiced in conjunction with language arts lessons, rather than as meaningless skill drills (Balajthy, 1988). The computer itself provides the hands-on, direct experience that helps children to internalize abstract concepts relative to word processing. The following is a list of key word-processing terms, which can be taught to the whole class in the beginning and later reinforced in smaller groups or one-to-one instruction.

*(continued)*

**Instructional Guidelines (continued)**

`iwnoaetim`

`wdiwtdfiwfiwoniwonaehtmthilraiwnohsili`

### I Went On An Elephant
### By Tim

One day I went to the fair.   It
was fun.   I went on the elephant.   He
took me to his home.   I went on his
swing.   I liked it there.

**FIGURE 8.3**   Tim's computer-written language experience story (Heller, 1993)

SOURCE: Reprinted with the permission of Visions for Learning from *The Writing Notebook, 10*(3), Jan/Feb, 1993. PO Box 1268, Eugene, OR 97440-1268.

| USING THE PROGRAM | THE KEYBOARD | FUNCTION KEYS |
|---|---|---|
| DOS (for IBM and IBM compatible | letters | control key |
| A, B, C *prompt* (>) | numbers | alt. key |
| word-processing software (i.e., Logo-Writer) | space bar | escape |
| command to enter the program (i.e., >logowr) | enter/return | print |
| main menu (for menu-driven software) | tab | underline |
| files | shift | move |
| work space or work page | caps lock | exit |
| command center or command space | delete | help |
| cursor | backspace | cancel |
| mouse | backslash (\) | list files |
| quit | arrow keys | merge |
| | page up | save |
| | page down | |

When Everyone Is Asleep In Manhattan
By
Rachael

When everyone is asleep in Manhattan, the bird 🦅 comes out. He 🦅 flies all around the village 🧱. He smells the flowers ◆🦅. Then he goes back to the tree 🌳 🦅.

**FIGURE 8.4**    First-grader's "shape story"

3. Use the computer to support the process of reading and writing. The computer can be a useful tool in virtually all of the teaching methods described in this text. During the prereading/prewriting stages, whole-class brainstorming suggestions could be entered, printed, and then stored on a disk, using either word-processing or database programs. Children could also store their own data, including personal lists of writing topics, reading interests, and books read during the year. When established properly, children's computer files can be retrieved whenever needed, added to, and deleted when no longer necessary. The hard, paper copy of the file can be made anytime, which is a real advantage because such lists are often misplaced by even the most responsible student.

Children should be encouraged to compose at the computer, rather than write their work on paper first and then type it into the computer. Typing

*(continued)*

**Instructional Guidelines (continued)**

from a handwritten copy has two major disadvantages. First, it requires eye-hand coordination that most elementary and middle school children have not yet acquired. And second, it can be a time-consuming, frustrating process, which leaves children exhausted and reluctant to use the computer as a vehicle to explore language.

When there is limited access to computers, as in a one-computer classroom, the children should work on only one piece at a time during their computer time allotment. One-computer classroom schedules ordinarily require the children to wait their turn for ten to fifteen minutes of computer time sometime during the day. They could also be working on other writing projects with the more traditional paper and pencil. Realistic goals should be set so that children will know how to pace themselves and their computer time. For example, in a fifth-grade class of twenty-five children in a one-computer classroom, a single computer-composed story every two weeks may be all that is possible. But if the children are scheduled in a computer laboratory for thirty minutes every day, they could conceivably write and revise one or more pieces per week, once they had become adept at word processing.

Hard copies of initial drafts can be used for whole-class instruction on refining editing skills, as well as for work at the Editor's Desk. Editing a printed copy heightens children's awareness of editorial matters when they are at the screen composing their own work. "Now, let's see, I have to put a capital at the beginning of the sentence. Where's the shift button?" is a familiar comment after children have had the experience of editing a hard copy (M. F. Heller, 1989b).

The ease with which children can revise and edit their final copy makes publishing their work much more appealing. Publishers of software are fully aware of the popularity of classroom publishing. Programs such as *The Children's Writing and Publishing Center* (The Learning Company) employ user-friendly screen layouts, color graphics, and word-processing capabilities that produce a professional-looking document, be it report, story, letter, or newsletter (Figure 8.5). Sign-maker programs, such as *Printshop* (Broderbund) can also be used to design creative book jackets for the children's publications. The computer truly makes desktop classroom publishing a reality, and thus the writing process can be brought to closure. As the children's individual and class collections of stories, poems, and nonfiction become available to their reading public, the connections between reading and writing are fully realized.

wstjrgztwr.

The soldier guards the tower

By Michael

The Dragon Fighter
By
Michael

Once upon a time
there lived a dragon and a
knight. And the knight
was trying to fight the
dragon. And the
knight killed the
dragon. He got a
medal for his good
deed. And he always
has been a hero.
That is all.

**FIGURE 8.5**   Children's Writing and Publishing Center examples: *(top)* kindergarten composition; *(bottom)* kindergarten dictation

## Emerging Technology: Hypermedia

***Hypertext.***    Hypertext, a term first used by Ted Nelson in the 1960s, refers to the process of connecting textual information in nonlinear ways. Nelson (1982) defines hypertext as "nonsequential writing that branches and allows choices to the reader [through] a series of text chunks connected by links which offer the reader different pathways" (p. 4). The organizational structure of a hypertext mimics the way in which we organize information in our memory (Jonassen, 1989). Information is accessed in a nonlinear fashion, depending upon the reasons we establish for retrieving data. For example, if we think about the concept of *communication,* our imaginations will take us in many different directions, from letter writing to telecommunications to simple conversation and discussion we've had in our lives. Computer software based upon the concept of hypertext may indeed be the ultimate practical application of schema theory.

When a hypertext involves more than text, it is referred to as *hypermedia.* Hypermedia connects verbal and nonverbal information. Thus, hypermedia extends the idea of *text* in hypertext by including visual information, sound, animation, and other forms of data. Verbal discourse can then be linked to images, maps, diagrams, and audio as easily as to another verbal passage (Landow, 1992, p. 4). Hypertext computer software is interactive in nature, allowing the user to manipulate information as desired. Interactive programs such as Broderbund's *Living Books* series, combine music, sound effects, and animation to create an environment whereby children are actively involved in the story. While viewing Mercer Mayer's picture book *Just Grandma and Me* (Broderbund, 1992) on a Macintosh computer, a child listens to the story unfold and at any time activates new information via mouse arrow. For example, to learn what Grandma is thinking, click on her bonnet; to hear the waves crashing, click on the ocean; to continue the story, click on the upturned corner at the bottom of the page. Interactive books are possible through the technology of Compact Disk–Read Only Memory (CD-ROM), which is capable of storing and accessing vast amounts of textual information, music, sound effects, and digitized speech.

*HyperCard.*     HyperCard™ (Apple, 1990) is a computer-application base developed by Apple Computers for use with any model of the Macintosh. *IBM Linkway 2.0* is a HyperCard program compatible with IBM and other DOS-driven computers. HyperCard translates the concept of hypertext into a computer program by organizing information into discrete units or stacks of cards that can be linked together in a variety of ways, depending upon the purpose of the program. For example, *The Amanda Stories* (Goodenough, 1987) are HyperCard narratives for children. "Your Faithful Camel Goes to the North Pole" is the story of two camels' adventures trying to get to the North Pole. In this program, the HyperCard stacks are a series of wordless pictures (or cards) accompanied by a few simple sound effects. The child navigates the story by using a mouse to move the arrow to any point in the picture (or card) and searching for preprogrammed "hot spots" that, when clicked upon, move the narrative along, scene by scene as depicted on each card in the stack. Figure 8.6 illustrates the decision-making process of moving from frame to frame in a HyperCard story.

Children can create their own picture stories using HyperCard™ 2.0 (1990) directly. In a study of fifth-graders' response to traditional narratives and HyperCard texts, Heller and McLellan (1993) paired students who then worked together to navigate several of the Amanda Stories, including "Inigo At Home" (Goodenough, 1987), the story of a house cat's home activities. The students were directed to tell each other what was happening as they took turns finding the hot spots and moving

**Frame 1**

*Scenario:*
*Jeff, a fifth grader, must decide which path*
*the character in the picture should take.*
*Using a mouse, Jeff moves the arrow to the*
*left path and clicks.*

**Frame 2**

*Jeff has moved the character to*
*the sunny and less-traveled path.*
*He then decides to take the boy down*
*the other road. He moves the arrow*
*to the right path and clicks again.*

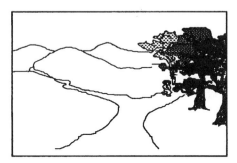

**Frame 3**

*Now Jeff has placed the boy on*
*the shady, more mysterious road.*
*Where will he go next?*

**FIGURE 8.6**  Navigating a HyperCard story

SOURCE: Courtesy of Karen J. Schmidt, Art Instructor, Manhattan Middle School, Manhattan, KS.

the story forward. For instance, John would say to Jamie, "Inigo is trying to catch the mouse. Click on the mouse to see what happens next." The HyperCard setting proved to be very motivating for the students who ultimately wrote and illustrated original narratives. The children's handdrawn illustrations were electronically scanned into HyperCard stacks. During the project, the children learned simple drawing and editing procedures using the HyperCard program. Once their pictures were scanned, the children could access them on the computer, edit to their liking, and program hot spots. Figure 8.7 (Heller & McLellan, 1993) is a fifth-grader's HyperCard story illustrations, which were electronically scanned into HyperCard stacks. Overall, HyperCard programs provide a unique environment for problem solving as well as oral language development, reading, and writing.

***Virtual Reality.***     Virtual reality (VR) is the newest innovation in interactive, computer-based technology. VR systems surround the user with sensory displays, such as 3-D graphics, 3-D sound, and touch feedback, thus conveying a feeling of immersion and a sense of presence (McLellan, 1994; 1993). A person experiencing virtual reality is able to move around in and manipulate the virtual world, to see things from different angles, "to reach into it, grab it, and reshape it." (Rheingold, 1991, p. 17). At present commercially prepared VR systems have limited capabilities with regard to educational applications (Bricken & Byrne, 1993). Yet the idea of manipulating an artificial environment is particularly intriguing with regard to language arts instruction. One day soon it may be possible for teachers to provide children with a wide array of direct experiences without ever having to leave the classroom. For instance, imagine taking your third-graders on a virtual field trip to the Grand Canyon where they can observe and manipulate rock formations and fossils. Such an imaginary journey could take place in the context of a thematic unit on the southwest. Virtual reality holds promise for innovative computer programs that would provide children with new experiences via head-mounted displays and three-dimensional computer graphics, which are beginning to make their way into video arcades. Because of virtual reality technology, our perspectives on play as a vehicle for language learning will have new meaning as we enter the twenty-first century.

## CLASSROOM ORGANIZATION AND MANAGEMENT

Although there is much more to organizing a classroom than time schedules, rules for behavior, and seating arrangements, the issue of when, how, and where lessons take place is nevertheless important. It is here that most teachers begin to get organized. Children need an appropriate amount of structure during the six to seven hours per day they spend in school. A structured school day gives children security, provided that within the overall framework of the day-to-day activities there is room for flexibility. Our understanding of how structure affects children's ability to learn is based on studies of the home environment and parenting. We have only begun research into how children seem to learn to read and write "naturally" in homes where literacy events are structured and shaped by parents (Teale, 1982). Further, the most positive kind of home environment appears to be *authoritative* in nature.

**FIGURE 8.7** Drawings scanned into HyperCard stacks

SOURCE: Heller, M. F., & McLellan, H. (1993). Dancing with the wind: Understanding narrative text structure through response to multicultural children's literature (With an assist from HyperCard). *Reading Psychology, 14*(4), 285–310. Reprinted with permission of the authors.

Authoritative parents are those who blend "structure and support with flexibility, open dialogue, explanations, and conflict resolution," (Jones & Jones, 1986, p. 65). A good deal of research supports structured yet flexible approaches. It is within this kind of environment that learning with the least amount of disruptive behavior takes place (Soar, 1983).

Elementary and middle schools are no longer simple settings where the three R's make up the total curriculum. Instead, they are complex social arenas with extracurricular activities as well as programs for children with special needs, including the learning-disabled, gifted, and speech-impaired child. An additional complicating factor is the often prescribed, text-driven curriculum filled with workbooks and practice masters to be completed in nine weeks. Unfortunately, the desire to get through *all* of the recommended (or required) school curriculum may take precedence over stepping back and breathing in new knowledge. Time, simultaneously a friend and a nemesis to learning, is a major consideration in classroom and instructional management. Both teachers and children need time to read and to write connected text and to reflect on ideas, new and old.

The process of assimilating and accommodating new information takes time, and this need must be recognized by teacher and administrator so that scheduling can be used to everyone's benefit. Whenever possible, special classes involving itinerant teachers should be scheduled at the *same time* every day so that children will not miss important whole-class experiences, direct instruction, and child-centered activities. When art, music, physical education, speech, learning-disabled, and gifted educators have regularly scheduled times, it is easier for the classroom teacher to manage a more flexible schedule for the remainder of the day. It is particularly desirable to integrate frequently into regular lesson planning concepts that the children are learning in their special classes. Art is a subject that carries over into all other content areas, especially in terms of illustration. Music can be an excellent motivator for listening to detail, and physical education provides a backdrop for real experiences involving gross motor activities such as field trips or games.

The schedules that follow illustrate how blocks of time for listening, speaking, reading, and writing can be managed in a variety of settings, across all subject areas. The examples illustrate how activities blend together to bring continuity and order to the day.

## Example Schedules

### Kindergarten (Half Day, A.M. or P.M.)

| | |
|---|---|
| *8:30–8:45* | *Children arrive, organize for the day; quiet play/talk;* |
| *8:45–9:00* | *"Morning Message." Review what will occur that day.* |
| | ***Focus on conversation:*** *Children share their news.* |
| *9:00–9:15* | *Story, poetry, nonfiction read-aloud.* |
| | ***Focus on listening/response:*** |
| *9:15–9:50* | *Whole-group lesson: Topics vary from day to day. This is the time to integrate language learning with other subjects, including science, health, social studies, art, music, and P.E.* |

**Focus on real experiences/listening/responding:** *This is a time for concrete experiences, as well as direct instruction, explanations, demonstrations, experiments, and discussion/reaction.*

9:50–10:20     *Individual and small-group activity, based on whole-group lesson above.*

**Focus on reading and writing connected text:** *This is the time for child-centered activity, when children choose books to read, work on picture drawing and writing, interact with peers or with teacher during informal conferences.*

10:20–10:40     *Snack, cleanup, outdoor or indoor play.*

**Focus on cooperation/social interaction.**

10:40–11:10     *Art, music, P.E. scheduled at this time.*

11:10–11:30     *Individual and small-group activity.*

**Focus on conferences and cooperation:** *This is the time for more direct instruction, if needed by individuals or small groups, independent reading and writing, and small-group interaction through dramatic play, computer tutors, book buddies, or teacher conferences.*

11:30–11:40     *Closing. Whole-group activity. Varies from day to day—music, movement, story, poetry related to the day's activities; review day's activities.*

**Focus on listening/closure:** *Class dismissed.*

### Primary Grades and Intermediate Grades (1–6)

8:30–8:40     *Organizing the day: Lunch count, quiet talk.*

**Focus on listening/cooperation.**

8:40–9:00     *Story, poetry, or nonfiction read-aloud. The selection is related to the concepts under study during the day or week.*

**Focus on listening/reaction:** *This is a time for listening and responding to prose and poetry, reacting to and discussing new ideas.*

9:00–10:15     *Reading and language arts block.*

**Focus on real experiences/reading and writing connected text/reaction:** *This is the time for concept-building experiences, whole-class direct instruction by mini-lessons and reading and/or writing workshop.*

10:15–10:30     *Recess.*

10:30–11:30     *Reading and language arts block continued.*
             *Independent reading and writing/conferences.*

**Focus on reading and writing connected text:** *This is the time for child-centered activity during which the children read self-selected books, work on their drafts, interact with teacher and peers, visit the library, use the computer, and so on. This is also the time that special programs are scheduled, such as those designed for the gifted, learning disabled, or speech impaired.*

| | |
|---|---|
| *11:30–12:00* | *Art, music, P.E. schedule varies daily.* |
| *12:00–12:30* | *Lunch.* |
| *12:30–12:45* | *Story, poetry, or nonfiction read-aloud.* |

> ***Focus on listening/responding:*** *This is a time to bring the whole group together to listen and react to a selection that readies them for the afternoon's activities. Emphasis is placed on concept formation through listening to a relevant piece of prose or poetry.*

| | |
|---|---|
| *12:45–2:30* | *Math, science, social studies, foreign language block.* |

> ***Focus on real experiences/listening/responding:*** *Whole-class or small-group work is appropriate here. This is the time for direct instruction as well as individual conferencing and cooperative learning. Time allotted per subject area will vary according to the lessons undertaken. For example, a math lesson may be integrated into a science experiment and thus consume the entire content area time.*

| | |
|---|---|
| *2:30–2:45* | *Recess.* |
| *2:45–3:20* | *Content area reading and writing.* |

> ***Focus on reading and writing connected text:*** *This is the time for more child-centered activity, including journal writing and independent reading and writing in the content areas. Computer time is again available. This part of the day is intended to bring closure to the subject area lessons of the day.*

| | |
|---|---|
| *3:20–3:30* | *Prepare for dismissal.* |

> ***Focus on cooperation/quiet talk.***

### *Middle School and Junior High Modular Scheduling, Weekly Example*

| | |
|---|---|
| *8:30–9:25* | |
| *9:30–10:25* | *Reading and language arts block.* |
| *Monday* | *Concrete experience/demonstration and accompanying short story selections (one or two).* |

> ***Focus on experiencing/listening/reading connected text:*** *Teacher introduces the concept under study through a real experience. Short-story selections are read silently and responded to in writing in the student's journals. Journal entries are read by at least one peer. Teacher reads and writes with students and confers with individuals as the need arises.*

| | |
|---|---|
| *Tuesday* | *Reading workshop (whole class).* |

> ***Focus on responding to literature/developing writing topics:*** *Response to short-story selections (either orally or in journals). Emphasis on story structure, particularly characterization, through direct instruction/modeling. Whole-class discussion of topics for writing. Possible assignments: nonfiction character sketch of a friend, relative, teacher, or person in history. Preliminary notes taken for writing project. Teacher confers with individual students as needed.*

| | |
|---|---|
| *Wednesday* | *Review concept under study. First/second draft writing.* **Focus on reading and writing connected** *text/reaction/listening: Teacher presents a model of the writing project. Students begin working on first/second drafts, responding orally or in writing to their partner's first work in progress. Teacher confers with students who need help, organizes, and conducts small-group mini-lectures to focus on problems in content or mechanics of papers in progress.* |
| *Thursday* | *Short-story selection. Second/final draft writing.* **Focus on reading and writing connected text/research:** *A second or third short-story selection is read silently to reinforce the concept of characterization. Students react to the story in their journals and read one another's reactions. Students continue working on their papers, researching any aspect of character that is not completely understood. Teacher confers individually with students needing assistance.* |
| *Friday* | *Writers' Workshop (whole class/small-group).* **Focus on listening/responding/reading/writing:** *Working in small groups, the students read and respond to one another's final drafts. Students work on editing either alone or at the Editor's Desk. Final copies are readied and turned in for assessment. Teacher confers with individual students.* |

## Closing Thoughts

Teachers have the power to create a classroom environment that positively affects the development of literacy among children in all grade levels. A key to successful classroom instruction, organization, and management is the amount of reflection undertaken by the teachers themselves. To be a reflective practitioner, one must first be a teacher-researcher, who questions what he or she observes and then seeks ways to answer the questions in simple and creative ways. For the reflective practitioner, who is also a thoughtful researcher, teaching becomes a risk-taking adventure that will be to every child's ultimate benefit.

### FOR YOUR JOURNAL

1. Write a model piece of fiction, nonfiction, or poetry for a specific grade level. How would you use your model in a workshop to teach language arts more effectively?

2. Observe a cooperative learning group in action. What are the basic characteristics of the children's interactions? How does this group setting differ from more traditional, homogeneous groupings or whole-class instruction?

3. Ask a random sample of primary, intermediate, or middle school children about their knowledge of computers. Characterize the computer literacy of these children. How comfortable are the children with the computer's word-processing capabilities?

4. Take a good look at the physical arrangement of a (your) classroom. Observe the desks, tables, chairs, bookshelves, bulletin boards, and so on. Based on what you see and what is available, describe (make a sketch) the best arrangement to facilitate a literate classroom environment.

## SELECTED EDUCATIONAL SOFTWARE AND MULTIMEDIA

### Word-processing Programs

*Apple Writer II* (6–8) (40 or 80 column)
Apple Computer, Inc.
20525 Mariani Avenue
Cupertino, CA 95014

*Bank Street Writer* (3–8)
Scholastic, Inc.
P.O. Box 7501
2931 East McCarty Street
Jefferson, MO 65102
Apple II, IBM-PC, Commodore, Atari

*Homeword* (3–8)
Sierra On-Line
Sierra On-Line Building
Coarsegold, CA 93614
Apple, Commodore, Atari

*LogoWriter* (K–8) (includes graphics tool, 40 or 80 column)
Logo Computer Systems, Inc.
330 West 58th Street
Suite 5M
New York, NY 10019
(212) 765-4780

*Magic Slate* (1–8)
Sunburst Communications
39 Washington Avenue
Pleasantville, NY 10570
Apple II

*Quill* (3–8) (includes mailbag, library, and planner)
D.C. Heath
125 Spring Street
Lexington, MA 02173
Apple II series

*Story Maker*
Bolt Beranek and Newman
10 Moulton Street
Cambridge, MA 02238
(617) 497-8173

*The Children's Writing and Publishing Center* (2-8) (includes graphics tools)
The Learning Company
6493 Kaiser Drive
Fremont, CA 94555-9985
(800) 852-2255

*WordPerfect* (4–adult)
Satellite Software International
288 West Center Street
Orem, UT 84057
Apple II, IBM, Tandy

*Writer's Helper* (6-8) (includes prewriter and analyzer)
CONDUIT
University of Iowa, Oakdale Campus
Iowa City, IA
Apple

*Writing a Narrative*
Minnesota Educational Computing Consortium (MECC)
3490 Lexington Avenue North
St. Paul, MN 55126-8097

*Writing Workshop* (3-8)
Miliken
1100 Research Boulevard
St. Louis, MO 63232

## Programs for Revising and Editing

*Bank Street Speller* (4-8)
Scholastic Inc.
P.O. Box 7501
2931 East McCarty Street
Jefferson City, MO 65102
Apple II, Commodore

*Grammatik* (6–adult)
Aspen Software
P.O. Box 339
Tijeras, MN 87059
IBM PC, TRS-80

*Master Spell* (1-8)
MECC
3490 Lexington Avenue North

St. Paul, MN 55112
Apple

*Sensible Grammar & Sensible Speller* (7–8)
Sensible Software
210 South Woodward, Suite 229
Birmingham, MI 48011
Apple II

## Typing/Keyboarding Programs

*Keyboard Cadet* (2–8)
Mindscape, Inc.
3444 Dundee Road
Northbrook, IL 60062
Apple, IBM, Commodore

*Typing Tutor* (4–8)
Microsoft Corp.
10700 Northrup Way
Bellevue, WA 98004
Apple, IBM

*PC-FASTYPE.* (1–6)
Trendtech Corporation
Wayne, NJ
Apple, IBM

## HyperCard

*HyperCard 2.0* (Voyager, for the Macintosh)
*Amanda Stories* (Amanda Goodenough, Voyager)
  Volume 1, *Inigo the Cat*
  Volume 2, *Your Faithful Camel*
  Volume 3, *Inigo at Home*
  Volume 4, *Your Faithful Camel Goes Underground*
*IBM Linkway 2.0* (Ztek Company, for IBM Compatibles)
HyperCard Stacks for *Portraits Bulletin Boards: Biographies of Authors* (Dale Seymour)

## Expanded Books (Macintosh with CD-ROM)

*Arthur's Teacher Trouble* (Marc Brown, Broderbund)
*Jurassic Park* by Michael Crichton (Voyager)
*Just Grandma and Me* (Mercer Mayer, Broderbund)
*The Complete Annotated Alice* (Lewis Carroll, Voyager)
*The Complete Hitch Hiker's Guide to the Galaxy* (Douglas Adams, Voyager)
*The Paper Bag Princess* (Robert Munsch, Ztek)
*The Tale of Peter Rabbit* (Beatrix Potter, Ztek)

## Videodiscs

*Africa's Stolen River* (National Geographic)
*Curious George* (Churchill)
*Frog and Toad Are Friends* (Churchill)
*Garbage Tale: An Environmental Adventure* (Churchill)
*How the Leopard Got His Spots* (Ztek)
*King: Montgomery to Memphis* (Ztek)
*Rain Forest* (National Geographic)
*Ralph S. Mouse* (Churchill)
*Red Balloon/White Mane* (Ztek)
*Strong Kids, Safe Kids* (Ztek)

## Videocassettes (Reading Rainbow Series)

*Digging Up Dinosaurs* (Aliki)
*Galimoto* (Karen Lynn Williams)
*Gila Monsters Meet You at the Airport* (Marjorie Weineman Sharmat)
*Mummies Made in Egypt* (Aliki)
*The Bicycle Man* (Allen Say)
*The Legend of the Indian Paintbrush* (Tomie dePaola)
*The Snowy Day* (Ezra Jack Keats)

## Paint Programs

*The Print Shop IIGS* (Broderbund)
*Print Shop Companion* (Broderbund)
*Kid Pix* (Broderbund)
*Kid Pix Companion* (Broderbund)

## Publisher Ordering Information

Broderbund Software
Dept. 93EC
PO Box 6125
Novato, CA 94948-6125
1-800-521-6263

Churchill Media
12210 Nebraska Avenue
Dept. 102
Los Angeles, CA 90025-3600
1-800-334-7830

Dale Seymour Publications
PO Box 10888
Palo Alto, CA 94303-0879
800-872-1100
FAX 415-324-3424

National Geographic Society
Educational Services
Dept. 5413
Washington, DC 20036
800-368-2728
FAX (301) 921-1575

Reading Rainbow: A Guide for Teachers
P.O. Box 80669
Lincoln, NE 68501

The Voyager Company
Laser Learning Technologies
3114 37th Place S.
Seattle, WA 98144
800-722-3505
FAX (206) 723-3497

Ztek Co.
PO Box 1055
Louisville, KY 40201-1055
800-247-1603
FAX 502-584-9090

# APPENDIX A
## Making Puppets

Box

Masks

Paper Bag

Glove

Tube/Cylinder

Sock

Stick

Original drawings by Mary Hammel
Graphic Artist
Kansas State University

Hinged Theater

Humanettes

Doorway Theater

Blanket Theater

Carton Theater

# APPENDIX B
## Making Books

MATERIALS
Cardboard
Masking tape
Stapler
Contact paper
Writing paper

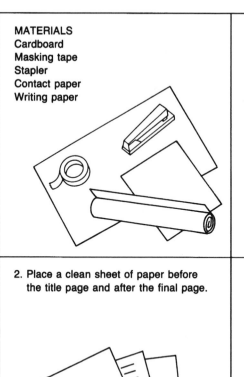

1. Write and illustrate a story, nonfiction, or poetry that you want to publish. Use any size paper, lined or unlined.

2. Place a clean sheet of paper before the title page and after the final page.

3. Staple the pages.

4. To make the book jacket, cut two pieces of cardboard a little larger than the text pages.

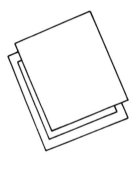

5. Attach with tape.

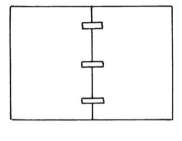

6. To make an attractive cover, cut contact paper one inch larger than the cardboard.

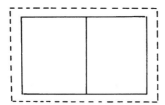

7. Seal the contact paper to the cardboard and press the corners down.

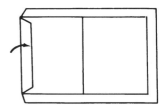

8. Seal the short ends and then the long ends. This is the book jacket.

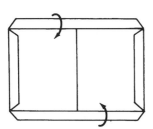

9. Attach the text pages to the jacket with tape.

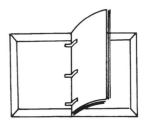

10. To reinforce the binding, cut two pieces of contact paper as wide as the ends of your pages and twice as long.

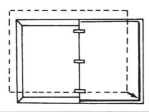

11. Seal the contact paper to the first sheet. Then smooth it onto the cardboard. Repeat on the other side.

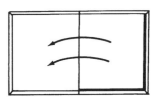

12. Share your book with a friend.

The Case
of the
Missing
Teacher

By Erin

Shape Books

My Journal

Original drawings by Mary Hammel
Graphic Artist
Kansas State University

# APPENDIX C
## Handwriting Models

## Zaner-Bloser Handwriting Model

SOURCE: Letter models are taken from *Zaner-Bloser's Handwriting: A Way to Self-Expression,* copyright © 1993. Reprinted with the permission of the publisher.

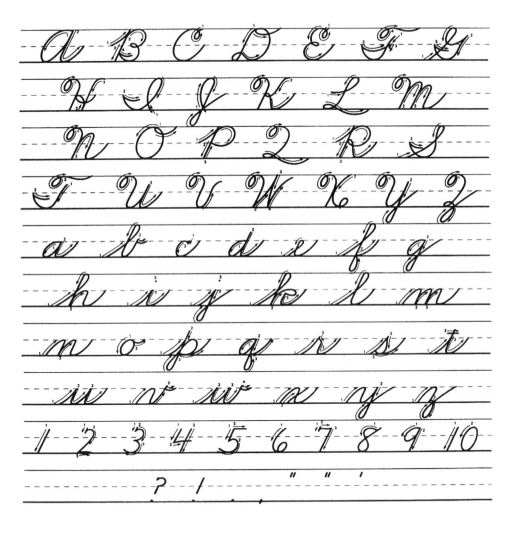

D'Nealian Handwriting Model

SOURCE: From *D'Nealian® Handwriting* by Donald Neal Thurber. Copyright © 1987 by Scott, Foresman and Company. Reprinted by permission.

# APPENDIX D
## Thematic Units

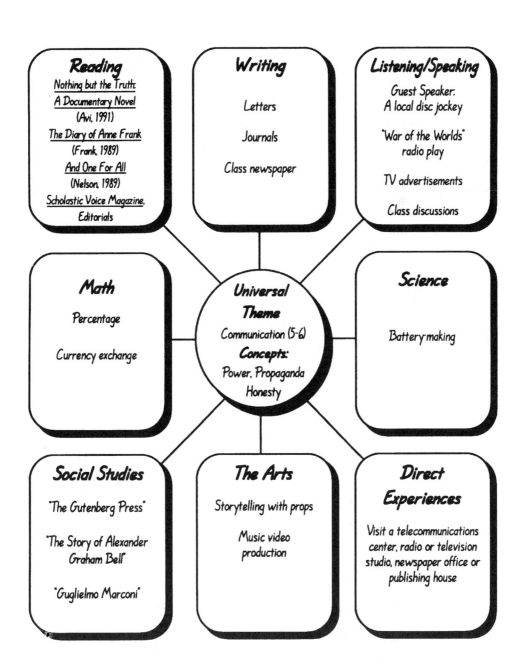

**Reading**
Nothing but the Truth:
A Documentary Novel
(Avi, 1991)
The Diary of Anne Frank
(Frank, 1989)
And One For All
(Nelson, 1989)
Scholastic Voice Magazine,
Editorials

**Writing**
Letters
Journals
Class newspaper

**Listening/Speaking**
Guest Speaker:
A local disc jockey
"War of the Worlds"
radio play
TV advertisements
Class discussions

**Math**
Percentage
Currency exchange

**Universal Theme**
Communication (5-6)
**Concepts:**
Power, Propaganda
Honesty

**Science**
Battery-making

**Social Studies**
"The Gutenberg Press"
"The Story of Alexander
Graham Bell"
"Guglielmo Marconi"

**The Arts**
Storytelling with props
Music video
production

**Direct Experiences**
Visit a telecommunications
center, radio or television
studio, newspaper office or
publishing house

The following thematic units are adapted from B. Eisele (1991), Managing the Whole Language Classroom, Cypress, CA: Creative Teaching Press, pp. 55 & 62.

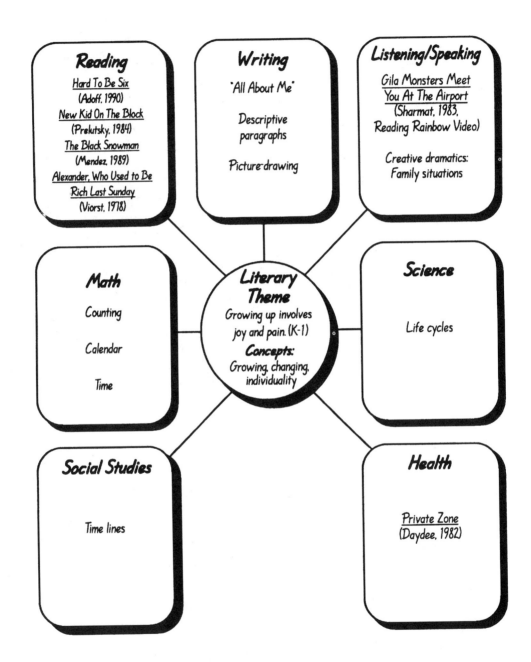

**Reading**

Hard To Be Six
(Adoff, 1990)
New Kid On The Block
(Prelutsky, 1984)
The Black Snowman
(Mendez, 1989)
Alexander, Who Used to Be
Rich Last Sunday
(Viorst, 1978)

**Writing**

"All About Me"

Descriptive
paragraphs

Picture-drawing

**Listening/Speaking**

Gila Monsters Meet
You At The Airport
(Sharmat, 1983,
Reading Rainbow Video)

Creative dramatics:
Family situations

**Math**

Counting

Calendar

Time

**Literary Theme**
Growing up involves
joy and pain. (K-1)
**Concepts:**
Growing, changing,
individuality

**Science**

Life cycles

**Social Studies**

Time lines

**Health**

Private Zone
(Daydee, 1982)

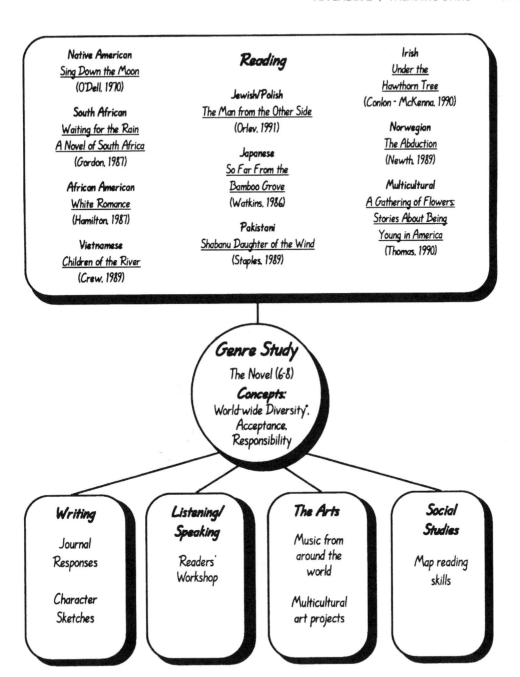

Native American
<u>Sing Down the Moon</u>
(O'Dell, 1970)

South African
<u>Waiting for the Rain</u>
<u>A Novel of South Africa</u>
(Gordon, 1987)

African American
<u>White Romance</u>
(Hamilton, 1987)

Vietnamese
<u>Children of the River</u>
(Crew, 1989)

*Reading*

Jewish/Polish
<u>The Man from the Other Side</u>
(Orlev, 1991)

Japanese
<u>So Far From the</u>
<u>Bamboo Grove</u>
(Watkins, 1986)

Pakistani
<u>Shabanu Daughter of the Wind</u>
(Staples, 1989)

Irish
<u>Under the</u>
<u>Hawthorn Tree</u>
(Conlon - McKenna, 1990)

Norwegian
<u>The Abduction</u>
(Newth, 1989)

Multicultural
<u>A Gathering of Flowers:</u>
<u>Stories About Being</u>
<u>Young in America</u>
(Thomas, 1990)

*Genre Study*
The Novel (6-8)
*Concepts:*
World-wide Diversity;
Acceptance,
Responsibility

*Writing*
Journal
Responses

Character
Sketches

*Listening/
Speaking*
Readers'
Workshop

*The Arts*
Music from
around the
world

Multicultural
art projects

*Social
Studies*
Map reading
skills

Professional Resource: *Multicultural Literature for Children and Young Adults*
(1991), Cooperative Children's Book Center, 4290 Helen C. White Hall,
University of Wisconsin, Madison, 600 N. Park Street, Madison, WI 53706.
(608) 263-3720.

## Reading

*A Great Big Ugly Man Came Up and Tied His Horse To Me* (Tripp, 1973)

*Father Fox's Pennyrhymes* (Watson, 1971)

*Tyrannosaurus Was A Beast* (Prelutsky, 1988)

*Sports Pages* (Adoff, 1990)

*Illustrated Poems for Children* (1973)

*A Light in the Attic* (Silverstein, 1981)

*This Same Sky A Collection of Poems from Around the World* (Nye, 1992)

## Genre Study

Poetry (4-6)

**Concepts:**

Rhyme, Rhythm, Meter, Free Verse

## Writing

Poetry Writing

Class Publication

## Listening/Speaking

Poetry Readings

Audiotape
Jack Prelutsky's Poetry

## The Arts

Musical Rhythms

African Drums

Choral Readings

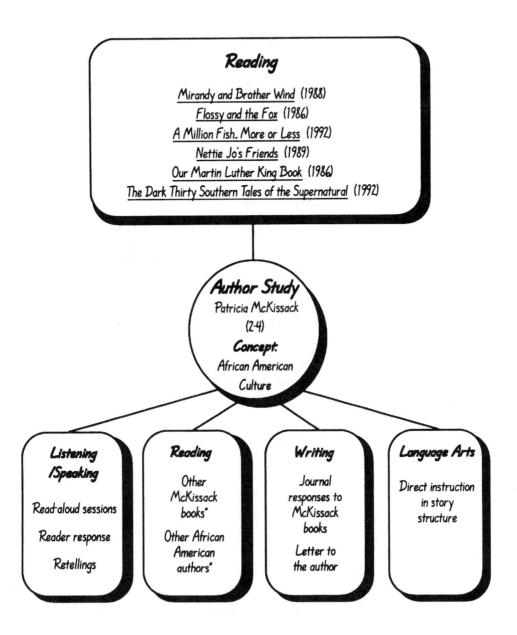

**Reading**

Mirandy and Brother Wind (1988)
Flossy and the Fox (1986)
A Million Fish.. More or Less (1992)
Nettie Jo's Friends (1989)
Our Martin Luther King Book (1986)
The Dark Thirty Southern Tales of the Supernatural (1992)

**Author Study**
Patricia McKissack
(2-4)

**Concept:**
African American
Culture

**Listening /Speaking**

Read-aloud sessions

Reader response

Retellings

**Reading**

Other McKissack books*

Other African American authors*

**Writing**

Journal responses to McKissack books

Letter to the author

**Language Arts**

Direct instruction in story structure

Professional Resource: *Multicultural Listing. Grades K–12* Perfection Learning. 1000 North Second Avenue, Logan, IA 51546-1099, 800-831-4190.

## Reading

<u>Come A Tide</u> (Lyon, 1990)
<u>Feelings</u> (Aliki, 1984)
<u>Tucking Mommy In</u> (Loh, 1988)
<u>Moira's Birthday</u> (Munsch, 1987)
<u>The Doorbell Rang</u> (Hutchins, 1986)
<u>On Grandaddy's Farm</u> (Allen, 1989)
<u>Abuela</u> (Dorros, 1991)
<u>The Quilt</u> (Jonas, 1984)

## Writing

Picture drawing,
written language
play

"My Friends"
"My Family"

## Topical Theme

Friends and Family (K)
**Concepts:**
Caring, Responsibility,
Memories

## Listening/Speaking

Storytelling and
retelling

Sharing a
special toy

## Social Studies

"How Do People
Make Friends?" in
Living With People
(Laidlaw Brothers, 1985)

## The Arts

Creative Dramatics:
"May I Introduce
My Friend?"

Paper friendship quilt

"Growing Up Together"
Gemini Records

## Direct Experiences

Field Trip to
nursing Home

Family member
guest speakers

## Reading

On Planet Earth,
"Unit One"
(Coronado Books, 1985)
Earthwatch Earthcycles
and Ecosystems
(Savan, 1991)
In the Beginning
Creation Stories from
Around the World
(Hamilton, 1988)
The Earth Is Sore: Native
Americans on Nature
(Amon, 1981)

## Writing

Poetry

Descriptive
paragraphs

Science logs

## Listening/Speaking

"The Planets"
(National Geographic
videodisc)

Discussions

## Content Area Unit

Earth Science (4)
**Concepts:**
Exploration, Investigation,
Ordering

## Social Studies

Globe reading
skills

Latitude and
Longitude

## The Arts

Recyclable art
sculptures

Planet mobiles

Audiotape:
"The Planets" (Holst)

## Direct Experiences

Field trip to planetarium,
natural area,
or recycling plant

Organize "Save Our
Earth Day"

# REFERENCES

Ahlberg, A., & Ahlberg, J. (1986). *The jolly postman or other people's letters.** Boston: Little, Brown.

Alden, R. M. (1985). The castle under the sea. *Flights of color, Level 6.* New York: Ginn & Company.

Allard, H. (1985). *Miss Nelson is missing.** Boston: Houghton Mifflin.

Allard, H. (1985). *There's a party at Mona's tonight.** New York: Avon Books.

Allen, C. A. (1988). Social interactions between a teacher and small groups of students working with a microcomputer. *Computers in the schools, 5*(1/2), 271-284.

Anders, P., & Bos, C. (1986). Semantic feature analysis: An interactive strategy for vocabulary development and text comprehension. *Journal of Reading, 29*(7), 610-616.

Anderson, R. C. (1977). Schema-directed processes in language comprehension. *Technical Report 50.* Urbana: University of Illinois Center for the Study of Reading.

Anderson, R. C. (1984). Role of the reader's schema in comprehension, learning, and memory. In R. C. Anderson, J. Osborn, & R. J. Tierney (Eds.), *Learning to read in American schools: Basal readers and content texts* (pp. 243-257). Hillsdale, NJ: Lawrence Erlbaum.

Anderson, R. C., & Armbruster, B. B. (1984). Content area textbooks. In R. C. Anderson, J. Osborn, & R. J. Tierney (Eds.), *Learning to read in American schools: Basal readers and content texts* (pp. 193-226). Hillsdale, NJ: Lawrence Erlbaum.

Anderson, R. C., Hiebert, E. H., Scott, J. A., & Wilkinson, I. A. G. (1984). *Becoming a nation of readers: The report of the commission on reading.* Washington, DC: U.S. Department of Education.

Applebee, A. N. (1978). *The child's concept of story: Ages two to seventeen.* Chicago: University of Chicago Press.

Applebee, A. N. (1986). Problems in process approaches: Toward a reconceptualization of process instruction. In A. R. Petrosky & D. Bartholomae (Eds.), *The teaching of writing* (pp. 95-113). Eighty-fifth Yearbook of the National Society for the Study of Education, Part II. Chicago: University of Chicago Press.

Armento, B. J., Garcia, J., & Erickson, R. (1985). *Living in our country.* Forest River, IL: Laidlaw.

Asimov, I. (1988). *Rockets, probes, and satellites.** New York: Dell.

---

*Books for children mentioned in text.

Atwell, N. (1984). Writing and reading literature from the inside out. *Language Arts, 61*(3), 240-252.

Atwell, N. (1987). *In the middle.* Upper Montclair, NJ: Boynton/Cook.

Axelrod, R. B., & Cooper, C. R. (1988). *The St. Martin's guide to writing.* New York: St. Martin's Press.

Balajthy, E. (1988). Keyboarding, language arts, and the elementary child. *The Computing Teacher, 15*(5), 400-43.

Balajthy, E. (1989). *Computers and reading.* Englewood Cliffs, NJ: Prentice-Hall.

Bartlett, F. C. (1932). *Remembering.* Cambridge, MA: Cambridge University Press.

Bauer, M. D. (1986). *On my honor.** New York: Dell.

Beardsley, L. V., & Marceck-Zeman, M. (1987). Making connections: Facilitating literacy in young children. *Childhood Education, 63*(3), 159-166.

Beck, I. L. (1984). Developing comprehension: The impact of the directed reading lesson. In R. C. Anderson, J. Osborn, and R. J. Tierney (Eds.), *Learning to read in American schools: Basal readers and content texts* (pp. 3-20). Hillsdale, NJ: Lawrence Erlbaum.

Birnbaum, J. C. (1982). The reading and composing behavior of selected fourth- and seventh-grade students. *Research in the Teaching of English, 16*(3), 241-261.

Birnbaum, J. C. (1986). Reflective thought: The connection between reading and writing. In B. T. Peterson (Ed.), *Convergences: Transactions in reading and writing.* (pp. 30-45). Urbana, IL: National Council of Teachers of English.

Bissex, G. (1980). *GNYS at work: A child learns to write and read.* Cambridge, MA: Harvard University Press.

Blume, J. (1972). *Tales of a fourth grade nothing.** New York: Dell.

Bondy, E. (1984). Children's definitions of reading: Products of an interactive process. Paper presented at the American Educational Research Association, Chicago.

Boning, T., & Boning, R. (1957). I'd rather read than . . . . *Reading Teacher, 10*(7), 196-200.

Bowers, C. A., & Flinders, D. J. (1990). *Responsive teaching: An ecological approach to class-room patterns of language, culture, and thought.* New York: Teachers College Press.

Braddock, R., Lloyd-Jones, R., & Shoer, L. (1963). *Research in written composition.* ED 003 374. Champaign, IL: National Council of Teachers of English.

Branley, F. M. (1984). *Comets.** New York: Harper & Row.

Branley, F. M. (1986). *Journey into a black hole.** New York: Harper & Row.

Branley, F. (1990). *Tornado alert.** New York: Harper & Row.

Bricken, M., & Byrne, C. M. (1993). Summer students in virtual reality: A pilot study on edu-cational applications of virtual reality technology. In Alan Wexelblat (Ed.), *Virtual reality: Applications and explorations* (pp. 199-218). Boston: Academic Press Professional.

Britton, J. (1970). *Language and learning.* Coral Gables, FL: University of Miami Press.

Brockway, C. S., Gardner, R., & Howe, S. F. (1985). *General science.* Boston: Allyn & Bacon.

Bromley, K. D. (1988). *Language arts: Exploring connections.* Boston: Allyn & Bacon.

Brophy, J. (1988). Educating teachers about managing classrooms and students. *Teaching & Teacher Education, 4*(1), pp. 1-18.

Brown, L. K. (1986). *Taking advantage of media.* Boston: Routledge & Kegan Paul.

Bruce, B. (1978). What makes a good story? *Language Arts, 55*(4), 460-466.

Bruner, J. (1986). *Actual minds, possible worlds.* Cambridge, MA: Harvard University Press.

Burnett, F. H. (1963). *A little princess.** Philadelphia: Lippincott.

Burnett, F. H. (1984). *The Secret Garden.** Dell.

Carle, E. (1969, 1987). *The very hungry caterpillar.** New York: Putnam.

Carnegie Council on Adolescent Development (1989). *Turning points: Preparing youth for the 21st century.* New York: Carnegie Corporation of New York.

Carr, E. (1985). The vocabulary overview guide: A metacognitive strategy to improve vocabulary comprehension and retention. *Journal of Reading, 29*(6), 588-595.

Carr, E., Dewitz, P., & Patberg, J. P. (1989). Using cloze for inference training with expository text. *The Reading Teacher, 42*(6), 380-385.

Carr, E., & Wixson, K. (1986). Guidelines for evaluating vocabulary instruction. *Journal of Reading, 28*(7), 684-689.

Carroll, J. B. (1971). Development of native language skills beyond the early years. In C. Reed (Ed.), *The learning of language* (pp. 97-156). New York: Appleton-Century-Crofts.

Caulkins, L. M. (1986). *The art of teaching writing.* Portsmouth, NH: Heinemann.

Cazden, C. B. (1981). Peer dialogues across the curriculum. Unpublished manuscript, Harvard University.

Cherry, L. (1990). *The great kapok tree.*\* New York: Harcourt Brace Jovanovich.

*The Children's writing and publishing center.* (1989). Fremont, CA: The Learning Company.

Chomsky, C. (1979). Approaching reading through invented spelling. In L. B. Resnick & P. A. Weaver (Eds.), *Theory and practice of early reading, 2* (pp. 43-65). Hillsdale, NJ: Lawrence Erlbaum.

Clay, M. (1975). *What did I write?* Portsmouth, NH: Heinemann.

Clay, M. (1982). Learning and teaching writing: A developmental perspective. *Language Arts, 59*(2), 65-70.

Clay, M. M. (1966). Emergent reading behavior. Unpublished doctoral dissertation, University of Auckland, New Zealand.

Clements, D. H. (1987). Computers and literacy. In J. A. Vacca, R. T. Vacca, & M. K. Grove, *Reading and learning to read.* Boston: Little, Brown.

Cobb, V., & Darling, K. (1980). *Bet you can't.*\* New York: Lothrop.

Collins, A., & Smith, E. G. (1980). Teaching the process of reading comprehension. Technical Report No. 182. Urbana, IL: Center for the Study of Reading.

Cooper, C. R. (1976). Empirical studies of response to literature: Review and suggestions. *Journal of Aesthetic Education, 10,* 77-93.

Cooper, E. K., Blackwood, P. E., Boeschen, J. A., Giddings, M. E., & Carin, A. A. (1985). *HBJ science.* New York: Harcourt Brace Jovanovich.

Cooper, J. D. (1986). *Improving reading comprehension.* Boston: Houghton Mifflin.

Crawford, L. W. (1993). *Language and literacy learning in multicultural classrooms.* Boston, MA: Allyn and Bacon.

Crowell, D. C., Kawakami, A. J., & Wong, J. L. (1986). Emerging literacy: Reading-writing experiences in a kindergarten classroom. *The Reading Teacher, 40*(2), 144-149.

Crowhurst, M. (1977). The effect of audience and mode of discourse on the syntactic complexity of sixth and tenth graders. Unpublished doctoral dissertation, University of Minnesota.

Daiute, C. (1986). Physical and cognitive factors in revising: Insights from studies with computers. *Research in the Teaching of English, 20*(2), 141-159.

Dale, E. (1969). *Audiovisual methods in teaching* (3d ed.). New York: Holt, Rinehart & Winston.

Davis, J. H., & Behm, T. (1978). Terminology of drama/theatre with and for children: A redefinition. *Children's Theatre Review, 27*(1), 19-21.

Day, A. (1985). *Good dog carl.*\* New York: Green Tiger Press.

DeFina, A. A. (1992). *Portfolio assessment: Getting started.* New York: Scholastic.

DeFord, D. E. (1980). Young children and their writing. *Theory into Practice, 19,* 157-162.

de Paola, T. (1972). *The cloud book.*\* New York: Scholastic Books.

de Paola, T. (1989). *The art lesson.* New York: Putnam.

de Paola, T. (1991). *Bonjour Mr. Satie.* New York: Putnam.

Dewitz, P., Carr, E. M., & Patberg, J. P. (1987). Effects of inference training on comprehension and comprehension monitoring. *Reading Research Quarterly, 22*(1), 99-121.

Downing, J. (1982). Reading: Skill or skills? *Reading Teacher, 35*(6), 534-537.

Doyle, W. (1978). Task structures and student roles in classrooms. Paper presented at the American Educational Research Association annual meeting, Toronto, Canada.

*Dreams.* (1989). New York: Harcourt, Brace, Jovanovich.

Duffelmeyer, F. A. (1980). The influence of experience-based vocabulary on learning word meanings. *Journal of Reading, 24*(1), 35-40.

Durkin, D. (1978-79). What classroom observations reveal about reading comprehension instruction. *Reading Research Quarterly, 14*(3), 481-533.

Durkin, D. (1984). Is there a match between what elementary teachers do and what basal reader manuals recommend? *The Reading Teacher, 38*(8), 734-744.

Dyson, A. H. (1981). Oral language: The rooting system for learning to write. *Language Arts, 58*(1), 5-55.

Dyson, A. H. (1982). Teachers and young children: Missed connections in teaching/learning to write. *Language Arts, 59*(7), 674-680.

Dyson, A. H. (1987). The value of "time off task": Young children's spontaneous talk and deliberate text. *Harvard Educational Review, 57*(4), 396-420.

Dyson, A. H., & Genishi, C. (1982). "Whatta ya tryin' to write?": Writing as an interactive process. *Language Arts, 59*(2), 126-133.

Early Childhood and Literacy Development Committee of the International Reading Association. (1986). Literacy development and pre-first grade. *Childhood Education, 63*(2), 110-111.

Edelsky, C. (1991). *With literacy and justice for all: Rethinking the social in language and education.* New York: The Flamer Press, Taylor & Francis.

Edelsky, C. (1992). A talk with Carole Edelsky about politics and literacy. *Language Arts, 69*(5), 324-329.

Eisele, B. (1991). *Managing the whole language classroom.* Cypress, CA: Creative Teaching Press, Inc.

Epstein, J. L., & Mac Iver, D. J. (1990). *Education in the middle grades: National practices and trends.* Columbus, OH: National Middle School Association.

Farr, R., & Carey, R. F. (1986). *Reading: What can be measured?* Newark, DE: International Reading Association.

Feldman, S. & Elliott, G. (Eds.). (1990). *At the threshold: The developing adolescent.* Cambridge, MA: Harvard University Press.

Fitzpatrick, J. (1988). *Wheels.** Englewood Cliffs, NJ: Silver Burdett.

Flavelle, J. H. (1976). Metacognitive aspects of problem solving. In L. B. Resnick (Ed.), *The nature of intelligence* (pp. 231-235). Hillsdale, NJ: Lawrence Erlbaum.

Flood, J., & Lapp, D. (1987). Forms of discourse in basal readers. *The Elementary School Journal, 87*(3), 299-306.

Flood, J., & Lapp, D. (1989). Reporting reading progress: A comparison portfolio for parents. *The Reading Teacher, 42*(7), 508-515.

Flood, J., Lapp, D., & Farnan, N. (1986). A reading-writing procedure that teaches expository paragraph structure. *The Reading Teacher, 29*(5), 556-562.

Florio, S., & Clark, C. M. (1984). The environment of instruction: The forms and functions of writing in a teacher-developed curriculum. In G. Duffy, L. R. Roehler, & J. Mason (Eds.), *Comprehension instruction* (pp. 104-115). White Plains, NY: Longman.

Friedman, I. (1984). *How my parents learned to eat.** Boston: Houghton Mifflin.

Fries, C. (1962). *Linguistics and reading.* New York: Holt, Rinehart & Winston.

Furner, B. (1969). Recommended instructional procedures in a method emphasizing the perceptual motor nature of learning in handwriting. *Elementary English, 46*(8), 1021-1030.

Galton, M., & Simon, B. (1980). *Progress and performance in the primary classroom.* London: Routledge & Kegan Paul.

Gander, F. (1985). *Father gander nursery rhymes.* Santa Barbara, CA: Advocacy Press.

Garelick, M. (1961). *Where does the butterfly go when it rains.** New York: Scholastic Books.

Geller, L. G. (1983). Children's rhymes and literacy learning: Making connections. *Language Arts, 60*(2), 184-193.

Geller, L. G. (1984). Riddling: A powerful way to explore language. *Language Arts, 58*(7), 669-674.

Gentile, L. M., & Hoot, J. L. (1983). Kindergarten play: The foundation of reading. *The Reading Teacher, 36*(4), 435-439.

Gentry, J. R. (1982). An analysis of developmental spelling in GNYS at WRK. *The Reading Teacher, 36*(2), 192-200.

George, J. C. (1972). *Julie of the wolves.** New York: Harper & Row.

George, P. S., & Alexander, W. M. (1993). *The exemplary middle school.* New York: Harcourt Brace Jovanovich.

Gibbons, G. (1987). *Dinosaurs.** New York: Holiday.

Gillet, J. W., & Temple, C. (1986). *Understanding reading problems: Assessment and instruction.* Boston: Little, Brown.

Ginsburg, H. P., Gustafson, D. B., & Leutzinger, L. P. (1991). *Mathematics: Exploring your world.* Morristown, NJ: Silver Burdett & Ginn.

Ginsburg, M. (1980). *Where does the sun go at night?** New York: Greenwillow.

Goldstein, B. S. (1986). Looking at cartoons and comics in a new way. *Journal of Reading, 29*(7), 657-658.

Good, T., & Marshall, S. (1984). Do students learn more in heterogeneous or homogeneous groups? In P. Peterson, L. Wilkinson, & M. Hallinan (Eds.), *The social context of instruction: Group organization and group processes.* Orlando, FL: Academic Press.

Goodenough, A. (1987). Inigo at home. *Amanda Stories,* Santa Monica, CA: Voyager Company.

Goodenough, A. (1987). Your faithful camel goes to the north pole. *Amanda Stories,* Santa Monica, CA: Voyager Company.

Goodlad, J. (1984). *A place called school.* New York: McGraw-Hill.

Goodman, Y. M. (1978). Kid watching: An alternative to testing. *National Elementary Principals Journal, 57,* 41-45.

Goodman, Y. M. (1989). Roots of the whole-language movement. *The Elementary School Journal, 90*(2), 113-127.

Gordon, C., & Braun, C. (1983). Using story schema as an aid to reading and writing. *The Reading Teacher, 37*(2), 116-121.

*A great big ugly man came up and tied his horse to me.** (1973). Boston: Little, Brown.

Graves, D. H. (1983). *Writing: Teachers & children at work.* Portsmouth, NH: Heinemann.

Graves, D. H., & Hansen, J. (1983). The author's chair. *Language Arts, 60*(2), 176-183.

Graves, M. (1987). The roles of instruction in fostering vocabulary development. In M. McKeown & M. Curtis (Eds.), *The nature of vocabulary acquisition.* Hillsdale, NJ: Lawrence Erlbaum.

Gray, W. S. (1960). The major aspects of reading. In H.M. Robinson (Ed.), *Sequential development of reading abilities* (pp. 8-24). Supplementary Educational Monographs, No. 90. Chicago: University of Chicago Press.

Greenfield, E. (1977). *Africa dream.** New York: HarperCollins.

Greenfield, P. M. (1984). A theory of the teacher in the learning activities of everyday life. In

B. Rogoff & J. Lave (Eds.), *Everyday cognition: Its development in social context* (pp. 117-138). Cambridge, MA: Harvard University Press.

Greenleaf, Ann (1983). *No room for Sarah.** New York: Putnam.

Griffin, P. (1977). How and when does reading occur in the classroom? *Theory into Practice, 16,* 376-383.

Grinnell, G. B. (1986). The dun horse. *Holt basic reading, Fifth Grade.* New York: Holt, Rinehart & Winston.

Hall, M. (1981). *Teaching reading as a language experience.* Columbus, OH: Charles E. Merrill.

Hallinan, M. (1984). Summary and implications. In P. Peterson, L. Wilkinson, & M. Hallinan (Eds.), *The social context of instruction: Group organization and group processes.* Orlando, FL: Academic Press.

Hamilton, V. (1969). *Zeely.** New York: Macmillan.

Harris, L. A., & Smith, C. B. (1980). *Reading instruction: Diagnostic teaching in the classroom.* New York: Holt, Rinehart & Winston.

Harris, T. L., & Hodges, R. E. (Eds.). (1981). *A dictionary of reading and related terms.* Newark, DE: International Reading Association.

*Heath American readers.* (1986). Lexington, MA: Heath.

*Heath English.* (1986). Lexington, MA: Heath.

Heller, M. F. (1986a). Directed reading and writing in the content areas. *Reading Psychology, 7*(3), 173-182.

Heller, M. F. (1986b). How do you know what you know? Metacognitive modeling in the content areas. *Journal of Reading, 29*(5), 415-422.

Heller, M. F. (1986c). Modeling critical thinking in the English classroom. *Highway One, 9*(2), 87-90.

Heller, M. F. (1987, October). Remembering writing. Paper presented at the meeting of the National Reading and Language Arts Educators' Conference, Kansas City, MO.

Heller, M. F. (1988a, September). College pen-pals: Models for literacy. Paper presented at the annual meeting of the National Reading and Language Arts Educators' Conference, Kansas City, MO.

Heller, M. F. (1988b). Comprehending and composing through language experience. *The Reading Teacher, 42*(2), 130-135.

Heller, M. F. (1988c). Reading and writing across the curriculum. Unpublished paper.

Heller, M. F. (1988d, March). The teacher as researcher: Putting theory into practice. Paper presented at the Association of Teacher Educators' Mid-America Mini-Conference, Kansas State University.

Heller, M. F. (1989a). The effective translation of theory and research into practice. Unpublished paper.

Heller, M. F. (1989b, September). Enhancing literacy through computer-assisted language experience stories. Paper presented at the annual meeting of the National Reading and Language Arts Educators' Conference, Kansas City, MO.

Heller, M. F. (1989c). Grammar in context. Unpublished paper.

Heller, M. F. (1991). The promise of whole language instruction. *Kansas Journal of Reading, 7,* 41-48.

Heller, M. F. (1992). What'd ya' think about that story? Children responding to literature. Paper presented at the annual meeting of the International Reading Association, May, Orlando, Florida.

Heller, M. F. (1993a). "Computer-Assisted Language Experience Stories." *The Writing Notebook, 10*(3), pp. 15-17, 32.

Heller, M. F. (1993b). Environmental children's literature. Paper presented at the annual meeting of the International Reading Association, April, San Antonio, Texas.

Heller, M. F., & McLellan, H. (1993). Dancing with the wind: Understanding narrative text structure through response to multicultural children's literature (With an assist from HyperCard). *Reading Psychology, 14*(4), 285-310.

Heller, S. (1987). Writing fiction to save your life. Paper presented at the Kansas Writers' Association annual meeting, Dodge City, KS.

Henderson, E. H., Templeton, S., Coulten, B., & Thomas, J. A. M. (1982). *Houghton Mifflin Spelling,* Book 3. Boston: Houghton Mifflin.

Hennings, D. G. (1990). *Communication in action* (4th ed.). Boston: Houghton Mifflin.

Herman, J. L., Aschbacher, P. R., & Winters, L. (1992). *A practical guide to alternative assessment.* Alexandria, VA: Association for Supervision and Curriculum Development.

Herman, P. A., & Dole, J. (1988). Theory and practice in vocabulary learning and instruction. *The Elementary School Journal, 89*(1), 43-54.

Hiebert, E. H. (1981). Developmental patterns and interrelationships of preschool children's print awareness. *Reading Research Quarterly, 16*(2), 236-260.

Hiebert, E. H. (1983). An examination of ability grouping for reading instruction. *Reading Research Quarterly, 18*(2), 213-255.

Higgins, J., & Kellman, A. (1979, January). I like Judy Blume; It's like she knows me. *Teacher,* pp. 12-15.

Hillocks, G., Jr. (1987, May). Synthesis of research on teaching writing. *Educational Leadership,* pp. 71-82.

Hipple, M. L. (1985). Journal writing in kindergarten. *Language Arts, 62*(3), 255-261.

Hoffman, J. V. (1992). Leadership in the language arts: Am I whole yet? Are you?. *Language Arts, 69*(5), 366-370.

Holdoway, D. (1979). *The foundations of literacy.* New York: Ashton/Scholastic.

Hough, R. A., Nurss, J. R., & Wood, D. (1987, November). Tell me a story: Making opportunities for elaborated language in early childhood classrooms. *Young Children,* 6-12.

Hoyt-Goldsmith, D. (1991). *Pueblo storyteller.** New York: Holiday House.

Hunt, K. W. (1977). Early blooming and late blooming syntactic structures. In C. R. Cooper (Ed.), *Evaluating writing: Describing, measuring, and judging* (pp. 91-106). Champaign, IL: National Council of Teachers of English.

HyperCard™ 2.0. (1990). Cupterino, CA: Apple Computers.

*Illustrated poems for Children.** (1973). Chicago: Rand McNally.

Johnson, D. D., & Pearson, P. D. (1978, 1984). *Teaching reading vocabulary* (2d ed.). New York: Holt, Rinehart & Winston.

Johnson, D. D., Pittelman, S. D., & Heimlich, J. E. (1986). Semantic mapping. *The Reading Teacher, 39*(8), 778-783.

Johnson, N. (1963). *What would we see?** Wichita, KS: Pheasant Books.

Johnson, N., & Mandler, J. (1980). A tale of two structures: Underlying and surface forms in stories. *Poetics, 9,* 51-86.

Jonassen, D. H. (1989). *Hypertext/Hypermedia.* Englewood Cliffs, NJ: Educational Technology Publications.

Jones, V. F., & Jones, L. S. (1986). *Comprehensive classroom management* (2d ed.). Boston: Allyn & Bacon.

Jongsma, E. (1971). *The cloze procedure as a teaching technique.* Newark, DE: International Reading Association.

Jongsma, E. (1985). Grouping for instruction. *Reading Teacher, 38*(9), 918-920.

Joyce, W. W., & Erickson, R. (1991). *People in time and place: Comparing communities.* Morristown, NJ: Silver Burdett.

Jukes, M. (1984). *Like Jake and me.** New York: Knopf.

Kaltsounis, T. (1986). *The world and its people.* Englewood Cliffs, NJ: Silver Burdett.

Kasten, W. C., & Clarke, B. K. (1993). *The multi-age classroom: A family of learners.* Katonah, NY: Richard C. Owen Publishers, Inc.

Keats, E. J. (1962). *The snowy day.*\* New York: Scholastic Books.

Keegan, M. (1991). *Pueblo boy: Growing up in two worlds.*\* New York: Dutton.

Kellogg, S. (1978). *The mystery of the magic green ball.*\* New York: Dial Press.

Kennedy, X. J., & Kennedy, D. M. (Eds.). (1982). *Knock at a star: A child's introduction to poetry.*\* Boston: Little, Brown.

Kiefer, B. (1988). Picture books as contexts for literary, aesthetic, and real world understandings. *Language Arts, 63*(3), 260-271.

King, M., & Rentel, V. (1981). *How children learn to write: A longitudinal study.* National Institute of Education Grant Number G-79-0137 and G-79-0039. Columbus: Ohio State University.

Kintsch, W., & van Dijk, T. A. (1978). Toward a model of text comprehension and production. *Psychological Review, 85*(5), 363-394.

Klein, A., & Schickendanz, J. (1980). Preschoolers write messages and receive their favorite books. *Language Arts, 57*(7), 742-749.

Koch, K. (1970). *Wishes, lies, and dreams: Teaching children to write poetry.* New York: Random House.

Koch, K. (1973). *Rose, where did you get that red? Teaching great poetry to children.* New York: Random House.

LaBerge, D., & Samuels, S. J. (1976). Toward a theory of automatic information processing in reading. *Cognitive Psychology, 6,* 293-323.

Landow, G. P. (1992). *Hypertext: The convergence of contemporary critical theory and technology.* Baltimore, MD: The Johns Hopkins University Press.

Langer, J. A. (1986). *Children reading and writing: Structures and strategies.* Norwood, NJ: Ablex.

Lee, H. (1960). *To kill a mockingbird.* Philadelphia: Lippincott.

Lesesne, T. S., Buckman, L., Chance, R., Covington, V. (1993). Books for adolescents. *Journal of Reading, 37*(1), 68-74.

*Living in our country.* (1985). New York: Laidlaw.

Loban, W. (1963). *The language of elementary school children.* Urbana, IL: National Council of Teachers of English.

Loban, W. (1976). *Language development: Kindergarten through grade twelve.* Urbana, IL: National Council of Teachers of English.

Long, R., & Bulgarella, L. (1985). Social interaction and the writing process. *Language Arts, 62*(2), 166-173.

Lynch, E. (1989). Parental approaches to transmission of language and literacy to young children with and without handicaps: A naturalistic inquiry. Unpublished research report, Moorhead State University, Moorhead, MN.

McGee, L. M., & Richgels, D. J. (1985). Teaching expository text structure to elementary students. *The Reading Teacher, 38*(8), 739-748.

McKeown, M. G., & Curtis, M. E. (Eds.). (1987) *The nature of vocabulary acquisition.* Hillsdale, NJ: Lawrence Erlbaum.

McKlosky, R. (1988). *Make way for ducklings.* New York: Puffin Books.

Maclean, R. (1988). Two paradoxes of phonics. *The Reading Teacher, 41*(6), 514-517.

McLellan, H. (1993, Winter). Virtual reality: Some guideposts for educators. *HyperNexus: Journal of hypermedia and multimedia studies, 4*(2), 4-6.

McLellan, H. (1994). Virtual reality and multiple intelligences: Potentials for higher education. *The Journal of Computing in Higher Education. 5*(2), 33-66.

*The Macmillan dictionary for children.** (1987). New York: Macmillan.

Maestro, G. (1984). *What's a frank frank?** New York: Houghton Mifflin.

Maleska, E. T. (1981). *A pleasure in words.* New York: Simon & Schuster.

Mandler, J., & Johnson, N. (1977). Remembrance of things parced: Story structure and recall. *Cognitive Psychology, 9,* 111–151.

Many, J. E. (1991). The effects of stance and age level on children's literary responses. *Journal of Reading Behavior, 23*(1), 61–85.

Marsh, G., Friedman, M., Welch, V., & Desberg, P. (1980). The development of strategies in spelling. In Uta Frith (Ed.), *Cognitive processes in spelling* (pp. 339–353). New York: Academic Press.

Martin, B., & Brogan, P. (1972). *Instant readers, Level 1.* New York: Holt, Rinehart & Winston.

Martinez, M., & Teale, W. H. (1987). The ins and outs of a kindergarten writing program. *The Reading Teacher, 40*(4), 444–451.

Martinez, M., & Teale, W. H. (1988). Reading in a kindergarten classroom library. *The Reading Teacher, 41*(6), 568–572.

Mason, J. M. (1980). When do children begin to read: An exploration of four year old children's letter and word reading competencies. *Reading Research Quarterly, 15*(2), 203–227.

Mavrogenes, N. A. (1986). What every reading teacher should know about emergent literacy. *The Reading Teacher, 40*(2), 174–178.

Mayer, M. (1977). *Oops.** New York: Dial Press.

Mayer, M. (1987). *There's an alligator under my bed.** New York: Dial Press.

Mehan, H. (1981). The role of language and the language of role in practiced decision making. Paper presented at the annual meeting of the American Sociological Association, Toronto, Canada.

Merriam, E. (1985). *Blackberry ink.* New York: Morrow.

Meyer, B. J. F., & Freedle, R. O. (1984). Effects of discourse type on recall. *American Educational Research Journal, 21*(1), 121–143.

Minot, S. (1993). *Three genres: The writing of poetry, fiction, and drama.* Englewood Cliffs, NJ: Prentice Hall.

Moldofsky, P. B. (1983). Teaching students to determine the central story problem: A practical application of schema theory. *The Reading Teacher, 36*(8), 740–745.

Morrow, L. M. (1989). *Literacy development in the early years.* Englewood Cliffs, NJ: Prentice-Hall.

Morrow, L. M., & Smith, J. K. (1990). *Assessment for instruction in early literacy.* Englewood Cliffs, NJ: Prentice-Hall.

Munsch, R. (1986). *The boy in the drawer.** Toronto: Annick Press.

Munsch, R. (1987). *Moira's Birthday.** Toronto, Canada: Annick Press.

Murray, D. M. (1985). *A writer teaches writing* (2d ed.). Boston: Houghton Mifflin.

Nagy, W. E. (1988). *Teaching vocabulary to improve reading comprehension.* Newark, DE: International Reading Association.

Nagy, W. E., & Herman, P. A. (1987). Breadth and depth of vocabulary knowledge: Implications for acquisition and instruction. In M. G. McKeown & M. E. Curtis (Eds.), *The nature of vocabulary acquisition* (pp. 19–35). Hillsdale, NJ: Lawrence Erlbaum.

Nakano, D. (1986). *Easy origami.** New York: Viking/Penguin.

National Commission on Testing and Public Policy. (1990). *From gatekeeper to gateway: Transforming testing in America.* Chestnut Hill, MA: National Commission on Testing and Public Policy.

Nelson, T. H. (1982). *Literary machines.* Swarthmore, PA: self-published.

Nicholas, C. (1978). *Hot rod.** West Haven, CT: Pendulum Press.

Olson, A. N. (1987). *The lighthouse keeper's daughter.** Boston: Little, Brown.

O'Neal, S. (1991). Leadership in the language arts: Student assessment: Present and future. *Language Arts, 68,* 67–73.

Orfan, L. J., & Vogeli, B. J. (1987). *Silver Burdett mathematics, Teacher Edition 4.* Morristown, NJ: Silver Burdett.

Otto, W. (1988). Here's looking at you kid. *Journal of Reading, 31*(4), 368–371.

Oxenbury, H. (1982). *Beach day.** New York: Dial Press.

*Oxford English dictionary.* (1971, 1975). Oxford, Eng.: Oxford University Press.

Palinscar, A. S., & Brown, A. L. (1984). Reciprocal teaching of comprehension-fostering and comprehension-monitoring activities. *Cognition and Instruction, 1*(1), 117–175.

Pappert, S. (1980). *Mindstorms: Children, computers, and powerful ideas.* New York: Basic Books.

Paulson, F. L., Paulson, P. R., & Meyer, C. A. (1991). What makes a portfolio a portfolio? *Educational Leadership, 48*(5), 60–73.

Pearce, D. L. (1984). Writing in content area classrooms. *Reading World, 23*(3), 234–241.

Pearson, P. D. (1985). Changing the face of reading comprehension instruction. *The Reading Teacher, 38*(8), 724–738.

Pearson, P. D. (1989). Commentary: Reading the whole language movement. *The Elementary School Journal, 90*(2), 231–241.

Perl, S. (1979). The composing process of unskilled college writers. *Research in the Teaching of English, 13,* 317–336.

Perron, J. D. (1977). Written syntactic complexity and the modes of discourse. Paper presented at the annual meeting of the American Educational Research Association, New York.

Peterson, B. T. (Ed.). (1986). *Convergences: Transactions in reading and writing.* Urbana, IL: National Council of Teachers of English.

Peterson, E. A. (1985). Frederick's alligator. In T. Clymer, R. Indrisano, D. D. Johnson, P. D. Pearson, & R. L. Venezky (Eds.), *Give me a clue.* Lexington, MA: Ginn & Company.

Pflomm, P. N. (1986). *Chalk in hand: The draw and tell book.* Metuchen, NJ: Scarecrow Press.

Piaget, J. (1952). *The origins of intelligence in children.* New York: W. W. Norton.

Piaget, J. (1955, 1973). *The language and thought of the child.* New York: World Book Company.

Piazza, C. L., & Tomlinson, C. M. (1985). A concert of writers. *Language Arts, 62*(2), 150–158.

Pinkwater, D. (1984). *Blue moose.** New York: Putnam.

Pinkwater, D. M. (1977). *The big orange splot.** New York: Hastings House.

Poe, E. A. (1938). The tell-tale heart.* In *The complete tales and poems of Edgar Allan Poe* (pp. 303–306). New York: Modern Library.

Prelutsky, J. (1988). *Tyrannosaurus was a beast: Dinosaur poems.** New York: Greenwillow.

Prelutsky, J. (1984). *The new kid on the block.** New York: William Morrow.

Prokofief, S. (1990). *Peter and the wolf.* New York: David Godine.

Purves, A. C. (1990). *The scribal society.* White Plains, NY: Longman.

Putnam, L. (1991). Dramatizing nonfiction with emerging readers. *Language Arts, 68,* 463–469).

Quayle, L. (1988). *Dolphins and porpoises.** New York: Gallery Books.

Raboff, E. (1988). *Renoir: Art for children.** New York: Harper & Row.

Rasinski, T. V., & Fredericks, A. D. (1988). Sharing literacy: Guiding principles and practices for parent involvement. *The Reading Teacher, 41*(6), 508–512.

Raskin, E. (1966). *Nothing ever happens on my block.* New York: Macmillan.

Read, C., & Hodges, R. E. (1982). Spelling. In *Encyclopedia of educational research* (5th ed., pp. 1758-1767). New York: Macmillan.

Readance, J. E., Bean, T. W., & Baldwin, S. (1981). *Content area reading: An integrated approach.* Dubuque, IA: Kendall/Hunt.

*The real mother goose.** (1916, 1982). Chicago: Rand McNally.

Reinking, D. (1988-89). Misconceptions about reading and software development. *The Computing Teacher, 16*(4), 27-29.

Rheingold, H. (1991). *Virtual Reality.* New York: Summit Books

Robinson, H. A. (1983). *Teaching reading, writing, and study strategies: The content areas.* Boston: Allyn & Bacon.

Roehler, L. R., & Duffy, G. G. (1984). Direct explanation of comprehension processes. In G. G. Duffy, L. R. Roehler, & J. Mason (Eds.), *Comprehension instruction* (pp. 265-280). White Plains, NY: Longman.

Rogoff, B., & Lave, J. (Eds.). (1984). *Everyday cognition: Its development in social context.* Cambridge, MA: Harvard University Press.

Rohmer, H., Chow, O., & Vidaure, M. (1987). *The invisible hunters (Los cazadores invisibles).** New York: Children's Book Press.

Rosegrant, T. J. (1986, April). Adult-child communication in writing. Paper presented at the annual meeting of the American Education Research Association, San Francisco.

Rosenblatt, L. (1978). *The reader, the text, the poem.* Cambridge, MA: Harvard University Press.

Rosenblatt, L. (1991). Literature—S.O.S.! *Language Arts, 68*(6), 444-448.

Roskos, K. (1988). Literacy at work in play. *The Reading Teacher, 41*(6), 562-566.

Ross, D. D., & Bondy, E. (1987). Communicating with parents about beginning reading instruction. *Childhood Education, 63*(4), 270-275.

Rumelhart, D. E. (1975). Notes on a schema for stories. In D. G. Bobrow & A. Collins (Eds.), *Representation and understanding studies in cognitive science,* New York: Academic Press.

Rumelhart, D. E. (1978). Understanding and summarizing brief stories. In D. LaBerge and S. J. Samuels (Eds.), *Basic processes in reading: Perception and comprehension.* Hillsdale, NJ: Lawrence Erlbaum.

Rumelhart, D. E. (1980). The building blocks of cognition. In R. J. Spiro, B. C. Bruce, & W. F. Brewer (Eds.), *Theoretical issues in reading comprehension* (pp. 33-58). Hillsdale, NJ: Lawrence Erlbaum.

Rumelhart, D. E. (1981). Schemata: The building blocks of cognition. In J. T. Guthrie (Ed.), *Comprehension and teaching: Research reviews* (pp. 3-26). Newark, DE: International Reading Association.

Ryan, S. M. N. (1986). Do prose models really teach writing? *Language Arts, 63*(3), 284-290.

Sadow, M. (1982). The use of story grammar in the design of questions. *The Reading Teacher, 35*(5), 518-522.

Samuels, S. J. (1976). Hierarchical subskills in the reading acquisition process. In J. T. Guthrie (Ed.), *Aspects of reading acquisition.* Baltimore: Johns Hopkins University Press.

Sanders, W. B. (1989). *HyperCard made easy,* 2d ed. Glenview, IL: Scott, Foresman and Company.

Scales, P. C. (1992). *Windows of opportunity: Improving middle grades teacher preparation.* Chapel Hill, NC: The University of North Carolina Center for Early Adolescence.

Scarry, R. (1966). *Storybook dictionary: A golden book.* New York: Western Publishing

Schmohe, K. (1990). A defense for teaching keyboarding. *Language Arts, 67,* 783-785.

Sendak, M. (1963). *Where the wild things are.** New York: Harper & Row.

Sendak, M. (1970). *In the night kitchen.** New York: Harper & Row.

Shannon, P. (1989). *Broken promises.* Granby, MA: Bergin & Garvey.

Sharmat, M. W. (1983). *Gila monsters meet you at the airport.** New York: Puffin Books.

Silverstein, S. (1974). Where the sidewalk ends. Harper & Row.

Silverstein, S. (1981). *A light in the attic.** New York: Harper & Row.

Simon, S. (1979). *Animal fact/animal fable.** New York: Crown.

Sippola, A. E. (1982). Story distance in basal readers. *The Reading Teacher, 35*(5), 550-553.

Slavin, R. E. (1987a). Ability grouping: A best evidence synthesis. *Review of Educational Research, 57*(3), 293-336.

Slavin, R. E. (1987b). *Cooperative learning: Student teams* (2d ed.). Washington, DC: National Education Association.

Sloan, G. D. (1984). *The child as critic.* New York: Teachers College, Columbia University.

Slobdkina, E. (1940, 1968). *Caps for sale.** New York: Harper & Row.

Smith, F. (1981). Myths of writing. *Language Arts, 58*(8), 792-798.

Smith, M., & Bean, T. W. (1983). Four strategies that develop children's story comprehension and writing. *The Reading Teacher, 37*(3), 295-303.

Soar, R. (1983). Impact of context variables on teacher and learner behavior. Paper presented at the annual meeting of the American Association of Colleges for Teacher Education, Detroit.

Spandel, V., & Stiggins, R. J. (1990). *Creating writers: Linking assessment and writing instruction.* White Plains, NY: Longman.

Spiegel, D. L. (1992). Blending whole language and systematic direct instruction. *The Reading Teacher, 46* (1), 38-44.

Spiegel, D. L., & Fitzgerald, J. (1986). Improving reading comprehension through instruction about story parts. *The Reading Teacher, 39*(7), 676-682.

Squire, J. R. (1983). Composing and comprehending: Two sides of the same basic process. *Language Arts, 60*(5), 581-589.

Stahl, S., & Fairbanks, M. (1986). The effects of vocabulary instruction: A model-based meta-analysis. *Review of Educational Research, 56,* 72-110.

Staton, J. (1980). Writing and counseling: Using a dialogue journal. *Language Arts, 57,* 514-518.

Staton, J. (1988). ERIC/RCS report: Dialogue journals. *Language Arts, 65*(2), 198-201.

Stauffer, R. G. (1980). *The language experience approach to the teaching of reading.* New York: Harper & Row.

Stauffer, R. G. (1981). *Directing the reading-thinking process.* New York: Harper & Row.

Steig, W. (1969). *Sylvester and the magic pebble.** New York: Simon & Schuster.

Steig, W. (1982). *Doctor DeSoto.** New York: Scholastic Books.

Stein, N. L., & Glenn, C. G. (1979). An analysis of story comprehension in elementary school children. In R. O. Freedle (Ed.), *New directions in discourse processing II.* Norwood, NJ: Ablex.

Stein, N. L., & Trabasso, T. (1982). What's in a story: An approach to comprehension and instruction. In R. Glaser (Ed.), *Advances in psychology of instruction* (Vol. 13, pp. 213-237). Hillsdale, NJ: Lawrence Erlbaum.

Steinbeck, J. (1976). *The acts of King Arthur and his noble knights.* New York: Farrar, Straus & Giroux.

Stodolsky, S. S. (1984). Frameworks for studying instructional processes in peer work-groups. In P. L. Peterson, L. C. Wilkinson, & M. Hallinan (Eds.), *The social context of education* (pp. 107-124). New York: Academic Press.

Stotsky, S. (1983). Research on reading/writing relationships: A synthesis and suggested directions. *Language Arts, 60*(5), 627-642.

Sulzby, E. (1985). Children's emergent reading of favorite storybooks: A developmental study. *Reading Research Quarterly, 20*(4), 458-481.

Sulzby, E. (1986). Kindergartners as writers and readers. In M. Farr (Ed.), *Advances in writing research, volume one: Children's early writing development* (pp. 127-199). Norwood, NJ: Ablex.

Surat, M. M. (1983). *Angel child, dragon child.*\* New York: Scholastic.

Taylor, B. M. (1982). A summarizing strategy to improve middle grade students' reading and writing skills. *The Reading Teacher, 36*(2), 202-205.

Taylor, B. M., & Beach, R. W. (1984). Effects of text structure instruction on middle-grade students' comprehension and production of expository text. *Reading Research Quarterly, 19*(2), 147-161.

Taylor, W. L. (1953). Cloze procedures: A new tool for measuring readability. *Journalism Quarterly, 30,* 360-368.

Teale, W. H. (1982). Toward a theory of how children learn to read and write naturally. *Language Arts, 59*(6), 555-570.

Teale, W. H. (1986). The beginning of reading and writing: Written language development during the preschool and kindergarten years. In M. Sampson (Ed.), *The pursuit of literacy: Early reading and writing.* Dubuque, IA: Kendall/Hunt.

Temple, C., & Gillet, J. W. (1989). *Language arts: Learning processes and teaching practices,* 2d ed. Glenview, IL: Scott Foresman.

Templeton, S. (1986). Literacy, readiness, and basals. *The Reading Teacher, 39*(5), 403-409.

Terban, M. (1982). *Eight ate: A feast of homonym riddles.*\* Boston: Houghton Mifflin.

Terban, M. (1983). *In a pickle and other funny idioms.*\* Boston: Houghton Mifflin.

Terban, M. (1984). *I think and I thought and other tricky verbs.*\* Boston: Houghton Mifflin.

Terry, A. (1974). *Children's poetry preferences: A national survey of upper elementary grades.* NCTE Research Report No. 16. Urbana, IL: National Council of Teachers of English.

Tiedt, I. (1970). Exploring poetry patterns. *Elementary English, 45,* 1082-1084.

Thelen, J. (1986). Vocabulary instruction and meaningful learning. *Journal of Reading, 29,* 603-609.

Thorndyke, P. (1977). Cognitive structures in comprehension and memory of narrative discourse. *Cognitive Psychology, 9*(1), 97-110.

Tierney, R. J., & Leys, M. (1986). What is the value of connecting reading and writing? In B. T. Peterson (Ed.), *Convergences: Transactions in reading and writing* (pp. 15-29). Urbana, IL: National Council of Teachers of English.

Tom, C. H. (1972). Paul Revere rides ahead: Poems teachers read to pupils in the middle grades. *Library Quarterly, 43,* 27-38.

Tomkins, J. P. (Ed.). (1980). *Reader-response criticism: From formalism to post structuralism.* Baltimore, MD: The Johns Hopkins University Press.

Trelease, J. (1989). *The new read-aloud handbook.* New York: Penguin Books.

Tutolo, D. (1981). Critical listening/reading of advertisements. *Language Arts, 58,* 679-683.

Twain, M. (1987a). *The adventures of Huckeberry Finn.* New York: Scholastic Books.

Twain, M. (1987b). *The adventures of Tom Sawyer.* New York: Scholastic Books.

Vacca, J. L., Vacca, R. T., & Grove, M. K. (1987). *Reading and learning to read.* Boston: Little, Brown.

Vacca, R. T., & Vacca, J. L. (1986). *Content area reading.* Boston: Little, Brown.

Valencia, S. (1990). A portfolio approach to classroom reading assessment: The whys, whats, and hows. *The Reading Teacher, 43*(4), 338-340.

Venezky, R. L. (1987). A history of the American reading textbook. *The Elementary School Journal, 87*(3), 247–265.

Viorst, J. (1972). *Alexander and the terrible, horrible, no good, very bad day.* * New York: Scholastic Books.

Viorst, J. (1978). *Alexander who used to be rich last sunday.* * New York: Macmillan.

Vygotsky, L. S. (1962, 1979). *Thought and language.* Cambridge, MA: M.I.T. Press.

Vygotsky, L. S. (1978). *Mind in society.* Cambridge, MA: M.I.T. Press.

Waber, B. (1972). *Ira sleeps over.* * Boston: Houghton Mifflin.

Wagoner, S. A. (1983). Comprehension monitoring: What it is and what we know about it. *Reading Research Quarterly, 18*(3), 328–346.

Watson, C. D. (1971). *Father fox's pennyrhymes.* * New York: Scholastic Books.

Welty, E. (1984). *One writer's beginnings.* Cambridge, MA: Harvard University Press.

Wertsch, J. V. (1985). *Vygotsky and the social formation of mind.* Cambridge, MA: Harvard University Press.

Wertsch, J. V., Minick, N., & Arns, F. J. (1984). In B. Rogoff & J. Lave (Eds.), *Everyday cognition: Its development in social context* (151–171). Cambridge, MA: Harvard University Press.

Whaley, J. F. (1981). Story grammars and reading instruction. *The Reading Teacher, 34*(7), 762–771.

Williams, K. L. (1990). *Galimoto.* New York: Mulberry Books.

Wixson, K., Bosky, A., Yochum, M. N., & Alvermann, D. (1984). An interview for assessing students' perceptions of classroom reading tasks. *The Reading Teacher, 37*(3), 346–353.

Young Adults Choices. (1992). *Journal of Reading, 36*(3), 213–220.

Young, R. E. (1978). Paradigms and problems: Needed research in rhetorical invention. In C. R. Cooper & L. Odell (Eds.), *Research on composing: Points of departure* (pp. 29–47). Urbana, IL: National Council of Teachers of English.

*Younger Kansas Writers.* (1992; 1993). Overland Park, KA: The Kansas Association of Teachers of English.

*Your English, Level 4.* (1984). San Diego, CA: Coronado Publishers.

Zarrillo, J. (1991). Theory becomes practice: Aesthetic teaching with literature. *The New Advocate, 4*(4), 221–234.

# INDEX